DATE DUE

FAC			
GAYLORD			PRINTED IN U.S.A.

25th Anniversary

EDUCATIONAL
FOUNDATION
An Investment in
Tomorrow

A Silver Anniversary Publication of the
Phi Delta Kappa Educational Foundation
Bloomington, Indiana

Cover design by Victoria Voelker

Library of Congress Catalog Card Number 91-62006
ISBN 0-87367-450-2
0-87367-453-7 (pbk.)
Copyright © 1991 by the Phi Delta Kappa Educational Foundation
Bloomington, Indiana

Table of Contents

Editor's Preface

Phi Delta Kappa commissioned this volume of essays to celebrate the 25th Anniversary of the Phi Delta Kappa Educational Foundation. While anniversaries are a time for celebration, they also are a time for reflection.

To reflect on public education in America, particularly over the past 25 years, Phi Delta Kappa invited 33 distinguished educators to contribute personal essays from the vantage point of their own careers. They are all senior educators (some more senior than others) and thus bring a historical perspective to their reflections. And they bring the diversity of experience of the researcher, the scholar, and the school practitioner (some are all three).

Many of the essays are highly autobiographical; others are more issue-oriented; some nicely combined both approaches. One of the interesting aspects of the essays is the authors' recounting of serendipitous events, which led to career decisions that ultimately brought them to prominence in their respective fields. Another is the role that mentors played in their careers.

A pervading theme in these essays is an abiding faith in the power of education to improve society. In some cases the authors report that this faith was instilled in them by their parents. In others this faith was their motivation to become teachers. Most of them began their careers as teachers, some in one-room schools. Taken as a whole, the 33 essays serve as a historical overview of public education through most of the 20th century, with several of the authors playing central roles in that often turbulent history.

Phi Delta Kappa is proud to present this volume of reflections by 33 distinguished educators. They offer the reader much to ponder.

Derek L. Burleson
Editor of Special Publications
June 1991

Wondering and Wandering in Education

BY WILLIAM M. ALEXANDER

An opportunity such as this to formalize one's reflections comes rarely, especially at an age when memory is supposed to be short and reminiscing all too long. I have wandered a great deal in my 50-plus years in education and have done a lot of wondering about many matters, even reaching some conclusions. My reflections, in brief form, follow.

My Formal Education

My public school, most of my undergraduate education, and my beginning years of teaching all took place in my hometown of McKenzie, a typical, small, west Tennessee town. In elementary and high school, I had some caring teachers and my memories are happy ones. At Bethel College in McKenzie, I really began to take advantage of educational and other opportunities, later successfully courting the college's new librarian, Nell McLeod. And I decided to go into teaching primarily, I must confess, because I could get a job teaching in my hometown when the broader job market for liberal arts graduates was almost nonexistent.

My real drive to go into teaching, however, came at Peabody College where, during the summers, I completed my M.A. in education and history and began doctoral work with Hollis Caswell, serving as his research assistant. During my first year with Cas, as his students and colleagues all called him, he accepted an appointment at Teachers College, Columbia University, and offered me the chance to continue my graduate work there and also a research assistant-

---

William M. Alexander is Professor Emeritus at the University of Florida.

ship. So, in late August of 1937, Nell and I began two of the most interesting and important years of our lives. Teachers College was suffering from the depression, too, but arrangements and opportunities for graduate students were superb. I had the great privilege of taking classes with some of education's most prestigious figures. And my experiences there included visits to many of the outstanding public and private schools in the area, work on school field surveys directed by Teachers College faculty, plus liberal participation in the many cultural opportunities available in New York City.

Among the ideas to influence my later career that came from my graduate work at Peabody and Teachers College, some perhaps even earlier, were these:

1. Close teacher-student relationships can have a great impact on every aspect of the learner's development.
2. Concentrated attention and study, the amount and type varying with individuals, are essential to learning.
3. The gaps between elementary, secondary, and college-level education are too wide and may discourage, even thwart, educational progress.
4. The multitudinous problems of our economy and of our multicultural backgrounds require both immediate and long-term improvements in education geared to the problems of present or future cultures.
5. Successful leaders in schools and colleges of education need a broad background of work experience in education at pre-college levels.

To be consistent with the last of these ideas, after completing my doctoral work at Teachers College, I chose to accept as my first job a position with the Cincinnati Public Schools rather than two offered me at the university level. In August of 1939, I left New York City and Teachers College behind to become assistant director of curriculum in the Cincinnati school system. My induction into the "real world" of education was just ahead.

From Theory to the Real World of Education

I have the greatest respect for the training my mentors and teachers provided at Peabody and Teachers College, but I could not have been, and was not, prepared adequately to move abruptly into the world of curriculum development in a large metropolitan school district. George Reavis, then Cincinnati's director of curriculum, with whom

I had become acquainted through my work with Caswell on *World Book Encyclopedia* studies, tried very hard to help me adjust to the situation. But it was not until several years later that I could fully appreciate his efforts, and acknowledge my own inadequacies.

Reavis, following the lead of top administration, was determined to produce printed courses of study to guide all instruction in the Cincinnati schools. To do this, he set up an elaborate system of committees, which were served by four of us who worked as his assistants. My understanding of curriculum development was that it was a far more deliberate process culminating in better instruction by teachers who were expected to adapt courses of study to their own situations. And so, I found myself in frequent conflict philosophically with my duties. Nevertheless, as I produced courses of study, I learned and wondered much about the problems of large city school systems and of teachers and principals serving schools with vastly different populations, ranging from the inner-city slums to affluent suburbs. Among the matters I wondered about, which I would later recognize as emanating from these experiences, were these:

1. The school programs of the late 1930s and early 1940s really did not come to grips with the educational needs of an urban community, where gross inequalities existed among cultural and economic groups. For example, at that time Cincinnati had both the traditional K-8 elementary schools and the newer junior high schools (grades 7-9), the former found predominantly in more affluent districts, the latter in downtown areas. For many of those downtown inner-city students attending junior high, where the curriculum emphasized prevocational training, completing the ninth grade was often the end of their formal education; whereas most of those completing the eighth grade in the suburban K-8 schools went on to high school and enrolled in the college preparatory program.

2. The conflict between the Essentialists and Progressives, which has permeated curriculum planning throughout this century, was evident in almost every curriculum committee and discussion during the years I was in Cincinnati. I have been trying to resolve some of the issues in this conflict throughout my career and do believe there is now much more recognition of individual differences among learners and of the need for curriculum and instructional options. In the public schools as I saw them in the late Thirties and early Forties, Essentialism prevailed, as evidenced by the dominance of the textbook and adopted courses of study and by the widespread emphasis on memorization.

3. The curriculum includes far more varied learning experiences than the typical course of study. At best, the course of study is a guide to help teachers and others plan the content of the curriculum.

My next career move brought me back to my home state at the University of Tennessee, where I became a professor of education in the fall of 1941. Thinking my wanderings were ended, I settled into my duties at the university; and Nell and I awaited the arrival of our first child. Pearl Harbor was to change all that.

My work with the university was very satisfying, especially the opportunity to be a member of the University of Tennessee board operating the new Norris School at Norris Dam for the Tennessee Valley Authority. This was one of the social experiments initiated under President Roosevelt's "New Deal" program. While helping to operate this school, I became an active participant in the new community school movement in the South and elsewhere. In those days schools served as community centers for administering the rationing program and other wartime services, including pre-induction training and work-study programs for essential war jobs. I benefited, too, from teaching a course in educational sociology with student field experiences in Knoxville social agencies, and from supervising student teachers.

In the summer of 1942, I was recruited as an Office of Price Administration (OPA) wartime consumer-information consultant and spent much time on the West Coast and in Washington, D.C. In the meantime, I had applied for a USNR commission and was notified of my acceptance about Thanksgiving in 1943. Soon thereafter I was off to Princeton University for Naval Orientation training and then to teach naval fundamentals at the Princeton Naval Orientation Center. From there I was assigned as executive officer of the Navy V-12 Training Program at Baldwin-Wallace College, with my final tour of duty at Yale University helping to close out the ROTC unit there at the end of the war. And so ended a most interesting and educative five years since leaving Cincinnati, in which I had wandered widely in the United States and in education and had achieved a little maturity in the process. I had also gained many additional impressions about education, including these I now recollect:

1. Despite seeming inadequacies, schools can make tremendous adjustments in order to cope with such emergency conditions as those created by U.S. involvement in World War II.

2. Compared with later conflicts, our people during World War II were thoroughly supportive of the war effort and of the ef-

forts by the schools to serve national defense and community needs at that time.

3. Community participation and service is of significant help to schools (and vice versa).

4. During World War II, students in military training had far greater motivation and learned much more effectively. There are lessons to be learned from that experience about motivation and incentives for regular academic programs in schools today.

5. Out of the community school experience, we have learned that both preservice and inservice teachers perform with enthusiasm and success when they take on tasks that contribute to community and national well-being.

While serving in the Navy, I was on military leave from the University of Tennessee. But instead of returning, I decided I wanted more public school experience and accepted an offer to become director of curriculum (later, assistant superintendent) in the Battle Creek, Michigan, Public Schools. The almost four years I spent there working with widely admired superintendent Virgil Rogers were challenging and productive. I managed to turn out (working nights, holidays, and weekends) the first of several books with Galen Saylor of the University of Nebraska, my long-time friend from our days working together with Caswell at Teachers College. I probably worked too hard; but being ambitious, I chose to go into public school administration all the way, becoming superintendent of the Winnetka, Illinois, Elementary School District.

This did not work out satisfactorily, although I learned much from this North Shore group of fine elementary schools, one of which was a grades 6-8 school (later to become one of my models for the middle school). So I accepted an invitation from John Beery, dean of the University of Miami's School of Education, to serve in a new position created by the university and the Dade County School District. The position was unique in that I served both on the university faculty and as curriculum advisor for this growing school system, where the number of schools tripled while I was there.

So I wandered again, this time to an ideal set-up, which I much enjoyed and from which I benefited for some eight years. Throughout this period, I worked with the mushrooming Dade County system, combining the direction and conduct of the system's inservice education with some campus teaching, particularly graduate courses in curriculum and supervision. Dade County was a fine laboratory in which to develop and test out innovations. With the help and cooperation of Dean Beery and my associates in Dade County, we were able to develop programs that served the schools well, even though the school system was going through many changes because of its tremendous growth. Among the ideas I first wondered about and then helped to implement successfully in Dade County were these:

1. "Basic education," a type of core curriculum typically embracing at least English and social studies, perhaps math and/or science, with one teacher per classroom group, was an effective way to help students make the transition from the self-contained elementary classroom to the high school departmentalized organization.
2. Curriculum development, in fact educational planning in general, for an area as large as Dade County, with so many schools and different cultural groups, is best done at the individual building level, with coordination of area schools (all levels) and direction at the county level through a coordinating council.
3. Summer workshops of one or two weeks are an effective means of providing orientation to rapidly growing faculties.
4. Special training seminars for prospective school principals and assistant principals are helpful in the orientation of those who would later be appointed to these positions.
5. Having curriculum assistants or assistant principals for curriculum and instruction is an effective way to provide for continuing school improvement.
6. Periodic self-studies by each school faculty, followed up by some type of visitation and feedback by personnel from other schools, helps in the process of improvement.

I wonder if these ideas are not still useful for many school systems.

Focusing My Professional Interests

In 1958 I succumbed to the temptation to work exclusively in higher education and wandered back to Tennessee to accept a professorship at Peabody College, one of my alma maters. By this time, our second son had arrived; and so the four of us traveled to Nashville.

Although I had profited greatly from the variety of educational experiences of the previous 20 years, there was still much to learn about my wonderings and to write about them in readable form. I was determined to narrow my focus and do more intensive work in the curriculum field. This was not easy with the chairmanship of Peabody's

Education Department and the presidency of the Association for Supervision and Curriculum Development (ASCD) being added to my load. However, my teaching of general curriculum courses, my work with graduate students in this field, much consulting with school districts on curriculum development, and the completion of the second edition of *Curriculum Planning* with Galen Saylor resulted in a crystallization of my ideas in this field, which have continued to be central in my work and publications. Among these ideas are the following, which in retrospect may seem obvious but are nonetheless significant:

1. The central goal of schooling, and therefore of curriculum and instruction, should be the development of self-directing, continuing learners.

2. Curriculum planning should be done at all levels, in this order of importance: 1) teacher planning for individual students as needed, for small groups of students, and for each class; 2) team, grade, or department planning for the teachers and student groups involved; 3) schoolwide planning by the total faculty or some representative group, such as a council on instruction; and 4) systemwide planning. Groups involved at each level of planning should understand their function and relation to groups at other levels, with frequent communication among groups.

3. The process of school improvement may be summarized using the acronym IDEAS and should include these steps:

I — Identify goals for improvement.
D — Determine means of achieving these goals.
E — Evaluate the selected model or change.
A — Act on the evidence.
S — Stimulate the process continuously.

4. The individual learner should be actively involved in planning his or her own curriculum in an open process that eliminates the "hidden curriculum" of passing the grade or meeting the other hurdles of the school's evaluation system.

5. The learner progresses in a continuum in each curriculum domain (basic knowledge, communication skills, and personal development), rather than up the steps (grades) of the educational ladder. Artificial barriers between the steps should be minimized because they interrupt the smooth progression of learning.

In 1963 I wandered back to the Sunshine State and the University of Florida, where I was to work with a long-time friend and colleague, Kim Wiles, who was soon to become dean of the School of

7

Education there. Curriculum was still my teaching focus, and my publications extended to include the third and fourth editions of Saylor's and my curriculum book (the fourth edition in collaboration with Arthur Lewis, also at the University of Florida), a book of readings on the secondary school curriculum, and several related to research in the curriculum and instruction field conducted with my colleague, Vynce Hines. But the more I studied both general and secondary curriculum, the more I became convinced that the concept of grade levels was a major barrier to continuous progress in learning. To overcome this barrier, major restructuring would be essential. And so I intensified my interest and efforts on the middle level of education between childhood and full adolescence and between elementary and high school.

The Middle Level of Education

At the University of Florida, we were fortunate to receive federal funding for an NDEA Middle School Institute for 1966-67. Emmett Williams, a former student of mine at Peabody and now a colleague, served as its director. The institute included persons nominated by the three cooperating school systems (Atlanta; Dade County, Florida; and Montgomery County, Maryland). Working with this group of prospective middle school personnel provided Williams and me and other colleagues the opportunity to explore in depth many knotty issues related to the middle school structure and curriculum. We soon discovered there was little literature to help us and tried to close this gap by producing *The Emergent Middle School* (1968), one of the earliest books dealing with middle schools. Assisting in this effort were Dan Prescott at the University of Maryland, Vynce Hines, and Mary Compton, then a Florida doctoral student and now at the University of Georgia. Joining us to work on the second edition (1969) was Ron Kealy, then a graduate student and now at Frostburg State University in Maryland.

Also with a small Cooperative Research grant and with Kealy's help, I was able to collect and publish much needed data on the number of "reorganized middle schools" (defined as a regrouping of former elementary and secondary grades into schools of from three to five grades including grade 7) and considerable information about their establishment, organization, and programs as of 1967-68. This survey yielded benchmark data, which I followed up periodically with various studies and publications from 1976 to 1989, collaborating with Ken McEwin at Appalachian State University, where I taught summers in 1976 to 1989.

In the early Seventies, Paul George joined the faculty at the University of Florida to give leadership in developing a middle school teacher education program. I continued to work actively with him in middle school education at the University of Florida until my retirement from full-time teaching in 1977. We co-authored the first comprehensive textbook in this new field, *The Exemplary Middle School*, in 1981, and are even now engaged in preparing a new edition.

My various experiences in teaching, research, consulting, and writing about middle-level education over the past 40 years has led to some generalizations about the new middle school (most commonly grades 6-8, but substantial numbers with such other patterns as 5-8 and 7-8). Let us start with the establishment of the middle school, which calls for a brief bit of history.

Establishment. The junior high school, established early in this century, had become widespread by 1960, when about four out of every five high school graduates had gone through a 6-3-3 school organization. By contrast, in 1920 about four out of every five had gone through the traditional 8-4 organization. But by the early 1960s, sufficient criticism had mounted over the high school's domination of the junior high program that some districts (an outstanding example was Upper St. Clair, Pennsylvania) were ready to experiment, or already were experimenting, with a new organization for the middle grades. (Some of the variations included senior elementary, intermediate, and some atypical junior highs with different grade plans.) The middle school movement was primarily a local development without the impetus of national committee reports, which had helped to accelerate the earlier growth of junior highs. Actually, the development of junior highs by many communities starting in the 1920s was simply a matter of expediency in order to handle the growing enrollments after the rapid rise in birthrates following World War I. Interestingly, the same type of housing needs was one of the reasons cited for some grade 6-8 schools established in the 1960s. My first status study, completed in 1968, identified 1,101 reorganized middle schools; and the most frequently cited reason given for their establishment was "to eliminate crowded conditions in other schools." The next most cited reason was "to provide a program specifically designed for students in this age group." In our 1988 survey, the order of these two reasons was reversed. Other reasons were given in both the 1968 and 1988 surveys, and still others mentioned in other sources. In way of summary, I believe the major reasons for the growth of middle schools and the decline of junior high schools to be the following:

9

1. The most cited and probably the most educationally sound reason for the establishment of a middle level of education is to provide a better transition from elementary to high school. Elements of the transition include the movement from childhood to adolescence and the need for greater continuity in the learning process. These factors, then, justify the need for a different, unique school.

2. Another reason, related to the first, is to overcome the weaknesses of the junior high school and the eight-grade elementary school. This negative reason is rarely cited but is, nevertheless, a major factor.

3. Another reason is to help solve school-enrollment and other administrative problems brought on by such diverse factors as burgeoning enrollment at the elementary and high school levels, new housing developments, making room for kindergartens, or meeting court-ordered desegregation guidelines. In addition, these new schools could serve as "guinea pigs" for innovations that also can be applied at other levels.

4. Also appearing in the surveys were scattered local reasons, such as getting grade 9 back into the high school, to create a consolidated upper school into which several elementary schools would feed, and to "be more like" some other school system.

Organization. Regardless of the grade-level organization of middle schools, they all typically have a principal, usually with one or more assistants with varying titles. Faculty may be organized by departments, grades, or teams. There has been considerable growth in the use of interdisciplinary teams from 1968 to 1988, but there has been little movement away from uniform period schedules. Middle schools tend to have smaller enrollments than the junior highs.

Programs. The program of middle schools has three components, two of which vary greatly among the schools. The first is basic knowledge (language arts, mathematics, social studies, and science), with each usually taught in all grades but varying as to whether it is departmentalized or taught on an interdisciplinary basis and whether it is taught in uniform periods or on a flexible schedule. The trend is toward interdisciplinary team organization, with each team teaching these basic subjects to the same group of students, and toward flexible scheduling within the team, although this is less common.

The second program component is exploratory subjects. The traditional junior high school subjects in this component (art, music, homemaking, industrial arts) have continued in the middle school; but many others, especially computer usage and reading, have become common as required or elective courses. Other courses, such as sex education, health, creative writing, and foreign languages, are popular in both middle schools and junior highs.

The third program component includes some clubs and activities adopted from the junior high, especially interscholastic athletics, but also more intramurals. Some of the newer activities in middle schools are of a shorter duration and meet less frequently than a regular class. Many of these grow out of student and teacher interests and range from "Current Events" to "Wood Carving," with teachers and community resource persons leading these activities.

Guidance. A major function of middle schools has been to provide more guidance for this critical age group, with a focus on both personal behavior and intellectual development. Increasingly the guidance responsibilities are shared by teachers and the full-time guidance personnel. Typically, the teacher guidance function is carried out under such designations as "A-A" (advisor-advisee), "home base," or "home room." A common organization is a daily session of 15 minutes or longer, which is used for school orientation, participation in school government, individual conferences, study or homework, and special activities relating to the interests and problems of this age group.

Staffing. Probably the most persistent, and troubling, problem of the middle school has been adequate staffing. Most personnel in middle schools have come from elementary and junior high schools, or they are beginners trained for these levels. Inservice education has helped some, and slowly teacher education institutions have added middle-level preparatory programs. Only 30% of the member institutions of the American Association of Colleges of Education responding to McEwin's and my 1981 survey had these programs; by 1986 only 33% had them. This situation worries me most! On a more positive note, interest in middle schools is evident by the fact that at both the 1988 and 1989 annual conferences of the National Middle School Association, some 8,000 persons were in attendance.

Evaluation. I believe that the majority of schools now classified as "middle schools" are working diligently to achieve the goals announced by the National Middle School Association in 1977. These widely cited "priority goals" for middle schools are:

1. Every student should be well known as a person by at least one adult in the school who accepts responsibility for his/her guidance.
2. Every student should be helped to achieve optimum mastery of the skills of continued learning together with a commitment to their use and improvement.

3. Every student should have experiences designed to develop decision-making and problem-solving skills.
4. Every student should acquire a functional body of fundamental knowledge.
5. Every student should have opportunities to explore and develop interests in aesthetic, leisure, career, and other aspects of life.

The recent survey Ken McEwin and I conducted comparing middle schools of 1968 with those of 1988, and the 1988 survey of schools by different grade-level organization that I have already drawn upon here, plus a 1988 survey by the Association for Supervision and Curriculum Development, which used approximately the same number of schools in its sample, yielded remarkably similar data regarding the middle schools' achievements. Certain characteristics or "earmarks" of good middle schools were used as criteria in both of these surveys. A summary of our findings and my wonderings about each criterion follow:

1. *An interdisciplinary organization, with a flexibly scheduled day.* As already noted, the use of interdisciplinary organization has increased greatly in middle schools, with about one-third using this organizational plan in 1988. However, the departmentalized plan still predominates; and uniform daily periods are still common in all middle-grade organizations. Those who have succeeded in getting interdisciplinary teams established are enthusiastic. The challenge now is to get the word out and persuade others to try it.

2. *An adequate guidance program, including a teacher advisory plan.* As previously noted, the popular "A-A" and "home base" plans have come from being almost unknown to use in about 40% of middle-level schools in 1988. Both "small group advisories" and teaming plans were recommended by the recent influential report of the Carnegie Task Force on Education of Young Adolescents, *Turning Points* (1989). We now need to seek out other funding agencies that will follow Carnegie's lead and provide grants to help implement these recommendations.

3. *A broad-based exploratory program.* By 1988 all middle-level organizational plans had in common an emphasis on careers, computers, health and sex education, plus a wide variety of newer courses and special-interest activities, including mini-courses on a multiplicity of subjects. Both interscholastic and intramural athletics are popular now.

4. *Curriculum domains providing for such broad goals as basic knowledge, continued learning skills, and personal development.* For

the basic knowledge areas, almost 100% required language arts, mathematics, science, and social studies (the last two being slightly less than universal) throughout the middle grades. For the continued learning skills area, we found increased requirements for reading instruction and computer skills. For the personal development area, the entire exploratory program and the guidance provisions noted under Criterion 2 and 3 as well as the health and physical education program serve these goals. What else does the curriculum need to reduce dropouts and illiteracy? I believe good teaching throughout is the best answer.

5. *Varied instructional methodology appropriate for the age group.* We did not attempt in our survey to get adequate data on this criterion. We did inquire about the independent study opportunities and found they had increased considerably over the 20 years between our surveys. However, we did not find much progression from grade to grade as might be expected, since students should become increasingly independent as they mature and progress through the grades. The future of middle schools will depend on a teaching force that can effectively use a variety of instructional techniques.

6. *Continued orientation and articulation for students, parents, and teachers.* By 1988 preparatory activities for opening new middle schools became more important and more prevalent. Also more common were efforts to articulate the middle school with the levels below and above it. Many innovative practices were reported by write-in responses to our 1988 survey. One word of advice I would offer here to middle school administrators and teachers is that they remember that each year, indeed each day in some communities, brings new students, parents, and school personnel, who will need orientation. Orientation efforts will need to be continuous, not just the first year or two.

Looking Ahead

In looking to the future, I would place middle-level education as one of our first priorities. Middle schools already have become a key link in our three-tier system of precollegiate education. We cannot let it suffer the fate of its predecessor, the junior high school. First, the public needs to be better informed about the purposes and programs of the middle school, although much progress has been made in this regard through the efforts of the National Middle School Association and allied groups. Second, it is essential that the teachers and administrators working at this level receive special training in middle-level education. This must occur at both the preservice and inservice levels. And many steps remain before all the criteria for good middle schools are met.

As I reflected on my career in writing this essay, I have said to myself, "I wish I could do it over" and "Why didn't I see this then?" and "What did I overlook?" For example, I have long been opposed to a national curriculum, but I wonder if we have outgrown the once very valid position that argued against central direction and standardization of education in the United States. Do today's perplexing problems call for nationwide standards for licensing school teachers and administrators? Or standards for high school graduation? Or literacy standards for employment? I continue to wonder, but I'm wandering again!

Public Schools and the Well-Being of America

BY ERNEST L. BOYER

I should note at the very outset that I came to education indirectly. My graduate work was in language development, with special focus on the pathologies of speech. And then, as a post-doctoral fellow at the University of Iowa Hospital, I studied new surgical procedures for middle-ear deafness. These experiences — especially my work with linguistically disadvantaged children — informed my vision of education and convinced me, early on, that language and learning are inextricably interlocked.

My more direct involvement in academic work goes back to the 1950s when, after a teaching stint, a college president friend of mine asked, almost in desperation, if I would become dean at what was, I suspect, the world's smallest higher learning institution. While this struggling little college closed its doors years ago, it was during this assignment that I began to ask questions about teaching and learning that have captured my curiosity to this day. What, in fact, does it mean to be an educated person? Is there a core of learning appropriate for all students? And if so, how should such a curriculum be shaped? What is an appropriate environment for learning? And how do we evaluate results?

While reflecting on these questions, I was invited in the late 1950s to a conference at the Center for Advanced Study at Palo Alto, California. There I met Ralph Tyler, then director of the center, who became a key mentor in my life. He, perhaps more than any other person, reinforced my understanding that goals, curriculum, and evaluation are the essential issues every educator must confront. More

---

Ernest L. Boyer is President of the Carnegie Foundation for the Advancement of Teaching.

than that, Ralph Tyler deepened my conviction that education was not only a socially consequential subject but can, and should be, intellectually compelling, too.

In addition, several other assignments significantly shaped my view of education. In 1960, I was asked to serve as director of the Commission to Improve Teacher Education for the Western College Association. Later, I accepted the directorship of the Center for Coordinated Education at the University of California at Santa Barbara. Both positions — coupled with the post-Sputnik push for school reform — helped me understand that the precollegiate years of education are transcendentally the most important and that the work of higher education is, above all, connected to the schools.

My time with the State University of New York (SUNY) also taught me lessons that persisted. During this period, for example, I became increasingly committed to nontraditional education and lifelong learning. As chancellor I launched, in the early 1970s, Empire State College as a noncampus institution, which made it possible for adults to complete their degree programs while working closely with a mentor.

While at SUNY my commitment to international education also deepened. Like most Americans of my generation, I had been profoundly influenced by World War II. While missing the draft, I did sign on to a United Nations relief ship in 1946 and traveled to Europe. I was shocked by the devastation I saw in war-ravaged Poland. Then during the darkest days of the Cold War, I worried, along with most Americans, about nuclear destruction. And as a young father, I began to reflect on how the nation's colleges and schools might extend human understanding and help build a safer, more peaceful world.

These concerns were still very much on my mind in 1972 when my wife, Kay, and I were invited to the People's Republic of China. We traveled alone to that far-off country still caught in the grip of the Cultural Revolution. In China I was challenged by traditions that differed so dramatically from our own, and I wondered: "How can we in America help our children understand just how much their destiny is tied to other cultures on our shrinking planet?" Later, in response to an invitation from another region of the world, I was pleased to sign an agreement to further student exchange between the State University of New York and all higher learning institutions in Israel. Then, in 1976, Rector Khokhlov of Moscow State University and I signed the first undergraduate exchange program between the United States and the Soviet Union.

16

In the intervening years the world has become a more crowded, more interdependent place. My concern about the urgent need for international understanding continues to grow. And I frequently find myself asking: Is education in this country becoming parochial at the very moment the human agenda is more global? How can we adequately prepare our students for the world they will inherit?

A crucial turning point in my career came in 1977 when, quite unexpectedly, I received a call from Joe Califano, newly appointed Secretary of Health, Education and Welfare, asking if I would accept the post of United States Commissioner of Education in the Carter Administration. I said "no" at first. After all, I genuinely liked my job as chancellor of SUNY. Further, I viewed Washington as a place concerned more with politics than education. But in the end, Secretary Califano was persuasive; and once again, I experienced a profound shift in my priorities for education.

It was during my term as commissioner that the crisis of the disadvantaged hit me with stunning force; and I began to understand more clearly than before just how wide the gap truly is between the privileged and the disadvantaged. As commissioner I was responsible for the administration of the Title I program of the Elementary and Secondary Education Act, the Bilingual Education Act, and the newly authorized Education for All Handicapped Act — all of which reinforced my conviction that the federal role in education must, above all, promote human justice.

But one event in Washington — a rather minor one it seemed at the time — influenced me perhaps more than any other. During the first days of his administration, President Carter instructed all agencies to prepare a "zero-based" budget. The goal was to go back to square one and "prioritize," as they said, all federal programs from top to bottom. In response, I scheduled a weekend retreat with members of my senior staff, suggesting that we take time off to debate the merits of the 146 separate programs administered by the Office of Education. As we examined various priorities, I was most impressed by Cora Beebe, the Office of Education's Director of the Budget, who argued eloquently that the Indian Education Program should be the "number one" priority for the office. The federal government, Beebe insisted, has both a legal and moral obligation to help Native American children who were suffering under pathetic, prejudicial conditions that we, as a nation, had tragically imposed. Her argument was profoundly compelling for me, and I remain deeply troubled by America's unwillingness to respond adequately to the needs of our Native American population.

After my service in government, I came to the Carnegie Foundation for the Advancement of Teaching. As president of this policy study center based in Princeton, I concluded that our goal should be to help shape the debate about American education, focusing our reports on consequential issues. But what issues should be addressed? For years, the foundation had focused primarily on higher education. But soon after I arrived, the trustees agreed that education is a seamless web and that while our concern for colleges should persist, perhaps the time had come for Carnegie also to look at precollegiate education. This became a mandate for our work; and during the decade of the Eighties, we focused on three essential themes.

First, Carnegie studies have stressed the *centrality of language* — a commitment that goes back to my work with children who were deaf. I remain convinced that proficiency in the written and the spoken word is the first and most essential goal of education, and that becoming skilled in the use of symbols is the means by which all students will socially and educationally succeed. In our reports we also argued repeatedly that writing should be taught in every class, since it's through clear writing that clear thinking can be taught. And we have insisted that all students must, above all, be able to express their convictions with clarity and coherence, to integrate ideas, and to listen with empathic understanding.

The second theme in our work has been the *essentialism of teaching*. There's a background story here that is worth recalling. In 1981 the late Bartlett Giamatti, then president of Yale University, invited me to give the presidential address at his institution. Almost on impulse, I chose as my theme "Teaching in America." Among other things, I said on that occasion that the teaching profession in this country is caught "in a vicious cycle, spiraling downward." I observed that, "Rewards are few, morale is low, the best teachers are bailing out, and the supply of good recruits is drying up. Especially disturbing is the fact that *good* teachers are not rewarded for their work."

Well, I was unprepared for the flood of responses I received. At that time, the image of teachers in this country was largely negative — with headlines about strikes, labor conflicts, and the like. But in response to my description of the pressures and problems of the profession, large numbers of teachers wrote to say how pleased they were that someone had given voice to their concerns. And I was especially impressed that many commented on how they were being called upon increasingly to do what the nation's homes, communities, and churches have not been able to accomplish.

Thus the working conditions of teachers became a centerpiece of our 1983 report, *High School*. And from that time on, excellence in teaching has remained a major theme in all our work. Indeed, it is now clear to almost everyone that teachers simply must be given a greater role in decision making and that in the next phase of school reform, classroom teachers must become more active partners in renewal. The good news is that the public attitude toward the profession seems to be improving. We still have a long way to go, of course; but the difficult and demanding work of teachers does appear to be better understood today. I eagerly anticipate the time when the profession of teaching in this country will be given the dignity and status it deserves. Only then will the nation's schools be vibrantly successful.

A third theme in our work at the foundation relates to the *engagement of students*. During school visits I became increasingly aware that this country has not just a *school* problem but a *youth* problem, too. Among far too many teenagers there is a disturbing sense of drift, a feeling of being unwanted, unneeded, and unconnected to the larger world. And I became convinced that if education truly was to succeed, the nation's young people must feel socially engaged and see a relationship between the classroom and the realities of life.

With this in mind, we urged that every student complete a community service requirement. We call it the "new Carnegie unit." The old Carnegie academic units measure time in class or "seat time," while the new Carnegie unit puts emphasis on service. The goal is to help all students see a connection between what they learn and how they live, and to understand that they are not only autonomous individuals but also members of a larger community to which they are accountable. Further, a community service program in the school would tap unused talent, suggest to young people that they are needed, and build bridges across the generations.

The good news is that the service idea is catching on. School districts from Vermont to California are including community service in the curriculum, and some have even included it as a requirement for graduation. Hundreds of colleges and universities also have made service a key part of the undergraduate experience. And just last year Congress passed legislation in support of national youth service, recognizing that such activity can enable students to live lives of dignity and purpose and to channel knowledge to humane ends.

But what about the future? What priorities should the nation's schools pursue in the decade of the Nineties?

19

First, I believe that American education now stands at a historic moment of transition. After years of unshaking faith in grassroots control of education, America now seems ready to support a "top down" national agenda for our schools. And for the first time in our history, the citizens of this country appear to be more concerned about national results than local control. Consider that President Bush, after declaring himself the "Education President," convened an education summit that brought together the governors from all 50 states. Consider also that in his first state of the union message, President Bush announced six goals for all the nation's schools. Consider, too, that according to a recent Gallup Poll, most Americans now support national goals, national testing, and a national curriculum for the schools. Thus the decade of the Nineties is ushering in a dramatic new phase of school reform, one dominated largely by *national mandates* for excellence and *state accountability* for results.

It is true, of course, that national goals can give focus and direction to our work. It's also true that local schools must be held accountable for the performance of their students. And who can argue with the proposition that this nation simply must have more reliable evidence that its $180 billion investment in public education is paying off. At the same time, there is just so much that can be accomplished by directives from above. Educational leadership must be school-based; principals need freedom and flexibility to do the job; and above all, teachers must be full partners in the process. Thus during the decade of the Nineties, American education must find a way to blend local school control with national results. And how we resolve tension between these priorities surely will shape public schooling − and the nation − for years to come.

A second crucial issue for the Nineties relates to the content of education. Is there a core curriculum for the schools? If so, how should it be defined? During the first phase of school reform, most states increased their requirements for graduation. Students were asked to complete more credits in English, in science, in mathematics, and the like. The push has been to help students become well grounded in traditional academic fields and achieve "cultural literacy," as E.D. Hirsch has proposed. Still, I find it disturbing that students can complete the required courses, receive a high school diploma, and still fail to gain a more coherent view of knowledge and a more integrated, more authentic view of life.

What then should be the core curriculum for the schools? In a world that is academically fragmented and culturally diverse, there is no simple answer to this challenge. But as we approach a new century, I am convinced we simply must not only introduce our students to the facts of history, literature, and science but also help them understand how the separate fields of knowledge relate to one another. Further, it is urgent that we help students think about the transcendent human problems, the environment, energy, population, hunger, and a host of other global issues, which they will inevitably confront as adults. And in our interdependent world, it is crucial that they learn about cultures and traditions other than their own in order to overcome prejudices that lead to conflict of unspeakable dimensions. In short, how can we shape a curriculum that is focused on the next century, not the last?

A related challenge is assessment. Is it possible to evaluate school results? I find it quite remarkable that after years of formal schooling, we still remain so confused about how to measure the performance of our students. Thinking back, I recall that when I was U.S. Commissioner of Education, the "minimum competency" movement was in full swing. Thirty-four states had, on their own initiative, mandated some form of testing to find out what was happening to students. This grassroots movement, driven primarily by politicians, should have been a warning about accountability issues. And then, as pressure for public accountability became increasingly intense, states added more tests, frequently using instruments that focused primarily on the recall of isolated facts. Meanwhile, the SAT emerged — inappropriately, I might add — as a national report card on public education. And in the early Eighties the Secretary of Education began releasing to the media the now famous "wall charts" ranking the educational achievement of all 50 states.

Looking down the road, it is clear that we simply must devise better ways to measure the full potential of every child. In pursuit of this objective, I would like to see a national R&D program on assessment — a kind of peacetime "Manhattan Project" — that would bring together scholars and classroom teachers from across the country to shape more appropriate methods of assessment, which would focus not just on knowledge acquisition but on knowledge integration, too. And I surely hope that by the year 2000 our assessment procedures acknowledge not just verbal intelligence but also the aesthetic, spatial, intuitive, and social intelligences in children. To neglect these essential talents is to do violence to the dignity and uniqueness of each student.

I have a final concern, one that is perhaps a backdrop to all others. In the search for educational excellence, I am convinced that we simply must give more attention to life *outside* the school, since many of the problems in the classroom reflect the pathologies in the community and home. Indeed, the longer it goes the more I am persuaded that the family is a much more imperiled institution than the school, and that we must focus increasingly not on schools but on the social crises that surround them.

Recently, at the Carnegie Foundation, we surveyed 22,000 teachers. More than half of the respondents wrote powerful, often poignant comments about their work, focusing frequently on the lives of children. One teacher wrote: "Today's children are living with many more stresses than children of a decade or even five years ago. Single-parent families, dual-employed parents, unemployment, and teen parents have produced children with little or no coping skills, and parents are too busy, too uneducated themselves to help." Another teacher told us: "I'm sick and tired of seeing my bright, achieving first-graders fade into the shadows of apathy and trouble by age 10. They need parents who care, who expect, and who appreciate. Teachers simply cannot do it all."

America wants, and surely needs, effective schools. But let's acknowledge that we cannot have an island of excellence in a sea of indifference. In order to achieve quality in the classroom, parents simply must become active partners in the process. Further, let's acknowledge that poverty and schooling are inseparably connected, and that poor performance in the classroom may, in fact, be connected to events that precede schooling — and even birth itself. Thus if this nation hopes to have all children "ready to learn," as President Bush proposes, mothers and babies must have good nutrition. And we must have full funding of Head Start and Chapter One programs, which focus on our least advantaged students.

There are, I believe, hopeful signs. I'm encouraged, for example, that today, after years of discussion and debate, we have a strong consensus about school reform. Almost everyone now agrees on these seven strategies for renewal: early intervention, proficiency in language, teacher empowerment, a coherent curriculum, thoughtful evaluation, motivation among students, and the partnership of parents. Clearly, we have the right *agenda* for good schools, but do we have the *will*? Will America stay the course or become beguiled by "quick fixes," easy answers, or, even worse, give up on the democratic dream of public schooling for the public good? We can launch experimental projects and tinker on the edges; but if we fail to support fully the nation's public schools, we run the risk of losing the *one* institution that is still helping us sustain the sense of community America so sorely needs.

I have been involved in education for nearly 40 years. Now, in the later years of an enormously rewarding career, I'm left with this deeply held conviction: More than ever before, the sustaining of a network of strong and vital public schools is crucial to the well-being of our nation. There should never be one child — let alone a generation of children — to pass through our schools intellectually unawakened and unprepared to live with confidence and compassion. Educating all children to their full potential is still America's first and most challenging obligation.

Melding Education
and Politics

BY JOHN BRADEMAS

Education is a matter about which I feel intensely. I am the son of a Greek immigrant father and a Hoosier schoolteacher mother. I was raised in a family for whom education was central. The Brademas family today includes, in addition to a former member of Congress and university president, a university professor, a public school teacher, and a successful businessman.

During my childhood, my two brothers, my sister, and I spent the summers in my grandparents' home in Swayzee, a small town in north-central Indiana. There we were exposed to my grandfather's keen interest in history and politics and to his library, which had nearly ten times more volumes (7,000) than Swayzee had people. I practically lived in that library, and those books enabled me to travel in my mind far beyond the borders of Swayzee, Indiana. So deep was my father's commitment to education that he used to say, "John, I'll never leave much money to my children, but I will leave you all a first-class education."

That education began for me in local public schools — James Madison Elementary and Central High in South Bend — and led to Harvard University. My four years at Harvard (1946-50) was like living in a magnificent treasure house of ideas and people. Not only did I study under great teachers, such as Samuel Beer, Raphael Demos, William Yandell Elliott, Carl Friedrich, Alvin Hansen, Louis Hartz,

John Brademas is President of New York University and served in the U.S. Congress for 22 years (1959-80) as Representative from Indiana. Portions of this essay are adapted from John Brademas (with Lynne P. Brown) The Politics of Education: Conflict and Consensus on Capitol Hill, Norman, Okla.: University of Oklahoma Press, 1987.

and Perry Miller; but I learned as well from the bright, intense students of the postwar generation.

A Rhodes Scholarship at Oxford opened another cornucopia of people and ideas as well as new places to visit – England, Holland, France, my father's homeland, Greece. Yet I was drawn to Spain and decided to write my doctoral dissertation on the anarchist movement in Catalonia from 1923 through mid-1937, which marked the end of the first year of the Spanish Civil War.

While in England completing my dissertation and wondering what I would do on returning to the United States, I considered three options: pursuing a career in the U.S. Foreign Service or the United Nations, becoming an Hispanic scholar, or running for Congress. This was the summer of 1953, a time of turbulence in American politics. The newspapers were filled with accounts of the assaults of Wisconsin senator Joseph McCarthy on, among other groups, the U.S. Foreign Service; and I decided that the life of a professional diplomat, constrained to suffer such senatorial abuse in silence, was not for me. I wanted to be where I could talk back.

So in 1954, at the age of 26, I sought a seat in the U.S. House of Representatives from my home district in Indiana, centering on South Bend. After winning the nomination in a field of several candidates, I lost to the Republican incumbent in the general election by five-tenths of a percentage point. Coming that close to winning, naturally, I decided to run again in 1956. In the interim during 1955-56, I worked in Chicago as Adlai E. Stevenson's executive assistant in charge of research for his second presidential campaign. Both Stevenson and Brademas lost their races in the Eisenhower landslide of 1956.

I started teaching political science at Saint Mary's College in South Bend; but still convinced that I could go to Congress, I ran a third time and was elected in November 1958. The following January, I was sworn in as a freshman member of the 86th Congress. I was re-elected 10 times, serving 22 years in all.

As this brief biographical sketch makes clear, the two strands of education and politics were firmly woven into the experiences of my youth and young adulthood. By the time I entered Congress, at 31, I already held firm views about education and its place on the national agenda. First, I was convinced that education was indispensable to happiness, defined by the Greeks as "the exercise of vital powers along lines of excellence in a life affording them scope."

Second, education had not only expanded my own capacities but was demonstrably a ladder to social and economic advance. That the son of an Indiana schoolteacher and a Greek immigrant should have been able to study at two of the finest universities in the world profoundly impressed on me the power of education for opening opportunities.

Beyond an appreciation of the power of education to shape an individual's skills and values and to enhance his mobility in society, I had by the time I went into politics another conviction: that education was the foundation for building a strong nation both in economic and material terms and in the quality of its intellectual and cultural life.

The year of my third and successful bid for Congress (1958) was also a momentous one for both education and politics in this country. In that year, under the leadership of President Eisenhower, Congress approved legislation that signalled a new federal role in education, the National Defense Education Act (NDEA).

Education: A View from Capitol Hill

My personal journey from South Bend, Indiana, to Washington, D.C., was such that by the time I entered Congress in 1959, I sought a seat on the Education and Labor Committee. Given my views, that committee seemed a natural legislative home. Moreover, the issues this committee would be considering would also have a major impact on the people I represented in northern Indiana (in my district were the regional campuses of two state universities, Indiana and Purdue; the University of Notre Dame; and Saint Mary's, Goshen, and Bethel Colleges). I also was convinced that in the years ahead the federal government would be giving much more attention to education.

The committee seat I came to hold (second-ranking member of the elementary and secondary subcommittee) had previously been occupied by a congressman from Massachusetts who had left the House to run successfully for the Senate and who in two years' time would occupy still higher office. His name was John F. Kennedy. As president, Kennedy was a vigorous advocate of federal support for education. Although his aspirations for a general school-aid bill were frustrated during his administration, his legacy includes several measures, signed into law in the weeks after his assassination, for medical and dental education, college academic facilities, and vocational education.

The most prodigious outpouring of education legislation came, of course, following the election of 1964, under the leadership of Lyndon Baines Johnson. Now there are some who say, in light of the fragmentary and incremental way in which presidents and Congresses inevitably make policy, that we did not really understand what we were doing when we wrote those laws and the ones that followed during the "Great Society" years. Not so.

We who worked in committee and on the floor to fashion legislative measures to support education and culture had clear and, for us, compelling objectives. Certainly our original intent was not always translated with precision into the final legislative product. Lawmaking in our system is too messy and porous for exact outcomes. Furthermore, an effective congressman learns during the process of legislating and, in response to new information and new ideas, often moves away from first judgments. Nonetheless, I can identify during my time in Congress the commitments that informed my approach — and that of many of my colleagues as well as presidents — to the legislation we passed. Listing such commitments may help to capture the rationale for the diversity of measures enacted in the years from 1959 to 1980.

First, we — and when I say "we," I include presidents, senators, and representatives of both parties — made a commitment to make education accessible to those otherwise likely to be excluded. Obviously, I think here of the Elementary and Secondary Education Act of 1965 (ESEA), which for the first time provided substantial federal funds to elementary and secondary schools, with particular attention to the teaching of disadvantaged children. The financial fulcrum of that act is Title I (now Chapter 1), which channels federal funds to school districts with large numbers of low-income families.

In addition to ESEA, Lyndon Johnson's proudest jewel, there were Project Head Start, Job Corps, Neighborhood Youth Corps, Upward Bound, and all the other components of the War on Poverty. Also, there were the vocational education and manpower-training initiatives and a measure on which I labored long, the Education for All Handicapped Children Act. Each of these programs grew out of a deep concern on the part of many of us about the education of children who were particularly vulnerable.

And to expand the opportunities for a college education, presidents of both parties (Eisenhower, Kennedy, Johnson, Nixon, Ford, and Carter) as well as Democrats and Republicans in Congress created, beginning with the National Defense Education Act of 1958 through a series of higher education laws, a fabric of grants, loans, and work-study jobs for talented and motivated but needy young men and women.

We made a second commitment during my time in Washington to support our institutions of culture. The milestones along this path included the National Endowments for the Arts and the Humanities as well as programs to assist libraries. I was proud to be a champion of these measures on Capitol Hill and to sponsor other programs, such as assistance for museums.

There was a third commitment: to strengthen international studies in our colleges and universities. Here I cite the International Education Act of 1966, of which I was also author, as well as other efforts to encourage teaching and learning about the peoples and cultures of the rest of the world.

A fourth commitment was to research. Support from the national government has been crucial in enhancing our understanding of ourselves and our universe through, among other entities, the National Science Foundation, the National Institutes of Health, the National Institute for Handicapped Research, and the National Institute of Education. I felt a special commitment to the last initiative. When I introduced the bill to create the National Institute of Education, substantial percentages of the annual federal budgets for defense, agriculture, and health were earmarked for research and development. Yet when it came to education, with its enormous impact on our society, there was negligible investment in the kind of research needed to generate thoughtful, objective evidence about and analysis of how people teach and learn.

These four commitments, then, guided and informed our actions as lawmakers for education. The result was a legislative record of which I remain proud.

But I must also note some failures. Although successful with a number of proposals, I had my share of defeats — legislative initiatives never enacted or fully implemented because of lack of money or lack of support — often from the executive branch. The Comprehensive Child Development Act, which then Senator Walter F. Mondale and I wrote and Congress passed in 1971 but which President Nixon vetoed, is an example. I am heartened to see the final passage — nearly 20 years later — of child-care legislation in the last session of the 101st Congress in 1990.

Other measures that addressed pressing concerns, which have only grown worse in the interim, include the Alcohol and Drug Abuse Education Act of 1971 and the Environmental Quality Education Act of 1970. Both have been on the statute books for almost two decades, but neither received adequate funds to fulfill its promise. These remain areas, of course, where we still desperately need action and federal support.

Education: A View from the Campus

Since 1981 I have been president of New York University, the largest private institution of higher learning in the nation. My experiences on a campus have only reinforced my judgment that the actions taken by the federal government over the last three decades in support of colleges and universities and the students who attend them have been indispensable to the building of a strong and vibrant system of higher education.

The record vividly demonstrates the impact of a national commitment to higher education:

- in providing an opportunity for a college education to millions of talented but needy students;
- in supporting research and a constant stream of scholars intent on pushing back the limits of knowledge;
- in advancing solutions to problems ranging from combatting disease to increasing economic productivity, to protecting the environment, to alleviating poverty;
- in enabling the interchange of scientists and scholars between and among nations.

As Stephen Graubard, editor of the journal *Daedalus*, has said, "American colleges and universities have shown a remarkable capacity for growth, innovation, invention and renovation." By any measure, the system of higher education in the United States is the envy of the world. But, Graubard warns, "No one would have made that claim in 1939 . . . and one cannot be certain that such a claim will still be made in 2039."

At New York University over the last decade, we have had our eye on the 21st century and our sights focused on one overriding aim: to become a research university of the first rank. Our progress toward that goal has been impressive − and offers an instructive glimpse into the opportunities and challenges facing a major modern American university.

First, we have launched an array of academic initiatives to build on current strengths and move the university forward in selected disciplines. These programs have ranged from U.S.-Japanese economic relations to Talmudic law, from film and television to ultra-computers, from Hellenic studies to neural science. An area of particular emphasis has been European Studies, where we are developing expertise in the sweep of countries extending from the Iberian Peninsula and Western Europe through Eastern Europe to the Mid-

29

dle East. Second, we have made a strong faculty stronger, establishing since 1981 more than 60 endowed professorships.

Third, we have built a genuinely residential university that attracts students from throughout the nation and from 100 foreign countries. Undergraduate applications and enrollment, student quality, and geographic diversity all increased during the 1980s. In 1981 just 16% of our undergraduates lived on campus. Today that figure is nearly 50%. Student residence halls have been only one part of an ambitious construction and renovation program, with more than $250 million invested in classrooms, laboratories, and computing facilities.

Fourth, we have been fortunate in generating funds in amounts unprecedented in the history of the university. We are more than halfway – and well ahead of schedule – toward our goal of raising $1 billion by the year 2000.

The result of all these developments has been the emergence of New York University as a leading national – and in some fields international – center of scholarship, teaching, and research. But if our institutions of higher learning are to follow the example of New York University, if they are effectively to carry out their responsibilities, they must have support from a wide range of sources: alumni and friends, private foundations, business and industry, and especially from federal and state governments.

Certainly the 1980s saw a weakening of the commitment of the federal government to education generally and higher education in particular. The administration of Ronald Reagan marked a sea change in the attitude of a modern American president toward the federal role in education. Evidence for this assertion was to be found in proposed budgets that called for deep slashes in student aid, in tax policies that imposed new burdens on institutions of learning, in the rhetoric of high-ranking government officials contemptuous of the values of a college education, and in an administration ideology that pointed to wealth rather than need as key to educational opportunity. Fortunately, both Republicans and Democrats in Congress joined to prevent the most destructive of Mr. Reagan's assaults on higher education. The administration of George Bush has brought kinder and gentler rhetoric but not significantly greater resources to the enterprise of education.

As colleges and universities enter the next decade, they are confronted, beyond declining federal support, by a number of other pressures and demands: strengthening the liberal arts, improving teaching about foreign countries and cultures, rebuilding graduate education, ensuring educational opportunity. Let me explain.

In response to perceived shortcomings in the undergraduate curricula and in international studies and research, many colleges and universities are taking steps to strengthen these areas. New York University, for instance, has put in place a core curriculum in the liberal arts and sciences. And we have reinstituted foreign language and other international studies requirements.

Another challenge facing colleges and universities is to reinvigorate a graduate studies enterprise plagued by problems – the loss of talented students, sharp rises in the proportion of foreign students receiving American doctorates, the deteriorating state of the physical infrastructure that supports research and scholarship, and looming shortages of faculty. And a final task is helping ensure access to talented but needy students, particularly minorities.

Education and the Nation's Future

As we move into the decade of the Nineties, the nation will be looking to our educational system as the key instrument for coping with new challenges. Can American industry and workers compete effectively in world markets? As we shift increasingly to high technology and service industries, can we produce the people with the skills these activities require? Are we, in an age of specialization, preparing persons with the perspective to look beyond the recommendations of the experts and technicians and make the judgments required of citizens in a free nation? In a nation more and more apprehensive about the future, it is not surprising that more and more attention is focused on the institutions that will shape that future: our schools, colleges, and universities.

Nor is it unusual that concern about education is spilling beyond classrooms into living rooms, boardrooms, and legislative committee rooms. For in speaking of education, we speak of values – what we as a society believe important and worthy of expenditure of resources. And when we talk of resources – how to generate and allocate them – we enter the realm of politics. Values, resources, politics – all these considerations are inextricably bound up in any discussion of education.

What challenged me as a member of Congress and still does as a university president is the opportunity to meld values with resources and translate the mixture into some sort of viable action. When that action results in advances for education, I find my job immensely rewarding.

Education Beyond
the High School

BY SAMUEL M. BROWNELL

Education beyond the high school level was available tuition-free to about anyone who wanted it and was qualified when I graduated from high school in Nebraska in 1917. The state university and the four state normal schools (now state colleges) admitted, without examination, graduates from accredited high schools who were recommended for college-level work. Graduates from unaccredited high schools were required to pass an entrance examination.

There was no tuition and only a few fees. The registration process was simple. I presented my high school transcript at the registrar's office. She checked it to determine if it was from an accredited high school, if I had passing grades in all of the courses required for admission, and if I had received my school's recommendation for college admission. She then filled out a class schedule form. All but one of my courses were required. She assigned me to class sections that I requested and sent me next door to the bursar's office. There I was told that my costs would be a once-only $5 matriculation fee, semester fees of $2 for library services and $1 for health services, and a $2 chemistry laboratory breakage deposit fee (partially refundable if my breakage was less than $2). The total was $10 as I recall it. This I paid in silver dollars.

As I stepped out of the bursar's office, I was greeted by an Innocent (a member of the Senior Men's Honor Society) who welcomed

---

Samuel M. Brownell was U.S. Commissioner of Education (1953-56), Superintendent of Schools in Detroit, Michigan (1956-66), and Professor Emeritus of Urban Educational Administration, Yale University (1973). He died in October 1990 at the age of 90, shortly after completing this essay.

me to the university. Beside him was a large carton containing green beanies. He located one that fit my head size and presented it to me for 75 cents, with the instruction that I was to wear it whenever I was on the campus during the first semester. I had become a full-fledged university freshman in about 30 minutes, and for $10.75!

High school graduation exercises in 1917 (my class) were much like those of the class of 1990. We seniors lined up outside the auditorium where parents and friends were gathered. As the strains of "Pomp and Circumstance" filled the auditorium, the audience stood and the seniors marched in. All remained standing while an invocation was delivered by a member of the local clergy. The National Anthem was sung, and the audience was seated. Two honor seniors each delivered a short oration, followed by a musical selection. An imported dignitary gave a too-long speech; there was another musical selection, after which prizes and awards were announced.

Then came the long-awaited presentation of diplomas, with the graduates crossing the stage one by one as their names were announced. The exercises closed with singing of the school's Alma Mater by the graduates and the audience, a benediction was pronounced, and the audience remained standing while the graduates filed out. Outside graduates, parents, and friends joyously greeted each other, congratulations were voiced, and tearful farewells were exchanged between classmates who now would be parting.

You recognize the scenario, as I do, for I have attended more than 300 high school and college commencements in the past 74 years and have enjoyed them all. Each is a once-in-a-lifetime experience for the seniors celebrating their attainment of a long-sought goal.

There was one difference between my graduating class in 1917 and those in 1990. We were in the midst of bitter fighting in World War I. All the nation's energies were concentrated on winning the struggle. No one knew how much longer the war would last. A number of the seniors had left before the end of the school year to enlist. Some of them had secured a furlough to come home for the graduation. Their presence, in uniform, brought forth special applause as they received their diplomas.

In the weeks following graduation most of the 18- and 19-year-olds enlisted. Some of us who were still 17 were torn between the desire to "join up" and the counsel from our elders to continue with schooling as long as possible so that the pipeline to the Officer Candidate Schools would be kept filled with college-trained youth, since no one could predict how much longer the war would last. A number of us opted for the state university in Lincoln, which had a Reserve Officers Training Corps program (in 1918 it became a unit of the Student Army Training Corps). We were barracked on campus and took university classes about half time. The rest of the time was spent in military drill and military science and tactics taught by officers detailed from the Army. Periodically, contingents would be sent to Officer Candidate Schools.

Although the graduation ceremonies of 1917 and 1990 looked much alike, the graduates of 1990 enter a world much altered from that of 1917. In the 1915-20 era, the world of work a high school graduate entered was heavily dependent on unskilled labor for the farms, the factories, and the building trades. The common pattern for a majority of youths was to leave high school after one or two years. Many continued as unskilled laborers all of their working life. Only a minority remained in high school and graduated. Of these only a few aspired to one of the professions or had the financial resources to go to college.

Youth on the farm and in the city started contributing to family support at an early age. On the farm there were endless chores to be performed; in towns and cities a youth might be stocking shelves in the family grocery store. Boys earned small sums by peddling papers, shoveling snow, cutting grass for neighbors, or as a bootblack. For girls there were opportunities for household help as "hired girls." Part-time jobs often led to full-time employment. In those days each child was perceived as a potential source of income for the family. Thus it was of concern to the family when a youth extended his dependence on the family rather than becoming self-supporting and/or contributing to family support.

It was not uncommon in a family of several children to have each child, after reaching the eighth grade, stay out of school for a year to help on the farm or to hold a factory or other job in order to help support the family. They were not "dropouts"; they were enabling their siblings to continue with schooling. Many of my contemporaries can recall their "turns" to stay at home, and their "turns" to attend high school or college.

Youths joining the labor force took low-paying jobs hoping that if they worked diligently and faithfully, they would "learn the trade" and receive promotions to higher-paying positions, for example, from office boy to eventually head of the firm, from water boy to foreman, from farmhand to farm owner, from clerk to marrying the boss's daughter. Males were proud of being "self-made" men. Some, of course, remained as unskilled laborers throughout their lives, moving from one job to another, knowing that they would nearly always be able to find temporary work in the harvest field, on the road gangs, or on building projects.

In the 1990s advances in science and technology have changed that labor picture dramatically. New machines enable a worker to do in minutes what formerly took hours or days. Many manual operations are now done by machines, faster and more precisely. Increasingly robots do what laborers or even skilled workers formerly performed. Also, science and technology have produced jobs requiring special training beyond the high school. It takes highly skilled persons to operate the machines and instruments and to supervise them. Persons in these positions command higher wages, which are offset by their increased productivity. And so it goes in the banking field, in the health services, in the communication industries, etc. − fewer and fewer unskilled jobs, more and more need for workers with highly specialized training requiring education beyond high school.

Early in our history, the leaders of this nation decided that an educated citizenry was necessary to develop its resources, to maintain its stability, and to promote its economy. To that end each state required that all towns and villages establish a school and required parents to send their children to school until they had completed six or more years or had reached the age of 14 or 16. The schooling was free so that all children − rich and poor − would be educated. Later on, this principle of publicly supported education for all was extended to include secondary schooling, particularly after the *Kalamazoo* decision of 1872.

As a result of this principle, families could send their children to high school tuition-free, and the rate of high school graduation began to increase, reaching more than 70% in recent years. Now the goal of most school systems is to increase this percentage by preventing dropouts, since at least a high school diploma is now required for more and more jobs.

Although the public schools already provide 12 or 13 rungs on the education ladder as an investment in the future of the nation, additional education will increase that investment. There is now a need for an education ladder of 14 to 16 rungs. There are many capable young people desirous of climbing the rungs, but they do not have the assets to buy the longer ladder.

The increased demand for persons with education beyond the high school is occurring in other industrialized countries as well. Since

World War II, many of them have established new, government-sponsored post-secondary institutions, many of which offer rigorous technological curricula. In addition, many students, both privately and governmentally supported, have come to the U.S. for advanced education. It is clear, then, that in the years ahead the United States will be competing more and more in world markets with persons whose education is beyond the high school level. The competitive edge would seem to lie with those who have invested in a better and more extended education.

For students the investment means delaying the time until they become independent, wage-earning adults. For families the investment means prolonging the support of their children, paying for tuition and other fees, as well as losing their children's potential contribution to the family income. For the public at large the investment means paying higher taxes to provide the staffs, facilities, and the general operating expenses for post-secondary education. Providing this needed education beyond high school involves considerable financial resources. The cost will be large from whatever sources it is derived. Nevertheless, it is an investment that is justified because with it the nation benefits. Without the investment the nation will not have the skilled workforce that it needs to maintain its economic strength, and many young people with ability and ambition will be prevented from fulfilling their hopes and dreams.

The reason many do not continue their education beyond high school is financial. Today tuition and fees run into several thousand dollars a year, even in publicly supported colleges and universities. It appears to me that this nation is cheating itself by failing to support the large number of students who have the ability and the desire to continue their education beyond high school in order to learn the highly specialized skills required in a technological age. Having already made the investment to enable students to climb the education ladder of 12 or 13 rungs, it would seem sensible to lengthen the ladder in order for them to harvest the fruit they can only reach from the higher rungs of the ladder. After all, we shall all share in the fruits of their labor.

To those who argue that, because more highly trained students will be paid more for the jobs they eventually enter, they should pay for their own training, I would respond that there is no more justification for their paying for schooling beyond grade 12 than their paying for each year of their earlier education. Each year of schooling contributes a part of their total education. If more years of school-

36

ing bring higher wages, then the nation benefits by being able to collect more income taxes. One could argue just as well that a better trained workforce provides benefits to all; therefore, rather than having all the costs of education falling on parents and their children, perhaps non-parent adults should pay a higher rate of school tax.

Be that as it may, it seems quite clear to me that we should be moving forward with a program for tuition-free education beyond the high school level. Our tradition of tuition-free schooling through high school has served the nation well in the past. Now the time has come to prepare our youth for the scientific and technological advances that are certain to continue and to train them to use these advanced technologies.

This will require new ways of financing schooling beyond the high school. The present ways are both inadequate and inequitable. Capable young people from families with limited incomes are finding it more and more difficult to afford the rising costs of post-secondary education. Furthermore, student loan programs are grossly underfunded. Those who do secure loans take on a financial burden that many are not able to handle once they enter the workforce. The default rate on student loans is evidence of this problem. For qualified students, equal educational opportunities should be as readily available at post-secondary levels as they are at the elementary and secondary school levels.

In essence, providing additional tuition-free education beyond the high school is an investment in our nation. Everyone has a stake in this investment, so everyone should help to support and pay for it. It takes no seer to realize that this nation now needs a workforce educated beyond the high school level. It now remains for each state to find ways to finance equal educational opportunities for all who have the ability and wish to continue their education beyond high school. Only in this way will our nation remain competitive in the international marketplace.

My Life in Reading

BY JEANNE S. CHALL

I taught my first class as a student teacher in New York City's Taft
High School in 1941. I had looked forward to teaching, having been
an education major. I had expected to like it, and I did — very much,
in fact. A year later I was introduced to educational research at
Teachers College, Columbia University. My love for educational research was unexpected and came as a complete surprise. I had no
idea that one could work in education doing research. Nor do I recall that any of my undergraduate instructors in education were engaged in research. If they were, I was not aware of it. When I began
working at the Institute of Psychological Research at Teachers College, I was smitten within a few days as I observed such notable
researchers as Irving Lorge and Sophia M. Robison. My role was
to keep notes and to calculate means, standard deviations, and corre-
lations — it was before computers. Although the work was tedious,
to me it was exciting to be working with a group of people who were
helping children and furthering knowledge in a disciplined way. I
knew, then, that I wanted to do the same.

Thus I came early to my two loves in education: teaching and inquiry. Although research and practice are often seen as different
pursuits, I found that for me they had great similarities and were
intimately related to each other.

At Teachers College, the project on which I assisted sought work-
able solutions to one of the pressing educational problems of that
time and today: how best to educate juvenile delinquents and thus
to prevent delinquency. Specifically, we investigated whether it was

*Jeanne S. Chall is Professor of Education and Director of the Reading
Laboratory at Harvard University.*

better to place them in separate schools or to provide them with psychological services and an improved curriculum in regular schools. Among the findings (which are still being confirmed today, 50 years later) were that counseling and social services and a curriculum that had a better match with students' achievement were effective in decreasing the number of delinquents in the regular schools — more effective than special schools. I realized early how practical research can be.

Several years later I learned a similar lesson at Ohio State University as Edgar Dale's research assistant. Our task was to assist the National Tuberculosis Association by finding ways to make their pamphlets and other print media more readable for the layman. This very practical mission led to basic research on readability and vocabulary (the Dale-Chall Readability Formula[1] was developed to help assess the difficulty of the pamphlets) and to the development of a manual on clear and simple writing. Research and practice were intimately related, with research leading to good practice and real problems leading to useful research.

Throughout my long career I have engaged in both practice and research — usually at the same time. Since educational practice does not leave tracks as does educational research, I should like to mention at least some of the practice I have engaged in. I have taught students of all ages for nearly a half-century. Much of it was at the college and graduate level, but much, too, has been with students at all levels who needed special help with their reading.

I also have worked as an advisor and consultant on a variety of educational projects, including children's encyclopedias, an educational comic book, computer programs, and Children's Television Workshop's "Sesame Street" and "The Electric Company." I have consulted with schools and school systems to help them ask and answer educational questions.

These practical assignments helped me gain perspective on the important questions in education being asked by teachers, administrators, educational publishers, and the media; and they kept me from being too theoretical, too removed from reality. I learned to make the most out of the knowledge that existed and not to resort, unless absolutely necessary, to the use of "we need more research" as an answer to questions. I realized early that even the most theoretical studies ultimately boil down to a yes or no response. Is this or that idea more useful? Should this or that be done? If neither, what should be done?

As a member of various investigative and policy-making committees and commissions organized by professional associations and state and national departments of education, and as a member of the boards of directors of various professional groups, I had further opportunity to blend research and practice and to broaden my educational perspective.

Focus on Reading

Most of my work, both research and practice, has focused on reading. From time to time I have wandered off to mathematics or to the non-print media, but I soon came back to reading. For me it offers great challenges related to vast and almost endless issues for research and practice. At the same time, I found reading to be very basic, the bread and butter of education. It is the oldest and most enduring of subjects taught in schools and is an essential foundation for learning almost all other school subjects. It is essential for most jobs in an advanced, technological society.

When reading does not develop as it should, when it lags behind the chronological and cognitive development of the individual, it brings serious personal frustrations and loss of confidence. It brings equally serious losses to society. In fact, the importance of reading for society and for the individual seems to have grown even during the years I have studied it. We are reminded almost daily by leading U.S. economists that we may slip from our status as a world-class nation if our workforce does not achieve a higher level of literacy. They remind us that when we were a manufacturing nation, fewer people needed to be highly literate. But a high-tech society, one that produces and disseminates knowledge and symbols, needs more people who are highly literate. There seems to be a growing mismatch between workers and jobs, with many jobs unfilled because workers are not literate enough.

But it is not for work alone that there is a mismatch. Responsible citizenship also requires higher literacy, and personal literacy needs seem to grow with time. The labels on food and medicine packages require considerable reading ability. Add to this the growing numbers of children reported to have reading and learning disabilities, the low levels of literacy found among minority students, the declining reading scores on the National Assessment of Educational Progress, the declining verbal scores on the SAT, and it is not difficult to see why I have stayed with reading and literacy.

There are still other reasons. The strongest, perhaps, is that we may lose our past if we cannot read it in the texts that record it. And we also may lose the pleasure and inspiration that come from reading great literature — a loss that more of us may experience as life expectancies increase. With a growing number of years in which we are less active, reading can be a deep source of joy and inspiration.

For me, there is still one other reason. The field of reading is so rich and varied that I have been able to change my focus within it, making it ever more interesting and challenging.

Studies in Readability

My first research efforts were in readability and vocabulary, an interest I acquired from the late Edgar Dale, my teacher and mentor at the Bureau of Educational Research at Ohio State University. There I worked with him on the development of the Dale-Chall Readability Formula[2] and on various studies of vocabulary during the four years of my graduate study. These formative years were followed by 40 years of collaboration on research and writing. In fact, one of our works is scheduled for publication in 1991, *Readability Revisited and the New Dale-Chall Readability Formula*.[3]

I found readability a fascinating subject for research and application. It was an excellent vehicle for understanding how reading proficiency develops by studying the changes that take place in the complexity of texts. Readability draws from many disciplines (humanities, psychology, statistics, language, semantics) and in turn can be applied to textbooks, newspapers, magazines, comic books, and other print media.

The four years of working closely with Edgar Dale on readability and vocabulary also taught me lessons about research that still remain with me. One of the first lessons was the value of past research, why it is important and how to use it. After a year as his research assistant, Dale suggested that I write an article reviewing existing research on readability. Although I had been assisting him for a year, I did not feel quite ready to write such an article. To be more accurate, I was terrified. I protested that I didn't know enough. "That is why you should write it," he said. "You will learn from your writing."

I started the research with much anxiety and much agonizing. Why should I do this, I thought. Reviewing past research is not original; I wanted to get on with the new. But after all the fussing, I finally finished it and had to admit it had been a good assignment after all.

I gained familiarity with the past research on readability and became comfortable working with the ideas of earlier researchers. I was exposed to different viewpoints on the topic, some of which were unpopular at the time they were first proposed but later were accepted and became the dominant view. I felt I knew the researchers whose work I reviewed and how they thought. When I met several during the ensuing years, I felt that we had been friends for many years.

I had beginner's luck with that first article. "This Business of Readability" was reprinted in two digest journals.[4] But more valuable was the taste for historical synthesis that I developed. My love for this style of research lead to *Readability: An Appraisal of Research and Application*.[5] My books *Learning to Read: The Great Debate* and *Stages of Reading Development* also have strong research reviews.[6] When I undertook *The Great Debate*, many of my colleagues were skeptical. The research I planned to review was so confused, they said, how could I find anything by going over it again? But I had confidence, from my earlier experiences, that if I stuck with it and found a structure, I would find something useful. Syntheses were out of fashion for a long time but have come back in favor during the past decade. *Becoming a Nation of Readers*[7] is a more current synthesis by a commission of which I was a member.

Dale knew that one has to know what scholars of the past knew on a subject if one is to make useful contributions to that subject. He never assumed that what was done in the past was useless or not worth knowing. He also knew that the new research does not always clear up all the problems of the past research. Indeed, the results of the new can be more confusing than the old.

Knowing the past research keeps one from being too swept up with the current fashion. One can assess trends in a field only from a deep grounding in its past theories, research, and writing. It is sad, therefore, to see that current publications tend to refer only to recent writings, omitting even the classic research on a topic.[8] Have we decided to lose our past? If we do not know the past and do not use it in formulating practice and new research, are we not in danger of repeating the past — the bad as well as the good?

I learned another important lesson from Edgar Dale: the importance of knowing the related research from fields other than one's own. When we planned a project, he asked if I had checked it out with the psychologists, the statisticians, the sociologists, the linguists. Before sending out an article for publication, he asked again if I had checked with those in other disciplines who might pick up inconsistencies, conflicts, and errors. Today, there seems to be little reference in the field of reading to the work of others rooted in other disciplines. Perhaps because the reading field itself is so rich in research and publications, no one person can keep up with all of it.

In the reading field, we seem to have at least five bodies of research: basic research (usually done by educational researchers, cognitive psychologists, and linguists); research on reading methods, materials, and classroom procedures (usually done by educational psychologists, reading specialists, and teachers); research on reading difficulties (by psychologists, neurologists, and special educators); research on the relationship of literature, writing, and reading (by linguists and students of literature and language arts); and research on reading tests (by psychometrists). There seems to be a tendency for individuals in each of these groups to talk almost exclusively with, and to write for, others within their own field. Seldom does one group refer to similar findings from the others.

Recently I read an excellent longitudinal study of children's reading in grades 1 to 4. The authors reported that phonemic development was of first importance in early reading without referring to similar findings by leading researchers on language and learning disabilities at least 15 years earlier; and by educational psychologists in the 1930s for beginning reading. Ignoring the relevant research of others is not uncommon in other areas of education. Can we afford to repeat studies when our research funds are so limited (unless, of course, the research is a deliberate replication)? And can we afford to ignore the relevant research that exists in our field and other disciplines?

Another important lesson I learned from Edgar Dale was to ask for whom one does educational research. For Dale the answer was always clear. All of his studies, including his most theoretical, were designed to be useful in the practice of education in school and out of school. I remember vividly how he helped me realize this after I had written one of my early research reports. He read it, made several editorial suggestions, then said, "Very nice, Jeanne. It is very scholarly. What do you think it will mean to the superintendent in Winnetka, the fifth-grade teacher in Oklahoma City, the English teacher in Cleveland?" I knew then that I was far from finished. I had much rewriting to do.

Reading Difficulty and Its Prevention

In 1950, when I joined the faculty of the City College in New York, my focus shifted from the readability of texts (in relation to readers' abilities) to the study of the readers (in relation to the texts they read). For 15 years my interests were concentrated on the teaching of reading, ways of assessing it, and the causes and treatment of those who experience special difficulties in spite of their adequate intelligence – about 10% to 15% of the population.

In collaboration with my colleague Florence Roswell, who was director of the City College Reading Center, I carried out numerous research and development projects, including auditory blending and its effects on reading achievement, why children of low-income families have difficulty, and what could be done to remediate their difficulties. We developed tests to help teachers adjust instruction to students' needs. My collaboration with Roswell has continued to the present.

It was at City College in the 1950s that I started to concentrate on the diagnosis and treatment of children, youth, and adults with reading problems. It has continued to the present. Indeed, the time I have spent diagnosing and treating individuals with reading problems, and teaching and supervising teachers in this work, has been extremely absorbing and enriching. It has influenced not only my teaching and research on reading difficulties but most of my other research as well, particularly the research I undertook in the early 1960s on beginning reading methods. Concerned with prevention of reading problems, I sought to find whether there was any evidence that certain beginning reading methods produce better results and help prevent reading failure. This research, which was carried out when I was at City College, became the book *Learning to Read: The Great Debate*, which was written and later updated when I was at Harvard.[9]

The study had many facets. It was a synthesis of the past research on beginning reading from the classroom, the laboratory, and the clinic. I also analyzed more than 20 beginning reading programs, the two most widely used basal readers and their teacher's manuals, interviewed authors and editors of various reading series, observed in hundreds of classrooms, and talked to as many teachers and principals. I was fortunate again, as I had been with my first synthesis article on readability, to get an almost immediate response. Although some of the reviews in the reading journals were critical, most reviews in the general educational and scholarly journals were very favorable. Even more satisfying was its early acceptance by textbook publishers in revising their reading programs, and its appearance on required reading lists for courses on methods of teaching reading and reading research. Twenty years later the satisfaction was mixed with pain. In spite of the fact that my update in 1983 confirmed my earlier conclusions and that my earlier and later findings and conclusions were confirmed by the research of linguists, cognitive psychologists, and child development specialists, misunderstandings and attacks on its findings and conclusions have appeared.[10]

My 25 Years at Harvard's Graduate School of Education

My move to Harvard in 1965 marked another shift in my concerns with reading. At Harvard much of my attention has been focused on building and directing a graduate program for master's and doctoral students with the dual purpose of providing training in both scholarship and practice. The Harvard Reading Laboratory, which I directed, was established as a training, research, and service center.

My teaching focused on both research and practice. Through the years I taught the doctoral seminar on reading research, which was a historical overview of the research on reading and practice in synthesizing various aspects of this research. I also taught courses in the diagnosis and treatment of reading disabilities and, with the assistance of doctoral students, supervised the testing and teaching in the Harvard Reading Laboratory. I also taught a general course on reading for administrators and planners and other non-reading majors that focused on social policy and, in earlier years, taught the general course on the teaching of reading. I also had the great pleasure of directing and advising the dissertations of doctoral students and the research training of many graduate students who worked with me on various research projects.

My research continued to be concerned with issues of theory and practice, but it moved somewhat to theory and social policy. Among my studies of reading and social policy was the one commissioned by the Panel on the SAT Score Decline and the College Board on the relationship of textbooks to SAT scores, published in 1977.[11] It was extended to a larger study, *Do Textbooks Challenge Students: A Case for Easy or Hard Textbooks*.[12] My interests in the medical aspects of reading failure became even stronger. I attended lectures at Harvard Medical School on neurology and language; and I edited, with Allan Mirsky, the National Society for the Study of Education Yearbook, *Education and the Brain*.[13]

The unanswered questions in *The Great Debate* led me to a theoretical study of the reading process, *Stages of Reading Development*, a work on how reading changes qualitatively as it develops.[14] This was an important study for me since many of the controversies on methods and materials seemed to stem from two theories of the reading process: a single-stage theory or a multi-stage theory. From my synthesis of the relevant theory and research on how reading develops and from my experience in teaching reading at all levels, I concluded that a developmental, multi-stage theory fit the data better and was instructionally more useful.

In *The Reading Crisis: Why Poor Children Fall Behind*, we attempted to find out why the literacy of low-income children begins to decelerate around grade 4 and how the deceleration can be prevented.[15] The theoretical basis for the study came from my *Stages of Reading Development*. The work was further enriched by collaboration with linguists and many faculty and graduate students at Harvard.

My interests in social policy brought me to studies of the trends in the reading scores on the National Assessments of Educational Progress, and I have tried to explain these trends by relating them to methods and materials used in the schools and to community support for reading.[16]

As I reflect on my various professional interests and activities, I am aware of different concentrations at different times. During my early years I concentrated on psychology, statistics, and research design, on objectivity in searching for knowledge about reading. Later I focused on problems in learning to read and took on the concerns of the teacher and clinician: why certain individuals have difficulty in learning to read, how to help those individuals, and how to prevent such problems. Thus my concerns with the science of reading turned to teaching and healing, and I delved into the neurosciences as well as into the art of teaching.

More recently I have been concerned with the broad social, cultural, and educational issues that are related to our reading problems and to their solution and prevention. Examples of this concern are found in my research on textbooks and publishing, on the trends in scores on the national assessments of reading and writing, and on the methods and materials that work with children from low-income families.

I have gained much from the people with whom I have worked. I have gained great satisfaction from my teaching and have reached the age when my former students are now full professors with students of their own. I have especially gained from my work in the diagnosis and treatment of reading disabilities. Helping children, youth, and adults overcome their reading difficulties has always given me direct and immediate rewards that are especially welcome when the research on which I work reaches a frustrating point. While one cannot always move ahead in research and writing, one can always help a child learn to read.

Current Concerns

In the more than 40 years of working in the field of reading, I have observed much growth in research and in professional activities. The public has become more conscious about the importance of literacy for children and adults. With these many advancements have come many problems. The reading achievement of too many children and adults is not what it should be. This has been reported by the National Assessment of Educational Progress, by the College Board for SAT verbal scores, by school systems over the nation, and by industry, which has long complained that employees are lacking the literacy skills needed for work.

I recognize this sad state is not the sole responsibility of the reading field or of teachers and that improvements will require efforts from many. But I do have concerns that our efforts, particularly those concerned with the methods and materials of reading instruction, may not be fruitful because we are paying too little attention to our hard-won knowledge and experience. We seem to be so pressed by the low literacy achievement of the nation that many of us are resorting to largely untested solutions and ignoring those procedures that are backed up by research and experience.

There also seems to be less confidence than in the past in the power of research and analysis to find better solutions. A single case study or a classroom observation or a "bright idea" is often considered equal or superior to the hard-won knowledge from research and experience.

There is also a loss of confidence in how we can best assess and evaluate reading achievement and progress, thus making it still harder to base practice on objective evidence. Often it seems as if the tests are being criticized because the results are not those we hoped for. Thus we seem to kill the messenger, hoping it will turn the bad news to good. While there is a need for better assessment instruments, it is hard to believe that better assessments will find the state of literacy in the United States to be any better than is now being reported.

Perhaps my concerns are colored by my long and positive experiences with the power of research to inform and serve practice. Do I see the past in a more rosy light? Perhaps. But I think we currently are going through a period in which less attention is paid to analyses of past research, which may, in the long run, lead to even lower levels of reading achievement. Many of the proposals for reform in reading instruction are made with little basis in theory, research, and practice. Indeed, many of the proposed changes have been used in the past, under different labels, and were found wanting.

With the loss of confidence in research has come a heightened emotionality among teachers, parents, and researchers. The stridency of the rhetoric has been labeled by some journalists as "reading wars" in which teachers, parents, and the media line up in different camps with respect to the best method for teaching reading. Certainly there have been differences of opinion about reading instruction during my 40 years in the reading field. But the almost religious fervor of the present rhetoric seems to go beyond what existed in the past. Why is this happening when the research in reading has grown so considerably? Perhaps this vast research base, which should be contributing to better practices, has also contributed to the loss of faith in its use. Perhaps it is too vast and confusing and not sufficiently interpreted and synthesized.

It is sad to think that we go through the same debates over and over again and that we seem to learn so little from the past. The tendency of researchers to use new labels for old concepts also seems to cut us off from the tested knowledge of the past. Thus the new research on phonological awareness seems to cut itself off from the earlier research on phonics; adult literacy seems to cut itself off from child and adolescent literacy; and emergent literacy seems to cut itself off from the vast knowledge and experience on reading readiness. Why do we need to use new labels for old ideas? It may earn immediate attention and interest, but it also cuts off teachers who are urged to do the "new" thing when they may already be doing it, but under an older label.

Where Do We Go from Here?

My present concerns, which are many, have not shaken my strong commitment to research and theory, to the value of analysis, and to experience. In the long run, the methods and materials that will prove to be most effective will be in line with research, theory, and experience. In the meantime, many children, particularly those from low-income families or children from any social level who are predisposed to having reading difficulty, are not doing as well as they can. Such children benefit most from a reading program that has been proven over the years. They need excellent teachers. They need extra help when they fall behind.[17] Children of middle-class families are not affected as much by the reading methods and materials used by their teachers, since their parents often supplement their child's reading instruction by their own teaching or by obtaining a private tutor.

To improve reading achievement I would hope that we can look more to what we know works and apply it wisely and well. For the past decades, study after study has found that certain classroom practices produce significantly better results (for example, setting high expectations, using books that challenge, making frequent assessments and basing instruction on them, providing a strong beginning reading program, attending to word meanings in the intermediate grades and later, and many others).[18]

Unfortunately, some in the reading field act as if the solutions to our pressing problems lie mainly in changing the old, usually tested methods to untested methods, which results in polarization among teachers, parents, and reading specialists. One wonders why we do not invest that energy and time into doing better, and more widely, what does work. Indeed, research study after research study has found that students need to read widely to grow in reading. Why then don't we put more funds into better school, classroom, and community libraries? Indeed, while we debate methods, these services seem to be declining nationally. Also, while we gain ever stronger evidence that extra instruction keeps children from falling ever more behind, the schools too often tend to underfinance special instructional services. There is also considerable knowledge about the kinds of programs that are effective with kindergarten and first-grade children that help prevent low achievement and reduce reading problems. Why do we not push for broader applications of these programs to improve reading instead of seeming always to be on a search for a single, charismatic solution?

Teachers need to know and understand this body of knowledge and how it is best implemented. But much of it they already know and need only the resources and encouragement to use. The present call for greater empowerment of teachers is highly constructive. But if that empowerment is to benefit students, it must be buttressed by knowledge and understanding by teachers.

There also is a need to look into the education of our researchers. The kind of personal, mentor-student relationship many of us experienced in graduate school several decades ago is rare today. If learning to do research is more than acquiring a body of knowledge and technical skills, if it consists also of attitudes, values, and commitments learned from an experienced researcher/mentor (which I think it does), then we must improve how we educate the next generation of researchers.

There is a need also for a greater simplicity in what we do. Our theories, research, and practice are becoming more complex and technical, requiring elaborate explanations, even videos, in order to communicate to other researchers and teachers. The manuals of the major basal reading textbooks, for example, keep getting larger and heavier, suggesting that the teaching of reading to six-year-olds requires ever more exacting directions and guidance. And the many suggestions made to differentiate instruction for children make one wonder whether it is humanly possible for a classroom teacher to carry them out. With all of these growing complexities, one wonders how a teacher can survive. Even more, one wonders how it was possible for anyone to have learned to read before all the new methods and materials were invented. Indeed, how did Thomas Jefferson, Abraham Lincoln, or John Dewey become such superb critical readers and writers? I think those of us who are professors of reading, scholars and researchers, and teachers of teachers must try to hone down what we are saying; we must try to simplify it so that it can be understood and used.

And finally, who is to bell the cat? Who is to be responsible? Can teachers use whatever procedures they prefer without being accountable for the results they produce? If standardized tests are not to be accepted, what other objective devices can be used in their place? What is the responsibility of textbook publishers? They work in a highly competitive atmosphere, but does that mean they can use any procedures that sell? To what extent should professional organizations take responsibility? And, perhaps foremost, what is the responsibility of the scholar? Is it solely searching for new basic knowledge about the reading process? Or should it also include the responsibility of helping to solve the grave literacy problems facing us today?

Footnotes

1. Edgar Dale and Jeanne S. Chall, "A Formula for Predicting Readability" and "Instructions," *Educational Research Bulletin* 27 (January and February, 1948): 11-20, 37-54.
2. Ibid.
3. Edgar Dale and Jeanne S. Chall, *Readability Revisited and the New Dale-Chall Readability Formula* (Boston: Houghton Mifflin, 1991).

4. Jeanne S. Chall, "This Business of Readability," *Educational Research Bulletin* 26 (January 1947): 1-13. Reprinted in *Education Digest* 12 (May 1947): 9-11, and *Correct English* 48 (November 1947): 11-16.

5. Jeanne S. Chall, *Readability: An Appraisal of Research and Application* (Columbus: Ohio State University Press, 1958).

6. Jeanne S. Chall, *Learning to Read: The Great Debate* (New York: McGraw-Hill, 1967; updated, 1983); idem, *Stages of Reading Development* (New York: McGraw-Hill, 1983).

7. Richard C. Anderson, Elfrieda H. Hiebert, Judith A. Scott, and Ian A.G. Wilkinson, *Becoming a Nation of Readers: The Report of the Commission on Reading* (Champaign: Center for the Study of Reading, University of Illinois, 1985).

8. Harold Herber, "The Heritage of Our Profession" (Paper presented at the Reading Hall of Fame, International Reading Association Annual Conference, Toronto, 3 May 1988).

9. Chall, *Learning to Read: The Great Debate*.

10. See Marie Carbo, "Debunking the Great Phonics Myth," *Phi Delta Kappan* 70 (November 1988): 226-40; Jeanne S. Chall, "Learning to Read: The Great Debate 20 Years Later — A Response to 'Debunking the Great Phonics Myth'," *Phi Delta Kappan* 70: 521-38. For confirmation of the findings in *Learning to Read: The Great Debate*, see, for example, Marilyn Adams, *Beginning to Read: Thinking and Learning about Print* (Cambridge, Mass.: M.I.T. Press, 1990).

11. Jeanne S. Chall, Sue S.Conard, and Susan H. Harris, *An Analysis of Textbooks in Relation to Declining S.A.T. Scores* (New York: College Entrance Examination Board, 1977).

12. Jeanne S. Chall and Sue S. Conard, *Do Textbooks Challenge Students: A Case for Easy or Hard Textbooks* (New York: Teachers College Press, 1991).

13. Jeanne S. Chall and Allan F. Mirsky, eds., *Education and the Brain, Seventy-Seventh Yearbook of the National Society for the Study of Education* (Chicago: University of Chicago Press, 1978).

14. Chall, *Stages of Reading Development*.

15. Jeanne S. Chall, Vicki A. Jacobs, and Luke E. Baldwin, *The Reading Crisis: Why Poor Children Fall Behind* (Cambridge, Mass.: Harvard University Press, 1990).

16. Jeanne S. Chall, "Could the Decline Be Real? Recent Trends in Reading Instruction and Support in the U.S." in *Report of the NAEP Technical Review Panel on the 1986 Reading Anomaly, the Accuracy of NAEP Trends, and Issues Raised by State-Level NAEP Comparisons*, ed. Edward Haertel et al. (Washington, D.C.: National Center for Education Statistics and U.S. Department of Education, 1989).

17. Chall, Jacobs, and Baldwin, *The Reading Crisis: Why Poor Children Fall Behind*.

18. Jeanne S. Chall, "The Importance of Instruction in Reading Methods for All Teachers," in *Intimacy with Language: A Forgotten Basic in Teacher Education*, ed. Rosemary Bowler (Baltimore: Orton Dyslexia Society, 1987).

My Incomplete Agenda
for Education

BY DAVID L. CLARK

Being invited to write a reflection on a long professional career raises a personal dilemma. What level of embarrassment need one acknowledge publicly about earlier views and products to make the point that my professional field has progressed remarkably over the past 40 years? I intend to dispose of the matter quickly.

My first major research study was one of a series of cost-quality studies conducted at Teachers College, Columbia University during the late 1940s and throughout the 1950s. This study of 126 New York State school districts added extensive student achievement test data to the observational data that had been characteristic of the earlier research in this series of studies. In this study, which the New York State Educational Conference Board distributed widely throughout the state and across the country, I established beyond a shadow of a doubt that the level of educational expenditure was related to student achievement.[1] Of course, I did not bother to take into account the socioeconomic status of the students or their communities.

I cannot reconstruct the naiveté that would have allowed such a variable to be ignored; undoubtedly, I still have similar blocks affecting my current views of schooling and teaching. But while I am in the mood of critical reflection, I want to explore other areas of ignorance or murkiness or confusion that seem to have marked the eras of my professional travels (and travails). For me, they have included:

- the characteristics of the student population served, or not served, by the common school;

David L. Clark is Professor and Chair of the Educational Leadership Program at the University of North Carolina, Chapel Hill.

- the assumptions that have driven the search for knowledge in the field of education;
- the theoretical bases that have dominated the consideration of how schools should be organized and administered.

The Exclusive Common School

In 1951, a 16-year-old girl led her 400-plus high school classmates out of an aging building and three tarpaper shacks that passed for an American public school for black children in Farmville, Virginia. They were on strike, on strike against the visible disparity between the black and white schools in their community.

I have no recollection of that startling act of courage and defiance. I read about it only recently in Taylor Branch's *Parting the Waters: America in the King Years 1954-63*.[2] One might have expected, however, that it would be a vivid memory since, in that year, I had just completed a teacher education program at the State University of New York at Albany (then Albany State Teachers College) and was already committed irrevocably to a career in teacher education. The most important educational event of the year escaped my attention!

This is an especially troubling reflection because my preparation program and my personal predisposition emphasized the concept of the common school as the priceless centerpiece of American education. How then do children and youth fall outside the concept of common opportunity and access; how do they become invisible? Handicapped children were not within my purview of free public education. Only a few had access to public school buildings, and those who did were segregated from the non-handicapped population. Girls and young women functioned on the periphery of the mainstream classroom, often being counseled away from academic work for which they were clearly capable, and which would subsequently limit their life opportunities. All these youngsters, suffering varying degrees of exclusion from the American common school, were invisible to me as a beginning professional.

In retrospect, I have no trouble identifying the achievements of American public schools in the past 40 years. Fewer children are invisible. As a matter of sustained public policy, we have reasserted the common school as a guiding principle of American education. And educators have played an important role in that achievement. In many instances they have risked local or regional disdain by providing convincing data to support the existence of inequities. For example, in 1954 Truman Pierce, then dean of Auburn University's

School of Education, conducted a study of discrepancies in educational support between black and white schools in the South.[3] Local teachers and school administrators were often the catalysts in making it possible for minority groups to enter majority schools. Many educators joined with parents in the special education coalition that resulted in Public Law 94-142.

Critics of American education need to re-examine this era of achievement. This nation has never been placed at risk by having too many of its youth in school. Average achievement test scores at an arbitrary grade level are an inadequate basis for comparing achievement across national school systems. Rather, the issue is how many students can ultimately achieve at levels that approximate their fulfillment as human beings.

In 1960, I attended one of the early meetings of national research directors and educational scholars from Western Europe, Israel, and the United States who were planning what ultimately became the longitudinal study of international educational achievement based at the UNESCO Institute at Hamburg. My most vivid recollection of that meeting was a conversation with Swedish researcher Torsten Husén, who subsequently directed the project. He emphasized repeatedly the pride Americans should take in the access offered to students in U.S. schools – not just initial access but continued opportunity to pursue education without being tracked capriciously into dead-end curricula.

Once again, as we enter the 1990s, we are faced with a large portion of our student population whose opportunities for self-fulfillment are being lost in the common school. Children of poverty have physical access to the schools, but their access in terms of opportunities for learning and development are severely limited. The efficacy of the common school will now be tested, not on the basis of who can attend but who can succeed. The test is already upon us and will be exacerbated over the next 10 to 20 years by statistics we can barely comprehend:

- 30% of children in metropolitan areas currently live in poverty; that will increase by a third by the year 2000.
- Twice as high a percentage of children age 0-6 live in poverty as do adults age 18-64.
- Between now and the year 2020, the percentage of white youngsters of school age will decline by 27%; the number of Hispanic youngsters will triple from 6.8 million to 18.6 million, and a large percentage will live in poverty.

54

- Unless a revolution in educational practice begins tomorrow, five million American youngsters will drop out of school by the year 2000.

These children must not be allowed to disappear silently into an adulthood that is not economically or personally viable. We must invent and implement ways to make schools into living places that fit children rather than continuing to operate schools for "good kids" who adapt to the existing structure. Time for change is short. Broadly based public interest in addressing the problem of saving poor children is lacking. We have to challenge long-standing school practices in ways that will jolt the complacent.

How can we continue to turn our least advantaged children out on city streets or into rural slums for three months a year? How can we ignore the major decrements in achievement that are associated with this "vacation" period — a vacation from which many of them never return? Why are our inner-city schools closed in the evening hours when poor children are in the greatest danger from their community environment? Why are these buildings restricted to keeping school when they could be youth centers housing inter-sector agencies that serve the developmental needs of children (health, nutritional, dental, psychological, social) as well as their obvious need for schooling in the traditional sense?

The challenge to the common school has arisen again. Can the American public school system be the route of access on the journey out of poverty to participation in the sunlight of this society? The alternative, the emergence of a bifurcated society with a permanent underclass is, on its face, unacceptable to everyone. However, the policy choices and paths of action and implementation required to avoid this condition are difficult and costly. Our current efforts to respond to the challenge foreshadow an unpromising future.

The Half-Life of Scientism

My faith in the potential of the scientific method to ameliorate the ills of education stood second to none in 1960, when I became director of the Cooperative Research Program of the U.S. Office of Education. I was in good company, since most of the scholars in education and the social and behavioral sciences of that era imagined the emergence of bodies of knowledge that would predict, at high levels of confidence, the relationship between interventions and outcomes. While most of us were predicting the half-life of knowledge that would

55

be created by our scientific discoveries, we would have been wiser and more accurate had we been predicting the half-life of positivism and the faith in quantitatively based research methods spawned by that philosophy of science.

Over the past three decades, education research has profited from, and occasionally contributed to, the development of a more sophisticated and heuristic view of how we can learn about our craft and science. Qualitative research methodologies, which differ from traditional empirical research rooted in quantitative methodology, have gained status in the field. My longtime colleague Egon Guba has played the role of missionary, as well as methodologist, in advocating a form of qualitative research that emphasizes naturalistic inquiry. More traditional forms of qualitative research have been refined for educators by such qualitative researchers as Robert Yin, Matthew Miles, and Michael Huberman and have been re-examined and endorsed by respected quantitative and experimental design scholars, such as Lee Cronbach and Donald Campbell.

The change that has taken place in inquiry has not been restricted simply to the issue of quantitative vs. qualitative methodology or objective vs. naturalistic views of the world. Researchers and theoreticians employing the tools of critical theory and feminist theory have identified questions for study that challenge the very discourse that has controlled the way we think about children as students, about knowledge as curriculum, and about pedagogy as teaching. The questions they are raising should make it easier for all of us to see today's invisible poor and minority children and the limits we have placed on our imagination as we strive to support these youngsters.

Before pushing this topic too far, I should be more modest in my assessment of progress. Although I believe it is true that most contemporary education researchers have reservations about the direct applicability of the research methods and structures of the natural sciences for the social sciences, it is not accurate to state that most studies in education are framed in qualitative or naturalistic terms. But it is reasonable to argue that the field of education research is responding to the pressures and new insights produced by non-orthodox methodologists, philosophers of science, and theorists. More diversity is evident in our doctoral programs, among our active researchers — especially those with recent training — and in the prestigious research journals in the field.

These developments in education research are promising because they provide a basis for practitioners and researchers to work together to better understand what is and is not happening in schools as they exist today. In his most recent collection of essays, *Teachers as Intellectuals*, Henry Giroux concludes with a call to critical theorists to complement critique with a description of practical future possibilities.[4] This same hope should spur the research community to assume its normative responsibility in the reconstruction of American education.

Unstructuring Educational Administration

My first book in educational administration, co-authored with Daniel Griffiths, Laurence Iannaccone, and Richard Wynn, was titled *Organizing Schools for Effective Education*.[5] In hindsight it probably should have been titled "Organizing for Efficient Education," since its basic purpose was to bring the traditional wisdom of business and public administration to education. In the late 1950s that wisdom reflected an uncritical acceptance of the usefulness of bureaucracy as a theoretical structure for organizing education.

The book attempted a synthesis of what was known about administration at the beginning of a decade in which social and behavioral researchers were engaged in literally thousands of studies of leadership, motivation, climate, decision making, power, conflict, planning, goal-setting – all you wanted to know about organizations and organizing. The dialogue within the field was exciting and each year produced another generalization or analytic tool that most of us could barely resist. We inundated superintendents and their staffs with Leader Behavior Description Questionnaires (LBDQ) and Least Preferred Co-Worker instruments. We examined roles, role conflict, and role ambiguity until no one wanted us around any more. We intersected studies of organizational climate (using, of course, the Organizational Climate Description Questionnaire) with the LBDQ to determine the effect of leadership on climate or the impact of climate on leadership – producing the unsurprising notion that leadership was situational.

Retrospectively, it is easy to snipe at the output of these neo-orthodox researchers who wanted to find out more about the inner workings of bureaucratic systems. But, in fact, they were breaking new ground, asserting propositions that had not previously been stated, generating theoretical structures that had not been imagined. Situational leadership seems obvious only after it is explicated. Prior to that point it seemed perfectly sensible to study leadership employing a traits approach. Social systems theory seems simplistic only after theorists and inquirers make it available as a perspective from which to view bureaucratic systems. Prior to its generation it seemed appropriate to treat individual dispositions and needs as well as the organization's external environment as either irrelevant to the organization or, at best, as perturbations of minor consequence. The 1960s and 1970s were a boom period in studies of administration and organization; and, in the process, the period supported some basic propositions that were to come back to haunt us, such as:

- Large organizational structures have natural advantages over small organizations.
- Structured technological systems of planning and managing, such as management by objectives and program planning and budgeting systems, will address and solve focal problems in organizations.
- Organizational accountability will be facilitated by strong executive centralization and effective systems of employee evaluation and reward.
- Rational planning will prepare us for the future.
- Strong leaders are the key to organizational performance.

Every period of thought produces its dissidents; and so did this period, in which mainstream thought was reifying a new, more complicated bureaucracy. But most of us paid scant attention to those who were challenging the role of goals in organizations (action usually precedes intent), or the utility of planning in facilitating change (hyper-rationality impedes the implementation of change), or the effectiveness of merit pay plans (most pay-for-performance systems have been counter-productive). The standard answer to those who challenged the conventional wisdom was simply that their challenges were premature. In due time we would be sufficiently advanced in the development of an administrative science so that the technological tools of that science would be precise enough to guide human behavior.

The 1980s brought a change in emphasis in organizational studies. While the predominant thrust of the empirical studies still emphasized conventional models and techniques, the dissident voices commanded more and more attention. Popular books claimed that effective organizations behaved in non-orthodox ways exhibiting a bias for action, emphasis on empowerment, deemphasis on structured systems, nurturance of product entrepreneurs, broadening of job responsibilities, transfer of decision making to the operating level, peer evaluation, self-supervision, encouragement of loose coupling, respect for non-designated leadership, and an emphasis on awards and rewards rather than merit pay systems.

As usual, education attached itself to the emerging developments in organizational studies. In this instance, however, education seems to be caught in a dichotomy. While the knowledge about effective organizations encourages smaller operating units, more autonomy and decision-making authority at the school and classroom level, teacher empowerment, job enrichment for teachers, and less emphasis on personnel evaluation and more on personnel development, the political climate within which schools are operating demands increased accountability in the form of more student testing, more competitiveness among teachers, schools, and school systems, and closer teacher and student supervision. Increasingly schools are becoming viewed as under-performers by influential political decision makers. This has created an ambiguous climate in which to undertake the most popular topic of the day, restructuring schools.

The ubiquitousness of restructuring may be its undoing as a reform strategy. The open question seems to be whether to restructure means to rearrange, to change, or to make anew. Of course, in popular usage it means all those things. Restructuring may be provoked by pressure to undertake a symbolic action toward reform, an internal response to a highly specific problem, or a commitment to rethink the structure of schooling that is appropriate for the developmental needs of children and youth as citizen-learners. If the interpretations of restructuring begin to focus on the latter commitment, it could lead education in the United States into a new era of vigor and productivity. If we are to carry out that commitment, we might be better off labeling it *unstructuring* rather than restructuring. Most of the difficulties confronting schools, as well as other organizations, is the excessive hierarchical structuring that derives logically from bureaucratic theory. To assume that bureaucracies that were designed for domination can be restructured into organizations emphasizing freedom may be impossible. Unstructuring may be the precursor to rethinking an appropriate structure for schooling.

My Incomplete Agenda

I have no illusion that my reflections cover the territory of this complicated field of education. In fact, they do not even cover my own areas of specialization. During my years in the field, I have worried about, and tried to work on, federal education policy development, the governance and structure of teacher education, the change process in schools and school systems, the national infrastructure to support education R&D, and the preparation of educational administrators. But right now my agenda has a three-fold focus that commands my attention, to wit:

1. I fear that we will lose sight of the common school, one that provides support to all children as they develop into adults who will share in the plenitude of this society. We must not be deterred in our pursuit of this end by the limited vision of our political leaders. By the nature of their positions and the source of their authority, they will propose incremental solutions to a problem of crisis proportions. My hope is that as educators we can link our cause to a populist base that sees schools as the only viable mechanism to overcome lifelong poverty.

2. At a more esoteric level, I view the upcoming years as ones in which a new, more complex and, consequently, more interesting explosion of knowledge about education may occur. The obstacles to this "explosion" are, I think, ones of conservatism, paucity of resources, and ineptness in execution. First, most of the research community is still invested in a relatively narrow range of research methodology and philosophic orientation. The investment is rooted in their training and experience. They need to turn their attention to, and lend their support to, diverse ways of knowing. Second, the federal interest in education research has waned for the past 15 years. The modest resources now available are insufficient to support the R&D needs of the field. That trend needs to be reversed. Finally, those who are employing emerging research methodologies and challenging traditional theoretical constructs have a special responsibility to display intellectual rigor and methodological meticulousness in their endeavors. In short, they should be asked to prove their worth.

3. Organizations in our society, including schools, provide less productivity, personal satisfaction, and freedom than is needed to nurture either economic growth or people. As we approach the year 2000, we are likely to see growing impatience with organizational forms in workplaces that are less free, less nurturing than the social, religious, family, and leisure structures of everyday life. If there is a target for human rights concern beyond race, ethnicity, religious affiliation, and age, that target should be the arbitrary use of power and authority in work life. Focusing on that target will provide educators with the essence of an effective learning environment — a free environment that encourages growth and supports achievement.

60

We must work together to support the development of the least well-served children in a setting that fosters individual achievement and freedom. That is my vision, my interest.

Postscript

I didn't learn everything I needed to know in kindergarten, but I did learn everything I needed to know about my adult work life in the first grade. During that year, I had a protracted illness requiring some six months of recuperation. Almost every day my teacher, Miss Tyler, visited my home to keep me up-to-date on the rigors of the first-grade curriculum. I decided irrevocably that year that schools were the best places for human beings to spend their lives. Never again did I question becoming a teacher. Nor have I ever questioned the desirability and utility of staying one. Every child should find school to be a safe haven, a place for growing, a place in which to learn, to succeed, to be valued. School should be the best place to live for every person regardless of ethnicity, gender, socioeconomic status, health, or individual idiosyncrasy. School is democracy's common meeting place for human development.

Footnotes

1. Note that there is no reference cited here, and copies are nearly impossible to obtain. As a point of personal privilege, please do not attempt to do so.
2. Taylor Branch, *Parting the Waters: America in the King Years 1954-63* (New York: Simon and Schuster, 1988).
3. Truman M. Pierce, James B. Kincheloe, R. Edgar Moore, Galen N. Drewry, and Bennie E. Carmichael, *White and Negro Schools in the South* (Englewood Cliffs, N.J.: Prentice-Hall, 1955).
4. Henry A. Giroux, *Teachers as Intellectuals: Toward a Critical Pedagogy of Learning* (Granby, Mass.: Bergin and Garvey, 1988), pp. 220-21.
5. Daniel E. Griffiths, David L. Clark, D. Richard Wynn, and Laurence Iannaccone, *Organizing Schools for Effective Education* (Danville, Ill.: Interstate, 1962).

Reflections on Schools
and Adolescents

BY JAMES S. COLEMAN

My life as a sociologist concerned with education began one evening at the dinner table. I was near the end of my graduate studies at Columbia University. My wife and I had invited to dinner my fellow student and co-researcher, Martin Trow, and his wife. The talk turned to our high school days. As we described our experiences, it was clear that each of us had lived in a somewhat different kind of cocoon during that period of our lives. My wife had gone to high school in Shelbyville, Indiana, a school that had won the state basketball championship in her junior year. Basketball was the focus of adolescent attention, rivalled only by the social escapades of the leading clique in school. Trow's wife had attended a private girls' school in Atlanta, a school designed to produce young ladies for the next generation of Atlanta's social elite, but also a school in which scholastic pursuits were taken seriously. Trow had gone to Townsend Harris High School in New York City, a public high school (no longer in existence) that was highly selective academically. Graduates who returned to speak at assemblies or commencement were Nobel prize winners and others who had distinguished themselves in intellectual pursuits; and Trow and his classmates had similar goals.

My own high school experience was in Louisville, Kentucky, where there were two boys' public schools, Male (with a college preparatory curriculum) and Manual (with vocational and pre-engineering curricula). I attended Manual. Male and Manual were locked in a fierce football rivalry, which culminated every Thanksgiving Day

---

James S. Coleman is University Professor of Sociology and Education at the University of Chicago.

but flavored the whole school year. The boys who counted in the school were the first-string varsity football players. This environment shaped my own investment of time and effort, all intensely focused on football, although arguably my comparative advantage lay elsewhere. (I had begun high school in a small town of Greenhills in southwestern Ohio, where school life had, for a few of us, a more academic focus, in retrospect surprisingly so.)

The diversity among the different worlds that the four of us had inhabited during our high school years intrigued me; each of us had been shaped by the particular world each had inhabited, and in my case by the two sharply different worlds. That dinner conversation caused me to ponder the research direction I would take the next year after completing my graduate studies. It raised issues that interested me greatly: How did such different subcultures come into existence and persist, and what kind of impact did they have on those young people who passed through them? As a research focus, it met three criteria important to me: First, it allowed study of variations among social subsystems, which the survey research that many of my fellow sociologists were undertaking did not. Second, it had potential implications for policy, for something that would make a difference. Third, it held intrinsic interest for me, for it might help me understand better my own childhood experiences, which had taken place in four quite different social environments.

Stimulated by the dinner conversation, I wrote a research proposal, which was subsequently funded by the newly created Cooperative Research program of the U.S. Office of Education. The research, carried out in 1957-58, consisted of the study of adolescent subcultures in 10 high schools in Illinois. During that year, I and my small research team visited these schools, interviewed students individually and in groups, talked to teachers and principals, and administered questionnaires at the beginning and end of the school year. The results were reported to the Office of Education in 1959 as "Social Climates in High Schools," and were published in 1961 as *The Adolescent Society* (TAS).

This research provided a perspective on educational institutions that was distinctly sociological and decidedly unlike that done by researchers concerned explicitly with educational policy (for example, the kind of research that had been carried out by Paul Mort of Teachers College, Columbia University on measures of school quality, where quality was defined by consensus among leading educators). My research looked at high school life not in terms of the goals of educators but in terms of the goals and interests of the adolescents occupying the school. In this respect it contrasts not only with the work of earlier researchers but also with much of the educational research that has occupied me later in my career. The perspective provided in TAS is important, I believe, because it attempts to get inside the lives of those who pass through the schools, helps us to understand why schools sometimes fail with students, and suggests what kinds of changes are needed in schools to refocus the interests of young people toward more appropriate educational goals.

The last chapter of TAS focused on policy implications of the research results. One very clear result was that the social structure of competitive interscholastic sports in high schools led to social reinforcement of sports activity on the part of other students: teams were cheered on, participation and effort was encouraged, and success was rewarded with popularity and hero status for the athletes. By contrast, the social structure of competition for academic achievement was not interscholastic but interpersonal. A second clear result of the research was that there was social suppression of academic activity on the part of other students: good grades were not rewarded by hero status, and their recipients were often chided for "grade grubbing." Academic achievement by itself did little to bring popularity.

A policy implication I drew from these results led to my next educational research effort in 1961. If all the foregoing were true, it seemed reasonable to me that organizing interscholastic academic competition around teams and games would create a social structure that would encourage pursuit of academic goals. So I embarked on a program of developing academic games for high school and middle school students (including one game for learning numbers for younger students). These games, mostly of the social simulation type, were intended to be part of a reconstructed curriculum, in which students would learn social studies through a structure involving cooperation and social reinforcement. Our research group developed about six games, tested them in Baltimore schools, and disseminated them to teachers who came to share our enthusiasm for this approach to learning.

How successful was this strategy? The results were mixed. My vision of a reconstructed learning environment where scholars gained status by bringing glory to their school through successfully competing in interscholastic academic games was not realized. Yet the kinds of effects we hypothesized, in terms of social encouragement for learning, increased motivation, and intrinsic interest in the subject matter, did occur. A parallel program developed by Layman and Robert Allen around games of logic (Wff'n Proof), algebraic operations (Equations), and other topics, has had greater success. A program at Johns Hopkins University called "Teams, Games, and Tournaments" was a spin-off from our Academic Games program, and the very successful cooperative learning curriculum developed by Robert Slavin at Johns Hopkins counts the Academic Games program among its forbears. Interscholastic academic competitions in the form of Quiz Bowls and a national "Academic Olympics" have grown in popularity in many schools around the country. A broad-scale program of interscholastic academic competitions (thus generating *intraschool* social support) has recently been initiated throughout the state of West Virginia. Initial results in West Virginia indicate that success in the academic games does, as predicted, increase popularity and status for the participants.

The basic principles are clearly correct. (I saw my fifth-grade son energized by his teacher's introduction of mathematics games, which induced cooperation, discussion, and intense effort.) Mathematics leagues and debate teams, where they exist, appear to bring all the benefits predicted from these principles. Yet academic competition in the schools remains largely interpersonal, and these principles find limited use in the schools. I remain puzzled why this is so.

In the midst of our Academic Games program, I received a telephone call (in February 1965) from Alexander Mood, a well-known statistician and then U.S. Assistant Commissioner of Education and Director of the National Center for Education Statistics. After extensive discussion and some hesitation on my part, Mood persuaded me to accept the assignment of directing a survey of equality of educational opportunity mandated by the Civil Rights Act of 1964. Ernest Campbell from Vanderbilt University and I directed this massive survey, which culminated the next year in the publication of *Equality of Educational Opportunity* (EEO). I saw this assignment as a detour in my research direction, but I undertook it for two reasons: It offered an opportunity to demonstrate the value of social research for policy making, and it had the potential for increasing the equality of educational opportunity for black children. As it turned out, both of my expectations were realized: The research helped create the mold into which much succeeding policy research in education has been cast, and the results were widely used in school desegregation policy over a period of years following its publication.

The principal results of the research with policy relevance were two: First, the usual measures of school quality (per-pupil expenditure, teachers' educational background, size of school library, age of textbooks, etc.) showed little relation to achievement when students of similar backgrounds were compared; while differences in students' family backgrounds showed a substantial relation to achievement. Thus to search for ways of equalizing educational opportunity through school "quality" measures was not likely to prove successful. Second, achievement was strongly related not only to a student's own family background, it was also related (albeit less strongly) to the family backgrounds of other students in the school. This has obvious implications for strategies used in equalizing opportunity through desegregation, implications that led to the EEO report being cited widely to support desegregation efforts.

It is useful to contrast EEO with the approach used in TAS. The EEO survey did not begin with the lives of children; it did not ask what was the school experience for black children and for white children in varying school settings. Rather, it began with administrative goals and asked questions about how well these were met. How effective were schools in bringing about achievement? Were there inequalities in the educational resources available to black and white children? Were there inequalities in the outcomes of schooling?

We might ask, were the policy-relevant questions better answered by taking this perspective, asking directly about achievement of administrative goals? Or would they have been better answered by starting with the lives of children and asking what the school experience meant for them? These questions remain difficult to answer, even 25 years later. The TAS approach could not have been adopted wholesale, since its focus was on the social system of the school, not on the outcomes for individual students. But EEO, by largely ignoring the social system of the school and focusing primarily on the administrative goals of delivering services to students, may have missed the most important differences between the school environments in which black and white children found themselves.

One could imagine a combined approach, in which the administrative goal of delivering services to children remained the primary focus but with attention also given to the social system of the school and its impact on children. To do this would require researchers to take a more indirect route. First, they would have to collect information from students (based on interviews, questionnaires, or observation) in order to reconstruct conceptually the social system of the school. This would involve determining the norms, the bases of popularity, the positive or negative status conferred by various activities, and the social location of each child in this system. Then this social system of the school would be regarded both as a factor dependent on the policies and practices of the school staff and, in turn, as a factor that has consequences for student outcomes. Most interesting and most important in the context of the policy issues surrounding EEO would be the way in which the social system of the school varied with the racial composition of the school (and with the interaction between racial composition of the school and school administrative policies and practices), and how this, in turn, affected the school experience for black and white children.

Had this been done — and its not having been done in EEO or in other research is in part a matter of lack of research vision and in part a matter of the inherent difficulty of conducting such research — our knowledge of how to overcome problems of racial segregation would be far more advanced than it is. This is not a trivial matter. With such knowledge the policies of school desegregation as carried out from the late 1960s until today might have been far more beneficial to the lives of black and white children than they have been, might have led to more stability in newly integrated schools, and might not have brought the backlash of the 1980s, which has exacerbated race relations on some college campuses and in some large cities. The challenge remains for sociologists to do this kind of research and to do it well.

The reception of EEO by the research community and in the political arena involved me in controversy over a period of several years. However, another problem began to occupy my attention. The time was the late 1960s and early 1970s, the emergence of the baby boom generation into youth and young adulthood and the period of youth revolt. The events of that period focused attention on the inadequacy of our schools, particularly in the role they played in helping young people make the transition to adulthood. The problems were principally at the high school level, a segment of schooling that has never been satisfactorily organized since mass secondary education began in the 1920s and 1930s. The problems of how best to organize the transition of youth into adulthood did not need extensive new research, but they did merit more serious attention than they had been given.

I was at the time a member of the President's Science Advisory Committee and in that capacity organized a Panel on Youth to review the implications of existing knowledge related to the transition of youth to adulthood. Our panel produced a report, *Youth: Transition to Adulthood*, in 1972. As one of three or four similar reports on this issue appearing at about the same time, the report reinforced some of the restructuring of high schools designed to reduce the discontinuity between school and work, between dependency and economic independence.

Later, in the mid-1980s, similar problems continued to beset a number of European countries, which had seen their youth unemployment rates rise and had experienced problems in their recently restructured secondary education. These problems led to a request from the Organization for Economic Cooperation and Development (OECD) to address, with Torsten Husén of Sweden, similar problems in a broader perspective. The report of our work, *Becoming Adult in a Changing Society*, was published in 1985 by OECD.

In 1974 another telephone call led me in a new research direction related to the EEO-derived school desegregation policies. The call was from William Gorham at the Urban Institute in Washington, asking if I would contribute a chapter on urban education to a bicentennial book that he would be editing with Nathan Glazer. (The book, published in 1976, was titled *The Urban Predicament*.) One topic I wished to investigate in the chapter was trends in the racial integration of schools, given the massive desegregation policies of the late 1960s and 1970s. As it turned out, the Civil Rights Commission had been collecting data annually since 1967 on racial composition of schools across the United States, and had data available in machine-readable form for the years 1968-1973. With two research assistants at the Urban Institute (Sara Kelly and John Moore), I analyzed these data to examine these trends. The results were published in 1975 by the Urban Institute as *Trends in School Segregation, 1968-73* (TSS).

We found the results disturbing: Although desegregation policies had led to less-segregated schools in central-city school districts in large metropolitan areas, the large cities had experienced another change that tended to negate these policies. The schools of the central-city districts were experiencing extensive losses of whites, primarily to predominantly white suburban districts. Most serious, our analysis showed that loss of whites was most extensive where central-city desegregation had been most intensive. Thus, the policies of school desegregation in central cities had acted to increase racial segregation between cities and suburbs. This was hardly welcome news, especially to those still working to extend desegregation policies, and especially coming from a researcher who, since EEO, had been counted an ally in the social movement to integrate America's schools. The familiar tendency to "kill the messenger" led to another period of controversy, which made the earlier controversy over EEO pale by comparison.

My next major foray into research on schools began in 1979. The National Center for Education Statistics issued a request for proposals on what would become the High School and Beyond study, a survey of 10th- and 12th-graders in a sample of 1,015 high schools throughout the United States. In the proposal we prepared at the National Opinion Research Center at the University of Chicago, we planned not only data collection but also 10 initial analyses on topics relevant both to fundamental issues in education and to current policy questions. Five of these were approved; and after the data collection was completed in the spring of 1980, we presented our analytical reports to the government in September 1980. Among these was a report on public and private high schools that I, with two research assistants, Sally Kilgore and Thomas Hoffer, had prepared. In the spring of 1981 the report was released by the Department of Education, and in 1982 it was published as *High School Achievement: Public, Catholic, and Private Schools Compared.*

As in EEO and TSS, this research challenged conventional wisdom; for example, it reported that private schools did not have more racial segregation than public schools and that achievement in private schools was higher than that in public schools for students of comparable background. That we found these same results for Catholic schools as well was particularly hard for some to accept. Again controversy erupted and subsided only when Thomas Hoffer and I showed (in *Public and Private High Schools*) with a second wave of tests on the same 10th-graders, now seniors, that growth in achievement between grades 10 and 12 confirmed the earlier results showing higher achievement.

This last research, however, did more than confirm the results of the 1980 survey. We searched for an explanation of why achievement of children in religiously grounded schools was greater than that of comparable children in public or even independent private schools. To find the answer involved using a sociological perspective to study the social structure of school, going back to the general direction I began in *The Adolescent Society*. This time, however, the social milieu that was relevant for explaining the effectiveness of religiously grounded schools was not the society of adolescents in the school; it was the community of adults outside the school. We found

69

that when that community was strong, as is more often the case in religiously grounded schools, it provided a resource (which we termed "social capital") that was important for students' achievement and for their staying in school until graduation. This research again focused attention on the point suggested in TAS: that educational outcomes are not merely independent consequences of institutional "treatments" or "delivery of services," but can be understood only as a complex consequence of the functioning of social systems of which the formal school activities are merely a part.

Now what? I am taking up the challenge I issued to sociologists earlier: I am tackling the difficult task of incorporating the informal social system of adolescents into the analysis of the effects of schooling on student outcomes. Perhaps Phi Delta Kappa will invite me to report on whether or not the attempt was successful in its next volume of *Reflections*.

Reflections on Child Development and Education

BY JAMES P. COMER, M.D.

A funny thing happened to me on my way to becoming a general practitioner in my hometown of East Chicago, Indiana. During my internship in 1960, I did some "moonlighting" in preparation for going into general practice with a friend. But I quickly noticed that a large number of his mostly poor, African-American and Latino patient population did not have physical illnesses. Many had psychosomatic problems, and there was a disproportionate amount of psychological depression. I also noted that a large number of young people – some of whom I had attended high school with – were among the depressed.

The incident that probably did the most to change my mind about general practice occurred during a late-evening house call in a low-income section of our town. As I entered the darkened house and turned on the light, thousands of roaches scampered out of sight. Two small infants who undoubtedly had been covered by the roaches lay in orange crates; their profoundly depressed mother was in the next room. As it turned out, she was a former classmate of my younger brother. She was bright and able but was now on a downhill course in life. Similar circumstances affected too many of my friends.

What was going on?

At that time, East Chicago, a steel mill town that once had a job for everybody, was already feeling the pinch of foreign competition. The handwriting was on the wall. Future job opportunities and the ability to meet life's task would require a good education. But too many people didn't see the handwriting or weren't prepared to do

---

James P. Comer, M.D. is the Maurice Falk Professor of Child Psychiatry at the Yale Child Study Center.

anything about it. All my siblings, as well as a number of other young black people with similar backgrounds and from the same community, were attending and finishing college. But far too many were not finishing high school and, as a result, were in jeopardy. I soon realized I wouldn't be satisfied passing out pills to the depressed without addressing the forces contributing to the depression. But I didn't understand the forces at work here. I needed time to think and learn. I retreated to the United States Public Health Service to do my military service time − and to think.

While in the service I worked as a volunteer in a "bootstrap" agency called Hospitality House in Washington, D.C., established by middle-income blacks and whites before the advent of official poverty programs, to help families that had lost their welfare benefits because of the infamous "man in the house" ruling. Without work or income, these mothers were under extreme stress. They were pushed around by housing, health, police, and postal officials and by every bureaucracy they had to deal with. Hospitality House had a small shelter where they could live temporarily. Their total belongings were generally piled on the sidewalk in front.

I often sat and talked with the children. They were bright and able − like many of those I had grown up with who had gone on a downhill course. One of the youngsters, whose mother had moved almost every day, went off to school asking, "Where will I find you after school?" It occurred to me that it must be very difficult to learn in school when you don't know where you're going to meet your mother or eat and sleep that evening. Meanwhile, across the street there was a day-labor market where uneducated and undereducated young black men lined up hoping to be selected for a day's work, reminding me of pictures I had seen of the slave market. It occurred to me that my young friends at Hospitality House were going to end up in similar lines unless they got a good education.

Because of my concerns, I decided to attend the University of Michigan School of Public Health rather than return home to practice. It was there that the notion began to take form in my thinking that the school could make a difference − could compensate for some of the impoverished conditions in the home. It occurred to me that in a democratic society, the school is the first place that "outsiders" have a right to make demands on families. The school is the first test of a family's adequacy in nurturing a child. The school provides the single, common pathway for all children; and therefore no stigma is attached to helping children there as opposed to help provided

72

by mental health, welfare, or correctional agencies. Thus I wrote my master's thesis on the preventive potential of schools. But I was a physician, not an educator, so I didn't see a future in this area. But by that time I had figured out that I wanted to help people help themselves and that psychiatry offered me the best opportunity for doing so.

Because of the interest in social psychiatry of several people at Yale University's School of Medicine, I chose to go there for my training. It was a fortuitous move. Not only did the program give me greater flexibility and an opportunity to enlarge the traditional training experience, but the city of New Haven was ahead of the rest of the country in trying to address the problems related to social change and poverty. During my general psychiatry training, I was encouraged by several faculty members to work in schools, to explore their potential to help children grow. So without a blueprint for how it should be done and without a research agenda and methodology that would limit my observations, I plunged in. My experiences led me to specialize in child psychiatry, but there still was no career role for me in education. Also, in order to finance my training, I accepted a position as a career officer in the Public Health Service at the National Institute of Mental Health in Washington, D.C.

It was 1967 and our cities were in turmoil. The race issue was center stage. But the research was about poverty; and it was survey and experimental design research focused on individual behavior more than on systems. My life experiences (from a poor but educationally successful African-American family) and my work with poor families told me that the focus had to be as much on systems as on individuals, and that we had to pay attention to the unique nature of the African-American experience in order to understand and address education, race, and other social problems. I had a sense that my colleagues, as a result of their training and traditions, were locked into a structure that would not allow them (or me) to look at the dynamic interaction between systems, groups, families, and children in a way that addresses the needs of youngsters like those at Hospitality House or those I grew up with who went on a downhill course.

Five months into a frustrating year at the National Institute of Mental Health, I received a call from Dr. Albert Solnit, director of the Yale Child Study Center, where I had trained for a year. He made me an offer I could not refuse, and so I returned to New Haven in 1968. He asked me to direct a preventive psychiatry program focused on schools serving mostly low-income, African-American students. Our approach was not to impose a conventional research and intervention design on the schools but rather to live in and learn about two schools, which would serve as a subsystem of the total school system. With the involvement of all in the school — parents, teachers, administrators, and support staff — we set out to develop a school improvement approach that would help the overall development of all students and, in time, prepare them to function adequately as adults.

We set out to develop a "portal model," one that could be replicated throughout the New Haven school system at the elementary, middle, and high school levels; and eventually to inform and influence public policy in education nationwide, particularly as it pertained to low-income, African-American youth. The goals were precisely the ones I had in mind when I decided not to pursue a career as a family practitioner. And the methodology was consistent with what I believed, because it met my objections to the way research and intervention were generally being carried out across the country. And most important, I was returning to a city where I was known and had already established credibility in low-income communities, which were increasingly developing greater distrust of mainstream institutions.

Despite the fact that I was on friendly turf, our group from the Child Study Center (psychiatrist, psychologist, social worker, special education teacher) ran into difficulty immediately and almost did not survive the first year. The school system's ambivalence about our project was expressed in indirect ways: no full-time project coordinator, personnel selection problems, reduced funding in important areas, broken promises to parents, and the like. And our Child Study Center strategy to live in and learn rather than manage the project ourselves left the two schools without an action plan or clear leadership.

The result was confusion, distrust, disappointment, conflict, and within five months, hopelessness and despair. These are the dynamics in poorly functioning schools, but rarely are they manifested within such a short period of time. These were good and able people — parents, teachers, administrators, students. And while it was painful to watch the high hopes and talents of very committed people deteriorate in such a short period, observing the rapid deterioration enabled us to conceptualize what would be needed to generate a successful school improvement process.

Witnessing the deterioration strongly supported our belief that successful school improvement requires a comprehensive intervention at the building level — supported by the larger school system — rather than interventions focusing on particular circumstances of students, parents, teachers, administrators, or the curriculum. Isolated, uncoordinated interventions may have some positive outcomes but generally do not have the power to make a significant and sustained impact on schools and schooling. It was clear to us that schooling is an ensemble production, and all of the players need simultaneous preparation and support to play their roles.

We had good people who wanted to succeed, but they were not prepared to interact with each other effectively. The resultant relationships interfered with rather than promoted appropriate child development and effective teaching and learning. And deeply ingrained cultural beliefs and attitudes adversely affected the behavior of staff, parents, and students.

In particular, three beliefs, although not often expressed overtly, were most harmful. First was the belief that learning is strictly a cognitive operation unrelated to prior experience, relationships, and affective forces. Second was the belief that learning requires a high level of intellectual functioning with winners and losers, with a disproportionate number of the losers among low-income, minority groups. (To some extent this belief is internalized within the groups themselves.) Third was the belief that motivation is a matter of will and that students either have the will to learn or they refuse to do so.

Although a few policy makers in the late 1960s had recognized that economic and social conditions in society had changed in a fundamental way and that all children would need to be better educated than ever before, the culture as a whole did not subscribe to this belief. Thus, despite the fact that the economy could no longer absorb large numbers of people without higher levels of education, there was inertia, in part rooted in the belief that nothing more could be done to educate African-American children, that nothing more needed to be done, that the world was unfolding as it should. An experience with a well-meaning teacher during the first year of our program illustrated the problem.

A bright but energetic and fun-loving student had irritated the teacher with his classroom behavior, and then did not do well on the mathematics quiz. The teacher retaliated with a large, angry "F" in red at the top of quiz sheet and huge crosses over the wrong answers. Because the youngster appeared bright, I decided to find out why he was making errors. It turned out he was making a systematic error consistently, adding one column rather than multiplying. The teacher, ordinarily positive and supportive, launched into an explanation, telling me about where these kids come from, why they cannot learn, and why it probably did not matter anyway because they would find a job in one of the factories (which at that moment were closing at an alarming rate).

We at the Child Study Center had to respond immediately to the anger and defensiveness of most staff as well as to the fury of the parents. I will not pretend that we had a well-developed theoretical framework to guide our actions at that time. I relied on my personal experiences and my training in child psychiatry and public health, and my two colleagues relied on their clinical backgrounds. We groped like clinicians and epidemiologists; and when we identified sources and patterns that were problematic, we applied our experience and training to develop useful responses.

In setting up the project initially, Dr. Solnit and Sam Nash, New Haven's special projects director, had created a steering committee, comprised of representatives of all the participating groups, to guide our work. We borrowed the steering committee concept and created a Governance and Management Team in each school, with representatives from staff, parents, and support personnel. This team was to develop a social and academic program for its building, coordinate and assess the overall work of the school, and make adjustments as indicated. Although we did not call it a school-based management team in 1968, it was indeed such a team. We cannot find an earlier reference in the literature to such an effort.

Effective functioning of the Governance and Management Team reduced many of our problems and stabilized the schools, but we still had no way to help the staff understand the developmental needs of students and how they related to academic learning. We also were faced with duplication and fragmentation of support services. Each support service provider was working independently. We discovered one student who was being "helped" by seven different professional and non-professional support staff.

Our response was to create a Mental Health Team made up of the social worker, psychologist, special education teacher, a parent assistant, and any other support staff in the building. As the overall climate of the school improved, the team members were able to shift from an emphasis on helping individual children and families to helping the staff understand how the organization and management of the school and classroom and their relationships with students and parents affect the development and behavior of children. From such understandings the staff would learn how to respond in a supportive and preventive fashion. The Mental Health Team became our second major change mechanism.

The third mechanism we created was our Parents' Program. Low-income, minority parents were (and are) distrustful of and alienated from a largely white, middle-class school staff and system. Previously, parent participation had been limited and often discouraged. Many parents had had difficult experiences in school themselves and were angered by the way our program got off the ground. In response, we renegotiated our working relationships with the parents, giving them a major role in shaping the social program of the school in particular, but also making an important input to the academic program.

These three mechanisms (Governance and Management Team, Mental Health Team, and Parents' Program) were put in place in the first year of our program in 1968-69 and continue to be at the core of our work, largely because they address the three critical areas of interaction from which most problems stem: interactions between home and school, among school staff, and between staff and students. The work of the Governance and Management Team eventually was refined into three key operations: creation of a comprehensive school plan, staff development to support implementation of the plan, and assessment and adjustment of the program. And three guidelines permeated all relationships within the Governance and Management Team and eventually the entire social system of the school. They were: 1) a no-fault policy that facilitates problem solving; 2) decisions by consensus rather than majority vote; and 3) true collaboration, where team members cannot block action by the principal or team leader but the leader also cannot ignore the will of the group. We called our process model the School Development Program (SDP).

By the third year of our work, these very difficult inner-city schools had become good places to live and work. Student behavior problems declined sharply. Staff and student attendance improved significantly. Staff turnover was greatly reduced. Parent satisfaction and participation in the program greatly increased. Over the years, several teachers have enrolled their own children in the schools, as have some of the handful of middle-class parents in the area. It took seven years before we obtained significant academic improvement, but in subsequent programs such improvement has occurred in two to three years.

After the third year we were able to step back and look systematically at what had happened and why. And we began to develop a theoretical framework for our work rather than simply applying our clinical and epidemiological skills to problems as we encountered them.

With the theoretical framework that emerged from our work, we rejected the notion that academic learning is an isolated cognitive function. Instead, we used a child-centered, ecological perspective that reads as follows:

Learning is a product of individual development, which is facilitated by attachment and bonding to adults who mediate child experiences, and in the process teach and motivate. Child imitation, identification, and internalization of adult attitudes and values facilitate learning. Learning takes place first in primary social networks and then in schools; and the quality of these learning experiences is influenced by the skill of the adults directly involved, but also by conditions and opportunities in the local and national political, economic, and social institutions, past and present.

The intervention that flowed from this theoretical framework puts in place mechanisms, conditions, and practices that promote student development and appropriate teaching that counter and compensate for problem areas.

We identified three major problem areas. First, our African-American students were the product of an environment that was more traumatic than that of other groups. A disproportionate number of our students and families were marginal participants in the social, political, and economic mainstream of American society. Even when families wanted their children to succeed in school, they often were not able to give them those preschool experiences that would make it possible. The children were not prepared to meet the expectations of the school and were underdeveloped in the areas that are critically important for academic learning. Many of these children developed in ways that led to success outside of school but to failure in school.

Second, although the staff was prepared to teach, they did not view their role as one of supporting the development of students or of helping them to meet the expectations of the school. As a result, staff often viewed any acting-out behavior as bad, or they believed that the students had limited ability for learning. The constant struggle to control behavior combined with low expectations for students led to conflict and a downhill course in school for all involved — students, parents, and teachers.

Third, the hierarchical, authoritarian organization and management of schools did not permit teachers and parents to respond to prob-

lems and opportunities or to plan and implement programs coopera-
tively and collaboratively. As a result, there was very little sense
of community among the staff and parents.

By developing responses to the three major problem areas identified above, we were able to overcome the alienation and distrust between home and school and to create a supportive climate that fostered
parent-student-staff bonding, thus facilitating teaching and learning.
Our Governance and Management Team, made up of elected
representatives of parents and teachers plus selected professional and
non-professional support staff and the principal, flattened the organizational pyramid without decreasing the power of the principal and gave
every adult in each school a stake in the program. The team coordinated and gave direction to the schools, using a management style
that was cooperative and collaborative, empowering all involved. The
collective benefits of the nine elements of our program (three mechanisms, three operations, three guidelines) had the power to change
the culture of the school and to promote development and learning,
thus counteracting the belief that these children couldn't learn.

The rap on our program was that it worked because of my charisma. (I had never been called charismatic earlier in my career. Why
now?) Some said it was because the Yale Child Study Center was
nearby and thus able to influence the schools. As a matter of fact,
the highest level of achievement in the two initial project schools
occurred three years *after* the process had been institutionalized at
the building level and our Child Study Center team had left. To
demonstrate that it was the process and not our presence, we developed a training approach that has enabled personnel in several school
districts across the country to learn the theory and gain the skills for
successfully implementing the School Development Program or process in their districts with minimum input from us and at minimum
cost to their districts.

Another rap was that the program was very expensive. This is not
so. We began as a research and development project with the intent
of influencing school improvement efforts beyond New Haven. This
has happened. Individual schools and school districts are successfully using the principles of the program with no official training
or relationship with our Child Study Center staff. Also, at the outset
we deliberately structured the program so that personnel already employed in schools, such as a social worker, psychologist, special education teacher with mental health skills — in fact, any educator with
good people skills — could implement the model in a school or at
the district level without outlays for additional personnel.

Another concern was that we were mixing education, child development, and mental health; and because educators were not trained in child development and mental health principles and their application, they would use their lack of training in these areas as an excuse to not find ways to help children from families under stress achieve at a reasonable level. The fact that large numbers of people working with children were not learning child development and mental health principles and their application was, and still is, amazing to me. But the level of understanding our model requires is just a bit beyond common sense, if beyond at all. I believe that everybody working with young people in schools should have this level of understanding and skill. Schools of education and other human-service institutions have an obligation to provide their students with the needed training and experiences. Should an auto mechanic be allowed to work on a car if he doesn't know its normal operations?

We eventually realized that we were developing a critical missing link in school reform. Other reform efforts have focused on more efficient and effective management or on emphasizing the principal as the leader. Still others have focused on teacher effectiveness, curriculum enrichment, longer school days, more homework, and on and on. No school reform effort that we know of focuses primarily on child development and bringing all the other elements to bear on it — organization and management, leadership, teacher training, parent participation, and the like.

Even when school reform efforts address relationship issues and child development concerns, it is usually done incidentally and secondarily. One leader of the Effective Schools Movement pointed out that a by-product of the teams organized in schools to focus on management and teaching was the improved relationships that developed among the parents and staff as they worked together, resulting in positive outcomes for the children. I would argue that instead of waiting for a "by-product," we focus first on creating a good climate of relationships among parents and staff. The difference in perspective may appear to be small, but we believe that it is a critically important difference with greatly different outcomes. Again, good adult relationships facilitate student attachment and bonding to the people and program of the school and enable adults to support the development of students in ways that facilitate teaching and learning. *No matter how good the administrators, teachers, curriculum, or equipment, no matter how long the school day or year, no matter how much homework is given, if the students don't attach and bond to the people and program of the school, less than adequate learning will take place.*

Recently, members of the National Commission on Children visited one of the schools in New Haven using our model. One of the visitors made an astute observation, pointing out that this high-achieving school had a very traditional curriculum, and that while the high achievement in this school can be attributed to the power of focusing on relationships and child development, the school could probably make even greater gains using some of the new curriculum and teaching methods. I agree.

We did not intentionally ignore curriculum issues in order to emphasize the importance of relationships and child development. Curriculum and teaching are not our areas of expertise, and we were not able to enlist the New Haven school system or a school of education to collaborate with us on curriculum reform. We do, however, point up the importance of age-appropriate subject matter; and we emphasize the importance of moving from concrete experiences to more abstract, rather than the other way around, as is so often the case. Children from families under stress, in particular, have not had enough mediated learning experiences with meaningful adults to handle the level of abstraction expected of them in school.

To address this problem we developed a curriculum (Social Skills Curriculum for Inner-City Children) designed to give low-income children experiences to facilitate more abstract thinking and, in time, to participate in the mainstream of the society. With the involvement of parents, we asked what kinds of experiences and skills children would need to be successful as adults. The staff and parents together agreed that they would need experiences in politics and government, business and economics, health and nutrition, and spiritual and leisure activities. In these areas we developed activity units that integrated basic academic skills, social skills, and appreciation of the arts — the latter as a way of channeling children's energy into constructive work and play. These activity units currently are being integrated into the curriculum of New Haven's schools from pre-kindergarten through high school in an effort to promote learning for mainstream life in an open, democratic society. We believe that such a curriculum is needed by all of our children.

We are now developing relationships with schools of education, which will enable us to address curriculum issues. But we will continue to focus on relationship and child development issues, since there is still too little attention being given to this area in the school reform efforts we know about.

What are the implications of our work for the future of schooling? After almost 25 years of work in schools, the metaphor that comes to mind is a boat without a rudder. There is no coherent, comprehensive theory of schooling that is widely supported and used to guide practice, training, assessment, and research. As a result, schooling policies and practices are swept one way or another by political, philosophical, and financial forces, none of which are child centered. This is still the case. For example, what does parental choice have to do with how children grow and learn? This idea, as it is being applied, rarely addresses the needs of children from families under stress, whose failure in school places them and the nation at risk.

Nonetheless, I am optimistic that the several current successful school reform efforts will soon coalesce into a coherent, comprehensive theory of schooling. When this happens it could set the stage for changes in training, practice, assessment, and research that are child centered. All these areas must be addressed more or less simultaneously if we are to have an effective educational system in a reasonable length of time. Earlier reform efforts have failed because their recommendations were not institutionalized in the places where the foot soldiers, the teachers and administrators, learn their profession and develop attitudes and values that are lasting and difficult to change − in their preservice education.

We have all heard the rap on schools of education, that they are resistant to change, tradition bound, and the like. But many people in schools of education already have moved to adapt their programs in order to respond to today's needs. Legislators, foundations, corporations, and others can exert influence to encourage schools of education and other preparatory institutions to focus on ways of helping young people grow and learn so that they will be prepared to assume adult responsibilities and, in turn, meet societal needs.

One component of the preservice education of teachers and administrators should be training in the skills of participatory management, wherein administrators, teachers, parents, students, and support staff work collaboratively to create relationships that allow adults to help the students develop and learn. The occasional teacher and principal who is able to do this intuitively will not be enough. They struggle, often unsuccessfully, against the resistance of colleagues who are unconvinced that change is needed or are fearful of change.

School people will need "clinical" skills in order to identify conditions and behaviors that interfere with teaching and learning and to be able to "fix" them through cooperative and collaborative efforts.

And administrators must encourage bottom-up, building-level management, with the central office organized to serve building-level needs. This calls for cooperative and collaborative efforts rather than hierarchical and authoritarian management structures.

Our work suggests that the traditional forms of research we do in education should be modified and/or broadened. Currently, quantitative experimental and quasi-experimental research designs and survey research are the preferred approaches. But it was a clinical, epidemiological, and qualitative approach with an ecological perspective that gave us insight into how schools worked and how to fashion a successful intervention program.

Much of the research about schooling focuses on individuals, groups, and things in isolation rather than in a dynamic interaction. With quantitative, experimental research designs, we are often left with outcomes without process knowledge, without an understanding of the dynamic contexts that produced them, or how to modify them. Because such work does not adequately consider social context variables, research findings in one setting often are not applicable to another.

Our need today is for research approaches that can address the uniqueness of every school yet enable us to generalize and transfer results from one situation to the next. The case-study approach used in business probably would be helpful in understanding what goes on in a particular school and in helping prepare prospective teachers and administrators to work in any school. I suspect that program audits, similar to program audits in business (not financial audits), would be helpful in understanding the people and dynamics in place in a school, whether they are effective or not, and how they might be changed to meet the goals of a school.

Finally, I am convinced that the kind of schools we need to meet the challenge of the 21st century can be created. The question is whether this nation will accept the premise that a greater investment in all our young is necessary. There is a point of no return somewhere in the near future. If we continue to produce young people who do not have the education needed to take care of themselves and their families, or even if we produce well-educated young people who put individual needs before societal needs, we will have created a situation that will not permit us to survive and thrive in the 21st century.

Educating All God's Children

BY ALONZO A. CRIM

A child is a person who is going to carry on what you have started. He is going to sit where you are sitting, and when you are gone, attend to those things which you think are important. . . . The fate of humanity is in his hands.

— Abraham Lincoln

An alumnus returning to campus for his 25th reunion was visiting with his favorite professor. The professor had to leave his office momentarily. Upon his return, the alumnus said, "Professor, I could not help noticing the stack of final examination papers on your desk. I am surprised that you ask the same questions you asked my class 25 years ago." The professor replied, "That is correct, but all of the answers are different."

I was delighted to be invited by Phi Delta Kappa to contribute to this volume because it allowed me to reflect over the past 25 to 35 years about the questions we asked about the schools and the answers we gave, and to speculate on how we will answer the questions during the next decade and beyond. Like the professor said, the answers are likely to be different.

In September 1954, a landmark year for expanding the educational franchise to a shamefully neglected segment of America's children, I showed up at Jacob Riis Elementary School in Chicago for a seventh-grade teaching vacancy along with three other candidates. Mrs. Gervaise Schnettler, the principal, made her selection by hav-

Alonzo A. Crim is the Benjamin E. Mays Professor of Urban Educational Leadership at Georgia State University and former Superintendent of the Atlanta Public Schools (1973-88).

ing the four of us draw straws. I drew the short straw and got the job. I was given a set of keys, directions to get to room 303, and the principal's best wishes for a good day. Needless to say, it was an interesting day. I spent nine years at Riis, which I subsequently labeled Riis "University" because it was there I served my apprenticeship and learned my craft.

Growing up during the Great Depression, I was from a generation that was fed up with being poor. Still, it was possible as a boy to find work. I started at age eight as a newsboy delivering 300 morning papers and 150 evening papers and collecting on weekends. A newspaper route that size would now be done by adults in most places.

At age 12, I was able to move up to a stock boy in the Chicago downtown wholesale district, making 35 cents an hour. After giving half of my salary to my parents, I still had enough left to purchase all of my clothes and pay for my personal needs and entertainment. Throughout my high school years I moved on to other part-time jobs, where my salary increased although the level of job remained relatively fixed. I know few youth today who have the opportunity to learn the job skills that I and many others in my age group learned during our high school years.

My parents inculcated in me the belief that it was important to work hard in school, but at the time I did not have the expectation that school would do anything special for me. Throughout my 12 years in school I cannot remember a teacher or an administrator encouraging me to go on to college. If we had counselors in high school (my former classmates tell me we did), I never saw one. My only visit to the main office was to receive notice that I had been selected for the National Honor Society.

Of the 40 persons in my class who graduated from elementary school, only 10 of us graduated from my high school. My parents wanted me to go on to college, but I wasn't convinced it was for me. It was my involvement in a Hi-Y Club at the Wabash YMCA (at the time it was the only YMCA branch in Chicago where blacks could join and participate freely) that changed my mind. From adults, paid and volunteer, in that YMCA program I received confirmation of my parents' belief that I had the ability to succeed in college. I may have gone later without their encouragement but not at the time of my graduation from high school. The YMCA, the Hull House settlements, Lincoln Center, and the Henry Booth House were so important in my adolescent life that I decided I wanted to become a group worker or social worker so that I could help other youth like me to make sense out of their lives.

With the exception of a year in the U.S. Navy, I pursued my career objective first at George Williams College and later finishing my bachelor's degree at Roosevelt College. Throughout my undergraduate years I was able to apprentice at the YMCA or Henry Booth House as a part-time worker and became a full-time employee upon graduation. A coal strike and lack of funds forced the closing of the agency where I worked, which precipitated my seeking a teaching position at Riis Elementary School.

Riis "University" served a racially mixed population, with the black students coming from one public housing project and the whites coming from another public housing complex. There were serious "turf" conflicts among neighborhood groups, which frequently overflowed into the school. Many times at the close of the school day, teachers were asked to escort the black students in one direction and the whites in the other.

Even with my experience in youth work, it amazed me to see how effectively my older colleagues coped with such difficult circumstances. They were predominantly white, single females who had been at the school for years. They got a lot from the students and had an instinct for sensing trouble and heading it off. Fortunately for me, they took me on as a project.

I took to Riis an ability to work with young people, but I had much to learn about teaching and how to reach more of the students. At the time neither my experience nor my training had prepared me for the challenge of educating all God's children and educating them well. They needed to know through my behavior that I considered each of them important and capable of doing good work. It was at Riis "University" that I realized I had lucked onto a career where I could pay back those persons who had invested in me by offering my "shoulders" to young people needing a confirming adult.

During my nine years at Riis, I continued my group-work practice through part-time and summer work at Henry Booth House of the Hull House Association. And I improved in my pedagogical skills by teaching at least one class at every grade level and by reading all the textbooks for all the subjects. This was all good preparation for beginning my graduate work at the University of Chicago.

At the University of Chicago two professors in particular pushed me to think about my role as a teacher and to refine my craft in ways that would improve instructional experiences for students. One of these was John Goodlad, who even in the 1950s was promoting multi-aged groups and team teaching. He urged me and others to consider

86

peer tutoring programs and to engage the community in the work of the school. The other was Allison Davis, who taught us to respect and believe in the ability of all children to learn. It was Dr. Davis who shattered my brainwashed mentality about how God distributed intelligence. What a revelation it was to learn that all children possess 13 billion brain cells, most of which are not used. Environmental stimulation, which includes the schools, is a primary factor in producing students who achieve.

The most satisfying aspect of my master's program at the University of Chicago was integrating the entire experience in order to prepare for the comprehensive examination. The ten separate courses I took became one and a part of me. I had at once found something that had been missing in my own education and in my teaching.

During the nine years when I was learning to become a more effective teacher, great teachers and preachers were transforming our nation into a classroom, with the lesson focusing on why and how all Americans can live together, work together, and go to school together. This noble lesson was heard in Chicago in the early 1960s, about the time I had decided to become a principal. Schools might be changed by laws and mandates, but would they be changed into places of learning for those who had been shut out, sorted out, or pushed out? Thus my educational mission had been cast.

In the 1950s when I decided to become a teacher, it was common practice in Chicago to seek the assistance of your ward committee man to secure a position. This practice was eliminated by a courageous general superintendent, Herold V. Hunt, who later as my professor at Harvard Graduate School of Education became a major influence in my life. The ward patronage system was changed to a rigorous written and oral examination system.

In 1961 approximately 800 persons took the written examination for the principalship. Only 105 persons survived both the written and oral examinations, with only five of those persons being black. I was one of them. At that time five was the second-greatest number of blacks ever appointed to the principalship in one year. Four of those persons went on to become general superintendents during their careers, and the fifth retired as an assistant superintendent in the Chicago system.

It took the Chicago newspapers a year and a half to learn that I had been appointed principal of Whittier Elementary School, a school with an all-white student body. It was fortunate that I had time to get to know the staff and the community before becoming a news item. The faculty tended to be younger than those under whom I apprenticed at Riis, but they were of the same mold. Most public elementary schools in Chicago had large enrollments, but the enrollment at Whittier was only 600. I could and did visit every classroom almost every day. Students and teachers expected to see me and would express disappointment if I failed to visit. Teachers looked forward to reading my brief written comments on what I had seen and heard. Most of our follow-up discussions on my written comments occurred on an informal basis.

During the years I was principal at Whittier, I encouraged teachers to form teams to work on certain projects; but my major task was as case manager for students who needed more help. Because of my frequent classroom visits, teachers viewed me as a partner. And my social work background served me well when referrals needed to be made.

My fondest memory of Whittier is the Christmas Community Song Fest. Whittier is located in an old area of Chicago, then populated by families of Slavic origin. Each enclave in the community had its own church, with its priest and nuns from Europe who spoke the native languages of the different national groups in the area. Most of the churches had small schools attached to them. There was little communication and less cooperation among the several schools. We could feel the community tension in the public schools because many of our students and their parents were members of the different churches.

It did not take much encouragement from me to gain the involvement of the several priests, community leaders, and PTA members in organizing a community song fest at which all the schools and the community could bring student singing groups to perform. It became an annual event that gave us a reason to work together. And that cooperation spilled over to other activities, including more persons joining the PTA and giving direct support and assistance to Whittier.

In 1965 I was offered an administrative assignment that I considered good enough to pry me away from Whittier. Superintendent Ben Willis and Welfare Director Raymond Hilliard had agreed to establish a day school for illiterate and functionally illiterate adults, and I was given unprecedented full discretion in selecting teachers and developing the program of instruction.

After apprenticing as a teacher at Riis and as a principal at Whittier, I was conditioned to instill in those hand-picked teachers the idea that they had a free hand in what they could teach and how they delivered instruction. But our mandate was to get these adults functioning at an eighth-grade level as quickly as possible. The phrase "teacher empowerment" had not been coined then; but if it had, it would apply to this staff.

Because we had no administrative rules to follow, we were able to develop the school schedule so that staff could meet mornings and afternoons if needed. An early success was the use of the daily newspaper as instructional material. Students told their teachers they enjoyed the shopping hints they learned from using the newspaper in class. It helped them manage their meager welfare grants. An early mathematics project was to compute their welfare grant. The percentage of errors made by social workers was so great that the welfare agency assigned a full-time person to the school to make grant corrections based on the much more accurate student calculations.

Perhaps the major motivation contributing to these adult students learning at three times the rate of younger students was our enlisting two large companies to provide jobs for graduates of our program. The payoff for the companies was two-fold: We trained the students at school using the companies' equipment and continued their education on the job with classes before and after work in classrooms provided by the companies. The two companies used success in the classroom as a criterion in making promotions.

After only three months the progress of the Adult Education Center somehow gained the attention of Superintendent Willis. He asked me to join a team of his top staff to go to Washington, D.C., to appear at the hearing of the Health, Education and Welfare Committee chaired by Congressman Adam Clayton Powell. I was honored to be invited but confused as to why this small new program had been singled out for attention.

The committee was courteous to all of us on the staff but spent most of the time interrogating Superintendent Willis on how the Chicago Public Schools were being responsive to its poor and minority constituents. Observing Willis deal with the committee's questions made me realize the importance of politics in education. Instead of avoiding politics, an effective leader and children's advocate must engage in politics to benefit students.

My next assignment came during my first year at the Adult Education Center, when I was asked to accept the principalship of Wendell Phillips High School. Phillips was similar to a few other large city high schools with names like Booker T. Washington and Paul

Lawrence Dunbar in that it was the first high school in Chicago designed for black students. It counted among its alumni many prominent black Chicagoans. With the school's long tradition of excellence, the value that an education was a privilege and not a right was firmly established. Nevertheless, dropout and "pushout" rates were high. Attendance hovered around 80%.

My predecessor, a distinguished and experienced principal, was promoted to district superintendent; and many experienced teachers elected to transfer, resulting in almost half of the faculty being first-year teachers. The school's greatest asset, however, was a small cadre of experienced teachers who had internalized the Phillips tradition and refused to give in to lower standards of conduct and academic performance.

Eighty percent of Phillips' almost 4,000 pupils lived in the several public housing complexes. The school itself was a three-story structure located on a square block with no outdoor campus. In order to accommodate this many students, the school operated on a 12-period day with three different starting and departure times and five lunch periods, the first beginning at 10:20 a.m. During the first months on the job, my only plan of action was to react to problems as they developed. My first move was to secure permission from my district superintendent to delay school opening one morning each month in order for the faculty to meet in large and small groups. We had to become a team.

There was faculty agreement that our toughest problem was the five lunch periods, which required us to send at least half of the students out into the streets for lunch between the hours of 10:20 a.m. to 2:10 p.m. My district superintendent supported our request for a cafeteria expansion and joined me in submitting the request to Superintendent Willis. He granted the request, which gave us the first victory we needed to begin making things better for students.

Another major thrust of the staff was to reduce the anonymity that pervaded such a large school. Students knew the senior staff by reputation, and some knew me because of my work in settlement houses located in the area. But new staff didn't know the students and the students didn't know them. Students from one housing project didn't know students from other housing projects. Some of the activities the staff developed to make Phillips a more friendly place included a "Getting to Know You" program with students and staff wearing name tags so they could call one another by name, writing autobiographies in English classes and sharing the information by reading them in class, and inviting successful Phillips graduates to school to share their life stories with students.

Still another major problem during my first semester was the threat of gang violence. It was 1965 and teen gangs were organizing and establishing their turfs. It did not take me long to realize that my immediate task was to create a safe environment at the school. The staff and I organized to respond. Our first step was getting two policemen assigned to the school, but we needed to eliminate the threatening environment. I sought and gained invitations to gang meetings. I argued the reasons for making the school a sanctuary. Over the year, one by one the gangs pledged no violence in school and supported the school staff's handling of isolated cases of violence without interference.

With the establishment of a safe and orderly school, other improvement projects were undertaken, including: improved attendance, departmentally developed lessons for students who attended irregularly, a closed campus lunch hour with the opening of the expanded cafeteria, and most important, a job placement program for seniors, with almost 90% being placed within six months following graduation.

So much had happened so quickly, but I felt a need for improving my own professional life, focusing on secondary education. I applied and was accepted at Harvard Graduate School of Education in the Administrative Career Program. I went to Harvard believing that I had risen in the ranks as far as a black administrator could go in the Chicago Public Schools. I was pleased with being a secondary school principal and aspired to be an outstanding one. I did, however, want to test my mind against the best in the country. I needed to affirm for myself my worth as a person and as an educator. I divide my professional life before and after Harvard. My perspective on who I was and what I could do was changed during my two years at Harvard.

Herold V. Hunt was my advisor at Harvard. Early on he began dismantling the protective wall I had built around my ego and emotions. By my second year at Harvard, he was instrumental in my being promoted to district superintendent while still on leave from the Chicago Public Schools. In addition, he had me apply and be interviewed for three superintendencies. He debriefed me after each interview and, in the process, taught me how to handle the hurt and suspicion of racism. He made me believe that I would become a superintendent. In fact, he promised that I would be placed in a superintendency within two years following my leaving Harvard.

Perhaps more important than raising my career goals, my Harvard experience introduced me to the joy of learning. We were encouraged to work in groups, and we discussed what we read and wrote. Still, there was time for introspection and the sorting and weaving of ideas and values for one's own purposes.

Dr. Hunt was prophetic. I received my degree from Harvard in June 1969, and in July I accepted my first superintendency in the Compton (Calif.) High School District. Six months later the high school district was merged with three elementary school districts, and I was elected superintendent of the Compton Unified School District. For six months my secretary and I were the only employees of the new school district. What a way to learn your craft!

Compton is located almost in the center of Los Angeles County and is contiguous to Los Angeles' Watts District. During the 1968 Watts riots, the citizens of Compton went to the edge of their city and refused entry to the Watts rioters. Compton's population was (and is) predominantly black and brown and took pride in electing the first black mayor west of the Mississippi and in declaring Cinco de Mayo (Fifth of May, a Hispanic holiday) a city holiday. Despite the pride of Comptonians, they lacked an economic base. They could govern, but there was little wealth other than real estate taxes to support their dreams.

They wanted all of the American dream, but their leaders could not deliver. Meetings of the city council and the school board were long and rancorous. Never before did the biblical passage, "That without a vision the people perish," become more real to me. I organized a series of town meetings to look at what the system could and should do. Each town meeting was attended by 1,000 or more people. After the fourth town meeting, it was clear that our mandate was to improve basic skills of all students, to increase the number going on to postsecondary education, to distribute equitably the resources of the school district, and to maintain communication between the district and the community in general.

Soliciting community input on the goals for the school district proved to be fortuitous. The Los Angeles Black Panthers determined that Compton was to become its headquarters and had selected Compton High School as its target for student recruitment. It was not long before they proposed a takeover of the campus with the goal of replacing the principal and instituting their own curriculum. Panthers went to every class to persuade students to join their cause. The campus was under siege. The 90-person Compton police force was of little assistance in controlling the situation.

I invited the Panther leaders to the school district offices to discuss their demands. After three days of negotiations, we agreed to present their 13 demands to a student vote and allowed them to present their position to students without faculty being present. The students supported the school administration by a three-to-one vote. Although the demands of the Panthers were rejected by the students, some of the reasons behind their demands, such as the inequity in resources, continued to plague the district.

Much of my time in Compton was devoted to the search for additional resources to augment the meager tax base in the district. Staff became adept at applying for grants from both public and private organizations, including the University of Southern California. We also forged productive alliances with the University of California-Los Angeles, where I was able to renew my relationship with John Goodlad dating back to my days at the University of Chicago. He included several of our principals in his special programs. Both USC and UCLA encouraged their professors to work with Compton students and staff.

In addition, we kept the pressure on the State Department of Education and the legislature. The state superintendent and the county superintendent became our partners in securing additional resources. As California moved toward 100% state funding of schools, Compton's fiscal condition improved. And although Proposition 13 imposed tax ceilings that sharply reduced revenues in most school districts, its equalization factor was a boon for Compton.

Just as I was preparing to begin a new four-year term at Compton, I was invited to be interviewed for the Atlanta superintendency. In less than a week I became a finalist and was then selected superintendent.

During my 15 years as superintendent in Atlanta, I enjoyed many opportunities, but none greater than the privilege of working with and learning from Dr. Benjamin E. Mays, who served as president of the Atlanta Board of Education for eight of my 15 years there and 12 years in all. To work with Dr. Mays was to know greatness.

Dr. Mays was the youngest of eight children. He attended school at a time when the school year for blacks was but four months a year from third grade on up. Yet, this son of a former slave turned cotton farmer was valedictorian in 1916 of the high school department of South Carolina State College. He went on to graduate with honors from Bates College in Lewiston, Maine, in 1920. He acquired his master's and doctoral degrees from the University of Chicago between 1925 and 1935. He served as president of Morehouse College in Atlanta for 27 years.

Dr. Mays was internationally respected as an educator, author, lecturer, and minister. He advised world leaders of every description, including Dr. Martin Luther King Jr. and former presidents Lyndon Johnson and Jimmy Carter. Noted historian Lerone Bennett fittingly characterized Dr. Mays as "the last of the great schoolmasters."

Shortly after beginning my "secular ministry" in Atlanta, Dr. Mays gave me a copy of his autobiography, *Born to Rebel*, which had been published in 1971. This book and some of his other writings helped me to form a vision that guided me throughout my 15 years as superintendent.

Like Dr. Mays, I was fortunate in having the support of my family and others, who encouraged me to complete high school and college, thus preparing me for leadership positions in the community. Because of my good fortune, I felt an obligation and desire to help others. Through discussions with Dr. Mays and by studying his life and the lives of others who succeeded in spite of great odds, I came to believe that "all God's children can learn." From this simple premise I developed the concept of the "Community of Believers," which posits four conditions that must be satisfied if we are to produce successful students:

1. Adults must demonstrate they care about our children.
2. We must engage students in their own education. They must become producers of education as well as consumers of education.
3. We must challenge our students. If we teach to the average, and many teachers do, let's average up and not down. Let's raise standards.
4. We must create opportunities for students. We must help them to attend postsecondary institutions and to secure jobs with growth potential. Students must feel that they have a piece of tomorrow.

Dr. Mays challenged the Atlanta Board of Education, the staff, the students, and members of the community to do our jobs so well that no person living or dead or yet to be born could do any better. Over the 15 years we gained the involvement of parents, students, business community, religious community, and representatives of government and higher education. With the assistance of thousands of persons, we responded to the four conditions of the Community of Believers concept. Our students improved significantly in basic skills, in attendance, in admissions to postsecondary institutions, and in lowering the dropout rate.

In 1988 when I retired as superintendent of the Atlanta Public Schools, I could take satisfaction in the progress the school system had made in meeting the old challenges. But the demands of the future present new challenges and will require better-educated people. School systems and their communities must do more for all students and do it better. I am convinced school systems can overcome their own resistance to change. And I am convinced we know how to educate children beyond the basic skills.

Over the years I have learned much from students, faculty, professors, mentors, and community members. I've tried to apply their teachings in my work. At Georgia State University where I now work with administrators and others engaged in serving our youth, I try to pass on what I have learned. You should not just keep the faith, you should pass it on. Some of the teachings are:

1. Use the principles of intentional administration based on research; that is, clearly enunciate objectives and expected achievement in measurable and/or observable terms.
2. Stress involvement in the decision-making process by those who will be affected by the decision. Obtaining their opinions up front rather than after the fact promotes morale and success.
3. Recognize that a process becomes more important when the expected product is achieved in a cost-effective manner.
4. Develop performance profiles for both students and staff. Try to derive the data for the profiles as outcomes in pursuing the objectives.
5. Foster a climate of open communication. Report regularly the activities and results.
6. Respect the dignity of each and every human being.
7. Demonstrate a caring attitude. Be sincere in actions.
8. Be patient, fair, and reasonable when pursuing stated objectives, but pursue them diligently.
9. Place decision-making responsibilities with those nearest to the point of action whenever it is practical.
10. Minimize predetermined, operational procedures and regulations and maximize the individual's creativity in attaining stated objectives.

11. Minimize the proliferation of activities in order to conserve human resources and to use resources efficiently.
12. Recognize and reinforce improvement in performance.
13. Challenge staff and pupils to improve their own performance. Seek quality performance.
14. Seek the contributions of volunteers from the larger community including parents and representatives of business, civic, cultural, religious, and higher education groups.
15. Form an active partnership between the school system and the various community groups, which is characterized by mutual service and open communication.
16. Provide opportunities for pupils, staff, and the public to express their opinions and concerns.

In summing up my career in education, I close with these words by the poet William Wordsworth, "What we have loved, others will love, and we will teach them how."

Reflections on a Career in Teaching

BY LARRY CUBAN

I am a teacher. Others might classify me as an "educator" since I have also been a director of a school-based teacher training program, a superintendent, an associate dean in a school of education, and a researcher. But it is teaching — not administration or research — that has defined my adult life. Teaching has permitted me to be a performer, a lifelong learner, writer, and a friend to former students and colleagues. Even as an administrator and researcher, it is the teaching aspect of those roles that I prize.

In teaching, I have experienced the deep satisfactions of connecting to others in ineffable moments, producing odd tingles, even goosebumps on my back and neck, when a class, small group, or individual and I become one — moments listening to students that provided me with an insight that upended a conventional idea, moments that forced me to rethink after I had closed my mind's door, moments when my students had touched me deeply. These rare instances are like the resounding crack of a bat that sends a ball soaring into left field or like the graceful pivot to avoid the outstretched arms of an opposing player that allows you to go for an easy lay-up. These moments I treasure.

Less treasured are moments that have left me sad and uncertain about teaching and schooling in our society. There were times when I knew in my heart that I had failed to reach some students. There were times when bright students stopped coming to class and dropped out of school despite my visits and phone calls to their home. There

Larry Cuban is Professor of Education at Stanford University. The author acknowledges Gary Lichtenstein for his helpful comments on this essay.

were times when a daily teaching load of 160 students with three preparations forced me to practice a crude form of triage: work most with those who had a solid chance of learning; work a little with those who might be helped; try to be civil to those who for various reasons did little more than attend class. These depressing moments forced me to think anew about my teaching, about how the schools where I worked affected both me and my students, and about the commitment of my community to improve schooling. I slowly came to see that teaching has its high and low moments, and both have strongly influenced me.

Teaching has also spilled over to the rest of my life. I look everywhere for lessons that can be taught and learned. I approach situations and think, How can I get my point across? What can I learn from this person? My wife and daughters have had to endure the questions, the pauses, the indirect and direct teaching style over dinner, during vacations, and pillow talk. Moreover, teaching history has forged my core personal and professional values. Knowledge of the past has shown me that both stability and change mark human affairs; and through a historian's eyes, the present has deep roots in the past. Thus, teaching in general and teaching history in particular have been paramount in my life and career.

Teaching in inner-city schools for a decade and a half gave me insights into the strengths and ravages of being black in America. Teaching at Glenville High School in Cleveland and Cardozo and Roosevelt High Schools in Washington, D.C., gave me a deeper understanding of (and disgust with) the nation's stubborn reluctance to deal with the lethal cancers of poverty and racism, which continue to poison public schooling in our cities. It is also within these urban schools that I began my career, learned my craft, and forged my professional values.

As a son of immigrants I believed in the American Dream in which the school is an escalator to personal success. I entered teaching with this belief intact. However, my experience in big-city schools as a teacher and administrator has shaken that belief. I am increasingly skeptical about the national will to improve urban schooling. Such thoughts diminish my core faith in the power of schooling and make me uncertain about the future.

What insights I have gained about teaching, learning, and the role of schooling have come directly from the classroom. These insights have matured and have been revised as I have shuttled back and forth between administration and the classroom. As an administrator, I came to understand more fully the complexities of teaching children and teaching adults. As a trainer of teachers, as a director of a district staff-development program, and later as a superintendent, I have been able to reflect on the nature of teaching in urban schools and its web-like connections to administration and policy making. As a scholar, the research questions I have asked over the last decade have emerged from the core experiences I have had in the classroom, but go beyond the classroom into the linkages between teaching practices, administration, and policy making. In this essay, I shall consider how teaching, especially in urban schools, has largely driven my career and how it has helped me see the important linkages between the classroom, the administrator's office, and policy making.

No master plan guided my shuttling between the classroom and administration and between practice and research for almost four decades. Since beginning my professional career in 1955, I have been a high school history teacher (15 years), an administrator in public schools and a university (13 years), and a professor (9 years). At three different times I chose to leave the classroom for administrative posts and, subsequently, chose to leave those posts to resume classroom teaching. Why?

Looking back, the temptation is to try to make it all seem rational. But as I recall it, unexpected opportunities arose to stretch my intellect and broaden my skills (for example, a job offer to be a master teacher in a federally funded project training returned Peace Corps volunteers to teach in inner-city schools and becoming director of the project after two years). It was also the growing awareness that teaching gets routinized over time and its intellectual demands shrink. Yet after spending time on administrative tasks, the lack of sustained contact with students and the chance to create new curriculum drew me back to the classroom. Both the push and pull of different challenges and satisfactions in and out of classrooms made me reluctant to disengage completely from teaching.

Shifting back and forth between the classroom and administration was something I prized because of what I learned from the journey. There were costs, however. Neither pay cuts nor wounded self-respect made the moves easy. I am unsure whether moving back and forth between teaching and administration is easier in the 1990s; but it was painful for me in the Sixties, Seventies, and Eighties. My attempts to stay in teaching taught me how perverse incentives within school organizations perpetuate the low status of teaching.

One example may illustrate what I learned. In 1970, after two years as a high-level district office administrator in the Washington, D.C., schools, budget cuts gutted my department, although my position was left intact. The cuts convinced me that returning to the classroom would allow me to make a contribution in an arena that was far more satisfying than the pervasive bureaucratic politics in which I had become a losing player. I asked for a transfer to the high school social studies position that I had previously held. What I got was a series of stinging bureaucratic slaps in the face.

I knew that my salary would drop by one-third; but I was surprised to learn from the Board of Examiners (the department that certified credentials and established salary level) that none of the four years I had served as administrator in the district counted for salary credit, and only seven of my ten years teaching experience met the system's standards. Next came the official board notification regarding employee transfers. It read, "demoted without prejudice." The phrase, of course, was correct. I was voluntarily moving to a lower rung on the organizational ladder. Still, the phrase is born in the vocabulary of failure; it rang of inadequacy.

Then the Board of Examiners told me a week before school began that I could not receive a regular contract because I had never taken a college course in teaching in the secondary school. Despite having logged over a decade of classroom experience in three cities, having spent four years preparing teachers to work in the district's secondary schools, and having authored a book and numerous articles on teacher education, I was told that unless I took an education course within two years, I could not teach in the system. After a pay cut, a demotion, and then a threat, I felt that I had committed some crime.

Of course, what I had smacked up against were the perverse incentives that drove big-city public schools in the 1970s. The organizational rewards of more money, status, and control of one's time were outside the classroom. Urban high school teaching was tough work. Signing in every morning, teaching five classes, reading papers for more than 170 students, hall duty, a half-hour to gulp down lunch, one period to prepare lessons, seeing students after school, and then evenings spent marking papers and preparing for the next day — this grinding routine left little energy for counseling students, for my family, or for intellectual growth. Schedules driven by clanging bells left little appetite for reflection, interaction with colleagues, and involvement in school decisions. And then there was the less than subtle question from friends at social gatherings asking: Are you *still* teaching? No, there was little recognition or incentives to do more than be a time-server within the system. What rewards I got from classroom teaching I extracted for myself in spite of the bureaucracy.

100

Are the incentives less perverse now two decades later? In some cases, yes. Although the workload remains largely the same, teachers in pace-setting districts apparently have ample supplies, instructional materials, and discretion to make classroom and school decisions. I found this to be the case when I taught a U.S. history class for a semester in a nearby high school in 1988-1989. Yet as I listen to the teachers I work with in various parts of the country, read the popular and scholarly articles in trade and professional journals, note the surveys of working conditions in urban schools, and acknowledge the efforts of the last decade to raise teacher status with higher salaries and more involvement in schoolwide decision making, much still remains familiar — especially in big cities. A recent phone call to the personnel department of the Washington, D.C., schools confirmed that the phrase "demoted without prejudice" continues to be used for those administrators who return voluntarily to classroom teaching (there are very few, I was told). The bureaucratic barriers imposed when one tries to move between teaching and administration are forbidding to teachers who seek a change of pace in a temporary administrative assignment and to administrators who yearn for contact with students through a short-term teaching assignment.

Although I have left public school teaching at different points in my career, my passion for teaching and for understanding the past has never left me. In thinking about my career, I have been struck by how much both have driven my work as an administrator and professor.

As an administrator in schools and the central office, I continued to have contact with students by either teaching at least one class, tutoring students, or teaching teachers. I believe my strong impulse to stay in touch with students during the 1970s came in part from the guilt I felt for leaving full-time teaching, in part from my desire to maintain credibility with teacher-interns I was then training and with the teachers I worked with in staff development, and in part simply to experience again the joy of teaching.

As a professor, I continue to teach. Much of what I learned as a high school teacher, my understanding of how people learn, the importance of grasping ideas rather than covering content, all have proved useful in teaching graduate students. Everything I teach in graduate school has a historical spin to it. And the part of teaching that is learning from others comes into play consistently as a professor.

As a professor, I also do research. This role is mind-stretching. The questions I ask myself as a scholar are shaped by my passion for historical understanding of puzzles growing out of practical experiences. As a high school teacher and administrator, I lacked the time to pursue such questions. Why, for example, did the high school classrooms in which I sat in the 1940s seem so similar to those in the 1990s? Why do some reforms stick and others disappear like tracks in sand? Why so much hoopla about technology in classrooms and so few teachers using the equipment? Why is it so tough to fundamentally change schools with large numbers of poor children? These and many more questions, often requiring an investigation of the past, are anchored in my daily experiences in classrooms and in administrative offices but have both a scholarly cast and policy-linked thrust to them.

In effect, as I look back on my career as a teacher/administrator and teacher/researcher, I see that it has been driven by the lure of trying to change ideas and behaviors of others. As I reflect on why I kept switching job tracks, I think it was because I was seeking different ways of helping students and adults grow, while also searching for experiences that would stretch my intellect and develop my skills in areas in which I had little initial competence. There was no master plan, but in retrospect it was a direction I sought for myself. The mismatch of jobs, the shuttling back and forth, the pain and the pleasure were all aspects of my stumbling to find a direction.

My writing helped. Cutting across my teaching, administering, and professing is writing. Writing has provided me a means for reworking experience and for understanding better what happens in the classroom and office. In writing social studies textbooks, newspaper and journal articles, and books on teaching and administration, I have been able to reach a deeper understanding of what I do, of who I am, and of what I stand for. By writing, re-examining my teaching experiences, conducting research on practice-driven questions, and having close contact with hundreds of practitioners, I have learned a few core lessons about schooling.

What I Have Learned About Schooling from Teaching

Simply stated, the classroom teacher is the hinge on which schooling swings. What makes teachers the central element of schooling is that they are the ultimate decision makers. They make and unmake policy daily when they plan lessons, improvise solutions to unexpected problems, and execute myriad decisions prior to teaching, in the classroom, and after class when they decide what to do the next day. Their practice makes policy. They are the quintessential street-level policy makers and bureaucrats uneasily switching back and forth between roles that are in tension with one another — like teenagers who want to be independent and conforming at the same time.

Policy makers' intentions are stated in the laws, rules, and mandates delivered to schools. Administrators translate policies into regulations and procedures. I was influenced by them when I taught. And when I served as superintendent, I was responsible for generating many of them. Yet during the 15 years I taught high school, when I closed my classroom door I was free to decide as I wished on matters crucial to me.

In my classroom, public policies got transformed. I was insulated from scrutiny. In the 15 years I taught, no more than 10 times did an administrator enter my class to evaluate my teaching. The most extreme example of the insulated teacher-as-policy-maker is the professor at a research university. As a professor at Stanford University, I can teach virtually any course I want within my expertise, at almost any time, and certainly in any way, without interference from colleagues or department heads and, for sure, the dean, provost, or president.

While the professor is an extreme example, public school teachers still retain much discretion in determining content and practice in their classrooms. Although the courses I taught in high school were required for graduation, student interests helped to determine the content of my courses. For example, in 1957 after one year of teaching at Glenville High School in Cleveland, I began to develop classroom materials in what was then called Negro History. This was necessary since the standard text I used lacked even an index citation for "Negro." Over the next five years, I continued collecting and organizing materials and did some of my own writing until I produced a classroom text. My department head could care less about what I was doing. My principal was aware of my work and secured a ditto machine to help me produce the daily readings and lessons.

This experience taught me that I could create new materials for my classes, use lessons not in the syllabus, and if I chose, avoid most of the textbook for months at a time. Reading the accounts of such classroom teachers as Patrick Welsh, Grace Paley, Eliot Wigginton, Herbert Kohl, James Herndon, Jaime Escalante, and dozens of others, plus the growing body of research reporting how effective teachers vary in their instructional practices, suggest that my classroom experience was not unique. When I taught for a semester recently in a suburban school, I had the same freedom to create lessons, depart from the text, and determine what approaches to use.

Teachers, then, are the arbiters of policy makers' intentions. I use "arbiter" rather than the more common term "implementer," because it suggests putting the teacher in the role of a judge, one who determines what to put into practice, what to ignore, and what to modify. "Implementer," on the other hand, suggests a less reflective, more mechanical, even bureaucratic execution of a policy. As an arbiter, I wrote lessons and created units designed to engage students intellectually and emotionally in a way textbook chapters could not. What I have learned as a teacher and administrator is that in judging what should be put into practice, many teachers become classroom policy makers in their daily decisions. But not all.

As an administrator, I saw that most teachers try faithfully to implement the district curriculum and to follow their superior's instructions. They view themselves less as arbiters and more as civil servants doing what the authorities believe is best for their students. When policy changes or innovations are adopted, these teachers try to implement them. Yet even such well-intentioned teachers will have to adapt, alter, and deviate from the new policies and programs, because they don't fit their particular students, are inconsistent with their beliefs about learning, or are incompatible with their teaching style. I have seen this happen firsthand as an administrator and researcher with the adoption of district reading programs, Advanced Placement courses, schoolwide assertive discipline policies, and state-mandated curricula. Even those teachers who conscientiously attempt to implement policies made at higher levels in the organization still must judge in the privacy of their classrooms what to keep, what to change. Most teachers are actually covert policy makers, often unaware of the autonomy they exercise in deciding what and how they teach.

But many teachers (how many I do not know) are arbiters. They scrutinize district and state policies and assess their intended effects against their own views of what is good for students. They decide how much, if any, of the new policies and programs they will use and in what forms. They might adapt the district's new higher-order thinking skills program for their history classes, or they might modify the computer lab in ways unanticipated in the school board's mandate to use technology in the classroom. In a sense, then, these teachers become active policy makers. In each high school where I have worked since the mid-1950s, a small cadre of teachers operated in this fashion. They were astute in making sure that they conformed externally to policy makers' expectations; but once having closed their classroom doors, these teachers selected content and used methods that in their view were best for their students and feasible to carry out given the demands of classroom teaching.

Finally, there are those few teachers who march to a different drummer. Every district I worked in had such teachers. Their successes with students in drama, music, art, carpentry, auto body shop, social studies, journalism, poetry, or science fairs have earned them celebrity reputations. Their highly personal style of teaching is such that few principals or parents would challenge what they do, even if they did depart from accepted policies. The prudent principal simply stays out of their way. Such rare individuals obviously are policy makers.

What I have learned directly from teaching and relearned from the study of the history of instruction is that the role of teacher as policy maker has endured since the establishment of the graded school in the mid-nineteenth century. The recent hoopla over teacher empowerment and an expanded role in decision making tends to overlook the durable and inescapable role of teacher as policy maker in the classroom. District, state, and federal policy makers might profit by being reminded that teachers are policy makers. However, the chances are remote that they will, because policy makers inhabit different worlds than do teachers. Nonetheless, I offer this opinion about teachers as both overt and covert policy makers because it bears so directly on those who want to improve, if not fundamentally change, public schooling.

The desire for improvement, for changing individuals and institutions, is central to the future of schooling. It has been central to my career as a teacher, superintendent, and professor. So I end this series of reflections on the persistent efforts to improve schooling.

What I Have Learned About Change in Public Schools

As a historian I have learned much about education reform movements over the decades. Since 1955 I have seen firsthand a variety of reform efforts, federal and state government interventions, and foundation-funded innovations come to districts in which I have worked. These waves of change, recurring at irregular intervals, have altered educators' vocabularies and introduced new programs and instructional materials.

In my own writing I have tracked recurring patterns of reform. For example, public support for more practical subjects to prepare students for the workplace has ebbed and flowed, as has interest among employers and educators to stem the tide of school dropouts. The issue of requiring all students to study a common core of academic subjects rather than allowing them to choose electives returns periodically. I have seen decentralization come, go, and return as a policy option for urban schools. When I began teaching social studies, the preferred mode was a chronological, fact-filled approach to teaching U.S. history. Within a few years we were urged to teach fewer units but in greater depth with themes cutting across the nation's history and to use the methods historians use to understand the past. By the mid-1970s and since, there has been a gradual return to a chronological, hero-centered, factual coverage of everything that happened.

Despite the recurring waves of reform and innovation, teachers did not necessarily alter their classroom practices to conform to what policy makers said ought to be done. More often than not, what I saw as a superintendent, researcher, and even when I returned to teach history a few years ago was the remarkable constancy of certain forms of instruction. This is not to suggest, however, that there have been no changes in public schooling.

Since the mid-1950s when I entered teaching, I have seen and been part of efforts to make massive changes in access to public schooling for minority and handicapped students. There have been significant improvements in adapting the curriculum to match the diversity of student abilities and backgrounds. The right of due process, unknown to earlier generations of students, is now accepted practice. These examples testify to the fundamental changes that have occurred since I began teaching. What has not changed, however, is the benign neglect in big-city schools enrolling large numbers of low-income minorities.

In the summer of 1956, just before I began teaching in a black neighborhood, I saw the popular film, *Blackboard Jungle*, featuring Glenn Ford as the well-intentioned high school teacher ill-prepared for his new assignment and Sidney Poitier as his adolescent antagonist. My experiences at Glenville were unlike that of Glenn Ford. In fact, I found the years I spent there to be filled with learning, excitement, close relationships with several students, and a rare camaraderie with like-minded teachers. Yet the persistent neglect of the needs of the mostly black schools on the East Side of Cleveland became clear to even a politically naive white man in his early twenties.

By the late 1950s and early 1960s, the civil rights movement, starting in the South, began to sweep across the nation, even touching

106

Glenville's curriculum, student body, and staff. Many of us went to hear Martin Luther King Jr. speak at nearby churches. Students' emotions, inflamed by televised accounts of Freedom Riders being beaten and police dogs attacking marchers in Birmingham, spilled over into the classroom as we aired the issues. Beyond heated discussions, however, little changed within Glenville or the larger school district. Subsequent hearings held in Cleveland on proposed civil rights legislation revealed gross inequalities in allocating resources to East Side, predominantly black schools and discriminatory teacher-assignment policies during the 1950s and lasting through the late 1960s. By then, I had moved to Washington, D.C., to join in federally sponsored programs to improve urban schools.

For a brief period in the 1960s, many reform efforts were introduced with the intent of fundamentally changing urban schools. These included programs to train energetic, young teachers to work with inner-city children, programs in organizing communities, efforts at decentralization and desegregation, alternative schools, open education, and dozens of others. While well intentioned, most of these reforms were haphazardly implemented. Idealistic but naive policy makers, without much grasp of the change process, attempted to attack the accumulated neglect of urban schools. They lost; inertia and apathy won.

For a decade I taught in and administered some of these programs in Washington, D.C., and saw close up what they could and could not do. I participated in curriculum and teacher education reform, dropout prevention programs, and staff-development efforts. I have no regrets for what I and other like-minded individuals did. I take pride in the many teachers and students participating in those federally funded efforts who were rescued from deadly, mismanaged schools and ill-taught classrooms. But with a few notable exceptions, the fact remains that most of these urban school reforms were like graffiti in the snow.

In Washington I lost my innocence. I learned that dedication, good intentions, and long work hours could not overcome every problem. It was then that I began to feel that maybe some problems are intractable, some problems are insolvable dilemmas. My early stirrings of despair were intensified with the murders of the two Kennedys and Martin Luther King, the urban riots, and the corrosive effects of Vietnam on our youth. All played a part in my loss of innocence about solving severe urban social problems through improved schooling.

Subsequently I have seen the deepening decay of big-city schools in the 1970s and 1980s. There are exceptions, of course, in small cities and perhaps in Pittsburgh and San Diego, where strong superintendents and school board leaders harnessed to political coalitions outside the schools have seemingly arrested and even reversed the deterioration. Moreover, even in the largest cities there are schools that are islands of competence among seas of ineptness and apathy. Nonetheless, schooling in most urban districts is a continuing disaster plaguing the poor. It is, at best, a salvage operation; at worst, it is warehousing of poor children and youth.

We cannot place the blame for these conditions solely on incompetent teachers or administrators or on shortsighted policy makers and city officials. In my view, the problem stems from public indifference and neglect. The problem, simply put, has been a lack of sustained national and state leadership to build political coalitions aimed at improving the conditions of children in general and their lot in schools. Even when there has been sufficient political muscle to introduce reforms, results are problematical.

From my big-city experiences in the 1960s and 1970s and my experiences as a superintendent, I learned hard, painful lessons about the fickleness of national and local political leadership with regard to school improvement; and I learned what happens when attempts at reform are foisted on practitioners.

I learned that bringing about change is both a social and political process. I learned that it takes three to five or more years of dogged work and continuing pressure to change adult behavior even modestly. I learned that those who are expected to change their behavior (teachers, principals, students) have to understand clearly what is expected of them. And even when they understand, they have to put their own signatures on whatever is to be done. I learned that external pressure combined with ample teacher and administrator support is essential when trying to change an organization. I learned that plans were made to be unmade, that desired changes would occur unevenly and often in unanticipated ways.

I learned that no one group has a monopoly on wisdom about what should be done to improve schools. Certainly teachers, administrators, and university faculty bring special insights; but they are not necessarily the best ones to determine what policy to follow, because, like any group, they often seek to protect what they have or to advance their own interests. And again I learned that teachers are the ultimate policy makers when they either ignore, modify, or deviate from reforms intended to improve schools.

For almost four decades I learned these lessons and others as a teacher and administrator. These experiences, especially the years I spent in Washington, D.C., and Arlington, Virginia, taught me that the process involved — from the generation of an idea through its implementation and institutionalization — for even simple reforms is filled with mine fields. The process takes many years and requires steady pressure, perseverance, careful listening, generous help for those who need support, and deep respect for those who are expected to alter their behavior.

As for more fundamental changes in schooling, the road is even tougher, requiring political coalitions outside the schools that press educators and suggest alternatives considered unthinkable by insiders. For big-city school districts, the lessons I learned are written in capital letters. Because of long-term neglect and decline of public support, the prospect of significant reform or major overhaul seems remote. Although an optimist at heart, such thoughts leave me pessimistic and at war with myself. My head tells me to be skeptical; my heart yearns for the impossible.

In the late 1960s and early 1970s, parents angered by the failure of school policy makers to improve the lives of their children were driven to try radical ventures, such as community control, alternative schools, and vouchers. Such experiments, although not widespread, were tried and most eventually failed. In the 1980s state-driven reforms mandating higher graduation requirements, curricular alignment, and a bevy of tests have been embraced by many urban schools. Yet the indicators reflected in high dropout rates and graduates who fail tests for entry-level jobs show little or no improvement. In the late 1980s and early 1990s, savvy coalitions of parent and community groups produced Chicago's dramatic experiment in local school control. Similar resentment has spurred parents and taxpayers to seriously consider schemes that will break off the mostly black neighborhoods in Milwaukee and Boston into separate school districts. And in Chelsea, Massachusetts, the operation of the school has been handed over to a private university. Only time will tell what the fate of these reform ventures will be.

As the 1990s unfold, the state-driven reforms of the previous decade have evolved into a set of national goals established by President Bush and the nation's governors. A strong movement toward national standards of performance as measured by the National Assessment of Educational Progress rolls on. Driven by a compelling rationale that views schools as the primary vehicle for making the nation competitive on the international economic front, sentiment grows among federal and state policy makers for reforms that call for a national curriculum and standardized textbooks. At the same time that efforts are being made to centralize the control of schools, we are hearing much rhetoric about teacher empowerment and school-site decision making. But the rhetoric pales when set against the actions taken in states and districts to maintain existing controls.

The proof of altering the tragic trajectory of an inner-city child's career in school is yet to be tested in newly minted Effective Schools programs. Enthusiastic promoters of this model launched ambitious, districtwide programs in the 1980s. The hard work by good-hearted educators in these programs to pluck students from almost predestined failure deserves the highest praise. While exceptional success stories garner media attention, most such efforts, sadly, have yielded mediocre results. The larger numbers of students, beginning around the third grade, continue their slide into truancy, poor academic performance, and a strong distrust of school.

The reforms of the 1970s and 1980s have largely bypassed urban schools like the new freeways that slice through a city isolating one neighborhood from another. Without a massive infusion of funds to help administrators and teachers, local leadership, and strict enforcement of enlightened policies, I am skeptical that national goals, national standards and testing, and a national curriculum will stem the growing isolation of big-city schools from the rest of the nation. This lack of progress in improving urban schools during my career and my knowledge of how schools in cities historically have been unable to cope with children whose color, language, and economic status differ from the majority leaves me somber about our future as a nation.

I believe in the American Dream. I believe that the schools must acknowledge and respect cultural differences without attempting to smooth out their uneven edges that jostle one another in this diverse nation. The enduring failure of urban schools cannot be remedied by such measures as better-trained staff or national goals or national tests. Neither can our schools assume sole responsibility for turning out qualified workers in order to regain supremacy in the international economic order. Schools in big cities are not slums awaiting gentrification; they are not do-it-yourself fixer-uppers. The problems of these schools are not theirs alone. The problems are linked to perennial neglect by the larger community and a political unwillingness to connect what happens in these schools with what happens on the streets, in city halls, state legislatures, and Oval Offices.

I end on this somber note because I have come to see how urban schools have become a metaphor for the conscience of the nation. Public apathy and inertia, despite occasional bursts of intense activity, help to perpetuate the neglect accumulated over time. The moral principle of helping others to help themselves seems to have been abandoned. The principle that appears to dominate in our big-city schools since the 1950s is to control the damage, seal off the effects of bad schooling, and salvage what is best.

These reflections on my career, on the role of teachers as policy makers, and on the process of change are rooted in the urban school setting where I began teaching, learned my craft, and forged my professional values. These urban schools are where the young start out believing in the American Dream, believing that the school can improve their lot; yet they live out their young years surrounded by neglect, crime, poverty, and racism.

This skepticism I express, which occasionally emerges as outright pessimism, occurs more and more frequently. I have seen so many efforts to improve urban schooling arrive in glamour and depart in disfavor. I suspect that educators of my generation share these bouts of pessimism. Yet, and here I speak only for myself, I continue to be involved in efforts to transform schools. The war between my head and heart persists. It reminds me of what I have learned from *Don Quixote* and the dozens of individuals I have come to respect who pursue ideals that have the barest chance for success because they are the right things to do.

Leadership and Vision

BY JACK A. CULBERTSON

*Those gazing on the stars are proverbially at the mercy of
the puddles on the road.*

— Alexander Smith

Vision is an essential dimension of leadership. Without it individuals
cannot perform the most critical of all leadership functions: direction setting. Given the centrality of vision to leadership, one might
expect to find a large body of literature on the subject. This is not
the case — perhaps because it is so difficult to observe, define, and
analyze.

The reflections I offer here about vision or intelligent foresight
are not abstract ones. They are derived from experiences I acquired
while serving as executive director of the University Council for
Educational Administration (UCEA). The mission of UCEA, as its
founders envisaged it, was to develop more effective programs for
preparing school administrators in its member universities. Central
to this mission was the concept of cooperation. The founders wanted
groups of talented professors from different universities to work
together to bring about needed changes. UCEA's strategy of change
was to generate, through cooperative research and development, ideas
and methods to improve administrator training programs and to disseminate these ideas and methods.

When I assumed the executive director post of UCEA in 1959,
some months after its official founding, my major immediate responsibility was to help envisage fruitful directions and program activi-

*Jack A. Culbertson is Professor Emeritus at Ohio State University and
former Executive Director of the University Council for Educational Administration (1959-81).*

ties for the organization. Although this responsibility was much more prominent in UCEA's early years, it was still a highly salient one at the end of my tenure in 1981. Accordingly, throughout my 22 years with UCEA I was continually engaged in implementing cooperative programs and in envisaging new ones. Since vision was required to conceive programs, especially the more innovative ones, my experience provides a relevant base for these reflections. Yet reflections derived from experience have limitations. They can be distorted by personal bias and by errors in memory. Thus, they are offered mainly for their heuristic value.

The generalizations that follow are linked largely to experiences gained in two major UCEA programs. In one I helped set in motion a series of events that generated new international networks of leaders and scholars and significant developments in the field of educational administration. In the other I sought to improve the preparation of urban school administrators by involving more than 150 professors in the simulation of administrative positions and problems in one of America's 20 largest school systems. Even though the two programs, one international and the other domestic, were markedly different, the role vision played in the two endeavors was similar. In fact, vision played much the same role, in my judgment, in the scores of other UCEA programs I helped conceive and initiate.

Vision often began with an awareness of specific occurrences that at first glance seemed disconnected. The vision for the international initiative noted above originated from such a set of events. While sitting in my office at Ohio State University in the summer of 1963, I found myself musing about such occurrences as the following: William Taylor in England had recently developed and was using simulated problems to teach school management at Oxford University; a few months earlier William Walker at the University of New England in Australia had launched the *Journal of Educational Administration*, and in his introductory editorial he stressed the need for writings with international appeal. The University of Alberta, under the leadership of Arthur Reeves, had just become the first university outside the United States to join UCEA; and at the University of Michigan, Dan Cooper, Claude Eggertson, and four graduate students were making plans to conduct a pilot study of school management in England.

While meditating on these events, I saw new meaning in them. Collectively, they reflected a need, as I saw it, for better means of international communication in the field. With the creation of new

113

networks, scholars and leaders from different nations could learn from one another, support one another in their respective initiatives, and cooperate in research, development, and dissemination activities. Through an inductive process, then, I arrived at new insights about the meaning of events occurring in different parts of the world and in different contexts and about their potential links to UCEA's mission. The result was a guiding vision for developing a new UCEA program.

The vision for simulating a large-city school system began to emerge in the fall of 1968 when each of nine UCEA universities sponsored regional planning meetings. About 20 professors, on average, attended each meeting with the purpose of developing a UCEA five-year plan. Among other things, attendees were expected to identify needs that UCEA should address during the 1969-74 period. In the second meeting, several professors confessed they felt ill-equipped to prepare administrators for America's large school systems, since they had acquired their own administrative experiences in non-urban school settings and had had little contact with big-city schools. And as we moved across the country with the regional meetings, other professors voiced similar concerns. The concerns expressed echoed the messages coming from urban school administrators, who were facing unprecedented educational problems. The professors' candid expressions of their concerns underlined a need that UCEA could not ignore. But several months would pass before I conceptualized the vision of a simulation of a large-city school system as a teaching tool and the widespread use of its components in training programs for urban administrators.

A vision was of limited immediate value unless an appropriate means for pursuing it was conceived and implemented. To develop and implement an appropriate means was always a demanding leadership task. Not only did the means have to be logically related to a clearly stated goal, it also had to be politically viable and mesh with existing constraints. One could easily err by selecting a conventional means to achieve an unconventional goal. For example, when I decided that a conference could address the envisaged international goal described above, I erred. Taking an easy route, I presumed that a one-week conference of leaders and scholars from Australia, Canada, New Zealand, the United Kingdom, and the United States could effect the desired outcomes. When I described the idea in 1965 to Emory Morris, president of the W.K. Kellogg Foundation, he listened politely and then informed me that the foundation did not support confer-

114

ences. Fortunately, he gave me a second chance by asking if I could re-think the proposal, which I agreed to do.

As I re-examined the conference idea, I saw its limits more clearly. The interactions it would generate would be too brief, too scattered, and too fleeting to effect the creation of a continuing network of international scholars and leaders who could forge transnational developments. A different means was needed to attain the hoped-for network. Thus, a three-week rather than a one-week program was projected. Beginning with a seminar at the University of Michigan, the program would feature a two-week period in which small groups made up of individuals from different nations would travel to U.S. and Canadian universities to observe and analyze training programs, research centers, and related phenomena. The endeavor would end at the University of Alberta, where participants would spend several days evaluating the UCEA program and brainstorming future possibilities. The altered program, which received the support of the W.K. Kellogg Foundation, did realize its objectives.

When an innovative program was proposed for pursuing a vision, there was a tendency to dwell on the problems the program might encounter rather than focusing on its positive potential. In February 1969, I had a breakfast meeting with one of America's leading educators to discuss the projected urban simulation. A specialist in urban education who had visited dozens of urban schools in various nations, he reacted somewhat skeptically to the simulation idea. Questioning the program's feasibility, he countered with several pointed queries: "What makes you think you can find a big-city superintendent and school board who will permit scores of professors to gather data, make films, and produce audio recordings about events and problems in the system? Even if you gain entry, how can you maintain a working relationship with the system for five years? How will you get enough funds to conduct such a large-scale and long-range project?" By the end of breakfast, my companion had laid out a number of perceived problems; and his concerns were apparently strong enough to push aside any thoughts about the potential benefits the program might offer.

Reactions such as those just described, which I encountered frequently when recommending new UCEA initiatives, were very helpful. They served as a partial inventory of potential problems down the road. By examining each of the problems, one could make judgments about the threat they posed to a program's success and plan accordingly. Therefore, it was important to listen carefully to descriptions of perceived problems; there was little value in challenging their validity, since there usually was no way of knowing whether or not the problems would emerge as described. My response when strong opposition to a program arose because of its perceived problems was to say that UCEA personnel would never know how serious the problems were unless the program was actually implemented.

Even though it was important to listen to the concerns expressed, I did not let them deter me from pursuing my vision of developing a simulation of a big-city school system. While some of the perceived problems proved to be accurate forecasts, others did not. For example, despite the reservations my breakfast companion had about securing the cooperation of an urban school system, when I asked a superintendent if he and his staff would cooperate with UCEA in developing the projected simulation, he responded promptly and positively. He and his colleagues wanted to help improve the training of administrators, and they saw in the proposed simulation a promising strategy. Not only did they facilitate the work of more than 150 professors who spent time in the system but, in addition, an associate superintendent, aided by other personnel, perused thousands of pages, observed more than 10 hours of films and videotapes, and listened to numerous audio recordings in order to "clear" the materials for reproduction, distribution, and use.

Cooperation continued throughout the five-year project, and developmental activity in the "Monroe City" school system was extended for another two years. Those who facilitated the creation of the simulation did not labor in vain. An estimated 45,000 practicing and prospective administrators have assumed one of "Monroe City's" simulated administrative posts, where they learned decision-making and negotiation skills using problems presented to them in letters, memos, notes, and telegrams in their in-baskets, in audio recordings of messages from their secretary, in filmed episodes of teacher and student behavior, and in filmed episodes where parents, teachers, or students posed problems to them.

Perceived problems often reflected one's experience in a particular setting. When the urban specialist questioned UCEA's capacity to create a fruitful, five-year relationship with a large school system, he was influenced by the experiences he had acquired in working with the school system in his own city. However, UCEA was not burdened with a history of "town-gown" antagonisms. Furthermore, his questions about UCEA's capacity to acquire the funds needed to execute the project were undoubtedly more closely linked to a single university's R&D operation than they were to UCEA's structure. The UCEA staff was able to involve professors from about 40 universities, who contributed their time and talent to the UCEA urban simulation effort. Such an arrangement would not have been feasible if personnel in a single university had conducted the project.

Although a vision's potential may have attracted little attention initially, its concrete realization often generated new visions and actions. For instance, after the participants from different nations had participated in the three-week international program, they decided that its benefits were such that similar programs should be repeated every four years somewhere in the world. In 1990 the seventh such program was held. The programs have supported an expanding international network of leaders, enabling many of them to learn much from one another. More important, these leaders have helped improve and extend programs for preparing school administrators worldwide, have created opportunities for professors to study and teach in nations other than their own, have participated in cooperative inquiry, and have created new organizations. Their attainments can be briefly noted by listing some of the organizations they have created.

At the second international program held in Australia in 1970, the Commonwealth Council for Educational Administration (CCEA) was born. William Walker of the University of New England in Australia and George Baron of the University London, who were members of the advisory committee for the first program, agreed as did other attendees that the new organization should advance school management in both the old and the new Commonwealth nations. CCEA, among other things, helped establish national professional associations for school administrators in many of the more than 30 nations it has served. At the third program held in the United Kingdom, the European Forum on Educational Administration was spawned. This organization enabled scholars and leaders from countries other than the United States and the Commonwealth nations to present annual programs and to exchange ideas. Many of the nations in the Forum were represented at the fourth international program held in Canada in 1974.

New visions and actions also emerged from the administrator simulation project. The first positions simulated in "Monroe City" were three principalships for "Janus Junior High," "Wilson Senior High," and "Abraham Lincoln Elementary." Before professors or school system personnel could purchase one of the simulated principalship programs for use in their communities, they had to attend one of approximately 20 training institutes held in different regions of the country. In the institutes, participants examined components of a simulation, made decisions as a "principal," and learned about methods for using the simulation materials. Having gained insights into the potential of the materials, scores of trainers persuaded their institutions to acquire the simulations. The first major impact of the newly created simulations, then, was on the preservice and inservice training of school administrators.

Another important impact was the development of future simulations. Some decided they wanted "Monroe City" materials that differed from those already developed or were in the process of being developed. One group, for instance, wanted a simulation to help trainees acquire skills in "problem sensing" and consensual decision making. Using the "Wilson Senior High" database, the group developed a set of materials in those areas. Another example was a professor of psychology who, after attending a training institute, decided that a simulation needed to be created for the post of school psychologist in "Monroe City." After many months of intensive work, a large "PSYSIM" set of materials was completed. Still another noteworthy impact of the materials was in the area of research. Graduate students and professors used them to study the effects of simulated experiences on the attitudes, skills, and understandings of trainees.

In sum, the UCEA visions for guiding action did not emerge from abstract ideals. They came from insights related to concrete events. At times the visionary import of events was not at all obvious, as in the case of the international networks that were established. At other times the visionary implications of events were more explicit, as in the case of the repeatedly voiced concerns of professors about their limitations in training urban school administrators. One can argue that when visions are arrived at inductively, the programs they generate will be more closely linked to practice and, therefore, will more likely be realized than will programs deduced from idealized and abstract conceptions. In any case, if pertinent courses of action cannot be envisaged and implemented, the immediate value of visions is limited.

The generation of programs to realize visions is a highly complex undertaking. Action programs can fail for various reasons; for example, when a familiar but inappropriate means is chosen to attain an unconventional end. When professors learned about a proposed UCEA program, they tended to dwell on perceived problems rather than to focus on its potential benefits. Even though the identified problems did not always develop as predicted, the airing of the problems was helpful in the planning and implementation process. As a rule, a vision's potential was taken seriously only after it had demonstrated itself in concrete outcomes. Realized outcomes in turn tended to spawn new visions and new actions.

Having offered some generalizations about the role of vision in leadership and some examples from my 22 years with UCEA, let me turn now to consider what can be done to improve the vision of school administrators.

The depth and scope of an administrator's vision is influenced by what he or she sees or experiences. Thus the first task in improving vision is to identify those factors that affect what the administrator sees or experiences. For example, principals who devote most of their time monitoring what occurs within their schools will have a smaller base for envisaging new needs and initiatives than will principals who view their role as interacting with both their school and the wider community. And if community is defined more in global than in local terms, the stimuli will increase still more. School leaders whose vistas encompass both the present and the future are more likely to generate richer visions than those whose outlooks are bounded by the immediate. A three-year look ahead will tend to generate more new visions and fresh initiatives than will a one-week look hence.

In addition to a broadened and future-oriented outlook, visioning requires certain criteria that will help the school leader to differentiate the significant from the insignificant. Perhaps the most critical criterion in this regard is a clear conception of the purposes that will guide education in today's and tomorrow's world. With such a conception, school leaders can assess whether particular activities are appropriate for achieving the stated purposes. Other important criteria are those related to human and organizational potential. For example, school administrators who understand and accept the visions of the teachers with whom they work should be in better position to nurture such visions and to facilitate their expression in school practice.

The elements of vision discussed here serve as a starting point for thinking about options for enhancing vision. Professors, for instance, could design their courses or training programs to give prospective leaders a long-range view of education and its future needs. Inservice programs for practicing administrators might focus on how they can help their teachers implement their own visions. Individual administrators might be encouraged to broaden the scope of their vision by adopting new patterns of reading, travel, or observation. Graduate programs in school administration might use the elements of vision as criteria when recruiting prospective leaders. To offer detailed suggestions for all these options is beyond the scope of this essay. Therefore, I shall offer only a few examples derived in part from experiences gained in working with professors in UCEA universities.

Professors who expect to develop vision in school leaders will first have to overcome or work around some well-established barriers in their institutions. Perhaps the most formidable one is specialization. In recent decades professors have drawn ever-narrowing boundaries around their courses and areas of inquiry. As a result of this specialization, the knowledge typically offered trainees applies to smaller and smaller segments of the larger world in which school systems function; and the perspectives of these purveyors of knowledge encompass less and less of the territory school leaders inhabit. Such conditions subvert the development of broad and discerning visions and tend to snuff out imaginative thinking about education and its management.

The major purpose of specialized inquiry is to produce knowledge, but it tends to turn trainees away from practice. This tendency can be seen in the dissertation, the culminating experience for those in doctoral programs. Prospective administrators engaged in dissertation research often are required to study narrowly defined problems using well-established canons of inquiry. The dissertation experience tends to focus more on meeting the requirements of research than on the realities of practice. We need to acknowledge that school administrators pursue purposes, perform functions, and work in contexts that differ markedly from the purposes, functions, and settings of professors. Thus new models for training school leaders will be needed in order to break out of the mold of narrow specialization.

Could the dissertation experience be structured in ways that might enhance the vision of future school leaders? I believe it could if: 1) the culminating experience for prospective administrators required them to focus on the needs of educational practice rather than on developing specialized knowledge, 2) if they were able to look at aspects of education broadly rather than narrowly, and 3) if they were allowed freedom to develop and implement visions that would point education in promising directions. Inherent in the visions would be new relationships between knowledge and practice.

Let me illustrate by describing a dissertation dealing with a vision of the kind of citizenship education students in a specific high school would need in tomorrow's world. The inquirer might begin by examining pertinent school district policy plus the course objectives and other experiences that have shaped the existing citizenship education in the high school. Data on the backgrounds and characteristics of a sample of the students also might be collected and analyzed. Through such activities the existing program of citizenship education could be mapped. Using the map to anchor the study in practice, the inquirer could then investigate what general knowledge has a bearing on the topic. Pertinent knowledge might be generalizations about changes in society, especially those in the political domain. For example, what import for citizenship education does the growing trend of using television images and "sound bites" in political campaigns have? By thinking about the implications of changes in society such as the example given, the inquirer could craft a practical vision for citizenship education, which would be informed by general knowledge.

Other viable training options might be independent study and problem seminars. Either of these options could be structured in ways that allow future leaders to grapple with current developments in education and to broaden their outlook on educational issues. In recent years, for example, governors in various states have launched education reform programs, which are driven by a vision that schools should be preparing students to make American business competitive in the international marketplace. Should educational leaders accept this vision unquestioningly? Or should they make the case that such a vision is too limited to guide reform and then counter with a more appropriate vision? Only when school leaders have many opportunities to examine such issues will they be prepared to offer clear and well-defined visions about the ends of education.

To discern the import of societal changes for schooling, leaders need well-defined concepts of educational purpose and of our society's core values, such as freedom, justice, and respect for human dignity. Although schools have traditionally been the means for transmitting these values, they must be re-interpreted and re-defined as society changes. Thomas Jefferson's eloquently stated views about the role of education in ensuring freedom still ring true. However, the relationships between education and freedom in today's large, complex, and computer-driven society differ from that which prevailed in the simple, agrarian society of Jefferson's time.

If tomorrow's leaders are to understand the evolving relationships between educational purposes and society's core values, they must look to the humanities, especially the works of historians, philosophers, novelists, and poets. Professors of social foundations and educational philosophy could make a distinctive contribution to the preparation of school leaders by joining scholars in the humanities to select readings and to follow up with seminars where discussion would focus on values and the purposes of education. In this way school leaders would be exposed to a wealth of ideas from which enlightened vision can emerge.

In summing up, then, this essay contains some reflections about the nature of vision, how it might be enhanced in school leaders, and some illustrations of how to broaden, extend, and make vision more discerning. Underlying these reflections are several beliefs. If effectively employed, vision can be a powerful instrument of leadership. Not only can it point education in more promising directions, but it also can generate beneficial outcomes from which new hope, greater confidence, and novel actions can spring.

During the writing of this essay, I have read a number of articles about schooling in the four newspapers I peruse daily. Almost all reflect a skeptical or pessimistic tone about public education. One article reported that both conservatives and liberals now share the view that alternatives to the public schools must be put in place. Another, describing legislation allowing state support for private schools for low-income students in Milwaukee, Wisconsin, emphasized that the public schools were about to feel the winds of competition. In fact, one objective of the legislator who was instrumental in getting the Wisconsin law enacted was to force the public schools to do a better job. Do such developments foreshadow change in public schools or the beginning of their end? It is unlikely that voucher systems will change our schools significantly or soon. Other influences will be more compelling. A critical one is whether or not public school leaders (and those who abet them) can escape from the imprisoning press of the immediate to envisage and pursue more promising directions for schooling. If so, and if the outcomes generated are better than current ones, confidence in the public schools will be restored, and citizens will rally to provide the needed support. If not, then the institution that historically has been the prized centerpiece of our democracy could languish and eventually perish.

Reflections on Education and Well-Being: A Fresh Start After 200 Years

BY LUVERN L. CUNNINGHAM

Prologue

Harold D. Lasswell, throughout his long years of productive scholarship, noted that leaders must look backward to see forward. That homely observation makes considerable sense and adds significance to Phi Delta Kappa's invitation to contribute to this volume of reflections. My reflections will concentrate on the issue of educational governance. It is difficult to avoid being autobiographical; but I will yield to that temptation sparingly, noting only that the economic, political, and social settings in which the governance of education took place when I entered the profession and the settings in which governance is now embedded are substantially different. Our provisions for governance, however, remain much the same.

My mother taught in a one-room rural school; my father served for years as a rural school board member. I rode a white horse (Florie) to Colby School in Washington County in eastern Nebraska. There were eight grades, an enrollment of 12 to 16 children, outdoor privies, and an eight-stall horse barn in back. That school gave way to the bulldozer in the Sixties when it was consolidated with neighboring schools, forming a K-12 district with an enriched curriculum, new buildings, school buses, and a larger tax base. A five-member school board replaced a three-member board, but its responsibilities were not altered. Provisions for governance were unchanged.

Luvern L. Cunningham is the Novice G. Fawcett Professor of Educational Administration (Emeritus) at Ohio State University and Director of the Ohio Commission on Interprofessional Education and Practice.

Introduction

The New York Times and the *London Times* carried stories on successive weekends in September 1990 highlighting the plight of children. Some children need help from the day they are born, especially the increasing numbers of newborns damaged forever by alcohol and drugs consumed by their mothers. The programs required for their health, welfare, and educational needs will cost billions. Then, billions more will be needed to incarcerate them, said noted pediatrician T. Berry Brazelton, writing in *The New York Times Magazine*. Brazelton goes on to propose that massive new education and health interventions, even new institutions to carry out these interventions, will be required. In Britain the problems are much the same. There are thousands of children, many of them homeless, disease prone, suffering from malnutrition and absence of parental love and direction. And those conditions prevail in the Soviet Union, the "democratizing" Eastern Bloc countries, as well as throughout the Third World.

These circumstances warrant "reflection." They are so overwhelming, so institutionally untidy, so beyond the training and experience of most educators — and other human-services professionals, for that matter — to render them non-solvable, at least in the short run. Their massive and complex nature invites troglodyte behavior; it is much easier to ignore them than to confront them.

Chester E. Finn Jr., in a recent address delivered at the Center of the American Experiment's Conference on "The New War on Poverty," said:

> We are dealing with threats to the commonweal, to the society itself. When significant numbers of five-year-olds enter school with their brains messed up, when law-abiding people fear walking down the street at night, when youngsters may be struck down by random gunfire outside their homes or in the school's playgrounds, and when packs of marauding teenagers go "wilding" in the park, it is no exaggeration to say we are facing a national emergency, different in kind but, perhaps, not in degree from threats posed by hostile nations. If, in the words of the National Commission on Excellence in Education in 1983, an unfriendly foreign power had done this to us we would have deemed it an act of war.
>
> We should, therefore, think about mobilizing to deal with it as we would a major menace to our national defense. We should expect to submit ourselves to the organizational arrangements,

the long-term resolve, the bold changes in familiar assumptions and practices, the inconveniences and perhaps even the inhibitions that we associate with answering grave threats to the nation's well-being. My purpose is not to be melodramatic or to advocate some sort of police state. It is to say that if we have any serious expectation of winning this new war on behavioral poverty, we're going to need not only the imagination to devise strategies suited to victory but also the resolve to see them through.[1]

Initiatives proposed or under way, directed toward institutional reform and restructuring, are so distant, so remote, so void of promise that they wilt in the presence of the imperatives Finn describes.

Reconstituting Local Government for Education and Well-Being

Over the past half-dozen years, I have witnessed as well as been a part of several attempts to enhance the life chances of children and youth through restructuring initiatives of one kind or another. These have been intended to be responsive in one way or another to the circumstances Finn described. But most of them, despite heroic efforts, fall short of improving the life chances of large numbers of persons for whom the future is bleak, for whom personal well-being seems so remote as to be unattainable.

In 1988-89, I directed a comprehensive study of two educational systems in an impoverished county in the South. The economic problems there were chronic and no doubt contributed to the poverty of spirit shared by persons of all ages. Recommendations for changes in governance were ignored in favor of half-hearted responses to state mandates calling for essentially traditional approaches to educational improvement. A year later Lila Carol and I served as lead consultants to the Governance subcommittee of the Kentucky Task Force on Education Reform. Our task was to introduce fresh ideas about governance that would strengthen the state's education and finance reform initiatives. These were in response to the Kentucky Supreme Court's finding of June 1989 that the entire educational system of Kentucky was unconstitutional.

Six models of governance were proposed during two days of public hearings in Frankfort in November 1989. The proposals were: 1) a total educational governance system for lifetime education, 2) a well-being system, 3) educational development territories, 4) several large regional operating districts, 5) fine tuning the old system, and 6) a single unitary district for the entire state. The models contained some similar features, such as site-based decision making and an appointed rather than elected state school executive; but in other ways they were starkly different. Some of the features of each of the models found their way into the reform legislation passed in the early spring of 1990, but none of the six was adopted as *the* model for Kentucky.

During the fall of 1990 and the winter of 1991, Lila Carol and I were "in the trenches" again, this time in Memphis and Shelby County, Tennessee, where controversy arose over the prospect of the Memphis City School District relinquishing its charter, thus throwing itself on the county commissioners, who were also responsible for the Shelby County School District. This would have created a single school system of about 140,000 youngsters. The Memphis proposal – in effect, to go out of business – provoked an incredible uproar in both the city and county, leading to the formation of a city-county task force appointed by the county mayor. This task force of nearly 80 members, representing diverse political, financial, educational, and racial perspectives, began exploring ways to improve city and county schools, concentrating on finance, education, governance, and legal issues.

Our task was to serve as facilitator-consultants with a task force subcommittee on governance. Governance soon became the basic and most contentious issue. In early February of 1991, after numerous meetings with city and county political, business, educational, health and human services, civil rights, religious, and other leaders, the subcommittee generated a fresh proposal to govern education for the metropolitan area. A set of governance principles was developed and subsequently converted into an educational Bill of Rights. A process was initiated for creating a metropolitan area Constitution for Education, consistent with the Tennessee Constitution, to frame the establishment of an Educational Development Authority. Within the authority, educational accountability is lodged at the building level through site-based decision making, including formal parent participation. And several educational service districts are to provide technical assistance to schools. Finance, business functions, school construction and maintenance, personnel, planning, environmental scanning, purchasing, warehousing, and transportation also are placed at the authority level.

If the Constitution is prepared and adopted, the existing Memphis and Shelby County districts would be phased out in favor of the authority. Our discussions also considered including libraries, state-sponsored tax-supported learning technologies, a number of human services, even community colleges as a part of the authority in the future. The governance structure is intended to facilitate the incorporation of all those services that contribute to the well-being of a broad spectrum of the population, and would lead naturally into a more and more formalized lifelong education. Developments in Memphis, although a long, long way from public acceptance (a lengthy public review, debate, and potential adoption of a Constitution for Education has to occur), represent a closer approximation of what I believe must take place than any other proposal for changing educational governance currently on the drawing boards.

In earlier writings I have argued the need for reconstituting local government for well-being and education. My choice of language here is very important. The process I call for is *reconstituting*, not restructuring, not reorganizing, although each of these will be required if we take reconstituting seriously. A reconstituted local government for well-being would govern such areas as mental health, physical health, public safety, preschool and nursery school education, adult education, libraries, museums, child day care, adult day care, K-12 schooling, job retraining, employment counseling and placement, literacy, community development, and provisions for the homeless. Today these public services are the responsibility of a mélange of agencies with little or no policy coordination or continuity of service for individuals over time.

In *Educational Leadership and Changing Contexts of Families, Communities, and Schools* (National Society for the Study of Education Yearbook, Vol. 2, 1990), I based my call for reconstituting local government around well-being and education on several arguments:

- The "general welfare" provision of the Preamble to the U.S. Constitution has never been adequately addressed at the local level, much less achieved.
- The general responsibilities for well-being at the local government or community level are essentially unspecified.
- Recent federal and state governmental policy has redirected the burden of social responsibility to the grassroots level.
- The mission and goals of local governments (townships, municipalities, counties, school districts, special districts) have remained constant, for the most part, since their establishment.
- State constitutional conventions, infrequent in recent times, leave local government untouched.

- Many current problems of well-being (poverty, homelessness, AIDS, substance abuse, teen pregnancy, family violence) dot local landscapes and present a clear delineation of public responsibility.
- Attempts at inter-agency cooperation, important as they are, often are incremental and lack support.
- New imperatives such as lifelong learning and national public service currently are without clearly defined institutional and administrative homes and should be included in reconstituting formulations.
- Leaders across the public service professions are excellent sources of insight about the reconceptualization of local governments and can play central roles in their reconstitution.

The concept of an Educational Development Authority in Memphis, mentioned earlier, is intentionally open-ended. It is based on the assumption that provisions for education will never be fixed or absolute. It is fashioned as an umbrella under which, and within which, the generation of new approaches to well-being can occur. James S. Coleman has argued persuasively for the invention of new "social capital" forming institutions. These would augment and, in many instances, replace the social capital formation previously provided by families and other community sources such as scouting and non-school-related clubs.[2] Coleman describes how, in sequence, fathers and then mothers exited the home to become wage earners. Fathers, lunch buckets in hand, left home in massive numbers, abandoning in large measure their social capital-forming responsibilities at the turn of the century. Mothers followed, entering the labor force in the middle to late 1900s, depleting catastrophically the opportunities for close, enduring social relationships with children that are comparable to those provided by earlier generations.[3]

Consequently, the range of interactions between parents and children about academic, social, political, and economic matters has narrowed. Millions of children enter the classroom bereft of human association so essential to self-esteem. They lack personal confidence about their emerging roles in life and the meaning that formal education can have in their lives. Coleman urges the creation of new institutions designed expressly for child rearing, which can serve as surrogates for those parent-child associations that are not likely to be reclaimed on a large scale by contemporary families. Coleman goes on to assert: "The general shape of the demand for a new institution is clear: It is a demand not for further classroom indoctrination, not for any particular content, but a demand for child care: all day; from birth to school age; after school every day until parents return from work; and all summer."[4] Coleman adds that these new institutions must be able to induce the kinds of attitudes, effort, and conception of self that children and youth need to succeed in school and as adults.

The Well-Being Proposal for Kentucky

Reference was made earlier to the 1990 educational reform legislation that created a "new" Kentucky state system of public education. One of the governance models proposed (but not adopted) was actually titled "Reconstituting Local Government for Education and Well-Being." In the opening paragraphs describing the model it was emphasized that although

> . . . the nation's commitment to general well-being is anchored in the Constitution, we have treated it casually, almost with indifference. We have created units of local government such as school districts, and charged them with part of the responsibility for well-being, but not the whole of it. Schooling may well be the flagship of a flotilla of approaches to well-being but it is not the all of it. Schooling must be joined more fundamentally by other contributors to well-being, many of them identified earlier. Physical and mental health, employment counseling, infant education, preschool, day care, extended day, criminal justice, libraries, museums, community cable, foster care, churches and synagogues are partners that must be integrated into an emerging concept of local community designed to address well-being. These contributors to well-being are reasonably well-known. Some are public, some private, but each addresses a part, not the whole. Schools focus on the intellect and skills dimensions of well-being primarily; museums on natural and human history; libraries on information sharing; preschools and day care on the early years of life; hospices on dying with dignity; foster care on special needs populations; employment on economic self-sufficiency. Each is noble and defensible in its own right and historically significant but as parts they fall short.[5]

The model called for rather radical structural changes. At the level of the Kentucky General Assembly, committees of the House and Senate would be altered to correspond to the focus on well-being, and a new permanent joint committee for Well-Being Oversight would be created. An annual Well-Being Stewardship Report to the citizens of Kentucky would be required. The State Board of Elementary and Secondary Education would be replaced by a State Board of Well-Being with responsibilities consistent with this focus. A chancellor of Well-Being would be selected by the State Board and have administrative responsibilities for a Division of Well-Being Services replacing the existing Department of Education and other state-level administrative offices.

Adjustments in postsecondary education responsibilities would follow, especially as demands for better trained, human-services professionals grew. Such persons would need to possess philosophical orientations for well-being and the commensurate knowledge, understanding, and skills essential to effective practice. Another recommendation was local control of reconstituted local governments. Seven-member local governing boards or commissions were suggested. The scope of their stewardship would be far-reaching, requiring thorough orientation and preparation for these public officials. The chief executive officers of well-being districts would need qualifications similar to those developed for the State Chancellor of Well-Being. Since education is likely to be the most prominent, enduring contributor to well-being, local administrators would need to be well-rounded in education but not limited to traditional conceptions of this field. They would need to be able to see the big picture and understand how to integrate a broad range of human services that contribute to individual and collective well-being of persons of all ages.

Authorization for Reconstituting

Proposals for change in Kentucky and Tennessee were generated out of local conditions absent enabling legislation to support such initiatives. For this to occur in other states, legislative provisions will be needed to stimulate the consideration of similar changes. The mission, philosophy, broad goals, and features of governance and management might best be worked out through local constitutional conventions convened specifically for reconstituting purposes. Through enabling legislation, state legislatures would authorize such local constitutional conventions. Again note the emphasis on local constitutional conventions, not state constitutional conventions. Thinking must be concentrated on local vision and responsibility and not be allowed to escape or drift toward state and federal levels, as so often happens when local citizens find it difficult to face choice and accountability.

Enabling legislation would provide a framework within which local assemblies could carry out their reconstituting plan. Guidelines would spell out how the reconstituting process would occur; for example, designating responsibility for initiating and carrying out a plan for widespread citizen participation and for establishing a timeline. Initially, some geographical parameters would have to be determined. Perhaps existing counties would be best. A recent legislative proposal in Minnesota, if passed, would consolidate more than 80 counties into 10 for efficiency purposes. Although this Minnesota proposal was not designed to reconstitute local government for purposes of well-being and education, it is entirely feasible that should county consolidation take place, reconstituting might well go forward within each of the 10 newly consolidated counties.

Tension Between Infrastructures

Local resources, augmented by state and federal dollars, are needed to sustain and refine the physical and social infrastructures. Needs are severe and, as noted earlier, becoming more so. Many communities are experiencing decay of both types. Streets, sidewalks, bridges, water systems, sewers, court houses, city halls, parks, beaches, school buildings, commuter railways are poorly maintained or wearing out. Streets of large cities (New York, London, Dallas, Cairo, Amsterdam, Newark, Cleveland) are dirty, with trash piled everywhere. Pot holes abound. Trash and garbage disposal, including hazardous wastes, seem to overwhelm local governments in many places.

Communities are battered simultaneously with deterioration and erosion of the human-services infrastructure. People are increasingly unhappy with schools, job training, provisions for physical and mental health, shelters for the homeless, halfway houses, foster care, adult day care, police protection, criminal justice, domestic relations, and custody provisions. Deinstitutionalization of mental patients has produced new problems. So has chemical abuse. Noise abuse, the undisciplined use of ghetto blasters and auto sound systems, has led to a spate of noise ordinances.

Both the physical and social infrastructures of communities are important. Cities, counties, towns, townships, villages, port authorities, planning commissions, and special districts are responsible primarily for the physical infrastructure. School districts construct and maintain school buildings, also an essential component of the physical infrastructure. Accountability for the social infrastructure rests with school districts, library districts, parks and recreation districts, as well as cities, towns, townships, villages, and counties. Among and within these various jurisdictions, there is sustained, sometimes bitter, competition for public monies to support basic physical infrastructure needs and basic social infrastructure needs.

Currently, there is insufficient delineation of physical and social infrastructure accountability. Consequently, some enduring and emerging public problems go unattended because of fuzzy designations of jurisdictional responsibility. Many deinstitutionalized mental health patients, for example, roam the streets; they are essentially unemployable, have been abandoned by their families, and in many instances are homeless. If there is a public duty, with what government agencies does it rest? Obviously, infrastructure tensions will flare up early in any reconstituting initiative. Turf questions will surface. It will be difficult to keep a focus on the larger civic issues that reconstituting is intended to address.

Six Premises to Guide the Reconstituting Process

In the enabling legislation for reconstituting governance structures, it may be helpful to include some premises on which to base discussions and proposals for the reconstitution process. Six come to mind.[6]

1. A new governance jurisdiction must reflect in philosophy and structure a total commitment to well-being, both individual and collective. Its leaders must construct and be guided by a vision of community well-being grounded in a philosophy that supports the "general welfare" provisions of the U.S. Constitution, encompassing the values of individual self-sufficiency and mutual dependence.

2. A jurisdiction that is devoted to well-being must be locally controlled, much in the fashion that school districts are the province of local school boards. The problems of human beings are across the street, next door, and down the road. They cannot be addressed by a remote state or federal agency. This is not to dismiss a federal or state role in achieving well-being, but rather to recognize that those closest to human needs on a day-to-day basis are the ones best prepared to address such needs head-on.

3. Local control with respect to well-being can fix responsibility for monitoring such major threats as hazardous waste disposal and other environmental problems. Also, citizens have an outlet for their concerns at the local level rather than carrying their causes to remote state and federal agencies. The threats to well-being by haz-

ardous waste disposal sites, for example, are real and local. Such threats are not national, although they often receive national attention. Remedial actions must happen there, on site, and must be in the hands of local officials at the place where lives are in jeopardy.

4. Creating new governance jurisdictions does not mean establishing a "welfare state" designed to solve problems that people have, but rather to provide an enabling capacity, leading to self-sufficiency and civic responsibility.

5. Education is now, and likely will continue to be, the central institution for achieving well-being. Thus it may become the organizing center around which other institutions contributing to well-being will gather. That being the case, learning must be lifelong and compulsory. Data-gathering for each individual should begin at birth, or even soon after conception, and continue throughout the life span. Edward Zigler of Yale University contends now that every pregnant female should register the unborn child at the local public school. In the future, following reconstitution, this registration might occur at an office of a new jurisdiction. The purpose of such registration would not be to increase public-sector regulation over private lives. Rather, Zigler's notion is based on the belief that child-service providers need a much more comprehensive view about the cognitive, physical, and psychological development of all children if effective prevention and early intervention services are to be provided.

6. New concepts of support must be developed to break away from traditional patterns of finance, many of which are inequitable and produce unintended negative consequences. A fresh concept of entitlement may be in order, one that would be lifelong and available to every citizen. It might include support for lifelong continuing education encompassing career re-training and help with adaptation to technological change. It might include support for physical and mental health needs, rehabilitation, employment counseling, social capital formation in Coleman's terms, information accessing and utilization, a range of diagnostic services, and even personal financial planning.

Collaboration as a Stop-Gap Measure

In the late 1980s and early 1990s, considerable interest in interprofessional and interagency cooperation and collaboration appeared. Ohio State University developed successful programs of interprofessional education and practice involving eight professions. The Institute for Educational Leadership stimulated the creation of the Education and Human Services Consortium, which in turn produced

133

in early 1991 a comprehensive and widely disseminated report on interagency partnership and other collaborative arrangements across the country.[7] And in February of 1991 the National School Boards Association sponsored a conference to promote collaboration among school boards, superintendents, mayors, township trustees, and city council members to address the needs of children and youth.

As important as these efforts are, they fall short of addressing the inadequacies of existing local governance structures. The imperfections in individual governance entities remain. Well-meaning persons paper and paste over such limitations and continue to enter into collaborative agreements with lofty mission and goal statements about serving the needs of people, when, in reality, they are little more than exercises in institutionalized delusions.

Closing Thoughts

Michael Kirst has expressed a proper skepticism about symbolic reorganization schemes, such as a creating a state department of children's services or creating a state code of children's law.[8] I join him in his skepticism. However, reconstituting, as I envision it, is far from symbolic. It calls for widespread citizen involvement, much in the town meeting spirit and tradition.

John Dewey believed that within American society there was an essential civic need for improving the methods and conditions of debate, discussion, and persuasion related to public problems.[9] He also observed that we should never consider existing structures to be fixed. He was, in fact, skeptical of our unwillingness to challenge the sanctity of the forms of government consecrated by the Founding Fathers. Unwillingness to challenge such traditions, in Dewey's view, was a severe stumbling block in the way of orderly and directed change, even an invitation to revolt and revolution.

Harold D. Lasswell supported Dewey and went further, designing mechanisms to expedite public learning that incorporated technologies (mechanical and human) as the means for achieving public awareness and ultimately public-sector problem solving. Lasswell described what he called "social planetaria," which were to be permanent facilities for community problem solving, constructed and maintained with public funds and administered in the public interest much as public libraries and museums are.[10] Planetaria were to be public utilities essential to achieving well-being in a society that was becoming increasingly complex and where citizens were becoming disenchanted with purely political solutions to public problems.

Planetaria were intended to expedite public understanding of complicated questions through the use of computer information accessing and processing, which would lead to superior solutions to the problems that individuals and institutions face.

Since Dewey and Lasswell are gone, it falls to others to examine their ideas afresh and build from them. Though neither proposed reconstituting local government as an objective, their thinking was not alien to this need. If they were with us today, I feel confident they would more than likely lend their keen intelligence to the effort.

Footnotes

1. Chester E. Finn Jr., *Ten Tentative Truths* (Minneapolis, Minn.: Center of the American Experiment, 1990), p. 9.

2. James S. Coleman, "Families and Schools," *Educational Researcher* 16 (August-September 1987): 32-38.

3. Ibid., p. 32.

4. Ibid., p. 38.

5. Luvern L. Cunningham and Lila N. Carol, *Preliminary Models of Governance* (Alexandria, Ohio: Leadership Development Associates, 1989), pp. 9-10.

6. "Reconstituting Local Government for Well-Being and Education," in *Educational Leadership and Changing Contexts of Families, Communities and Schools*, vol. 2, edited by Brad Mitchell and Luvern L. Cunningham (Chicago: National Society for the Study of Education, University of Chicago Press, 1990), Chapter VII.

7. Atelia J. Melavitle and Martin J. Blank, *What It Takes: Structuring Interagency Partnerships to Connect Children and Families with Comprehensive Services* (Washington, D.C: Institute for Educational Leadership, 1991).

8. Michael W. Kirst and Milbrey McLaughlin, "Rethinking Policies for Children: Implications for Educational Administration," in *Educational Leadership and Changing Contexts of Families, Communities and Schools*, edited by Brad Mitchell and Luvern L. Cunningham (Chicago: National Society for the Study of Education, University of Chicago Press, 1990), p. 84.

9. John Dewey, *The Public and Its Problems* (Denver: Alan Swallow, 1927), p. 34.

10. Harold D. Lasswell, "Sharing the Experience of Permanent Reconstruction: A Policy Science Approach," in *Essays on Modernization of Underdeveloped Societies*, edited by A.R. Desai (New York: Humanities Press, 1972), pp. 536-46; and Harold D. Lasswell, "Studying the Future: The Idea of a Social Planetarium," unpublished manuscript (1976).

My Educational Passions

BY ELLIOT W. EISNER

The invitation to reflect on educational matters without constraint, save space, is a rare and daunting opportunity. It is rare because most editors impose focus. It is daunting because the lack of constraint provides what can seem like an insurmountable task: How does one choose? What does one say when asked to say something — anything — one would like to say about education, a field and a form of practice that I love. After a while the insurmountable was surmounted. The focus became clear. I chose to write about ideas I love. I chose to write about my educational passions.

The centerpiece of my work in education has been and is the arts. I was trained as a painter when I was young and, even more, used the arts to secure the deepest satisfactions in my life in school. The arts were where I succeeded in school. They provided for me a special sort of haven, an important source of nourishment.

The experience that I secured in the arts is not afforded to most students in school. Although recognized as one of the primary repositories of "culture," the arts are marginalized in American schools. Why are they marginal? What do they have to offer? How can the arts be used to think about, study, and improve educational practice? Just what do the arts have to do with the development of mind; and what, pray tell, do they help us understand? My educational passions are directly related to the questions I have just raised. These questions provide the foci for my reflections.

One of the key functions of schooling is to induct the young into the legacies that culture has provided and to develop their ability to

---

Elliot W. Eisner is Professor of Education and Art at Stanford University.

think. Unlike dogs, chimps, and even dolphins, human beings build a cultural network of ideas, tools, and images that influence not only their own lives, but the lives of their children. Ideas developed in Greece more than two thousand years ago are a part of our philosophical resources today. The theories developed by Newton in the seventeenth century, by Pasteur in the nineteenth century, and by Einstein in the twentieth century have influenced and continue to influence the way in which we understand our world. The works of Toynbee, Darwin, and Freud have given us portraits of human nature that help us organize our thoughts about the flow of history, the evolution of man, and the motives beneath human action. They help us understand what we might not.

These ideas, imbedded as they often are in theories of nature, human and otherwise, are the intellectual plums on which all of us feed. But they are not the only plums. The images created by Giotto on the walls of the cathedral at Assisi, the sculpture of Donatello three centuries later, the music of Mozart, Stravinsky, and Elgar also are a part of our cultural legacy. Furthermore, this legacy is not limited to the Western world. The bronze pottery of the Han Dynasty, or the clay masks of the Ife in fourteenth century Nigeria, or the ceramic figures of the Zapotecs in seventeenth century middle-America are also potentially powerful resources for insight and pleasure.

Yet these resources to which our children have an entitlement most likely will be for them someone else's pleasure. Most adults in America have never heard of Giotto, have never seen a sculpture by Donatello, do not listen to Mozart, have never encountered the music of Stravinsky, and do not know that the music that stirs them when they see their children march down the aisle to receive their diploma was composed by an Englishman by the name of Elgar (who, incidentally, wrote other stirring music as well). As far as the Han Dynasty is concerned, the art of the Ife, or the sculpture of the Zapotecs, well, that is simply another world.

In a culture in which more people watch "Family Feud" in one night than attend concerts of classical music all year, the marginal place of the arts is understandable. Yet, one hopes that educators would do better. Can those of us who work in education provide the intellectual leadership to give our children a chance to know and perhaps love what only a few know and love? One of my passions is trying to make that happen. We have a long road yet to travel before we rest.

My second passion deals with the business of legitimizing the use of artistic paradigms for thinking about teaching, preparing teachers, and studying teaching. Even more broadly, I aspire to legitimize the use of artistic methods for the study and improvement of schooling.

American educational practice has been regarded as a form of applied social science (Broudy 1976), a type of rule-governed behavior (Rosenshine 1976), a species of worker-processed raw material that turns out educational products designed to meet consumer specifications (Callahan 1962). None of these notions, with the implicit values and conceptions of human nature they harbor, are or can be adequate for understanding and improving so highly nuanced an enterprise as teaching. Children are not raw materials and teachers are not processors. The practice of teaching is not a form of applied social science and it is not something that can be managed by appealing to algorithms, formulae, or rules. Life in classrooms is far too dynamic and emergent to fit such an unrealistically orderly model of teaching.

All of the foregoing models have been predicated on the belief that efficiency in schools could be increased if practice can be harnessed to them. Some rules, in the form of prescriptive generalizations, were to come from the social sciences, others from a factory model of worker productivity: follow these seven steps, state your objectives at the outset in behaviorable and measurable terms, don't call upon a student until you first raise a question. These efforts to align educational practice to the security of rules is understandable; dependency upon judgment can be unsettling. Yet, the best of teachers are not driven by rules but by their sensitivity to context, by understanding their students, by knowing when an instructional situation requires subtle forms of pedagogical adjustment on their part. These teachers know what counts and they know what to neglect. They know what to emphasize and what to underplay. Indeed, the forms that excellent teaching take are numerous; they bear individual signatures. At its best, teaching is an art; and the arts that keep teachers in the classroom are similar to the arts that keep painters working in their studios. It is the application of such arts that are among the deepest forms of satisfaction.

We are finally seeing artistic paradigms being exploited as a way of thinking about, studying, and improving teaching. It is reflected in the work of Donald Schoen (1983), Louis Rubin (1985), George Willis and William Schubert (1991), and Madeline Grumet (1988). It has long permeated Maxine Greene's (1978) views on education, and it appears in William Pinar's (1988) efforts to bring a phenomenological perspective to education. We are making headway.

The emergence of the artistic paradigm reflects a growing recognition of its relevance for the study of teaching and schooling. It also reflects the growing recognition that many of the assumptions and models that have been used in the past are a bit too tidy to adequately address and improve educational practice. The aspiration, once held, to get teaching "down to a science" is giving way to a more complex and richer picture of teaching. We are on the threshold of accepting a wider and less formulaic conception of what teachers do, or what they ought to do. Increasingly we are recognizing that the best of them are engaged in an artistic activity and that the criteria employed in appraising artistic work have relevance for assessing a teacher's "performance." The emergence of the artistic paradigm represents the opening of a new conversation concerning the nature of educational inquiry. To my mind, it represents a kind of watershed in the history of American educational research.

My third passion is related to the second. It has to do with the relationship of the arts to human cognition and to the ways in which we come to understand and convey to others what we have experienced. There has been, and in some circles there still is, a view of cognition that regards thinking as a form of sub-vocalization, a kind of inner speech dependent upon language. Language, in turn, is regarded as a fundamental means for the exercise of intelligence: if to think is to use language, then surely language must be the primary ingredient of intelligent action. Pushing things even further, since language is the primary means through which intelligence is expressed, logic becomes the primary criterion for its regulation and, by implication, a necessary means for the exercise of intellectual activity. To be smart, in this view, is to be smart in language.

The reduction of intelligence and human reason to linguistically mediated thought and action diminishes our understanding and appreciation of the breath of human cognition. The mediation of image and the creation of forms that do not depend upon language falls by the wayside.

Clearly, the ways in which humans perceive, imagine, and represent their experiences are wider than words. As cognitive pluralists (Goodman 1978; Cassirer 1961) have long argued, human reason exceeds the limits of language; and as Polanyi (1967) reminds us, "We know more than we can tell." Indeed, in Jacob Bronowski's words, there is nothing in the head that was not first in the hand; the sensibilities, he implies, are the first avenues to consciousness.

By breaking the monopoly that language has had on our conception of cognition, we widen the arena for children with aptitudes in other areas to find a place in our educational sun. The artistically gifted, the athletically able, the mechanically competent, the socially skilled, also have an opportunity to be recognized. They too display forms of thinking and modes of intelligence that are socially important. The high road traverses much more than what the verbal and mathematical sections on the SAT measure.

Related to the expanded conception of cognition is a wider, more generous view of knowledge. In the standard view, knowledge is regarded as warranted true belief. To have warrant, one must frame a claim — a proposition — that can, in principle, be verified or, if not verified, at least not refuted. The standard model of knowledge is a scientific one. Such a conception of knowledge leads to the view that it is science alone that defines the parameters of human understanding. And it is language that defines the parameters of cognition. This view dismisses the variety of other ways in which the world is known.

These other ways include the works of the poet, the novelist, the painter, the actor, and the teacher as among those who create forms that help us grasp the way the world is or imagine how it might become. Badly taught, the sciences tend to present a packaged conception of truth, housed in textbooks and imparted to the young, measured by tests, and necessary to possess in order to move through the educational system. Such teaching treats knowledge as, at the most generous level, "temporarily fixed." Rather than acknowledging the multiplicity of ways in which we come to know, a scientifically grounded hegemony occurs, and a measured one at that. The task I see before us is to create schools that make it possible to honor forms of knowing that cannot be measured, or at times even articulated. As E.E. Cummings (1938) put it:

> While you and I have lips and voices which
> are for kissing and to sing with
> who cares if some one-eyed son of a bitch
> invents an instrument to measure Spring with?

Yes, Horatio, there is more in heaven and earth than is dreamt of in our philosophy.

Another of my educational passions is to create schools that are not hell-bent on getting all students to run a race toward the same goals with the garlands going to the swiftest. Speed is an overestimated virtue: the things we like to do the swiftest are typically the things we don't like to do. Nor is it a particular virtue to regard the "production" of students who have the same skills and forms of knowledge as our main achievement. While there are some common skills, themes, and bodies of knowledge that ought to be a part of the students' educational legacy, the cultivation of those special aptitudes that define us as unique and special people is, I think, more important. Can we create schools that value productive idiosyncrasy and that offer students opportunities to "follow their bliss," as Joseph Campbell would say?

Much of what we teach in our schools dampens idiosyncrasy. So much of it is highly rule-governed. The students' task is to learn the rules, to get them right. School learning becomes a matter of taking in the conventions of the culture and knowing when to employ them. This, of course, is a part of the task of any school; but it is a tactical, not a strategic aim. It is what students do with the cultural conventions they learn that matters. What should matter to us is how they make those conventions their own, how they give them their own personal signature. For this to occur schools ought to do at least two things. First, they should provide a school week that affords students time to work in depth in areas in which they have special interests. Schools can multi-age group students for such purposes. Students who are interested in biology or in music should be given opportunities to pursue these interests. Such a program constitutes what I call a *personally referenced curriculum*. It provides a complement to the *culturally referenced curriculum* that all children study.

What occurs in the curriculum in which students are engaged is of critical importance, and here I wish to emphasize a theme I will return to later. The arts provide a stunning example of a form of human activity that virtually requires students to draw upon their own personally imaginative resources. The arts provide the expressive side of human nature with opportunities to find its place in the world. They evoke the personal and give it a place of honor. At their best, other fields do this as well; the sciences, history, literature, and even mathematics (a subject that appears as rule-governed as one might imagine) can provide students with expressive options. The curricular task is for us to invent the kinds of activities and provide the kind of educational climate for such expressiveness to emerge. Put another way, one of my educational passions is to create schools in which students can know the subject matter in its deepest sense, know how to be creative with it.

The development of this kind of attitude toward the subject requires a transformation of our attitude toward students. Rather than seeing students as material that we (that is, teachers) do something to, we need to see students as people who do something to what they study. In other words, our view of the student shifts from a person to be processed, as one might process a raw material in a factory, to a view that sees the student as a kind of artist who works on a set of ideas or materials in order to make something for himself. Our task becomes something less directly instructional and more facilitative. We become less concerned with what Philip Jackson (1986) calls mimetic ends and more interested in transformative ones.

Tacit in all that I have been saying is an image of the virtues of the arts and the processes that lead to their creation. In a significant sense these processes can serve as aspects of educational practice that are worthy of emulation. What specifically might be emulated? What kinds of processes and outcomes do the arts yield and how might they infuse and invigorate what we teach?

The lessons to be learned from the arts are several. First, the arts teach us that there are a multiplicity of ways to solve a problem and a host of possible solutions. At a time when the appetite for standardized outcomes is so salient an aspect of our educational expectations for students, the realization that some educational virtues do not require converging on a single destination is particularly important. Virtually any subject in the curriculum can be designed to heighten the student's awareness of this way of thinking about problems; the pity is that so few do. The arts remind us that homogeneity of outcome is not necessarily the highest good. In fact, it can be cogently argued that the good school increases individual differences, it does not reduce them.

The importance of diversity in a population can be analogized to the importance of the instruments in an orchestra. With only violins, regardless of how broad their range, our musical experience would be impoverished. Each instrument, both individually and in concert with others, makes its distinctive contribution to the whole. Recognizing diversity and acknowledging the multiple ways to be and to act is a potential source of strength to our culture, as long as we provide for multiple perspectives and encourage students to use them.

The arts teach us that attention to nuance is important and pride in craft critical. Tolstoy once said that in art, "It is the wee bit that counts." Indeed it is. The difference between the merely well made and the truly excellent is in the wee bit. God, someone once said, resides in the details. The arts emphasize attention to detail, but not

142

detail detached from context. Always in artistic activity, whether as a creator of form or as a perceiver, perception of *configuration* is crucial; for it is in the oscillation between the part and the whole in which it participates that gives a work its aesthetic form. The lesson here is as important in working on a scientific report as in writing an essay. It is as significant in the design of a research study as in the creation of a collage. Neglect of the relationships that constitute a whole and inattention to nuance and detail is the surest way to court artistic disaster. Such inattention to form leads to the creation of essays that sound like square-wheeled carts moving along a yellow brick road.

The modes of perception that the arts teach are unlike our customary modes. Typically when we perceive the world we are pragmatic, that is, we treat the objects of our perception as instrumentalities; they are there to be used. In the arts, perception is more an act of consuming; we are there to take the work in, to experience its conformations, to relish its subtleties. In a world that is dominated by the pragmatic, the arts provide a needed relief. In a sense, they slow us down and ask us to have a look. No, even more, they ask us to see.

The arts also remind us that nothing replaces judgment. Precisely because in the arts, as in all practical affairs, there are no rules on which one can depend, judgment must be exercised. And because such judgment is always focused on unique configurations, there is always some degree of novelty in the task. Judgment in the arts, perhaps more than elsewhere, takes its cues not simply from how something looks or sounds, but how the look or sound of something makes you feel. The qualities that constitute art function in the service of feeling, thus the viewer or creator must tune into both form and feelings. Detachment, in this arena at least, leads to a loss of sight.

Because of the nature of artistic action, the results of one's activities cannot be wholly predicted. As a result, opportunities arise in the course of work that had not been nor could have been anticipated. The exploitation of these happy accidents is an important part of artistic thinking. "Art," wrote Aristotle, "loves chance. He who errs willingly is the artist." What attention to the potentialities of chance provides is new opportunities; it leads to flexibility in purpose, a willingness to shift gears, to take roads not yet traveled, and to entertain surprise. It helps students move away from a dependency on the formulaic aspects of work so that they can push the boundaries of their own thinking. In a word, the arts encourage intellectual risk-taking.

Intellectual risk-taking is a virtue that permeates all serious intellectual efforts. Flexibility is another. The arts emphasize both and to that extent can serve as a model for what genuine intellectual life is about.

Finally, if the arts celebrate anything, they celebrate sensibility and imagination. By sensibility I mean that sheer pleasure of experiencing the qualitative world. By imagination I mean the ability to take leave from the immediate and the immediately practical and to allow oneself to consider what might be. Without attention to sensibility, the world itself is dimly known. It is sensibility that makes the subtle vivid. It is sensibility that makes possible what we normally regard as perceptivity. Indeed, sensibility is the first road to consciousness, and its refinement is an important human achievement. We give little attention to the development of the sensibilities in school.

Imagination allows us to free ourselves from the press of the immediate, the practical, and the literal. It is through the imagination that the ability to read is made possible, and it is through the imagination that new possibilities emerge. The arts put a premium on both.

My educational passion is to make a genuine and significant place for such features of human capacity within our schools. We can design tasks and even programs that cultivate sensibility and stimulate imagination. To create the kind of world we need, surely we will need to have both.

These, then, are my educational passions. As I reflect on American education today, these passions provide direction and remind me about what really counts in schools. Perhaps one day we will create schools that provide the features that reflect the passions I have described. We shall see.

References

Broudy, H. "In Search for a Science of Education." *Phi Delta Kappan* 58 (September 1976): 104-11.

Callahan, R. *Education and the Cult of Efficiency*. Chicago: University of Chicago Press, 1962.

Cassirer, E. *The Philosophy of Symbolic Forms*. Translated by R. Manheim. 3 vols. New Haven, Conn.: Yale University Press, 1961/64.

Cummings, E.E. *Collected Poems*. New York: Harcourt, Brace, and Co., 1938.

Goodman, N. *Ways of Worldmaking*. Indianapolis: Hackett, 1978.

Greene, M. *Landscapes of Learning*. New York: Teachers College Press, 1978.

Grumet, M. *Bitter Milk*. Amherst: University of Massachusetts Press, 1988.

Jackson, P. *The Practice of Teaching*. New York: Holt, Rhinehart and Winston, 1986.

Pinar, W. *Contemporary Curriculum Discourse*. Scottsdale, Ariz.: Gorsuch Scavisbrick, 1988.

Polanyi, M. *The Tacit Dimension*. London: Routledge and Kegan Paul, 1967.

Rosenshine, B. "Classroom Instruction." In *The Psychology of Teaching Methods: Seventy-Fifth Yearbook of the National Society for the Study of Education*, edited by N.L. Gage. Chicago: University of Chicago Press, 1976, pp. 335-71.

Rubin, L. *Artistry in Teaching*. New York: Random House, 1985.

Schoen, D. *The Reflective Practitioner: How Professionals Think in Action*. New York: Basic Books, 1983.

Willis, G., and Schubert, W. *Reflections from the Heart of Educational Inquiry: Understanding Curriculum and Teaching Through the Arts*. New York: SUNY Press, 1991.

What It Took Me 10 Years to Learn About Retirement

BY STANLEY ELAM

Like marriage, retirement is one of those landmark events in one's life that nowadays call for a camcorder where once a Brownie would do. At my own retirement party on December 17, 1979, someone snapped a dozen color photos showing me puffy and gray but obviously pleased. It was my last day as editor of the *Phi Delta Kappan* after nearly 25 years on the job. I was burned out.

The next day I started for Green Valley, Arizona, pulling a U-Haul behind the white Zephyr. I sang along with the country western stars through Illinois, Missouri, Oklahoma, Texas, and New Mexico. I felt great. After four days on the road, I arrived in Green Valley, where Elizabeth, my wife of 53 years, was already living in the townhouse we had bought the previous August. I bragged that it had taken me less than 10 minutes to adjust to retirement.

The boast was almost true. Successful retirement requires homework, and we thought we had done ours. But we made some mistakes. The rest of this little memoir will include some things I have learned about retirement since 1979, both from my own experience and from quizzing people I came to know while editing the *Kappan*.

Preparations for my own retirement began in earnest in 1977 when, because of declining health, Elizabeth resigned her job as director of the Indiana University Education Materials Center. Inflation was already firing up to its double-digit peak of the period, so we wondered how to ensure a measure of financial security on the fixed income we assumed we would have as retirees.

Stanley Elam was Director of Phi Delta Publications and Editor of the Phi Delta Kappan *from 1956 until 1980. Currently he is a Contributing Editor to the* Phi Delta Kappan *and Coordinator of the PDK/Gallup Poll of the Public's Attitudes Toward the Public Schools.*

One step I undertook was to put the maximum allowable contribution into my TIAA-CREF retirement account. Participants may choose what portion of their retirement contribution goes to CREF and what portion to TIAA. The latter guarantees a minimum yield, but CREF yields depend entirely on stock market trends. Being cautious in financial matters, I chose to allocate only 25% of my retirement contributions to CREF. This proved to be a mistake. Since I retired, CREF income has risen by 251% while inflation over the same period totaled only 61%. Despite the mistake, my TIAA-CREF income has, overall, risen by 84%. Even my income from the Illinois Teachers' Retirement System and the Illinois Universities Retirement System has grown faster than the Consumer Price Index, and Social Security income has kept pace. So much for the myth of fixed income for retirees. But who can say whether the trend my wife and I now enjoy will continue? I can only say that we have been lucky so far.

Retirement planning is only as good as one's self-assessment — and spouse-assessment. Early on I asked myself, am I one of those people whose identity and self-esteem are largely determined by what they do for a living? Would the end of my life's work mean a loss of identity and sense of purpose? I didn't think so. I had several other interests I was eager to indulge. For example, I had always been something of a frustrated jock, too busy to pursue my interest in sports through most of my working life. So I was a willing victim of the standard come-on of geriatric ghetto promoters: a snowy-haired golfer with tight stomach muscles is pictured against matching snow-capped mountains. The Green Valley brochure also featured bowling, tennis, billiards, swimming, shuffleboard — whatever the ancient athlete can handle. As for Elizabeth, her dream of paradise was enough leisure time to lie quietly, listen to good music, play Scrabble, and read, read, read. You can do these things anywhere.

But I recognized that this self-indulgence was not enough. I also understood that a workaholic — and against all my youthful inclinations I had become one — has trouble going cold turkey. That was half my motive for bombarding boss Lowell Rose with a series of retirement job proposals during my last year at Phi Delta Kappa. He agreed with each one and soon began asking, with his usual high good humor, "When will I get the next five-year plan?" In the end I undertook a number of writing and editing chores for PDK, amounting altogether to a quarter-time assignment. This treatment for my disease, renewed annually in diminishing doses, has allowed me the luxury of continuing the kind of work I like best without the burdensome routine and relentless deadlines of magazine production.

During our two years in Green Valley I completed *Cream of the KAPPAN*, a collection of memorable pieces published in the journal during my tenure; a subject-author index for 10 volumes of the *Kappan*; a bit of investigative journalism of the kind I had always advocated; and continued coordination of the annual Gallup-PDK polls of public attitudes toward education. I even did some writing, speaking, and consulting outside of PDK. But with each passing year my ambitions faded, until now I am satisfied to do the poll and write this piece on retirement. The workaholic has recovered.

The other half of my motivation for continuing to work part-time was financial. The extra income would allow me to make investments to cushion the blows of ill health, which continues to afflict Elizabeth, and to buy that new high-resolution TV without guilt; the rainy days, I hope, are cared for.

It took Elizabeth and me nearly two years to realize that a retirement community was not our Shangri-la. We had chosen southern Arizona — Green Valley is 25 miles south of Tucson — partly because her doctor had recommended "a moderate, dry climate" to soothe Elizabeth's chronic bronchitis. We soon discovered, however, that her basic problem was lupus, not bronchitis; and Arizona's bright sunshine is anathema to lupus sufferers. Other factors too tedious to detail here contributed to our change of heart. We sold our townhouse one Sunday in January 1982; I bought a condo back in Bloomington the next Sunday; and we moved in April. We have since learned that one authority, at least, ranks Bloomington among the top 10 retirement cities in the U.S. Ironic? You bet.

In preparing to write this essay, I solicited reflections on retirement from 25 friends and acquaintances, mostly educators I came to know while editing the *Kappan*. One respondent, Egon Guba, who retired from his professorship at Indiana University in May 1989, wrote, "I'm surprised that you allowed yourself to be inveigled into another writing assignment. I suppose that having realized how much work it was going to be, you decided to take the easy way out and rope in a bunch of your friends to help. Well, OK."

You guessed it, Egon. This could become a small cottage industry. But as a labor-saving device my plan backfired. Here I am with an embarrassment of riches, repeatedly sifting through 25 often lengthy responses in search of common threads, and not finding many. I can identify them in four short paragraphs.

1. Educators who have been leaders in their fields do not, to paraphrase Dylan Thomas, go gently into that good night of old age. They tend to remain active, usually in the areas where they made their best professional mark. Most of my respondents are writers. Would they agree with Soyatoslav Fyodorov, the world-famed surgeon who said, "I can tell you that [writers] lose their capacity to think originally after the age of 45"? Perhaps. But they know, too, that there is a difference between originality and wisdom. Wisdom can come with age and experience. That was the insight George Reavis was pursuing when he started the Phi Delta Kappa Educational Foundation. His fondest dream was that the Foundation would make the wisdom of aging educators available to the profession.

2. Asked what they like most about retirement, nearly all of these educators alluded in some way to the freedom it provides: freedom to pursue one's major interests, to develop hobbies long neglected, to travel, to visit with friends and family, to sleep late, to attend a movie matinee in mid-week, to let one's beard grow, to throw away all one's neckties (except perhaps a conservative one for the funerals of friends and self).

3. Asked about worries and problems, several respondents mentioned declining health and physical energy, fear of monetary inflation, and insufficient savings to handle the cost of catastrophic illness. Egon said the IRS "scares the hell out of me."

4. And quite a number of my respondents said, "Don't retire!" I will allow these eccentrics to speak for themselves.

What follows is culled from 13 of the 25 responses to my retirement questionnaire. I apologize to the 12 people whose good comments I cannot include here because space doesn't permit it. (Yes, one's judgment can be clouded by age.)

In about every way Bessie Gabbard is the first lady of Phi Delta Kappa. She was the first woman to be initiated into the fraternity after the 1973 constitutional change that permitted the admission of women. She now chairs the Board of Governors of the fraternity's Educational Foundation. Her interest in and contributions to Phi Delta Kappa's summer institute program are so great that the series is named in her honor.

At the time of her retirement in June 1965 , Bessie was supervisor of primary grades in the Cincinnati, Ohio, school system and was teaching at the University of Cincinnati. For 10 years before retirement she had her own radio program on Cincinnati Station WLW, where she was known as "the Story Lady." She also produced TV programs for the Cincinnati schools on Station WCET.

When she left the Cincinnati schools, Bessie became an assistant to George Reavis, who had retired many years before from the same school system after a varied and distinguished career in education. She accompanied Reavis on his trip to PDK Headquarters in the fall of 1965, when he proposed the PDK Foundation to Maynard Bemis, then executive secretary of Phi Delta Kappa, and me. Before Reavis died in 1970 at age 87, he gave Bessie a life trust in two Ohio dairy farms. She has since bought another.

Today Bessie says, "Retirement is GREAT! But there are never enough hours in the day for all the things I like to do." She suggests taking early retirement, if you can, so that you can make the most of the years ahead. "Try something different, perhaps a second career. Plan for a diversity of interests and hobbies. In my case," she says, "I have ownership in three dairy farms. I do all the IRS forms without an accountant's help." Besides her PDK Foundation work, Bessie remains active in the National League of American Pen Women, serves as an American mother to foreign students, teaches Bible study groups, travels, plays the organ, reads, explores art, and participates in a number of organizations too long to list here. (It exhausts me just to read about them.)

Bessie concluded her response with an anecdote: "My Ohio funeral director calls me when I am in Florida [where she owns a condominium on the ocean in Fort Lauderdale]. Do you suppose he is trying to hasten my demise? He invites me to come and have tea with his family when I return to Ohio in the summer. He says he has never had a client like me. What does he mean?"

I would guess he means, Bessie, that you are a Renaissance woman, and perhaps that your good health comes from good works. Long may it last.

Let's look next at two educators who have done the kind of work in retirement that George Reavis hoped the PDK Foundation would encourage. Now in their eighties, both have recently written books on how to improve the schools.

First, Bob Gilchrist. I first met Bob when he was superintendent of schools in University City, Missouri, and gave a talk at the 1959 PDK Biennial Council on promising practices in education, which I published in two *Kappan* articles the following year. In the speech he advocated such things as ungraded elementary schools, an idea that had its heyday in America a decade or so later — and is now ready for recycling.

Bob retired gradually. At 64 he left school administration and began teaching educational leadership at the U.S. International University in San Diego, where he worked for 10 years. The job then tapered to teaching half-time for two quarters a year.

He writes, "I was advised when I finally retired, 'Do only things you like to do.' It took me four years to discover that I wanted to do something in schools. For three years, then, I coordinated a program in which senior citizens were recruited to help public school teachers. The half-time I spent doing this was most satisfying and led me into a project which has kept me as busy as I want to be for the last five years."

That project was a book. It began soon after Bob visited three schools recognized by the U.S. Department of Education as outstanding: an elementary school, a middle school, and a high school. In a leisurely manner, Bob observed their activities, taped interviews, attended meetings, visited classes, made copious notes. It took him two years to write up what he found out. He discovered that it was necessary to revisit the schools. He wrote dozens of letters and spent hours on the phone. Then he worked with two editors on the manuscript and began contacting publishers.

Finally his five years of work paid off. Today Bob is reveling in the success of *Effective Schools: Three Case Histories of Excellence*, published by the National Educational Service of Bloomington, Indiana. It has already sold 6,000 copies — unusual for a book in education — and is in a second printing. Bob Gilchrist would be my candidate for the George Reavis Retiree of the Year award, if there were one.

I first published a Burton Gorman manuscript in the May 1958 *Kappan*. A couple of years before Admiral Hyman Rickover began telling us how poorly U.S. schools compared with those of Switzerland, Burton asked, "How Can We Learn from the Swiss Schools?" At the time he was head of the Department of Secondary Education at Kent State University. His vita already included classroom teaching, a county superintendency, two principalships and a city superintendency, and various visiting professorships. Burton retired from Kent State in 1972, but retirement was only partial. He was a professor of education for four more years, two at George Peabody and two at Stetson University, where he developed the second year of graduate study for administrators.

Burton's most recent work, *Successful Schooling for Everybody*, a book on which he has worked for more than a dozen years, with some help from William H. Johnson, was accepted for publication by the National Educational Service in 1990. Ralph Tyler has written a foreword.

Burton's advice to educators contemplating retirement: "Continue your interest in human development and educational theory and be useful on a part-time basis wherever you can. If you ever had real intellectual interest in education, keep it alive!"

Gilchrist and Gorman wrote for publication throughout their careers. But they were not in William Van Til's league as writers. Bill wrote hundreds of articles, books, columns, critiques, and the like over a long career. Since retirement in 1977 as Coffman Distinguished Professor of Education at Indiana State University, Bill continues to write. In his advice to those who expect to retire in the next few years, he says: "As retirement age approaches, decide whether you want to end your relationship with education or to continue with some aspect of your former work. The majority choose the first of these alternatives; I chose the second. . . . I have long described myself as both an educator and a writer. Since my retirement, mandated by university policy, my published books have included a textbook, *Secondary Education: School and Community*; two editions of *Writing for Professional Publication*; an anthology, *Van Til on Education*; and my autobiography, *My Way of Looking at It*. Shorter publications include a contribution to history, *ASCD in Retrospect*; literary essays titled *Sketches*; an essay in a Kappa Delta Pi anthology, *Honor in Teaching: Reflections*; plus retrospective articles and interviews. No one can retire me from writing except myself.

"I am glad I took the road less traveled. I write as I please and when I please and on what I please. I live in both Indiana and Puerto Rico, participate in conferences, and travel whenever I wish."

Two of my respondents say, in effect, "Don't retire; retread." Both have been enormously successful in careers they took up at the age when many of their colleagues were looking forward to rest and recreation.

The first of these is Emery Stoops, at 88 the oldest living past president of Phi Delta Kappa. He presided in the mid-Fifties when Phi Delta Kappa built its new Headquarters in Bloomington, Indiana, and went international with the installation of a Canadian chapter at the University of Toronto.

I'll let Emery tell the story, because he tells it well.

"Don't retire. With your wealth of training and experience, the world — your world — needs you. Emptiness leads to decay. Be successful in your second career and the bluebird of happiness will come and rest upon your shoulder. . . .

"Opportunities will open when you are available. Some will come by chance and others by careful planning, whether in volunteerism or in a paid second career. On a personal note, mine came by chance. While I was in my preretirement years at the University of Southern California [where Emery was for many years a professor of educational administration and supervision], a wealthy retired builder consulted with me about a book manuscript he had written. He wanted it edited for publication and already had two bids, of $3,000 and $4,500. I offered my services without cost, and his book was published. Mr. Gregory was elated!

"A year later, Gregory and his nephew invited me to serve on the board and help organize the San Fernando Life Insurance Company. I later became its interim president, before the company was merged and sold.

"This insurance experience opened my second career: searching for the best annuities for educators. I got my licenses, worked hard, and for a year was number one in annuity sales for one of the largest companies in the world, Aetna. In this second career, I have made more than 500 acquaintances and friends, and in 20 years have made four times as much money as I made in 38 years in education.

"I said the world needs you after age 65. Did it need what I have done? Well, by my best calculation my clients and their families will receive about $335,000,000 because I helped them secure annuities and investment-type life insurance. My role for them has been not that of a high-pressure salesman but, as with my students, that of a counselor. I help in estate planning and in establishing financial security.

"Aetna far exceeds school districts and universities in rewards for superior performance. I have received four rewards each year, some of the greatest being trips for my wife, Joyce, and me to Bermuda, Acapulco, Sun Valley, Las Vegas, Kuaui, London, and many more."

Emery Stoops' approach to life shines through his response to the question, Why didn't you go to Sun City (the generic term) for retirement? "Neighbors who are inactive, complaining, depressed, waiting to die depress me. I thrive on activity and success."

Also advocating a second career at retirement age is Thorwald (Tory) Esbensen of Edina, Minnesota. Author of three books and numerous articles for professional journals (including the *Kappan*), Tory has taught at all grade levels, kindergarten through graduate school. He has been an elementary principal, a secondary school coordinator, an assistant superintendent, a superintendent, a university professor, and a college dean of instruction. In 1980 *Executive Educator* magazine named him one of the top 100 school executives in North America.

But in 1979, at age 55, Esbensen left school administration and was "magically reincarnated" – his phrase – as owner of MicroEd, described as a pioneer publisher of educational software and a company that takes pride in new ways of doing things. For example, soon after it was formed the company began work in the field of interactive video disks. Tory was a member of Minnesota's statewide task force charged with looking into the instructional implications of interactive video disks.

Between January and July of 1984, Tory authorized MicroEd to make software donations totaling more than one million dollars, to be used by school systems interested in establishing free lending libraries of microcomputers for families. *Closing the Gap*, a national publication dedicated to exploring the uses of microcomputers by handicapped persons, devoted a long editorial to Tory's mission and said he was setting a standard for the software industry to follow.

The October 1986 issue of *Amazing Computing* featured Tory and his educational software for the new Commodore AMIGA. The magazine said, "Here is one man making a difference . . . the realism and impact of Esbensen's educational programs have to be seen to be believed."

Another satisfying role for Tory Esbensen is that of cheerleader for his wife, Barbara, who is a successful children's book author. Her sixth book was published last spring; her fifth won the Minnesota State Book Award for Children's Literature. She is under contract for four more books by such publishers as Harper & Row and Little, Brown. At age 64 she gives talks on how to be a late bloomer. (The Esbensens had their sixth child when Barbara was 46.)

Tory's letter ends with this comment: "These are exciting years in which to live. At age 66, I look forward to seeing what I might be able to contribute during the next 30."

One of Phi Delta Kappa's most gifted and urbane past presidents is Gordon Swanson, who at age 69 continues his professorship at the University of Minnesota and also serves as associate director of the National Center for Research in Vocational Education at the University of California, Berkeley. A citizen of the world, Gordon has been a consultant to the World Bank, the Ford Foundation, the OECD, and the USOE Bureau of Research. Following his work as program officer for UNESCO's Department of Education in Paris, he visited some 67 different countries. For half a dozen years he served on the Board of Governors of the PDK Educational Foundation and was its first chairman.

Gordon's somewhat roguish approach to my first questions (When did you leave full-time employment? "Most people think I left 30 years ago." What did you do to prepare for retirement? "Became nicer and nicer to my wife.") soon turned serious. After saying that his advice is worth exactly what I paid for it, he wrote as follows:

"This is the advice a 69-year-old gives to himself:

"A. Don't grow mentally stale. Know what the flow of ideas is about. Subscribe to the *New York Review of Books*, the *New York Times Book Review*, and the *Wilson Quarterly*. Don't leave proximity to a good library. It's the best way to keep current with ideas — good, bad, or flagrant.

"B. Write something that tests your creative capacities, something for the scores of editors who want material and want to give you a deadline. Try some make-believe stuff and you'll see how good you are at telling big lies (if Garrison Keillor can do it, so can you). Write something about what you'd do differently if you could replay your first 10 years as a parent. Write something — anything which captures some thought.

"C. Take some classes in painting/drawing. You will not be happy with your painting, but you'll be impressed with how the effort improves what you thought was already good, your powers of observation."

To me, Roy Wilson, whom I have known since college days when we were both student newspaper editors, has always personified good organization and careful planning. These were among the attributes that made him a highly effective head of the National Education Association's communications division for many years and the successful first director of the National School Public Relations Association. They also make his advice to prospective retirees particularly worthy of attention.

After leaving NSPRA in 1976, Roy was not ready for full retirement. "I knew my wife had married me for better or worse, but not for lunch," he says. "So I located a desk in another organization [Educational Research Services] and signed on as a volunteer. I checked in there after the morning rush hour and departed before the evening crunch. It was challenging part-time work, with fine fellowship but no budgets to balance.

"Age 65 to 75 is a period of choice," Roy continues. "John Gardner once wrote, 'Man should be re-potted about every 10 years.' The chance to take days that have been carefully packaged to the demands of a career and completely rearrange them to fit personal pursuits reveals a new world that you had dreamed about while awaiting re-potting. The epitaph requested by Malcolm Forbes applies: 'While alive, he lived.'

"For adventure, lift a dream from an old lock box and make it happen. Midway between the summit years of 65 to 75, Ruth and I joined two other couples for a trip through the Inside Passage to Alaska, using an economy formula that included ferries, planes, and rental cars. Such events need to be scheduled before arthritis, faulty plumbing, or other restrictions create road blocks.

"Beyond 75, depending on one's personal circumstances, I believe serious consideration should be given to locating in a life-care community. If you are grounded unexpectedly by health problems, you spare your family agonizing decisions on how to provide the type of care you might need.

" 'Retired' is defined by one dictionary as 'withdrawn or secluded'; also as 'withdrawn from business or public life.' The word can even mean 'to go to bed.' Retirement for older Americans today can often mean a dynamic new phase of life, especially if these definitions are recast to 'doing something satisfying that you have chosen yourself'."

Gerald H. Read, who inaugurated Phi Delta Kappa's extensive program of travel seminars with a trip to the USSR in 1958, retired from his endowed professorship in comparative education at Kent State University in 1976. Today, after frequently feigning efforts to reduce his commitments, he is as busy as ever. And he is surprised that other professors don't share his enthusiasm for work in one's advancing years. He says:

"I am always amazed at the number of Ph.D.'s who retire and completely separate themselves from their lifetime work. It would seem to me that retirement would provide them with the leisure to investigate their special fields of interest further. For 10 years I gave most of my time to the Chinese seminars and tours sponsored by Phi Delta Kappa. In 1986, I agreed to update a Ford Foundation project: *The Changing Soviet School.* Dr. Brian Holmes of the University of London is retired and we are teaming up with Dr. Zoya Malkova of the Academy of Pedagogical Sciences in Moscow to work on this project for the next five years. I went with the PDK Research Team on Underachieving Children to Moscow to help them in structuring their joint project with the Academy of Pedagogical Sciences.

"When in Prague in September 1989, as the guest of the Ministry of Education and Charles University, I met the director of the Institute of Educational Research of Vietnam. We agreed to explore the possibility of exchanges between PDK and the educators of Vietnam. A letter in January from Hanoi indicated that the Politburo had the proposal under consideration. If we get an invitation, I shall go to Hanoi to develop the program.

"I am invited to lecture at many universities and to meet with classes. I find all this stimulating. It provides an opportunity to meet with many of my former colleagues in comparative education. I am still active on the Executive Council of the World Council of Comparative Education Societies and the planning of the world congresses of the Comparative Education Societies. So it is still an interesting, challenging, and exhausting life!"

It should be noted that Read contributed generously to the PDK Educational Foundation by establishing the Read International Seminar Scholarships in 1978. His wife, Vicki, founded the Foundation's Adopt-a-Scholar program in 1988.

In the quarter-century spanning my *Kappan* editorship, I published at least eight satirical or humorous pieces written by Ken McIntyre, the University of Texas professor and author of highly regarded works in school administration. When Ken returned my retirement questionnaire, he included half a dozen engaging pieces he has written on retirement in the past few years, some of them excerpted from *The Rest of McIntyre*, published in 1989. (I think "rest" in the title means "retirement.") Here's a sample:

A Bit of Imbecility

I've noticed my waning ability
At tasks that demand some agility.
I find that a growing debility
Leaves questions about my virility,
Which once — I must state in humility —
Had clearly a certain utility.
But now, at great cost in tranquillity,
And even in mental stability,
As well as verbal facility,
I acknowledge my rampant senility.

Ken has proclaimed four basic rules for successful retirement. The first and most important is: "Say no — or hell no — to everything you don't really want to do."

Don Thomas retired on January 1, 1987, from his position as Deputy State Superintendent of Public Instruction in South Carolina and returned to his home in Salt Lake City, where he was school superintendent for many years. Don echoes Gordon Swanson in his advice to prospective retirees:

"Write a lot about your work, the current state of affairs in America, and about what needs to be done to improve education. This will force you to read and keep current.

"Retirement is not a separate existence from work, or shouldn't be; it can be simply an extension of one's work life. The work may change, of course, but is work nonetheless, whether it is a new job, consulting, or mowing the lawn. The main consideration is doing what one enjoys doing. There is so much to be done that retirement to do nothing is an impossibility for a thinking man."

Today Don is a senior partner with Harold Webb Associates and serves as an education consultant to Governor Ned McWherter of Tennessee.

Don closed with these words: "One should be proud of having been an educator and having been associated with a great profession."

William H. Fisher left full-time employment as a professor of educational foundations at the University of Montana in the spring of 1983. He reports that he helped a colleague, Jim Cox, persuade the Montana state legislature to authorize a program permitting professors to continue teaching one-third time. "This enabled those of us who opted for it to phase into full retirement gradually, and that's a boon to one's psyche. Frankly, for me teaching is a form of therapy," he says, but quickly adds, "No one should be teaching who doesn't get a good evaluation from his/her peers, students, and administrators — whether 'retired' or not."

Bill believes both state-supported and private colleges and universities should make provisions — financial and otherwise — for the kind of gradual retirement he has achieved.

I have saved a cautionary tale for last, and it involves a friend and colleague at Phi Delta Kappa. Wilmer Bugher joined the staff in 1973 after successfully desegregating the schools of Evansville, Indiana's fourth-largest city, where he was superintendent for three years. Lowell Rose asked him to develop a new division for the dissemination of innovative programs. Although his mission was to develop and disseminate ideas and materials not considered to have much commercial potential, Wilmer built a division with sales approaching one million dollars annually by the time he retired in 1985 at age 65.

Wilmer and his wife, Sal, were aware of most of the pitfalls they might encounter in retirement. Phi Delta Kappa's excellent retirement supplement program, developed in the late Seventies, is largely Wilmer's work. He and Sal had been planning retirement for nearly 12 years.

But something happened that neither anticipated. I'll let Wilmer tell it in his own words, which I have edited down from the 17-page letter he sent me.

"My work at PDK required extended air travel throughout the U.S., Canada, and several foreign countries. Sal and I wanted to see more of the U.S. from ground level. So we abandoned our apartment, bought a motor home, and set out. For nearly four years we traveled throughout the country, first in a 31-foot custom-built Barth and later in an even bigger one. We got in the habit of spending January through March in Yuma, Arizona. For the first time in our lives, we did nothing but play. We even learned to dance, something we had never had time for. I hooked redfish and speckled trout in Louisiana and Texas. I caught flounder and red rock crab in Washington. I hunted quail in New Mexico. I bought metal detecting equipment and learned all the tricks of using it (but Sal had all the luck; she even found a half-ounce gold nugget with it). And I participated in senior Olympics.

"For two and one-half years, retirement was unbelievably good. Many times, while driving the motor home, I would say to myself, 'Why didn't I retire earlier? There simply isn't enough time to do all the things I want to do.'

"But then I would begin feeling guilty. Why should I have all this fun when so many people need help? Why wasn't I helping? I also realized that during my career an important source of motivation was recognition from my peers; I wasn't getting that ego stimulus in retirement.

"Then it happened; the dreaded retirement syndrome hit me. The lyrics of a popular song of the day kept ringing in my head: 'Is that all there is?' I was sinking into depression, and with it was the feeling that something was physically wrong. This was new, because my biennial physicals had always been encouraging. I took time out for another and very thorough physical. No single cause for depression was found.

"My symptoms were loss of appetite, insomnia, and low self-esteem. I tried medication, and I suffered the side effects: more loss of appetite and weight. Finally I was hospitalized, with strict control and increased levels of medication. But this too failed. Negative feelings begat more negative feeling until the cycle reached dangerous levels.

"After much reading, praying, consultation with experts, and discussions with my wife, I was convinced that the medication route was not for me.

"A change in hospitals and a drastic change in therapy was the next step. Medications were removed and therapy intensified. I sometimes felt as if I were trying to learn to walk again.

"Were it not for the loyalty of a dedicated and loving wife, the prayers of several concerned people, and the skills of therapists and doctors, I doubt that I would have survived this experience.

"But within days after medication was stopped, my appetite began to improve. With appetite came some joy and ambition. My stamina gradually returned. Then came opportunities to do something for someone else. Thus began the road to recovery. Lowell Rose helped me greatly by assigning me some special projects for Phi Delta Kappa. Other plans call for an expansion of volunteer work and participation in church activities. I am exercising regularly and watch my diet and weight. I continue to participate in senior Olympics. Certainly good physical condition enhances one's chances of recovering mental stability and optimism.

"How does one avoid depression? If I knew the answer for everyone who suffers from it, I could make a fortune. Depression is much more widespread than most people realize. Obviously, it is not confined to the retirement years. At the risk of being wrong, I suggest that, at least for personality types like mine, the transition to retirement be gradual. I should have continued some of my professional activities on a limited basis. Another route, of course, is to start a new career. It can give the ego boost that is so necessary for some of us to survive. Volunteer work can also be very fulfilling for certain people.

"I now realize that learning the art of retirement is not easy, but it should be part of everyone's preretirement tools. Learning about it after the fact is much like learning to be a parent after one has children. You can make a lot of mistakes in the process.

"We often hear the adage, 'All work and no play makes Jack a dull boy.' For me, all play and no work proved devastating. Writing about it is not easy, but if sharing this experience will help even one other person avoid the retirement syndrome, it will certainly have been worth the effort."

As the experience of these friends and colleagues suggests, there is no success formula that applies with equal merit to every person who faces retirement here at millennium's end. Each of us is likely to respond to the retirement challenge much as we responded to the challenge of our life's work — resourcefully or unimaginatively, optimistically or cynically, with self-direction or other-direction, with quiet hope or quiet desperation. In the small hours of morning, when we elderly folk are wont to relive the first six Shakespearean stages, when we enter that strange state of consciousness between sleeping and waking, when the mysterious ribonucleic acids of memory swish about in our skulls, recognition dawns: Today may be the last! Make the most of it! *Carpe diem!*

Reflections on Principles
of Educational Leadership

BY JACK FRYMIER

During the years since I finished my doctoral program, I have been a college professor, public school administrator, consultant, researcher, writer, and editor. In addition, I have been active in professional organizations. I thought a little and talked a lot about what people in leadership roles in education ought to do. It would have been better, probably, if I had thought a lot and talked a little; but my style was otherwise.

Some of the ideas that I thought were useful and true when I left graduate school have been confirmed by experience. Others have been repudiated by that same experience. From these experiences has evolved a set of principles about educational leadership. Some grew out of reading and reflection. Others emerged as a direct consequence of research studies or development projects in which I have been involved. Still others were an outgrowth of my work with people in the public schools.

For example, during the time that I served as director of instruction in Orlando, Florida, I worked with more than 4,000 teachers and administrators in 85 schools on improving the instructional program. We conducted research studies in curriculum, adopted and adapted innovative programs, initiated special projects, and organized teachers and others in ways that focused their energy and creativity on instructional improvement.

By contrast, between 1972 and 1984 I worked with a small group of teachers and the principal in just one school in Westerville, Ohio,

Jack Frymier is a Professor Emeritus at Ohio State University and currently Isaacson Professor of Education at the University of Nebraska at Omaha and Phi Delta Kappa Senior Fellow.

trying to improve the instructional program. During our years together, we conceptualized and implemented a practical way to individualize instruction. It is called the Annehurst Curriculum Classification System, named after the Annehurst School where it was developed. The Annehurst system we developed was a collaborative effort involving staff in that one school building and faculty at Ohio State University, who worked together regularly over a period of more than 10 years.

The practical principles of educational leadership that I set forth here are a product of what I knew when I left graduate school and what I have learned since. They are a product of personal experience, thought, research, and professional involvement, and thus are true for me. They might or might not hold true for others. They are not elaborated sufficiently enough to be dignified as theory, but they represent a beginning effort along that line. Time, research, reflection, and more experience may verify these principles; but I share them because they represent the best that I now know.

Let me begin by listing some assumptions that undergird my own belief system regarding educational leadership:

1. Each person is unique.
2. Every person has worth.
3. All people can learn.
4. Schools exist to help students learn.
5. Curriculum is the major means by which the schools help people learn.
6. Curriculum includes what is taught and how it is taught.
7. Curriculum can and must be improved.
8. Those most directly concerned with curriculum (students, teachers, parents, and administrators) should be involved in curriculum improvement efforts.
9. Those who willingly work on curriculum improvement will be influenced by the developmental efforts.
10. The basic responsibility of those in educational leadership roles is to improve curriculum.

In other words, I assume that the major responsibility of those who work in leadership roles in the schools is to work directly with teachers, students, administrators, and parents to improve what is taught and how it is taught. All other things are secondary.

As I have thought about how to make these assumptions operational, I long ago came to the conclusion that there is no one best way, no *right* way for leaders to function. People are different. Communities are different. Schools are different. Times change. These realities make me approach the task of improving schools with few preconceived strategies. In fact, I think it unwise, even professionally wrong, to begin a school improvement effort with a detailed plan of action. Plans must evolve *during* the leadership activity rather than before.

During the 10-plus years that I had worked with the principal and teachers at the Annehurst School, I learned a lot about curriculum development and staff development. And the hundreds of workshops I have conducted have given me the opportunity to talk through and clarify what I have learned with educators across the country. What follow are 12 principles of educational leadership that are valid for me — at least for today. Each principle is explained briefly, without supporting rationale.

1. *Take the long view.* People responsible for instructional supervision, curriculum development, and staff development will be most effective if they take the long view. Teaching and learning are complex human activities. Schools are complex institutions. Schooling is an involved and involving process. To bring about significant school improvement takes a long time.

In remodeling a home, if a light switch is changed from one wall to another wall, it takes most people about three weeks to learn where the new switch is located and to use it consistently. Similarly, helping teachers learn to think differently about students or to select or use curriculum materials differently takes time. To upgrade the competence of an entire staff is an extremely complex and demanding job. Anyone who has ever worked with a group of teachers just to change the report card knows how difficult it is to bring about even minor changes in school programs.

Some schools have one-day inservice programs before school starts each September. In the morning an out-of-town speaker is invited to give an inspirational address to all of the teachers assembled in the high school auditorium. After the speech there is coffee; teachers meet in grade-level or subject-matter groups, then have afternoon free in their classroom before students arrive the next day. Typically, that constitutes half of the inservice program for that school year. During late January the same format will be repeated, the assumption being that teachers need a boost; and the second one-day shot-in-the-arm is supposed to last until school is out in early June.

To describe such activities as "inservice education" or "staff development" is to make a mockery of the terms. Professionals need to come together and stay together and work together over long periods if they ever hope to develop new understandings or acquire new skills or change old attitudes. Curriculum-development and staff-development efforts require a long view.

2. *Work at the building level.* For many reasons, it is important for curriculum development and staff development to occur at the school building level. Individual classroom teachers are too "hemmed in" to make much progress on their own. They have access to too few materials and they have too little flexibility with time and other resources to bring about significant improvement working in isolation.

For example, if we accept the fact that students are different, then teachers need great variety and quantity of curriculum materials if they are to meet each learner's unique learning needs. A single teacher is not likely to have an adequate range of materials. However, if six or eight teachers pool their materials, the possibility of finding the right kinds of materials for students who differ (even dramatically) is increased.

Teachers who work together in the same building with the same students become members of an educational team. They see each other every day. They meet in the cafeteria, the teachers' lounge, and in the hall. They participate in faculty meetings. If they work together on concerns that are common in the areas of curriculum development and staff development, they learn to know one another as professional colleagues and as human beings.

Curriculum-development and staff-development programs conducted at the school district level may result in logical groupings rather than psychological affiliations. The net result is pressure for uniformity and evenness, agreements and compromises, or grade-level or subject-centered standards rather than teacher-oriented or learner-oriented activities.

Typically, the faculty of a school building is large enough to guarantee diversity but small enough to make a productive working group. Within the total faculty there are enough ideas, talent, and ingenuity to develop effective approaches to their own areas of concern. Further, they are close enough to the problems to identify and deal with the issues under consideration. Finally, if they assume responsibility for their own development, they will generate a sense of ownership that will guarantee success.

When mandates for improvement are "handed down" from the central office or "needs assessments" are delegated to persons from afar, the chances of securing meaningful participation essential for significant improvement are diminished. If central office people become involved at the building level, important changes may be possible; but if they insist on districtwide programs or innovations, many things may be initiated but few will mature or endure.

3. *Building principals must initiate change*. Too often building principals play a gatekeeper rather than initiator role in curriculum-development and staff-development efforts. They react to ideas or proposals that come to their attention rather than taking the lead and initiating their own. It may be too strong to describe this as "leadership by veto," but this is the way many principals function. Rather than being attuned to promising ideas or projects, their approach is likely to be, "We have to be careful; that probably would not work in our school."

I am convinced that curriculum development and staff development must not only focus on the building level but must be initiated at that level, too, by the principal and/or the staff. When people work at improving their own understandings, skills, or programs, they have a different attitude and are receptive to change. Those whose posture is one of reaction rather than initiation are more likely to be cynical and to reflect an "it won't work here" attitude than those who decide in their own minds that they can make a difference and things can be improved, "so we better get started."

Those who want to "keep their hand upon the tiller as well as the oar," who take charge and initiate their own developmental activities, are less likely to have mandates imposed on them from higher up. And even when mandates do come down, they seem to be able to incorporate them into a program they already have under way or to redirect their emphasis altogether. In other words, if a building principal and staff already have curriculum-development and staff-development ventures under way, they are less likely to be diverted from these ventures than if they had no programs working at all.

4. *Proceed on a broken front*. Even if curriculum-development and staff-development programs are focused at the building level, in my judgment, they are most effective and most likely to succeed if they involve small clusters of like-minded persons rather than the entire staff. Principals tend to want to achieve consensus among staff regarding policies and procedures, and no doubt some agreement is desirable and necessary. However, for a principal to say we need to have a uniform policy about, say, use of curriculum materials or homework generates dissension among staff and usually results in compromise and dissatisfaction. Further, it presumes that there actually is "one best way."

166

It is better to proceed on a broken front. Small clusters of people within a building can come together and work together over long periods of time if they are not expected to persuade all other staff to come around to their point of view, and if they are not expected to modify their own ideas to suit other peoples' expectations.

The school is a social institution, and give and take are an essential part of a professional activity. Even so, if a building principal adopts a broken-front approach and encourages subgroupings of faculty to generate their own directions and to follow their own hunches, two things typically result, and both are positive. First, there is diversity within the school. Second, people are energized and mobilized by their own commitments; and they work hard to achieve their own goals.

Diversity within the building means that parents and students are more likely to find a meaningful match between their expectations and what the school offers than if everything is uniform within the building. Having several "schools within a school," so to speak, will increase the probability of satisfying both parents and staff who have a specific orientation regarding what is "best" for any particular student. Second, enabling staff to pursue areas that are of interest to them capitalizes on their commitments as professionals and uses the creativity and energy that is there. People will work hard to pursue objectives to which they are committed; they are reluctant to work toward somebody else's goals.

5. *Focus on possibilities rather than problems.* One approach to curriculum development and staff development is to begin with the identification of problems that staff members face. Such an approach has a long and honorable history, and there is some merit to the strategy. But there are difficulties, too. Problems tend to immobilize people, turning them off rather than turning them on. Problems are reminders of past difficulties and proof of failure. They sap people's energies, drain their enthusiasms, and blunt their interests. For many people problems are negative motivators.

Possibilities, on the other hand, get people excited, mobilize their enthusiasm, and unleash their creative capacities. Focusing on possibilities rather than problems sustains people over extended periods and defuses the cynics and the "I told you so" crowd. Accomplishments are more likely to result in positive feedback. Focusing on possibilities enables people to exercise their strengths rather than reveal their weaknesses, and participation and productivity are generally high.

6. *Tasks must be intellectually exciting*. Of the many motivations for entering teaching, two stand out: an interest in young people and an interest in ideas. Any curriculum-development and staff-development venture that is successful will capitalize on those interests. One thing that I learned in my work at the Annehurst School was the importance of the intellectual dimensions of the staff-developmental effort.

Teachers know that teaching and learning are complex tasks. They realize that personality and motivation are multi-faceted phenomena. They recognize the intricacy of ideas and the complexity of knowledge. They are suspicious of simplistic solutions to problems that are obviously complex. They object to being "spoon fed" or talked down to.

Successful curriculum-development and staff-development programs are intellectually exciting; they come to grips with the nuances and complexities inherent in teaching and learning. Such programs make demands on staff. They grapple with ideas. They relate theory to practice. They seek out additional information and alternative explanations and draw on their own experience to support or refute a particular point. They analyze the parts and synthesize the whole. When such demands are placed on teachers and administrators, they rise to the challenge; they work hard; they are creative. They achieve.

7. *Staff must enter school improvement projects with the expectation that they will change*. Some people set goals that can be achieved only if somebody else changes their behavior. An illustration would be the person who says, "I would go to church more often, if the people there would be more friendly." When people establish goals that can be realized only if *other* people change, they are likely to end up frustrated or cynical.

Those involved in curriculum development and school improvement must establish objectives and chart courses of action that enable them to change rather than making somebody else change. When we focus our energies on making it possible for us to acquire new understandings, develop new skills, and adopt new attitudes, then we are in a position to learn and to improve. Rather than manipulating other people, our energies can go into changing and improving ourselves.

8. *Do not overplan*. Those responsible for curriculum development and staff development need to have a general idea of what they hope to accomplish but should avoid overplanning. Breaking down broad goals into specific activities, then sequencing those activities,

specifying timelines, and spelling out interrelationships, lines of authority, evaluation protocol, and reporting procedures often means that so much effort goes into planning nothing else gets done.

Being too specific in planning locks in activities in such a way that when promising alternatives emerge, they are rejected because they are not in the plan. Leaders need to learn from experience as they go along. They should not allow themselves to become imprisoned in their own timetables or evaluation schemes. Planning is important, but it must not be overdone.

9. *Use "hard" money.* Over the past 30 years or so, many of the curriculum-development and staff-development projects have been funded with "soft" money from the federal government or foundations. There is nothing wrong with accepting outside funding for worthy projects, but it has resulted in an attitude among educators that goes something like this: If you (federal government or private foundation) will give us extra funds, then we will engage in curriculum-development and staff-development programs. We want to do better. Just give us the money, and we'll show you. If you do not give us the money, then we will not be able to do it.

This kind of thinking has resulted in psychological dependency on others (especially the federal government) for school improvement programs. Because the press for funds is so great, people can easily persuade themselves into thinking that if they can get "extra" money from some outside funding source, that will solve the problem. It does not work that way. Unless school districts spend their "own" money (regular tax dollars, "hard" money) for curriculum-development and staff-development programs, few long-term results are likely.

In my judgment, $5,000 of local money will almost always accomplish more than $50,000 of outside funds. Rather than "chasing the funding buck" and then hiring a special administrator and staff to get the project off the ground, it is better to use regular funding and regular personnel to improve the regular program. The probability of success is greater, and the probability of maintaining the gains is much improved.

10. *Use good group processes and good data.* We have learned a lot in the past 30 years about the role of group process and group dynamics in curriculum-development and staff-development efforts. Issuing mandates, writing memoranda, or other unilateral pronouncements do not make schools better. Helping people change requires group activities: meetings, prolonged discussion, problem identifi-

cation, generation of alternative solutions, and careful evaluation. Group process involves being sensitive to other people and finding ways to bring their talents and abilities to bear on significant problems.

Good data also are important. Good processes may make people feel good; but without good data, school people will not be able to make significant improvements in curriculum.

11. *Produce a product.* As important as good group processes and using good data are in curriculum development and staff development, it is equally important to produce a product. That product may be a new schedule or teaming arrangement, a new set of curriculum materials, or an evaluation plan. At some point a product ought to be forthcoming. People need some tangible product to point to and say, "We developed that."

12. *Use the resources of the community.* Every school is part of a larger community. School people cannot − dare not − go it alone. They need all of the intellectual and material resources they can get, starting with the resources that are already there. Draw the businessmen and farmers and parents into the school. Get people from the state department of education to help. Get people from nearby colleges and universities to share their expertise and knowledge. Use the resources of the community that are already there.

The staff at Annehurst School learned to use the resources of the community, not for public relations purposes or as a way of sensing or influencing public opinion, but because that was where the knowledgeable people were − people with ideas, people with skills, people with time to share and help to give. The staff considered Ohio State University within their community sphere and reached out and pulled in faculty to help them.

I cite the example of Annehurst School using resource people from the university, because the principal and staff did it so consistently, creatively, and collegially. There are probably 300 or so schools within a 50-mile radius of Ohio State University, but fewer than half a dozen have looked to the university as a resource or used that resource effectively. Public school people may invite a university professor to give a "pep talk" on inservice day or to conduct a facilities study before they build a new building, but devising working relationships that last for years is a rare occurrence.

Every community has human resources that the schools can tap. People believe in schools. They want their schools to be first-rate. Finding a way to use those human resources effectively and over extended periods of time is an important thing for educational leaders to do.

Conclusion

Let me restate the assumptions on which these 12 principles for school improvement are based. The first is that schools exist to help young people learn. Second, the major responsibility of people who work in leadership roles in education is to do everything they can to improve the curriculum in the public schools. All other things must be secondary. Now, how do these principles square with what has been going on in education in recent years?

My reading of what has gone on in the name of curriculum development and staff development during the past 30 years leads me to conclude that two forces have been at work. Almost every effort at school improvement since Sputnik has been the result of 1) financial inducements from the federal government and 2) coercion from the state governments in the form of legislation or mandates issued by the state departments of education. In other words, the prime forces for improving the public schools have been the positive attractiveness of federal funds and the negative press of state actions.

As a profession, we have failed to look at the effectiveness of new programs except in terms of these two forces. As a profession, we have not asked the most fundamental question: Does the new program help students learn? Instead, we have asked questions about whether we can get special monies if we do it or whether we will be in trouble with the state department of education if we do not. We have been more concerned with being fiscally reimbursed or legally correct than we have with being educationally effective. We have assumed that if the federal government made all of those monies available, it must be all right. Or, if the state department of education required it, it must be for the better. Neither of those assumptions is necessarily correct.

It is terribly important for those of us in the profession to look at the problems and complexities of curriculum development and staff development in new and thoughtful ways. Many schools are dull and boring places. Most secondary students are bored to death. If it were not for their peer groups and extracurricular programs, most adolescents would be climbing the walls. Furthermore, many of those who teach and work in schools day after day are bored to death. There is seldom any intellectual excitement about what they are doing. That is a tragic state of affairs.

Ralph Tyler has made the point that progress in education has always come during periods of economic decline. He cites the developments that grew out of Dewey's notions of child study during the panic years of 1907 and after and the remarkable activity that occurred during the Great Depression of the 1930s. Then Tyler asked: "And what will we work on now?"

That question poses a genuine challenge to those who are dedicated to improving the public schools. During the Sixties and Seventies we pursued more and more dollars under the assumption that money would improve the quality of education. During the Eighties we accepted the constraints and additional demands laid on us by the state legislatures and state departments of education. Neither of those tactics has made the kind of improvement that all of us hoped for and that we know is possible to achieve.

The educational slice of the national economic pie has increased almost four-fold during the past 50 years. During the 1930s, for example, 1.9% of the gross national product was devoted to education. By 1975, 7.9% of the GNP was devoted to education. In 1985 that percentage went down slightly; and given the current state of the economy, the odds are not great that schools will get much more money.

But do we do need more money or do we need better ideas? In my view, money will not do it. Ideas and innovation will. We can make a difference. This is a time for great opportunity and great risk. We must stop pursing an elusive goal that someone else has defined for us. Improving the public schools is a task that must start at the building level with the people who work there. It must go on over a long period of time and must use the resources that are available in the school and community. Yes, we can make a difference. But if we don't do it, it won't get done.

Reflections on Research
on Teaching

BY N. L. GAGE

Whence, whereat, and whither are the themes of these reflections: where I came from and how I got into the field of research on teaching, where that field stands now, and where I see it going. Along the way, I shall mention some of the people (outside my family) who have been most significant in my work.

Whence

As I see it, my career began when, at the age of 10, I was swept up in the airmindedness that followed Lindbergh's flight across the Atlantic in 1927. This aviation mania immersed me in reading about flying (especially in *American Boy* magazine), gave me a juvenile's knowledge about the theory of flight, and started my fascination with science and technology. In high school, mathematics, chemistry, and physics gave me an appreciation of what I later learned to call "elegant cognitive structures." Sinclair Lewis's *Arrowsmith*, Paul De Kruif's *Microbe Hunters*, and Bernard Jaffe's *Crucibles* made me long for the romance and adventure of scientific research — the quest for truth and even, perhaps, the bestowal of great benefits on mankind.

In high school, I took a second year of Latin instead of biology, with the lamentable result that I have never felt at home with matters zoological or botanical. And somehow, I wasn't able to get as absorbed in college calculus or physics as I realized I should if I were to aim at a career in the physical sciences. By 1936, when I had finished my sophomore year at the College of the City of New York,

N.L. Gage is the Margaret Jacks Professor of Education and (by courtesy) Professor of Psychology Emeritus at Stanford University.

I realized that I was oriented toward benefiting society more directly than the natural sciences seemed to be.

During the summer of 1936, my brother, who was about to transfer from Columbia to Cornell, gave me the idea of transferring, too. So I applied for admission to the University of Minnesota, which was then (at $36 per quarter for a non-resident) one of the least expensive universities in the country. There I would no longer have a one-hour commute twice a day, could enjoy much more the companionship of fellow students, and take a long step toward maturity by getting away from home. This institution, far away in America's Heartland, seemed to beckon me. As someone who had grown up in New Jersey, on a street just across the Hudson River from 72nd Street in Manhattan, and had never been west of Philadelphia, I was embarking on a great adventure.

At that point I was leaning toward economics − I would be the next Adam Smith or Karl Marx rather than the next Lavoisier or Newton. But three courses in economics at Minnesota made me think that an economics major (at least as I perceived it then) would lead me into the business world and not toward making a revolution in economic theory that would save the world from future depressions.

During my first fall quarter at Minnesota I took Psychology I to round out my liberal education. The course was taught in a large lecture hall by the department's chair, Richard M. Elliott, supplemented with lectures from other professors in the Psychology Department. Strongly attracted to the subject and motivated to achieve, I studied hard and at mid-quarter, for the first and only time, got a perfect score on an exam. In return for this sterling achievement, I was offered membership in an honors section being taught by an instructor, newly arrived from Harvard, by the name of B.F. Skinner.

During the same quarter I was earning 50 cents an hour from the National Youth Administration, a New Deal agency created to help needy college students eke out a living. My work was clerical: making tally marks for the item analyses of multiple-choice tests used in Minnesota's General College. I found the work boring and, because I was slow and error-prone, frustrating. When I learned of the possibility of shifting to another job, perhaps working for a faculty member, I offered my services to Skinner for whatever tasks he needed done, with my pay provided at no cost to him. Recognizing an excellent bargain, Skinner took me on.

Beginning about February 1937, and through most of my senior year, I served as what might be called, somewhat expansively, Skinner's undergraduate research assistant. My duties included making pellets for the rats Skinner used in his conditioning experiments. I recall using a gadget with razor blades for cutting $^3/_{16}$" segments of wet Purina Dog Chow to fit into the food tubes of the Skinner boxes. I used a lettering machine to draw the labels, such as "Responses" and "Time in Hours," for the axes of the figures in his then-being-written *Behavior of Organisms*. I counted the occurrences of words in the Kent-Rosanoff lists of associated words and of words referring to colors and flowers in a Shakespeare concordance (an alphabetical index of all the words used by Shakespeare, showing each word's context). Skinner used these counts in verifying G.K. Zipf's then recently published finding that, when plotted on double-log paper, the frequency of the words would have a straight-line relationship to their rank in frequency, thus showing something important about the distribution of associated words.

I also learned from lots of other little things while working for Skinner. He set out food to attract pigeons to his office window, apparently beginning to think about using them instead of rats as the organism of choice for his experiments on behavior. I remember that he trained a rat to climb a ladder, pull a chain that released a marble, carry the marble across the cage, deposit it in a funnel, and receive a pellet of food. This feat brought a visit by a reporter-photographer team from *Life* magazine, giving Skinner his second big coverage by the media. (The first was his article, "Has Gertrude Stein a Secret?" in the *Atlantic Monthly* in 1934, in which he speculated that her style was a form of automatic writing, done without her conscious direction.)

More important to me, of course, was my incidental learning from casual conversations with Skinner, from watching what he did when I gave him a new batch of data, from his answers to my questions, and from the readings he casually suggested. For example, he gave me a copy of P.W. Bridgman's *Logic of Modern Physics* so I could learn about operationalism. He asked me to read the manuscript of chapter 12 of his *Behavior of Organisms*, in which he argued that an independent science of behavior was possible and desirable and that it could be linked to a science of neurology whenever the latter matured enough.

I remember his telling me that he had devised a "paradigm" for conditioning that differed from Pavlov's. (This is how I was first exposed to the term and the concept of paradigm before Thomas Kuhn's use of it. My writing a chapter on "Paradigms for Research on Teaching" for the first *Handbook of Research on Teaching* in 1962 apparently made some writers wonder at my seeming prescience.) He had pictures of the great physiologists Sherrington and Pavlov on his office walls. He took pride in being mentioned alongside such eminent learning theorists as Hunter, Hull, and Tolman in an article in *Philosophy of Science* by Saul Rosenzweig. In short, I had through blind luck stumbled onto what I later realized was a mentor — one who was to become the most famous psychologist of his time. All these experiences made me realize what it is like to lead the life of a scientist. The idea of making a living, of getting paid, for doing the kinds of things that Skinner and other professors did was irresistible. How fortunate were these scholars and scientists, who enjoyed so much the daily challenges of their work. Often, like Arrowsmith, they came back to work after hours because they wanted to, because their work was so absorbing. What a far cry from my summer jobs, where I worked with men and women who could hardly wait for five o'clock to come. So, envisioning my life as a scientist, I decided to major and seek a Ph.D. in psychology.

But first I had to be admitted to graduate school. During the winter quarter of my senior year I applied for admission to 10 universities for graduate work and for a fellowship or assistantship. My grades were good (I was elected to Phi Beta Kappa). But as the returns trickled in, I realized that I had received 10 rejections. I was not ebullient that spring.

Then, on June 15, 1938, my despair was relieved when I received a letter from H.H. Remmers, a professor of psychology at Purdue University, to which I had not applied. Remmers had obtained my name from the University of Iowa, which had turned me down. Purdue's doctoral program in psychology was only a year old and apparently needed more applicants. Remmers had presumably asked his own graduate school, Iowa, for the files of its rejects. (A week later I received an acceptance and offer of free tuition from Floyd Allport at Syracuse University. Who knows what I would have become if Allport's letter had reached me first?)

Remmers' letter offered me admission, tuition, and a readership paying $25 a month, which I later was able to supplement with income from another National Youth Administration job. Thus began my 30-year relationship with Remmers — a warm and collaborative one that shaped my research interests and, most important, bolstered my shaky confidence in my worth. As my second mentor, Remmers gave me what I needed most as a fledgling researcher: criticism tempered with constant encouragement.

176

When working with Skinner I had proven inept with his lettering machine and was less than brilliant with a laboratory experiment he suggested on learning concepts without awareness, that is, without the learner's being aware of the distinguishing features of the concept. And I had difficulty seeing human significance in Skinner's work — a significance that became apparent to me only with the publication of his *Walden Two* in 1948 and *Science and Human Behavior* in 1953. By contrast, Remmers seemed to approve of just about everything I did. I did well in whatever tasks were laid before me — writing, editing, statistical analysis, test construction, and the like — and their relevance to education and society was plain to see.

Early in 1940, Remmers asked whether I would be interested in co-authoring a textbook on educational measurement with him. Having security uppermost on my mind and realizing that the invitation promised employment for a year or two, I immediately accepted. The book came out in the spring of 1943 as *Educational Measurement and Evaluation*. It had respectable sales, went through four editions, and added an impressive bulk to my collected publications.

During World War II, I was an enlisted man. After completing basic training and working as an interviewer, I was assigned to the Army Air Forces Aviation Psychology Program, where I worked with Gerald S. Blum, Stanley Blumberg, Douglas W. Bray, Stuart W. Cook, Robert Glaser, Albert H. Hastorf, Harold H. Kelley, George S. Klein, and others who were to make their careers in psychology. Here again I was lucky in that my work allowed me to use, and even improve, my training in psychology. After the war, at the 1946 meeting of the American Psychological Association, I was invited to do graduate work at Indiana University by Skinner, who had just become chairman of its Psychology Department. But I was too close to completing my Ph.D. work at Purdue by then, and felt too beholden to Remmers to want to move.

In addition to my courses in psychology, my minors in biology (genetics and physiology) and economics, and writing the measurement textbook with Remmers, my work as a graduate student took me into achievement testing, test reliability theory, surveys of high school students' opinions, and attitude measurement. My 1947 Ph.D. thesis used Guttman scaling, factor analysis, and factorial design in the analysis of an opinion poll of high school students' attitudes toward minority groups. By the 1947-1948 academic year, which I spent as assistant professor at Purdue, I was eager to move out from under Remmers' wing and to begin a career all my own.

An invitation came in the spring of 1948 from the University of Illinois, which was expanding its Bureau of Educational Research. I accepted and moved there in September of 1948. Another newcomer to the Bureau that year was Lee J. Cronbach, who within seven years was to be elected president of the American Psychological Association; at 39, he was the youngest APA president since John Dewey. So I did not lack for a nearby example of dedication, productivity, rigor, and integrity.

My research during my first 10 years at Illinois focused on what has variously been called empathy, accuracy in person perception, or social sensitivity. My idea was that teachers who had more empathy would make better teachers. Before long I became aware of artifacts and other pitfalls in measuring empathy and became expert at detecting them. Most of the work was correlational: get measures of teacher empathy and then correlate them with other variables, such as measures of how well the teachers were accepted by their pupils.

In 1953, when George S. Leavitt and George C. Stone joined me as full-time research associates for two years, the work became especially productive. Then I wanted to see whether improving a teacher's empathy would improve the teacher's effectiveness. This idea led to an experiment carried out in the late 1950s by Philip J. Runkel, Bishwa Chatterjee, and me. We gave feedback, consisting of pupils' ratings of their actual teacher and their ideal teacher, to one set of about 80 sixth-grade teachers and withheld it from a randomly equivalent group. After a three-month interval, the teachers who received the feedback were rated more favorably by their pupils than the teachers in the control group. Subsequent investigators confirmed the effect, especially when the feedback was accompanied by the teachers' consultation with a respected advisor.

But what turned out to be more important for me was an invitation in 1950 from Remmers to serve on the AERA's new Committee on the Criteria of Teacher Effectiveness, which he was to chair. I agreed to serve, and the subsequent events drew me into research on teaching with a new scope and intensity. Here again, my career path exemplifies the way in which chance meetings and referrals, combined with serendipity and one's own proclivities, can lead to the field that will occupy one professionally for many years.

Whereat

From the beginning, my interest in research on teaching rested on the assumption that teaching is central to the process of education.

It is the main way societies have developed for giving children and youth the knowledge, understanding, skills, and appreciations needed to live productive lives as individuals and as citizens. Most teaching occurs in classrooms. Classroom teaching goes on wherever schools exist around the world. It will probably be supplemented but not supplanted by technology now foreseeable.

During the late 1960s and early 1970s, the centrality of teaching seemed to be challenged by such large-scale surveys as *Equality of Educational Opportunity* (commonly referred to as the Coleman Report, after its principal investigator, James S. Coleman), which examined the factors that related to student achievement in school and beyond. The surveys were widely misinterpreted as showing that teaching had little effect on achievement. But the surveys did not compare teaching with no teaching. Rather, they compared various kinds of teachers as to their effectiveness and seemed to show that one teacher was just about as effective as another. The interpretation seemed to be that variations in such factors as teacher selection, teacher education, and teaching practices would make little difference in student achievement.

After studying these surveys, I began to realize that they were largely irrelevant with regard to understanding the importance of variations in teaching. The investigators had not gone into classrooms to watch teachers at work; they had simply used questionnaires to collect information on teacher characteristics rather than teaching practices. They had not measured student achievement of goals that the teachers had explicitly set. Instead, they had used vocabulary tests as a measure of student achievement – just as such tests are used to measure intelligence – and with the same result, that is, minimizing teacher effects. And the surveys had used correlational methods – whose interpretations can be argued almost endlessly – as bases for determining whether different teachers *cause* differences in achievement.

Despite the survey studies that seemingly challenged the centrality of teaching, the centuries-old intuition that one way of teaching might be better than another – at least for some purposes and some students – survived. Educators and society at large continue to consider variations in ways of teaching to be important.

Although Edward L. Thorndike, the father of American educational psychology, had focused on teaching in only two or three of his 600 publications, a considerable amount of research had been done on teacher effectiveness by the 1950s, particularly by Arvil S.

Barr and his students at the University of Wisconsin, as well as by many dissertation authors around the nation. By 1950, from many small-scale, one-shot studies, enough research had appeared to make it possible for Simeon J. Domas and David V. Tiedeman to compile a 1,000-item annotated bibliography of research on teacher competence. In 1954 Joseph E. Morsh and Eleanor W. Wilder published a review of hundreds of reports on the characteristics of effective teachers. In addition, the AERA's Committee on the Criteria of Teacher Effectiveness, with Remmers as chair, published reports on the topic in 1952 and 1953.

In 1955, a new AERA Committee on Teacher Effectiveness was appointed, with me as chair. Pondering what the committee might undertake and benefiting from my familiarity with respected handbooks in psychology, I proposed that the AERA produce a handbook of research on teaching. The new committee accepted and elaborated that idea, and in 1957 the AERA's Council accepted the proposal. The *Handbook of Research on Teaching* appeared in 1963. In the meantime, David G. Ryans had published in 1960 his impressive *Characteristics of Teachers*, in which he reported factor analyses of trained observers' ratings of teacher and student behavior and also the correlates of the resulting factors. And Ned Flanders had initiated his seminal program of classroom-interaction analysis, noting every three seconds the occurrence of one of 10 kinds of carefully defined teacher and student behavior and correlating their frequencies with pupil achievement and attitude.

The appearance of the *Handbook of Research on Teaching* apparently awakened many educational researchers and their students to the promise and feasibility of doing research on teaching. In increasing numbers, they began to conduct such research and contribute to the literature on its findings, substance, and methodology. Some of the *Handbook's* chapters were later published separately. The chapter by Donald T. Campbell and Julian C. Stanley on experimental and quasi-experimental design became a best seller in the behavioral and social sciences.

In reflecting on the status of research on teaching before and after publication of the *Handbook*, I recall that, at the 1957 AERA meeting, I ran into Harold E. Mitzel (a member of the *Handbook's* Editorial Advisory Board) in an elevator. I remarked that he and I alone represented research on teaching at that AERA meeting, since ours were the only two papers being presented in that field. But by the mid-1960s, owing to the AERA's growth and, I think, the *Handbook's* influence, the number of such presentations began to grow. In recent years, each AERA convention program has listed hundreds of papers on research on teaching.

In 1962, after 14 years at the University of Illinois, I accepted an invitation to join the faculty at Stanford University. There I became deeply involved in the federally funded Stanford Center for Research and Development in Teaching, which existed from 1965 to 1976. Led by Robert N. Bush and me, the center involved other faculty members and many graduate students in research on teaching. Many of the students − David C. Berliner, Christopher M. Clark, Lyn Corno, Ronald W. Marx, Alexis Mitman, Penelope Peterson, Barak V. Rosenshine, Dale H. Schunk, Richard J. Shavelson, Nicholas G. Stayrook, and Philip H. Winne, among others − went on to build careers in the field. Although the center's substantive and methodological products were considerable, these students give the center's impact on education an inestimable longevity.

In 1967 I began work on a textbook in educational psychology, a course I had been teaching since 1948. In this book I intended to redress the grievous neglect of teaching in the textbooks then available. By 1970, however, I realized that I needed help and was lucky enough to attract David C. Berliner as co-author. The book was published in 1975, and as I write we are working on the fifth edition. Berliner was to become a good personal friend, whose temperament, intellectual orientation, and values were extraordinarily compatible with mine. When I think of the haphazard way in which I conducted this bit of personnel selection, I am again struck with the importance of luck in human relationships.

By 1971 Barak V. Rosenshine was able to locate and review about 100 process-product studies, that is, studies of the relationship between teaching practices and student achievement and attitudes. By 1974 Michael J. Dunkin and Bruce J. Biddle were able to review and categorize (using a model originated by Mitzel) the results of several hundred studies of teaching, both process-product studies and other kinds, many of which were fairly recent.

In 1974 I was invited to Washington, D.C., for eight months by Garry L. McDaniels of the National Institute of Education to plan the ten-panel structure (with 110 participants) of the week-long NIE Conference on Studies in Teaching. The Dunkin-Biddle book helped to broaden my conception of the field in planning that conference.

The conference had some noteworthy outcomes. It led to increased use of two previously underemphasized approaches to research on teaching: studies of teachers' thinking, a concern originally suggested for the conference by Lee S. Shulman, who chaired the panel on teaching as clinical information processing; and qualitative studies of teaching as a linguistic process in a cultural setting, the focus of a panel chaired by Courtney B. Cazden.

During the 1970s and 1980s, the pace of these and other kinds of research on teaching increased; and the studies reached new levels of sophistication. Process-product studies flourished under Jere E. Brophy, Carolyn Evertson, Thomas L. Good, and Jane Stallings, among others. Teachers' thinking received creative attention from such investigators as Christopher M. Clark, Penelope Peterson, Richard J. Shavelson, and Robert J. Yinger. Anthropological, including ethnographic and sociolinguistic, studies of classroom cultures began to appear in greater numbers. More of these kinds of studies also began to be done in Australia, Belgium, Britain, Canada, Finland, Germany, the Netherlands, Sweden, and other countries. The International Association for the Evaluation of Educational Achievement (IEA) organized an international Classroom Environment Study, which was carried out, beginning in 1979, in eight countries. The study was reported by Lorin W. Anderson, Doris W. Ryan, and Bernard J. Shapiro in 1989.

Interest in research on teaching grew rapidly enough to lead in 1984 to the formation of a new division of the AERA: Division K on Teaching and Teacher Education, whose membership quickly exceeded 3,000. Two encyclopedias, the AERA's 1981 *Encyclopedia of Educational Research*, edited by Mitzel, and the 1984 *International Encyclopedia of Education: Research and Studies*, edited by Torsten Husén and T. Neville Postlethwaite, devoted far more attention than previous encyclopedias to research on teaching. The *International Encyclopedia's* material on teaching and teacher education was extended and published separately in 1987 in a one-volume *International Encyclopedia of Teaching and Teacher Education*, edited by Dunkin. This volume, and the AERA's 1973 and 1986 *Handbooks of Research on Teaching*, edited by Robert M.W. Travers and Merlin C. Wittrock, respectively, constitute the most comprehensive treatments of the field and epitomize much of the progress during the past three decades.

During the 1980s, the field of process-product research came under heavy criticism. Margaret Needels and I collated and reviewed these criticisms in 1989; among other things, we were able to review some 15 field experiments that demonstrated fairly convincingly the causal efficacy of research-based teaching practices in improving student achievement, attitude, and conduct. Also, a much more adequate appraisal of the overall yield of the research became possible with the advent of meta-analysis (the quantitative synthesis of research results across replications) as originated by Gene V. Glass in 1976. Herbert J. Walberg, in the 1986 *Handbook of Research on Teaching*, and others applied meta-analysis to research on teaching and showed that many previously derogated sets of results actually add up to significant and substantial findings with important implications for the theory and practice of teaching.

The 1980s saw increased attention to the application of research on teaching in the preservice and inservice education of teachers. Some writers considered process-product research, for example, to imply a technological rather than a reflective orientation to teacher education. Berliner and I took pains in 1989 to correct this misapprehension; we said that, when teachers consider the implications of research on teaching for practice, they should engage in critical, practical, and artistic thinking, rather than follow those implications unthinkingly.

Other educators have concerned themselves with the sheer amount of use of the research on teaching. Many believed the research was resting on library shelves rather than entering into the curriculum of teacher education and the practice of teaching. Some reports suggest that concepts and findings from research on teaching have already become important parts of the teacher education curriculum. But evidence of its effects on the practice of teaching seems insufficient to permit more than a surmise. Nonetheless, it is clear in the 1989 Gage-Needels review of criticisms that most of the teachers involved in the 15 field experiments were able and willing to use research-supported teaching practices once those practices were explained and justified. And the teachers' use of those practices over a semester or a school year did enhance student achievement, attitudes, and conduct.

Whither

Nowadays, we hear many voices on ways to improve teaching. The nation does not lack for eloquent and persuasive purveyors of such ideas. But we still have an inadequate way of assessing proposed improvements. In pharmacology, agronomy, engine design, and surgery, the proponent of a new practice or product is ready to meet a demand for empirical evidence of effectiveness. In those fields, it is routine to try out a new idea as carefully as possible and collect valid evidence of its effectiveness before expecting it to be adopted by practitioners. Regrettably, the same kind of assessment does not seem to characterize teaching — as was indicated in 1989 by Robert E. Slavin's account of the widespread adoption of new teaching practices that were not accompanied by research-based evidence and were supported mainly by the charisma and salesmanship of their proponents.

The empirical evaluation of educational practices has become a complex, subtle, and artistic discipline, heavily involved with measurement, statistics, sociology, anthropology, cognitive and social psychology, economics, politics, connoisseurship, and philosophy. But too few teachers and administrators have learned to insist on rigorous evaluative evidence before they install new practices. I expect education to see consequential improvements in teaching only as we learn to require evidence from research on teaching, just as we now demand evidence on the effectiveness and safety of new medical treatments.

The nation now receives reports from the National Assessment of Educational Progress (NAEP) on the achievement of its elementary and secondary school students. The reports show what students have achieved in major areas of the curriculum: reading and writing, mathematics, science, U.S. history and civics, and geography. (In a 1990 report on NAEP's findings over the preceding two decades, Emerson J. Elliott characterized the changes in achievement as "only modest . . . only rudimentary . . . stagnant.") These evaluations of our children's achievements come from applications of curriculum analysis, educational measurement, sampling theory, and statistical analysis. They provide an altogether estimable portrayal of the product, by way of knowledge and intellectual skills, of our educational system.

What I see as lacking is a comparably detailed and rigorous portrayal of the teaching and learning processes that go on in our classrooms. The NAEP reports do give us a picture of some of the educational practices in our classrooms, as obtained from questionnaires filled out by students, teachers, and principals. The resulting information tells us such things as the amounts and kinds of reading students do for homework and in school, how much they discuss their reading and writing, how often and how much students write, how much time teachers spend on writing instruction and assistance, and the availability of and enrollment in science and mathematics courses.

But we need additional evidence produced by what might be called a National Description of Classroom Processes (NDCP). An NDCP would use trained observers in classrooms and carefully analyzed videotapes to obtain a comprehensive and detailed portrayal of teaching practices, learning activities, and teacher-student interactions. It would also use trained interviewers to elicit from teachers and students the beliefs, the implicit theories of teaching and learning, and the conceptions of their subjects that can be hypothesized to affect teaching and learning in our classrooms. Such observations and interviews in carefully drawn representative samples of the nation's classrooms, when added to what is now obtained with questionnaires, would tell us much of what we ought to know about the significant events that bear upon what our students learn. And, of course, with proper planning, the findings from NAEP could be correlated with those from NDCP to help us learn more about the connections between what teachers do and what students learn. (Andrew C. Porter's article, "Creating a System of School Process Indicators," in the Spring 1991 issue of *Educational Evaluation and Policy Analysis*, greatly advances what I have in mind.) If, as some believe, such classroom observation would be too threatening to teachers if it were done by the federal or state governments, it should be done by privately financed enterprises.

Where will teaching and research on teaching go in the years ahead? Prediction is hazardous, but I can say what I see as possible and desirable. It is commonplace to say that teaching should become more professionalized. The low status of teaching, reflected in its low pay and its difficulty in attracting and retaining the academically able, should come to an end. What is not so widely understood is that the improved professionalization will come only when teachers have a better body of theory and knowledge based on research concerning the relative benefits and costs of alternative ways of going about their tasks. The body of theory and knowledge will need to become more similar − in its validity, depth, complexity, coherence, and relevance to practice − to those that give other professions their standing.

It may turn out that the "anti-naturalists" − those who hold that science of the kind that has been built for the natural world cannot be built in the realm of human affairs − are right. If so, the ensuing years will see no increase in any cumulative body of knowledge and theory. Even in that event, however, much of scientific method can still prove to be powerful in applying reason to the evaluation of alternatives in educational policy and practice, including teaching.

185

The trends in educational research between the 1950s and the 1990s will continue. The quantitative change is, of course, enormous. The increase in AERA membership has been tenfold, and the number of its publications and program events has increased correspondingly. Whereas AERA meetings were once held in three moderately large rooms, they now fill large convention centers.

But it is in the depth and variety of educational research that the two decades truly differ. In the 1950s, the three roomsful of AERA members were occupied with administration, curriculum, and measurement and statistics. In the 1990s, these three old subjects are still important, of course; but we now also have philosophers of curriculum and the social sciences, historians, anthropologists, sociologists, economists, and political scientists — in addition to the educational psychologists who have always contributed. If knowledge, theory, and reason can help with educational problems, the chances of our seeing improvement in education must surely be increasing.

Yet we are also more aware of education's embeddedness in politics and of what that means for actualizing what reason tells us is desirable. Just as medicine and public health could do a vastly better job of improving our well-being from our prenatal days to old age if only the right political decisions were made, so could education mitigate our malignant social-class, ethnic, and gender inequities if only the political powers would heed what we offer.

One small example: As a lifelong Democrat, I was chagrined that it was a Republican administration that in 1986 produced *What Works*, which brought together research-based ideas for improving education and carried the imprimatur of President Ronald Reagan and his Secretary of Education. Whatever its inadequacies, this first brave attempt at truly widespread and accessible dissemination of educational research findings should be applauded. We need even better efforts to show the world what it has gotten in return for its support of educational research.

As I write this in the autumn of 1990, the prospects of improved support of educational research are slightly better. Deficit-reduction, higher taxes, budget-cutting, and the Middle East properly preoccupy the President and Congress. And, hypnotized by the upward creep of the Asian and European shares of American markets, our business leaders seem unable to shift their gaze from this year's bottom line to that of the decades ahead, when today's children will take over our economy. But what it takes by way of research to improve our ways of educating preschoolers, preventing adolescents from dropping out of high school, helping teachers be more effective, and capitalizing on the varied strengths of all students, especially the gifted, is increasingly being recognized as well worth its cost. Let us hope the President, the Congress, and the state governors and legislators will see it that way.

Reflections on Schools: Tidying the Mind in an Untidy World

BY JOHN I. GOODLAD

Writing reflections on one's own career presents some rather disquieting problems. The first is the difficulty of standing back in order to get a perspective on activities that have engaged one's attention, somewhat akin to standing on the shore in order to observe oneself paddling a canoe in the moonlight. Then, there are the invariable distortions resulting from one's selective memory of past events. (I always marvel at the seeming clarity of memory and insight of all those, young and old, who write their memoirs.) Finally, there is the inescapable tedium of turning to one's own published work for some possible verification of how one viewed the world — in my case, the world of schooling — at various points in time. For this aspect of my narcissism, I apologize in advance.

In seeking perspective on this exercise in introspection, I found myself recalling how a student described John Dewey's classroom behavior: At the end of a rather long, dull lecture during which he often gazed out the window but seldom at his audience, Dewey concluded, "Thank you, ladies and gentlemen, I think I am a little clearer on these matters now." On concluding this essay, I also hope to be clearer on some matters.

My reflections here are on schools — on understanding them in order to improve them. It is a given, I believe, that one must have considerable understanding of something in order to improve it, whether one has in mind diesel engines, gardens, or schools. And for those seeking to study schools and the practices that go on there, I recommend messing around in them — a great deal.

John I. Goodlad is Professor and Director of the the Center for Educational Renewal in the College of Education at the University of Washington.

Dewey addresses this issue in *The Sources of a Science of Education*, where he sets a higher test of value for educational research than whether it adds to the understanding of the researcher or satisfies scientific principles:

> [E]ducational practices provide the data, the subject-matter, which form the *problems* of inquiry. . . . [T]hese educational practices are also the final *test of value* of all researches. To suppose that scientific findings decide the value of educational undertakings is to reverse the real case. Actual activities in *educating* test the worth of scientific results. They may be scientific in some other field, but not in education until they serve educational purposes, and whether they really serve or not can be found out only in practice. The latter comes first and last; it is the beginning and the close. . . . The position of scientific conclusions is intermediate and auxiliary.[1]

More recently, Elliot Eisner put forward essentially the same argument: educational research must inform educational practice. Such research, he argues, requires the construction of our own unique conceptual apparatus and research methods. "The best way I know of for doing this," he writes, "is to become familiar with the richness and uniqueness of educational life."[2]

My formative learnings about schools were derived from teaching in them. In a one-room school, where classroom and school were virtually one, I became painfully aware of the relentless intrusion of the norms of schooling into classroom life: the requirement of teaching each subject to each grade, which directed me to prepare and teach 56 lessons a day (an average of seven subjects with each of eight grades); the expectation that the several pupils at each grade level would be marked according to a normal curve; and the pass/fail system that already had resulted in Ernie spending seven years in the first grade.[3]

I carried into my next assignment as teacher/principal of a small elementary school a resolve to change what I later learned to be fearsome regulations of schooling. "We must do something about them," I said to my colleagues. More experienced with the ways of schooling than I, they were monumentally disinterested. I began to realize then, as our recent research has confirmed,[4] that interest in educational improvement on the part of most teachers extends very little beyond their own classroom. More often than not, where principals want to begin and where teachers want to begin to effect change are quite far apart. My mind tidied up a little; I realized that if a principal wants to get anywhere with school renewal, he or she must begin with teachers' perceptions of how the regularities of the school impinge on those of the classroom.

Bruised but undaunted, I moved to a setting where the consequences of schools' inadequacies were crowded together in small space. As Director of Education at the Provincial Industrial School for Boys in British Columbia, I endeavored to kindle some spark of academic learning in boys up to the age of 18 who had been committed by the courts. Most had repeated grades at least twice; by the sixth grade the average level of retardation exceeded two full grades. Immersion in this setting for four years, teaching each morning in essentially a one-room elementary school and each afternoon in a one-room secondary school, was a maturing experience. Mark Hopkins on one end of a log and a pupil on the other is a folksy image that does nothing to tidy up one's mind regarding schools.

My greatest problem with the students was their initial lack of confidence in my ability to teach them anything and their deep distrust of the schooling enterprise. Their records showed that they had been, with few exceptions, at the periphery of classroom life and had paid the price of isolation and negative recognition by repeated failure. The considerable success we had together of getting back on a track of academic progress was attributable largely, I now believe, to the fact that they were in this special setting, where they were the center of classroom life. But I was too much a part of the pond to perceive more than a little of its ecology, let alone to explain it.

Later, I encountered Dewey's advice to students of educational phenomena (which I paraphrase here): Immerse yourself in the phenomena and then retire from them in order to reflect on their meaning. This is a luxury not easily attained by the practitioner. Reflective luxury for me came during one of these early years in my career, when once a week I would make a long trip to the University of British Columbia, where I was enrolled in a course on criminology. It provided the basis for what came to be a master's thesis inquiring into certain characteristics of my incarcerated students. The inquiry strengthened my growing belief that there is much more to be learned about the human condition than can be acquired by studying individuals.

The quintessential luxury came a little later, at the University of Chicago. Since I never before had been in full-time attendance at a college or university, the headiness of the library in Judd Hall, my own designated study desk, the two-week reading period without classes near the end of each quarter, the coffee klatches in the commons rooms, and more, were overpowering. There I discovered Dewey and Thorndike, Whitehead and Hull, with whom my previous encounters had been only in snippets of required reading. And, of course, just down the hall, upstairs, or across the midway were Bruno Bettelheim, Benjamin Bloom, Guy Buswell, Chester Harris, Harold Dunkel, Kenneth Rehage, Cyril Houle, Maurice Hartung, Herman Richey, Joseph Schwab, Newton Edwards, Robert Havighurst, Virgil Herrick, William S. Gray, Lee J. Cronbach, Claude Reavis, Mandel Sherman, Ralph Tyler, and more. What a feast for the mind! Yes, a disparate lot; yet they had a common mission — tidying the mind.

But it was not they who directed me to what I most wanted to understand and, indeed, change. It was the eight years of immersion in the stuff of educational practice in those Canadian schools. My doctoral thesis became a study of some of the effects of promotion and nonpromotion, a practice of schooling that confounded my life as a teacher in a one-room school, as a principal, and when working with students for whom rejection and nonpromotion had been part and parcel of schooling. The methodology addressed the individual as the unit of selection, but the understandings I intuitively sought were of a larger ecology.

Fortune smiled. Over the next quarter-century I was deeply immersed in three projects that profoundly shaped my study and understanding of school ecology. They were the Atlanta Area Teacher Education Service, the Englewood Project, and the Study of Educational Change and School Improvement. The third of these was accompanied by inquiry deliberately designed to recognize the untidiness of such human enterprises as schools from the perspective of researchers preoccupied and transfixed by the compulsion to be a camera that stops the world and holds still what is captured through the lens. My colleagues and I decided that there is no way of tidying up the world of schooling and simultaneously understanding it. One seeks, instead, to tidy up the mind as best one can through listening, looking, and reflecting. Because of this mind cleaning, we were able to shape a study of schooling in the late 1970s, which many have told us helped them to understand a place called school and some of what is required for it to be a better place for young people to spend so many formative years.

The Atlanta Area Teacher Education Service

My brief period of luxurious mental "idling" (to use Mortimer Adler's evocative word) at the University of Chicago was followed by seven years that uniquely embraced the norms of both academe and educational practice in schools. The Atlanta Area Teacher Education Service (AATES), an unprecedented collaboration of six school districts and six colleges and universities, had been founded soon after World War II for purposes of upgrading the academic and instructional qualifications of a fast-growing teaching force. The individual, then, was the unit of selection for educational improvement.

I have documented elsewhere the rich personal learnings derived from these years of part-time association with the AATES.[5] High among them was the genesis of belief in the principle — as the scientist accepts a hypothesis as a principle in the pursuit of evidence[6] — of the individual school as the center of educational improvement. The shaping of this hypothesis into a principle was heavily influenced by experience in the child-study program of the AATES.

Daniel Prescott's child-study program, begun at the University of Chicago in the late 1940s, subsequently flourished at the University of Maryland and became a nationwide movement during the 1950s. A teacher studied one child for an entire year and then a child and children in an expanding social context for two additional years. The coordinator of the AATES version of the child-study program and I introduced a fourth year, during which the three-year veterans of the program were to examine the implications of what they had learned for their teaching. Instead, they persisted in focusing relentlessly on school regularities that restrained them from doing what they now wanted to do.

By this time, huge numbers of teachers had acquired bachelor's or master's degrees through the AATES and, it appeared to me, had disappeared without a trace into the grey haze of schooling. Then, some countervailing schools came to my attention. These schools shared something in common: the principal and several teachers had come through the entire AATES child-study program as a cohort group. When those teachers enrolled in the fourth year of the program discussed their frustrations, both the principal and a team of teachers from each of these schools participated in the dialogue — and apparently continued the dialogue in their home schools — and then acted on the basis of these discussions. By the mid-1950s these schools had become recognized as places where "things were happening" and were, more than most, centers of considerable inquiry.

The principals, too, had several things in common. They had deviated from the standard pattern of administrator inservice training by enrolling in what was designed primarily to be a program for

192

teachers. Closely related, they apparently perceived advantages to be obtained for their schools and for their roles as principals by joining a cohort group of their own teacher colleagues. In effect, they were leaders closely tied to the instructional programs of their schools and cognizant of their leadership role with teachers and students. Shades of the effective school characteristics so much lauded in recent years! To the concept of the school as the center of change I added to my learning that of the principal as catalyst for change. Thus I concluded: key setting and key person are the basis for educational improvement.

The Englewood Project

Bureaucratic intrusions, more than teachers' professional beliefs, determine the context of teaching in schools. In *Contradictions of Control*, Linda McNeil has nicely documented the bureaucratic influences on the daily lives of teachers.[7] When one takes the school as the center of improvement, whether as a researcher seeking understanding or as a change agent bent on reform, one inevitably becomes entwined with these bureaucratic influences and their consequences. The encounters take many forms, and I experienced a fascinating array of them, beginning in the first half of the 1950s and extending into the 1960s, with the Englewood School in Sarasota County, Florida.

During these years, I held appointments successively at Emory University, the University of Chicago, and UCLA and served as director of what came to be known as the Englewood Project. My teacher colleagues in the school and I designed a flexible-space classroom facility adjacent to the original egg-crate building, created what some students of the so-called continuous progress plan believe to be the first fully nongraded and team-taught school in the United States, and fashioned a curriculum based on our values and beliefs about learners and learning.

It was during these years that the hypothesis of the school as the center of inquiry and change hardened into a principle for me. This evolution represented a paradigm shift and reflected, I believe, Joseph Schwab's notions of long-term, fluid inquiry as differentiated from short-term inquiry. Both are necessary. But the former is risky. Not only does it involve delayed, personal gratification but it "calls for the political-rhetorical-scientific hard work of obtaining acceptance of a new conceptual scheme by one's fellow scientists."[8] Although increasingly many professors of education express interest in messing around reflectively in schools, they are more concerned about getting out of the process the kinds of publications likely to be approved by their colleagues, many of whom respond in their research to quite different drumbeats.

Ironies and paradoxes abound. There would appear to be enough countervailing evidence to allay fears. Some of our most respected colleagues have taken such risks (probably with little or no reflection on the prospect of unhappy consequences) and enjoy professorships in prestigious universities. Some who come to mind are Seymour Sarason, Dan Lortie, Philip Jackson, Larry Cuban, Elliot Eisner, and Sarah Lawrence Lightfoot. And Ralph Tyler, early in his distinguished career, broke much new ground in the Eight-Year Study.

Let me inject here a comment designed to correct possible misunderstandings regarding the school as the center of inquiry and improvement. This is not to rule out the importance of renewal by individuals and of individuals as the focus of inquiry. Indeed, in my judgment, the long-term health of our civilization depends more on the adaptation and creativity of individuals than on the institutional bones of our civilization. But it is my belief, supported by the experiences I am describing, that human beings renew in a context, a context in which they find purpose and meaning extending far beyond whatever individual goals of security and happiness they may have set for themselves. These large purposes and meanings create the culture in which individuality finds expression. The Englewood School came to be a renewing school culture in which those attracted to it experienced personal renewal.

Englewood, Florida, in the 1950s, constituted a community of a few hundred families enjoying the semi-isolation of being a few miles off Highway 75 connecting Sarasota, Venice, Fort Myers, and Naples. There were few eating places, no movie house, no spectator sports — just those everlasting joys of nature: beautiful beaches, an abundance of sunshine, and warm gulf water inhabited by large shrimp and an extraordinary variety of fish. It was a wonderful place for indolent living and putting one's brain on hold, but hardly a place conducive to generating professional and personal potential. Nonetheless, almost all of those recruited to be the principal or teachers went on to secure their doctorates and some to achieve substantial regional, national, and even international reputations.

The Study of Educational Change and School Improvement

Begun in 1966, the Study of Educational Change and School Improvement (SECSI) involved 18 schools (The League of Cooperating Schools) in 18 different school districts and the research division of the Institute for Development of Educational Activities (/I/D/E/A/), which I directed throughout its existence. The overall strategy was designed to effect the renewal of schools while tidying up our minds regarding both the process and the nature of healthy, renewing schools. It represented considerable synthesis of previous learnings: 1) the individual school as the center of change; 2) a process of inquiry in each school similar to the one developed in embryonic form with the Englewood School faculty, which was refined in the League Schools as dialogue, decision making, action, and evaluation (DDAE); 3) "alternative drummers," those supportive individuals not connected with the reward and approval system of the districts to which the participating schools belonged; 4) a deliberate networking of the 18 schools, not only for the exchange of ideas among principals and teachers but also to sustain the generation and support of innovative practices likely to be ground-breaking and threatening to the status quo; and 5) a university-connected research and development system designed not only to increase our understanding of the whole but also to provide a flow of data to the schools for corrective feedback in making and evaluating decisions.

Since descriptions, findings, conclusions, and recommendations appear in books and articles written by many of the SECSI participants, I make only a few observations. First, great as my expectations were, I did not fully anticipate the extraordinary power that is unleashed when teachers come to believe that they can do "it," when the likelihood of making mistakes is legitimated, and when they are trusted to accomplish whatever "it" may be.

Next, being part of the network provided for each League School a larger legitimation, which was crucial when the "rate-buster syndrome" began to appear with a vengeance. By sharing with their counterparts in League Schools, principals learned ways to handle such questions as, "How are things on the funny farm?" encountered at meetings in their own districts. What I had not at all anticipated was the discomfort of some superintendents with increasing deviance from standard practice on the part of their League Schools. Many preferred uniform practices throughout their districts. The lesson learned from this is built into the strategy of our present work at the Center for Educational Renewal, which I currently direct at the University of Washington. The superintendents of the school-university partnerships constituting the National Network for Educational Renewal sustained by the center are active participants.

195

Surprising, too, was the difficulty experienced by the principals in seeking to set school improvement agendas. For two years, during which they came together as a group for a full day on the first Monday of each month, nearly all believed that, ultimately, I would tell them what to do. They came into the League wanting to fly but had been in their cages so long that their wings had atrophied. What one must do in such circumstances is move the cages down to ground level so the birds can walk out. Ultimately, "the magic feather principle," with its assurance that "I can do it all by myself," takes over. Interestingly, the teachers came to believe in it first, creating a kind of confidence and self-assurance that some of the principals found threatening to their presumed authority. Changing the norms of schooling is not just difficult; it is threatening to almost everyone in positions of authority.

The most perplexing, yet provocative, learning for me during the six years of this endeavor was the difficulty of getting to bedrock problems of schooling − to changing those most entrenched practices that had plagued me for more than 25 years. We have ample data to support the conclusion that very worthwhile things were accomplished and that the most success was in schools that best refined the process of inquiry we labeled DDAE. Most of the schools became ones where I would have liked our two children to be enrolled. This was largely because the human connections in them were so obviously humane. But such considerations hardly enter at all into public judgments regarding the quality of our schools.

We were getting well into the work described above when the winds that had propelled school reform died down. The "education decade" following the launching of Sputnik was over. It was now a propitious time, it seemed to me, to heed Dewey − to back away from direct involvement with schools in order to tidy up the mind a little more. We should have spent more time writing about our experiences in seeking to effect change in the League Schools, but what we had already written was disappearing into an educational community pummeled on all fronts with the admonition, "get back to the basics." Almost overnight, change and innovation had become dirty words. Evaluation and accountability were in.

Once again, the rhetoric appeared to me to be not only simplistic but misguided. Our "Behind the Classroom Door" study,[9] coinciding in time with a large part of our experience with the League Schools, had convinced me that back to the basics was largely where our schools were. The call for more basics appeared to me to be a

196

prescription likely to exacerbate educational pathology already present in the schools.

As we were finishing up our work with the League of Cooperating Schools, several colleagues encouraged me to pursue this hypothesis. I drafted a memorandum, which became the genesis of A Study of Schooling, and out of this study emerged four books and many papers by colleagues, *A Place Called School*,[10] and a sizable clutch of technical reports and doctoral dissertations. The agenda of necessary school reform emerging from this work is markedly different from that proposed in the back-to-basics rhetoric.

A Study of Schooling began at a time of retreat from educational improvement agendas, especially at the federal level. To my surprise, *A Place Called School*, published a few months after *A Nation at Risk*, became a political document in the heated educational debates then occurring in state capitols. *A Nation at Risk* was in many ways a manifesto regarding state and local responsibility for what the report described as a national crisis. Calvin Frazier aptly described what was happening: "The educational train has returned from the nation's capitol and for the foreseeable future the driving force for educational change is going to be the state."[11]

Although the reform-minded state commissions quoted frequently from *A Place Called School* to support this or that position or purpose, the major messages of the book were ignored, perhaps because they do not lend themselves easily to legislated mandates or quick fixes. How do governors and legislators incorporate into their intentions the proposition that schooling in the United States must be improved school by school through unleashing the human energy residing in each? Chapter Eight, titled "The Same But Different," revealed that the schools we found to be most healthy differed from those we found to be most unhealthy in the ways the people within them related to one another and took care of the school's business. Paul Heckman of our research team, coming at the same data from a somewhat different perspective and heavily influenced by Sarason's work, concluded that the healthiest school cultures were significantly more self-renewing than were those we perceived to be the most unhealthy. This finding appeared to be only moderately correlated with the socioeconomic level of the surrounding community. Correlation with school size was considerably greater and favored the smallest schools.

Although, quite understandably, few of the schools selected to constitute our purposively representative sample were as far along in

197

the renewing process as were those in the League of Cooperating Schools after six years, there were two interesting similarities. First, the features characterizing the healthiest schools in the sample, like those demarcating the League Schools from schools generally, cluster around a rubric I have chosen to call "the human connection." Second, the conditions that generally eluded our efforts to get truly significant breakthroughs with the League Schools and that clustered very close to the means among the schools of our research sample also clustered around a common rubric: namely, curriculum and instruction. There was depressing conformity from school to school regarding the didactics of teaching and the substance and organization of the curriculum — those elements most central to what schools presumably are for.

We are directed once again to that bedrock agenda of school reform shaped by the relentless standardization of schooling that persists with or without endless mandates and passionate exhortations to reform. Messing around in schools has convinced me, however, that these conditions are amenable to change through mutually supportive processes of internal renewal and sensitive intrusions of external stimuli, both conducted in a spirit of rigorous, shared inquiry. But when I find myself becoming crystal clear in my mind regarding such convictions, I conclude that it is time to mess around in schools again.

Footnotes

1. John Dewey, *The Sources of a Science of Education* (New York: Horace Liveright, 1920), pp. 33-34.
2. Elliot Eisner, "Can Educational Research Inform Educational Practice?" *Phi Delta Kappan* 65 (March 1984): 447-52.
3. Ernie's situation is described in some detail in the Introduction of John I. Goodlad and Robert H. Anderson, *The Nongraded Elementary School* (New York: Harcourt Brace, 1959), pp. v-vi.
4. John I. Goodlad, *Teachers for Our Nation's Schools* (San Francisco: Jossey-Bass, 1990).
5. John I. Goodlad, "School-University Partnerships for Educational Renewal: Rationale and Concepts," in *School-University Partnerships in Action*, edited by Kenneth A. Sirotnik and John I. Goodlad (New York: Teachers College Press, 1988), pp. 14-18.
6. James B. Conant, *Two Modes of Thought* (New York: Trident Press, 1964), pp. 30-31.
7. Linda M. McNeil, *Contradictions of Control* (New York: Routledge, 1988).
8. Joseph J. Schwab, "The Structure of the Natural Sciences," in *The Structure of Knowledge and the Curriculum*, edited by G.W. Ford and Lawrence Pugno, (Chicago: Rand McNally, 1964), p. 43.

9. John I. Goodlad, M. Frances Klein, et al., *Behind the Classroom Door* (Worthington, Ohio: Charles A. Jones, 1970).

10. John I. Goodlad, *A Place Called School* (New York: McGraw-Hill, 1984).

11. Calvin M. Frazier, "The 1980s: States Assume Educational Leadership," in *The Ecology of School Renewal. Eighty-Sixth Yearbook of the National Society for the Study of Education, Part I*, edited by John I. Goodlad (Chicago: University of Chicago Press, 1987), p. 108.

The Educational Philosopher's Quest

BY MAXINE GREENE

When I joined the faculty at Teachers College, Columbia University 25 years ago, my experiences in teacher education had been diverse, to say the least. My undergraduate major at Barnard College was in American history with a minor in philosophy; and I had no thought of becoming a teacher. Some years later (with children at home), I enrolled for graduate studies at New York University because it was convenient; and there I finally earned my master's and Ph.D. in philosophy of education.

While doing my course work, I taught history and philosophy of education until the advent of a department chairman who decided I was too "literary" to teach in his field. (Only later did I realize that to him "literary" implied female, soft, and unscholarly.) So I was transferred to the English Department, even though I had never taken a course in literature. While there, I taught everything from composition to introductory English to something called "Educational Values," and one I concocted for myself called "Philosophy and Literature." On occasion, I took to the road and did inservice teaching in the "field," as it were. Sometimes it was educational philosophy; just as often it was something like "Perspectives on World Literature," ranging from the *Bhagavad-Gita* to Virginia Woolf.

At the time I received my Ph.D. in educational philosophy, it was extraordinarily difficult for a woman to find a place in either philosophy or philosophy of education, so I took a position in the English Department at Montclair State College. This propelled me into a year

---

Maxine Greene is Professor of Philosophy and Education and the William F. Russell Professor in the Foundations of Education (Emeritus) at Teachers College, Columbia University.

of self-study, during which I tried to learn enough to teach such texts as the *Iliad*, the Greek tragedies, the Old and New Testaments, *Beowulf*, John Donne's poetry, some of Shakespeare's plays, Wordsworth's poetry, George Eliot's *Middlemarch*, and Herman Melville's *Moby Dick*. This meant delving into the literature of criticism and literary history as much as I could, not to mention learning approaches to the teaching of reading for young undergraduates.

Two years later, when I was appointed to a program in Educational Foundations at Brooklyn College, I was convinced of the significance of imaginative literature when it came to the opening of new teachers' perspectives and their individual pursuits of meaning. I had read the work of the social phenomenologist Alfred Schutz and was struck by what he had to say about the "multiple realities" that were disclosed as one entered different "provinces of meaning"[1] and mastered their cognitive styles. Today, people like anthropologist Clifford Geertz make the point that "thought is spectacularly multiple as product and wondrously singular as process" and talk of how important it is to consider the translation of meanings in different systems of expression[2] — certainly of the first importance in contemporary education. In an earlier period, to suggest that imaginative visions ought to be granted as much integrity as empirical descriptions was to be considered less than scholarly. Clarity, rigor, detachment — these were the primary qualities associated with analytic thinking. It was difficult to venture into realms where accepted measures of validity seemed to be ignored.

I was moved, as I still am, by the importance of Dewey's comment in *Experience and Nature* (one that might elicit more regard today than when it was published in 1925) that "the realm of meanings is wider than that of true-and-false meanings; it is more urgent and more fertile. When the claim of meanings to truth enters in, then truth is indeed preeminent. . . . Poetic meanings, moral meanings, a large part of the goods of life are matters of richness and freedom of meanings, rather than of truth . . ."[3] Not only was this an affirmation of range and multiplicity, it was a call for fullness of experience — always a crucial Deweyan concern.

My interest in the "realm of meanings" in its widest sense certainly intensified my fascination with existential and phenomenological thought, which began in graduate school. Influenced though I was by Dewey's philosophy and, most particularly, by his social concern, I felt something lacking in his work. Perhaps it was lack of concern for ambiguity; perhaps it was the absence of a tragic sense of life.

201

In any case, I found in both the philosophies of Jean-Paul Sartre and Maurice Merleau-Ponty a concern for the centrality of consciousness and the problematic nature of freedom. Their awareness of mortality and paradox affected me, as did their resistance to accepting blandly what is usually taken for granted. Their emphasis on situatedness and vantage point seemed to me to add a dimension to what Dewey had been saying over the years.

Also, it was important to me to pose questions about unwavering reliance on the scientific method, about some of the fearsome uses of science in service to technology, and about the arrogant confidence exhibited with regard to the rational control of behavior. Like many others, I was deeply troubled by the depersonalization in our society, by the effects of bureaucratization and what existentialists called "the crowd."[4] The existential preoccupation with the dangers of objectness and the need for subjective awareness seemed to me to be significant supplements to Dewey's instrumental or pragmatic thinking. It directed attention to presentness and to being in the world.

I arrived at Teachers College when the student protests and the anti-war movements were surging to the surface. As editor of the *Teachers College Record* as well as a professor (for the first several years, of English education), I found it impossible to ignore or belittle what was happening outside the gates of academe. Indeed, much of what was being said by student protesters related closely to existentialism. Not only did it seem to be necessary to be oriented to the concrete, but I was convinced that we had to take human subjectivity into account if we were to understand the actions of civil rights and anti-war protesters. In my thinking, this did not signify a subject/object separation; it simply was that the meanings of the so-called "objective" world are contingent on subjective interpretation, on vantage point, on location. It also meant that official definitions and interpretations were susceptible to challenge and critique by those whose voices had rarely been heard before.

Many of these preoccupations fed into my first book, *The Public School and the Private Vision*.[5] I was dealing with (and still am attending to) a changing American culture as seen from the perspectives of imaginative artists as well as educational reformers. It struck me that there was a dramatic contrast between the righteous and prescriptive optimism of reformers like Horace Mann and Henry Barnard and the tragic vision often presented by our novelists and short story writers. I am thinking of the peculiar doubleness of Nathaniel Hawthorne, the truly dark insight of Herman Melville, also Mark

Twain, Edith Wharton, Stephen Crane, Ernest Hemingway, F. Scott Fitzgerald — they all saw and wrote about the gaps in the American Dream, what Fitzgerald described as the "valley of ashes."[6] Dewey and others had been critical enough of the injustices and cruelties of an industrializing nation; but it was our great writers who enabled readers to see further and, at once, to visualize alternative possibilities.

When literature is introduced into a class on educational history or educational philosophy, students are able to tap the wellsprings of their own experiences as they lend their lives to works of fiction. By doing so, they are likely to pose questions they would not otherwise pose; they are likely to discern what confinement to the discursive would never reveal. Through fiction, voices become audible that heretofore have long been repressed or buried in official history, voices like Melville's Bartleby,[7] or Ralph Ellison's Tod Clifton,[8] or Edith Wharton's Lily Bart.[9] Through literature it becomes possible to look at American history through a variety of lenses with no single perception dominating.

It has struck me that many of the consequences of "revisionist history" involved the consideration of experiences traditionally ignored: those of working people, minority members, newly landed immigrants, and adolescents. Even as I welcomed — and learned from — the new histories and the new sociologies in the Sixties, I was wary enough to take issue with their incipient determinism. I recall in my vice presidential address for AERA's History Division, titled "Identities and Contours," stressing the importance of framework and structure even in quests for emancipation.

In the course of such explorations, I rather belatedly became conscious of the feminist perspective and of the significance of the woman's "voice."[10] What some had described as a somewhat skewed and even "non-cognitive" approach on my part now appeared to me to be peculiarly feminine. If it is true that women are more likely to perceive in terms of relationship, if they are less likely to take a detached, autonomous view of events, then the feminine standpoint allows for more far-ranging vision and becomes the source of a new critique. And over time, despite all the differences of opinion within and around feminism and questions of gender, the importance of women and children in America's social institutions has drawn more attention than ever before. Whether it is their voices in the conversation[11] or the significance of an ethic based on "caring,"[12] it is unthinkable today for solely male definitions to articulate the direction of American public schools.

A concern for the feminine as well as for the interpretive fed into my work in philosophy of education during my presidency of the Philosophy of Education Society in 1967 and, later, into my courses in the philosophy of education and social philosophy at Teachers College. Because my presidency coincided with the protests of the Sixties, I could not avoid the connections between educational philosophy and public policy, anymore than I could ignore the importance of ideology for a philosophical understanding of American schools. Aware of the conflicting ideologies in American education, especially the increasing emphasis on the technocratic and the quantifiable, I tried to open in my classrooms (as I did in my writing) the contests between those primarily interested in training a skilled work force and those committed to personal and social growth. Even today, with the proponents of "empowerment" at odds with the proponents of "economic competitiveness," the problems continue to be as much philosophical as they are sociological and economic. With each position there are differing views of knowing, differing approaches to the nature of the human beings, and profound differences with regard to definitions of what is valuable and moral.

Problems of this sort and others stemming from the Sixties were haunting me in the early Seventies when I wrote *Teacher as Stranger*.[13] The title and theme of the book were suggested by an essay by Alfred Schutz, called "The Stranger."[14] Using the immigrant as one of his analogues, Schutz was interested in the point of view of someone not yet enmeshed in a particular social situation, yet drawn into it. I wanted to suggest that the stranger's vision brought a kind of acuity unlikely to be found in a person whose vision was dulled by familiarity. In effect, I was asking the teacher to take the view of the critical onlooker, someone attentive to inequities, false pieties, groundless promises. Today, I would probably alter that approach by taking seriously Michael Walzer's warning against a radical detachment that motivates so much social criticism.[15] His idea of a "connected critic" now seems more appropriate, using standards "internal to the practices and understanding" of one's own society and at the same time being properly critical.

Now that we understand more than we did about the effects of bureaucracies on teaching, the ease with which one becomes submerged into an organization, and the difficulties involved in standing off and reflecting on one's life situation, the critical orientation seems more important than ever. I am convinced that freedom can be achieved only when one can open a space sufficient for reflecting upon a situation lived with others. Thus I find optimism in the fact that this concern for reflectiveness is currently finding expression in the emergent interest in teacher research in the classroom, in journal writing, and the like. These developments are certainly at odds with the common assumption that the teacher is and ought to be a kind of functionary, a clerk without much sense of efficacy.

With my involvement in existential and phenomenological thought and my interest in the development of critical consciousness on the part of teachers, I wanted to enlarge teachers' social vision and to make it a responsible vision. Like Paulo Freire, I was eager to find ways of enabling people to understand and overcome their internalized oppression and to identify the grounds on which persons could come together freely to create a fluid community. If possible, I wanted to reconcile Dewey's notion of the articulate public and the public space with Freirian and existential conceptions of resistance and collaborative change. At once, I was trying to develop a grounded and accessible moral philosophy in the face of what I experienced as an always impinging meaninglessness.

In the 1970s, due to Watergate, the Vietnam War, and other events, there was considerable interest in moral education. As an educational philosopher, I thought a great deal (and spoke a great deal) about what it meant to be ethical in a society whose moral foundations seemed to be slipping. Impressed as I was by Lawrence Kohlberg's cognitively oriented approach to moral education, I had difficulty with its abstractness, its conception of autonomy, its neglect of concrete instances of moral choice. (It took some years before Kohlberg's colleague, Carol Gilligan, enlightened me with regard to the neglect of women's experiences in connectedness and mutuality as a factor in moral development.[16])

My own particular insistence on addressing moral issues in a situated context (often moral issues arising out of social exclusions and other forms of inequity) probably derived from my interest in existential and phenomenological treatments of what it means to be alive and in the world. Writers like Sartre, Merleau-Ponty, Heidegger, and de Beauvoir did not lay out constructive ethical philosophies. However, they did at least move people to realize the importance of responsibility when confronting moral issues. To think existentially about concentration camps, resistance movements, civilian bombing, and violations of the powerless was to recognize at some level the connection between identity and the courage to choose. While sympathetic to Kohlberg's emphasis on principles of justice and human rights, I knew that something more than rational capacity was needed for moral commitments of consequence. Not only did one have to be engaged, concerned, and willing to take responsibility; one had to resist what Albert Camus called "the plague,"[17] defined as indifference, blank resignation, or thoughtlessness.

On occasion at Teachers College, sometimes in the Department of Nursing Education, sometimes in Continuing Education, I taught courses in Health Ethics or Nursing Ethics. Not only did these experiences (and some writing I did in those fields) impress me with the compelling moral/ethical issues in the health field, I came to understand better what was entailed in empowering diverse persons to make ethical choices. Over time I became more and more doubtful about the likelihood of finding any objective ground or reference point, thus exacerbating the difficulties inhering in moral education. When I thought about moral issues in the contexts of health services or schools, it seemed important that health professionals and teachers take action against all bureaucratic structures that eroded their sense of agency. Indeed, it seemed to me that one form of Camus' "plague" might well be exemplified by bureaucracy, which Hannah Arendt once described as "rule by Nobody,"[18] where no one is ready to take responsibility for anything. The very idea of agency, of being personally present to what is happening, became more important to me than ever before, even as did the idea of human consciousness (if it were to be a moral consciousness) being open to the common connectedness in the world.

During the same period, I became deeply engaged with the Lincoln Center Institute for the Arts in Education and remain so to this day. Serving on the staff of the Institute's annual three-week summer programs for public school teachers (sometimes with 1,000 attending), teaching my own class in Aesthetics and Education, and speaking at many campuses on the meanings of aesthetic education, I became increasingly convinced that it had a great deal to do with the critical consciousness I was so eager to see develop in teachers.

Aesthetic education refers to a deliberate effort to nurture an informed awareness and a discriminating appreciation of art forms. As we have worked it out at Lincoln Center Institute and its satellites, the effort demands not only talk about the arts but also genuine participation in aesthetic experiences. Teachers attend workshops led by professional artists — in dance, music, drama, and the visual arts — to learn the "languages" of the various arts. They attend performances and exhibits and, before long, discover that their acquaintance,

206

say, with the language of movement enables them to attend to dance performances quite differently than they would have without their experiences participating with choreographers and performers. When the teachers go back to their schools, artists come and translate into their own idioms plans developed by the teachers. The artists also work with the children to prepare them to attend exhibitions or performances; and the children, like their teachers, find themselves becoming articulate in languages they scarcely knew existed.

My role at the Lincoln Center Institute and other settings has been as "philosopher in residence." Over the years, I have been addressing teachers about the role of imagination, perception, feeling, as well as cognition in bringing works of art to life in human experience. Much influenced by Dewey's *Art as Experience* and by such phenomenological studies as Mikel Dufrenne's *Phenomenology of Aesthetic Experience*, I stress the encounter or the transaction that must take place between a human consciousness and a work of art. The fundamental idea is that a work of art — a canvas hanging on a museum wall, a sequence of movements on a stage, an ordering of gestures and spoken dialogue — is transmuted into what is called an "aesthetic object" by a certain mode of attending to or discharging energy into the work at hand. The Cezanne landscape or the Balanchine pas-de-deux or the scene from *Romeo and Juliet* exists only as a possibility until it becomes an object of someone's live experience, or until it is grasped by an attending consciousness. I find this relationship between subject and object (the person attending and the work on the wall or the stage) something analogous to the kinds of confrontation with subject matter I want to make possible. Not only is there a conception of the ways works of art *ought* to be attended to, there is an emphasis on the interpretive action of the one attending. Also, because the works, whatever they are, emerge from social contexts at particular moments of history, and because the person attending is a member of some existing (and developing) community, the learning that takes place becomes a type of participant learning by someone who is a potential member of a community existing over time.

As the critical theorists make so very clear, this kind of membership requires a particular kind of reflectiveness and critical understanding of the mystifications and commodifications that characterize a consumerist society like our own.[19] In my teaching I want to release students to use their imaginations, to look at things as if they could be otherwise; and I am convinced that the arts provide the richest opportunities for this to happen. At once, I want to empower persons to make intelligent judgments, to choose themselves against what is often a mystifying enterprise.

In my Social Philosophy as well as my Aesthetics courses, I try hard to provoke my students to engage in the kind of reflectiveness that will allow them to understand the impact of ideologies, stereotypes, and illusions on their consciousness. In a time so dominated by media, this takes on special relevance for education, as it does for the arts and humanities. Linked to this is my encouragement of interpretive or hermeneutic approaches to texts as well as art forms — readings from lived vantage points, "namings" from actual locations in the world. Eager as I have been to affirm and reaffirm the need for a strong liberal arts background for teachers, I have always wanted to infuse that background with the capacity to interpret authentically and always with a critical attentiveness to prevailing norms. I take seriously Paulo Freire's reminder that education for liberation is cognitive education;[20] but, for me, it has always appeared necessary to conduct cognitive education with reflectiveness, so as to avoid any form of new hegemony.

Over the years, I have spoken on various themes that concerned me, popular or not: the problem of meaninglessness; student rebellion; civil rights and the matter of "invisibility"; moral choosing and "wide-awakeness"; curriculum issues; the articulateness (or inarticulateness) of the public; educational standards; and, always, the arts, with a special concern for literature. In the early 1980s I was both surprised and honored to be nominated for, and later elected to, the presidency of the American Educational Research Association. Yes, I had been president of the Philosophy of Education Society and the American Educational Studies Association; but AERA meant a different sort of challenge. For one thing, I had always separated myself from the empiricists and the positivists who dominated the organization, even as I admired much of their work. For another, I never considered myself part of the educational research community. Also, it was the time of the Reagan Administration and a feared domination by the Right. All that I valued when it came to educational reform and remediation (including the widening of opportunities for women and minorities) was being attacked or cut away; and there was something overwhelming about the thought of testifying before unfriendly committees, making pleas that would go unanswered, writing reports that would remain unread. I accepted the nomination, of course, in part because I was the first woman to be nominated in 31 years, in part because they had never had a humanities nominee before, and because I was amused by the AERA membership electing an existentialist without quite realizing it.

The three years of close involvement (as president-elect, president, and past-president) were enormously instructive. I learned to respect a great many colleagues who spent their professional lives in research institutes with minimal experience with the reality of schools. I met a surprising number of people who had been working for equal opportunity for years, others who brought remarkable insight into the politics of education, and still others very open to interdisciplinary thinking and a more multiplex approach to literacy. Of course, there were thin-lipped technicists and soft-money specialists; but the meetings of the Council of AERA, the work with the staff, and even the contacts with federal officials and congressional committees gave me, I believe, insights into the workings of education in its larger contexts unlike any I had had before.

I realize now when I scan my *Landscapes of Learning*, a collection of essays published before my time with AERA, I would not have eliminated the essays on the humanities, on ethics, on reflective teaching, or on feminism; but I might well have included an essay on the larger socio-political world of education, something I came to know and write about in my years with AERA.

Through it all, of course, I was interested in and concerned about what Dewey described, in *The Public and Its Problems*, as "the eclipse of the public." As a matter of fact, we made the "opening of public spaces" one of the major themes of our annual AERA meeting during my presidency. My presidential address was titled "Public Education and the Public Space"; and we had more than a few panels and papers on public policy, human rights in the public space, education and community, and so on. And, given my predilections, we also had a kind of convention within a convention devoted to the arts, including a production of David Mamet's one-act play, *Duck Variations*. There is no way of determining whether any of this had a lasting effect. Most likely it did not, since every presidential term is in one sense shaped by the major interests of the individual concerned and in another by her or his response to the demands of the historic moment. What can be said (and all this has been largely due to changes in the world around) is that there has been far more hospitality to qualitative research and to critical theory in recent years, and that far more women have served on the AERA Council. In fact, AERA is about to have its third woman president in a decade. I would like to think that these changes are positive straws in the wind.

In 1988 my John Dewey Lecture was published under the title, *The Dialectic of Freedom*. It most clearly integrates my interests in literature, politics, philosophy, feminism, art, imagination, and critique. I continue to speak in many places about the arts and humanities (for example, at a conference organized by the Organization for Economic and Cultural Development in Paris), on morals and ethics (as in the Kohlberg Lecture at the Moral Education Association's annual conference), on art education (as at the National Art Education Association's convention), on peace issues and women's issues (as in New Zealand during a recent Fulbright lectureship), and on such issues as post-modernism, pluralism, cultural literacy, and technology and the arts.

In many ways the foregoing list suggests what I believe to be the major themes in the educational conversation today. For example, to speak of post-modernism is to refer to the collapse of traditional rational frameworks in which all conflicts in belief could presumably be resolved. It is to expose the encompassing master stories or "meta-narratives" that purported to incorporate and explicate all sorts of random events: the idea of progress, for instance; what was called the "Enlightenment Project," with its stress on reason and order and control; aspects of the Eurocentric tradition, with its enthroning of Western male authority. In the history of literature, the meta-narrative can be found inhering in the Christian myth that articulated the modernist poet T.S. Eliot's many works, or the "Vision" that unified W.B. Yeats' work. As much as anyone, Toni Morrison dramatized the damage a master story can do in *The Bluest Eye*. She wrote of the destructiveness of the basal readers' "Dick and Jane" and of the meta-narrative focused on a blue-eyed Shirley Temple as a totality of acceptable human reality. "Let us wage war on totality," wrote Jean-Francois Lyotard,[21] a statement that is certainly one of the guideposts of post-modernism. Post-modernism requires, too, that sharp-edged questions be posed with regard to ideas like consensus on social visions for reform and transformation, with attention focused on the dispersal of power, as well as on the connections between power and knowledge, power and discourse.[22] Interested in diversity and multifariousness, if not relativism, post-modernism also calls attention to the newly audible voices sounding on the culture's surface and in its depths.

Necessary as I believe it is to maintain touch with these insights and to test them out in educational dialogues, I still continue to search for some viable consensus, some shared vision of a common world.

Significant though it may be to speak of language games and what Mikhail Bakhtin describes as "heteroglossia,"[23] it is also necessary to discover some new coherence in the affirmation of educational purposes. What with the surge in immigration from many countries not previously represented in the United States and with the new (and understandable) assertiveness on the part of numerous minority groups, the problems associated with pluralism and cultural diversity are going to confront American educators with increasing urgency. We are going to have to acquaint ourselves with a great range of background stories, as well as with the arts and humanities of many nations and cultures. Acknowledging the multiplicity of perspectives, making it possible for different kinds of persons to come together "in speech and action," to bring into being an "in-between" and, in time, a public sphere,[24] we need to provide occasions for dialogue and for open conversation. At once, we have to do more than we have ever done to enable the young to think for themselves and choose for themselves, especially as curricula become more and more inclusive. And somehow the young have to be empowered to teach themselves. I recall the Lady in Brown in Ntozake Shange's choreodrama remembering how she ran into the Adult Reading Room in the St. Louis Public Library, the room where at last she found her own "reality."[25]

If I had time left to me, I would want to do much more to release students to move beyond in that fashion, to reach beyond themselves, to find their own "reality." I believe, however, that there are dark days ahead, due to the financial plight of schools and the draining of so many billions of dollars for military ends. As before, we face the stark alternatives of using diminishing resources for technology and military machines or for committing ourselves to education for democratic citizenship, for wide-awakeness, for art experiences, and for growth. There are two streams running side by side: the stream of collaboration, teacher research, whole language, aesthetic education; and the stream of computerization, technicalization, measurement, control. In some manner, we will have to find a way of uniting those streams in the interests of limited growth and a new humane ecology. It still seems to me that we cannot avoid the call of community in this country, the demands of a democracy always in the making. There are spaces still to open; there are voices still to be heard. The faith in public education may be an absurd faith; but it sustains our vocation, which has to do with human reality — and with keeping it vivid, wise, and free.

211

Footnotes

1. A. Schutz, "On Multiple Realities," in *Collected Papers, I: The Problem of Social Reality* (The Hague: Martinus Nijhoff, 1967), pp. 207-14.

2. C. Geertz, *Local Knowledge* (New York: Basic Books, 1983), p. 151.

3. J. Dewey, *Experience and Nature* (New York: Dover, 1958), pp. 410-11.

4. S. Kierkegaard, "The Individual," in *The Point of View for My Work as an Author* (New York: Harper Torchbooks, 1962), pp. 109-20.

5. M. Greene, *The Public School and the Private Vision* (New York: Random House, 1965).

6. F.S. Fitzgerald, *The Great Gatsby* (Philadelphia: Franklin Library, 1974), p. 22.

7. H. Melville, "Bartleby the Scrivener," in *Billy Budd, Sailor and Other Stories* (New York: Bantam, 1986), pp. 95-130.

8. R. Ellison, *Invisible Man* (New York: New American Library, 1952), p. 379.

9. E. Wharton, *The House of Mirth* (New York: New American Library, 1964).

10. C. Gilligan, *In a Different Voice* (Cambridge, Mass.: Harvard University Press, 1984).

11. J.R. Martin, *Reclaiming a Conversation* (New Haven, Conn.: Yale University Press, 1985).

12. N. Noddings, *Caring* (Berkeley, Calif.: University of California Press, 1984).

13. M. Greene, *Teacher as Stranger* (Belmont, Calif.: Wadsworth, 1973).

14. A. Schutz, "The Stranger," in *Collected Papers, II: Studies in Social Theory* (The Hague: Martinus Nijhoff, 1964).

15. M. Walzer, *Interpretation and Social Criticism* (Cambridge, Mass.: Harvard University Press, 1987), pp. 36-40.

16. C. Gilligan, *In a Different Voice*, op. cit.

17. A. Camus, *The Plague* (New York: Alfred A. Knopf, 1948).

18. H. Arendt, "On Violence," in *Crises of the Republic* (New York: Harcourt Brace Jovanovich, 1972), p. 137.

19. See, e.g., Jurgen Habermas, *Knowledge and Human Interests* (Boston: Beacon Press, 1971).

20. P. Freire, *Pedagogy of the Oppressed* (New York: Herder and Herder, 1970).

21. J-F. Lyotard, "The Postmodern Condition," in *After Philosophy*, edited by K. Baynes, J. Bohman, and T. McCarthy (Cambridge, Mass.: MIT Press, 1987), p. 89.

22. M. Foucault, *Power/Knowledge: Selected Interviews and Other Writings*, edited by C. Gordon (New York: Pantheon, 1980).

23. M. Bakhtin, *The Dialogical Imagination* (Austin, Tex.: University of Texas Press, 1981).

24. H. Arendt, *The Human Condition* (Chicago: University of Chicago Press, 1958), pp. 182ff.

25. N. Shange, *For Colored Girls Who Have Considered Suicide When the Rainbow Is Enuf* (New York: Macmillan, 1977), p. 26.

Reflections on People
and Pedagogy

BY ASA G. HILLIARD, III

Four circumstances of my life during my childhood years in Texas have strongly influenced me as a professional educator. First, I was fortunate to be born into a family of educators. My father, Asa G. Hilliard, II was a high school principal, as was his father, Asa G. Hilliard, I. One of my father's brothers and two of his sisters were teachers. As a result, I was surrounded by educators and talk of education. I might add that they were successful educators; their students thrived even under difficult circumstances.

Second, because I lived in then segregated Texas, I began my formal education in segregated schools, attending them through the fifth grade. The memory of those early experiences is still very fresh in my mind, including the endless discussions by the educators in my family about the injustice and inequities of segregation and the adjustments and adaptations that we had to make in order to survive.

Third, after my parents divorced, my mother and I remained in Texas for a few years; but at the beginning of my sixth grade, we moved to Denver, Colorado, where I attended integrated schools. From that point until the completion of my graduate education, I spent nearly every summer in Texas and the school year in Colorado. This provided me experiences for making an abundance of comparisons revealing the absurdities of segregated education. Merely by crossing the state line, I, the same person, would receive radically different treatment. I paid close attention to these absurdities. Later, I would

---

Asa G. Hilliard, III is the Fuller E. Callaway Professor of Urban Education in the Department of Educational Foundations at Georgia State University.

213

use these experiences as my basis for analyzing equity issues in education as they presented themselves in other parts of the country.

Finally, my family life alternated between poor and moderate income environments. Once again, I, the same person, received quite different treatment depending on the economic status of my family. Thus early on, I was involved in natural "experiments" that started me thinking about equity questions raised by educators and sociologists. In these experiments I myself was a subject, as were those students around me.

Early on, I learned from these experiments that intellect has no correlation with race or economic status. I saw many brilliant classmates derailed simply because of the absence of nurturance from their teachers or from their families, or because they chose inappropriate strategies to cope with the stresses and strains of daily life. Whatever their problems were, they had nothing to do with intellect. Moreover, having been taught by teachers who were black, white, yellow, and brown, I learned that race was not a factor in teaching competence. Luckily, I had numerous excellent African-American teachers, and, through my father, I met dozens of others.

I did not plan to become a teacher. In fact, I had decided it was the one occupation I could rule out. In my second year of college, though, I began to gravitate toward education. I think the fact that both my father and my mother were, in their own ways, social-service oriented had a lot to do with my change of heart. They were concerned with the problems of others and felt an obligation to contribute to the betterment of our people.

I entered teacher education with high hopes, but I was impatient. I had difficulty with what I perceived to be a gap between the real world of teaching and learning and the formal systems being taught in institutions of higher education. I did not feel that the world of students — or the world of teachers, for that matter — was accurately described in classroom lectures or in the literature. I felt that many of the requirements for professional training were more hurdles to overcome than sources of enlightenment or empowerment.

At that time, I could not understand why professionals in education appeared to be so preoccupied with the capacity question. Why were educators and psychologists investing so much time and resources trying to discover, mainly through I.Q. tests, how much mental ability their students had? Enormous resources, then as now, were spent attempting to measure the capacities of students. To me, the magnitude of effort exerted on this question demonstrated a fundamental lack of faith in the capacity of the majority of students to learn. This capacity question takes on even more serious consequences when directed at minority students. It was later that I arrived at what I believed to be an explanation for this preoccupation.

I believe, but have been unable to prove, that the preoccupation with methodology in the training of teachers — to the exclusion of in-depth study in academic subjects — is a way of avoiding a commitment to high-quality education. For example, one would think that there would be a major payoff for a nation that expended so much money and energy in the "scientific" study of methodology; surely we should be number one. While I do believe that the study of methodology is worthy and will yield important benefits for teaching and learning, I remain unconvinced that we have advanced very far in this field. After all, human beings have been teachers for thousands of years. In a crunch, we appear to be able to teach what needs to be taught to virtually all those who need to learn.

It seems to me that there are things that we must do in order to have a science of pedagogy. I have observed that elite private schools and a few elite public schools place high value on depth of academic background for their teachers. These teachers have made a commitment to the academic subjects they teach. That commitment is reflected in how they spend their spare time; they continue to upgrade their knowledge in their chosen field. It seems to me that pedagogical strategies evolve naturally when teachers develop a depth of understanding of their field. Certainly, one is more comfortable with the things one knows well. This comfort allows one to enter into dialogue. And dialogue, of course, is at the root of the learning process.

As professionals, we operate within systems or structures; this is true of all professions. These systems and structures lead us to dispositions that are difficult to change; they tend to have great inertia. Moreover, professional opinion tends to perpetuate existing structures. In America such systems or structures as slavery, segregation, anti-immigration laws, and other forms of societal inequity are part of our legacy. Our schools have not escaped the influence of these structures. A case in point is the I.Q. ideology that undergirds the practice of tracking and other forms of segregated or differentiated services to children.

We speak today of restructuring. In fact, there is abundant activity already under way under the rubric of restructuring. However, it seems that we want to restructure systems without any guiding philosophy. We know that something is wrong; we know that major changes are needed. But we have not been open to restructuring the ideology or belief system that produced the structures in the first place. No real restructuring is possible without first examining the existing belief system. For example, do we have a true commitment to equity in education? Do we believe that excellence in educational outcomes is a priority goal for all our students? The way we answer these questions determines the approach we will take to the whole restructuring question. It determines what is an open and what is a closed issue.

As I read more about the history of education in America, I have come to realize that education of the masses was not a high priority at the time this nation was founded, at least not at the national level. It was many years before the concept of universal public education was accepted. Yet even today the concept of universal public education has not lived up to its promise. America remains a nation with enormous, but untapped, potential. Brilliant minds are rotting in prisons, in the dropout population, and even among the general population in individuals who are working at levels far below their actual potential. Educators and the general public must believe this if we are to marshal the energy and commitment needed to address the problem of fundamental change in the educational structure.

As with students, I believe we also have lowered our expectations for teachers. And just as I believe that there is untapped potential in students and the general population, I also believe that there is a tremendous amount of underdeveloped professional potential in teachers. I believe that the existing teacher force can be transformed into a powerful force for producing excellence in student achievement. In fact, I have seen such transformations take place on a limited basis under the right circumstances. I think it is accurate to say that American teachers have too little self-respect and receive too little respect from the general population. In fact, it is probably more accurate to say there is active disrespect for teaching as a profession. I am convinced that this is a consequence of the nature of our teacher education programs. We have been too timid in our demands for academic excellence among teachers and too lacking in pedagogical strategies for developing that academic excellence. We seldom provide power models of teaching in our teacher education institutions, so we fail teachers in training on both counts. Academic depth and power pedagogy are within reach of the masses of American teachers, provided that we are willing to restructure teacher education.

The capacity question (concern about innate intellectual ability) is still very much with us. Any review of the research priorities of our best and brightest teacher educators will show that much of their activity still centers on the capacity question. Recently this was brought home to me when I attended a seminar for teachers in the Chicago Public Schools. Some 20 teachers had been selected to participate in a seminar taught by the leading professors from one of the prestigious universities in Chicago. The content of the seminar was both professional and academic. The academic reading load required the teachers to read three or four difficult books in a week. During the seminar, the teachers, across the board, demonstrated an in-depth understanding of the reading assignments and were able to hold their own in analytical discussions with their professors. Moreover, they were creative in developing strategies for imparting basic understanding of the high-level concepts to students in the public schools where they taught. Later, I had the opportunity to observe their classrooms where these concepts were being taught. The work was extremely rigorous; and for the first time in a long time, I saw a true respect exhibited for the academic content these public school teachers were presenting as well as respect for the teachers.

Something has to happen now to unhook us from previous conceptions of teaching and learning and the environment within which they take place. The high purposes of democracy and the higher purposes of human fulfillment demand that we create educational systems to serve all the people. The democratic principles manifested in our laws and governance structures must be embedded in belief systems of the total populace. Realization of these democratic principles should be the outcome of an appropriate education and socialization process.

Our nation needs an excellent educational system in order to guarantee its national defense and to provide skilled workers whose productive capacity can exceed unprecedented international competition. More important, however, is that our democratic nation needs education for human and spiritual development, which prepares people for functioning beyond the market place in human communities. That is the true wealth of a nation.

As teachers and teacher educators, we can contribute to this outcome provided we are able to develop a new vision rooted in faith in the potential of people and faith in the power of the pedagogy. If I know anything at all, it is that no pedagogical barriers need stand between human beings and their highest achievements. Wherever we see failed potential, we see failed pedagogy, not because powerful pedagogy is not available, but because political inequities make powerful pedagogy unavailable to the masses. And when pedagogy fails, the masses begin to suffer.

I am delighted that I chose to become a teacher. Looking back, I would not have it any other way. Teaching is a vibrant, energizing profession. Being a part of a learning community and becoming involved in the lives and destinies of learners is something I treasure highly. And I have come to respect deeply those thousands of educators who demonstrate in their daily lives the power to lift the human spirit.

Reflections on
Education and Schooling

BY HAROLD HOWE, II

If someone had asked me 10 years ago to define education, I might have replied, "Education is the process by which schools and colleges equip young people with learning skills, and then help them to use those skills to acquire knowledge and eventually to become independent learners." If I had said that, I now think I would have been wrong.

Education is much more than schooling. Many people have become educated without schooling, and I have never encountered a person who was educated by schooling alone. But too many of us, particularly we educators, have a tendency to forget, or at least to underestimate, the significance of those aspects of education we don't control — the family, the community in all its manifestations, and all the other experiences of a young person's life outside the classroom. Indeed, education goes on throughout life.

None of the above is a surprise to anyone. Tennyson captured the idea neatly in his poem, "Ulysses," which starts with the sentence, "I am a part of all that I have met." Also, Lawrence Cremin, in his multi-volume history of education in America, documents the varied sources of learning beyond schools — sources that are frequently so powerful that they dwarf schooling.

Why, then, belabor this well-known truth? My answer is that the school reform movement in the 1980s has tended to ignore the truth we know so well about the sources of education outside schools. In very large part, school reform makes the assumption that the schools can be fixed, and they in turn can fix children and youth, no matter

---

Harold Howe, II is the Francis Keppel Senior Lecturer Emeritus at the Harvard Graduate School of Education.

219

how seriously these young people are shortchanged by their families and communities. That assumption is erroneous, in my view. Unless schooling can be supported by powerful, positive supports from both family and community, it will continue to be unsuccessful with some proportion of our young people and less successful than it might be with most of them.

The evidence for this assertion comes from three main sources: 1) recent data reflecting major changes in the lives of children and youth, changes having a powerful negative impact on their prospects for a successful passage through childhood and adolescence; 2) the current efforts to make families and communities more effective educational entities; and 3) the record of the school reform movement in underplaying and sometimes ignoring the significance of sources of education beyond the schools. Let's take these points one at a time, and then reflect on the adequacy of our educational efforts in family, community, and schools.

Changes in the Lives of Children and Youth

Most American children and youth have been powerfully influenced in the last 30 years by the steady increase in working mothers — a major economic shift in our society. This has come about for two main reasons. First, the women's movement has encouraged women in the name of equity and women's rights to aspire to all aspects of the world of work. Second, as middle-class families encountered the inflationary pressures of the 1970s and 1980s, they found that the only way they could remain in the middle class was to have two parents working. Parents in poor families worked when they could find jobs, but with little prospect that their work would elevate them from poverty. The growing number of single parents, mostly women, experienced special pressures and either ended up in poverty or found that maintaining a full-time, well-paying job meant compromises with family life.

It is quite clear that these changes result in parents having less time with children. Conscientious parents struggle to provide adequate day care in order to avoid the latchkey alternative, and they try to find ways to make the time they have with their families as meaningful as possible. Some succeed in making their families work well, in spite of the demands a job makes on their time. Others don't. The net result is a new demand for community services to support families, because families can't do all that they once did for children and youth.

Another major economic change is the growth of poverty in America. Poverty has a drastic effect on families, making it more difficult for them to provide the four main elements of a stable family life after the necessities of food and shelter: 1) consistent affection, 2) regular stimulation through participation in family experiences together, 3) strong encouragement as youngsters face difficulties in the community or school, and 4) established and sensible routines for family living. These elements of stable family life have eroded among the growing proportion of children living in poverty in the U.S.A. In 1970, one in seven children could expect to experience poverty during their years through age 18. By 1980, it was one in six. Today it is one in five. By the year 2000, it is expected to be one in four.

Poverty threatens the ability of families to function as families. Some poor families provide the four elements mentioned above; poor parents love their children just as much as do more fortunate parents. But the hazards of poverty put the daily necessities of life at risk. Hunger, lack of medical attention, homelessness, and other accompaniments of poverty make it hard for a poor family to provide consistently for the needs of the young. Half of our single-parent families live in poverty; many are headed by a very young mother who doesn't know how to be an effective parent.

Still another economic change contributing to the growth of poverty has been the decline in well-paying jobs in our manufacturing industries. In effect, these industries went outside the U.S. seeking cheaper labor, some to Mexico and others overseas, especially Asia. These were the jobs that allowed non-college-bound high school graduates to get started with some hope of earning enough income to support a new family. More than two million such jobs have disappeared. Today's high school graduates get the same dead-end jobs without health insurance that dropouts find.

The real wages of heads of young families have dropped by almost 30% in the last 15 years. These families now spend about two-thirds of their income for rental housing and are pinched for food and other necessities. They enlarge the ranks of the working poor in the U.S., and their children suffer many of the same deprivations as families maintained by our inadequate system of Aid for Dependent Children. Its payments, never generous, have been eroded by a failure to keep up with inflation.

Whether family poverty is caused by inadequate government programs, by low wages, by unemployment, or by lack of marketable job skills, its effects on children are the same. They are less likely to receive the care and attention a better-supported family might provide.

Reflecting on all these recent changes in the circumstances affecting families, I have come to two conclusions: 1) Almost all working parents, whatever their economic status, are less able than they once were to be an effective presence in the lives of children and youth. 2) Special hazards creep into the lives of the growing number of children whose families are poor, as they and their parents are confronted by circumstances over which they have little control.

Taken together, the total effect of economic changes in recent years has reduced the ability of families to provide the back-up support children and youth require in order to make steady growth toward maturity. Increasingly lacking in the lives of the young is the elusive element that comes from spending time with adults in a variety of experiences: family picnics, birthday or anniversary celebrations, sing-a-longs at the piano, board games, home renovation projects, even activities in which the young act as mentors for their parents and relatives. An example of the latter is my grandson teaching me to operate a Macintosh computer.

These special relationships, in which young people gain confidence, self-esteem, and the feeling that what they do is respected by older people, are essential for growing up. They were readily available in the 19th century when many families operated farms. In those times children and youth played significant roles in the social and economic life of the family, while simultaneously developing a sense of responsibility. Such experiences are difficult to replicate in today's changing family environment. Families are less able to provide them, and communities struggle to take their place. A few schools have been successful in finding ways to offer learning opportunities with these characteristics. Most others are so busy jamming the answers to test questions into the heads of children that they don't stop to consider the limited usefulness of that process.

James Coleman, a noted sociologist and student of American society and its young people, calls the combination of family and adult influences that children need "social capital." He sees it in short supply on the modern American scene and questions whether we can deliver it given the economic and other pressures on the hectic lives of today's families. If we cannot, we are then stuck with another question: What can be done in our communities to provide the young the social capital that families are increasingly less able to deliver?

In responding to that query we have to consider what families and communities can do on their own and what additional role state and national governments can play. These issues lead to my second topic.

Can Families and Communities Do More for Young People?

The answer to this question is yes. Of course they can, but will they? Nobody knows, but they might. To carry this discussion further, let me present an oversimplified structure for examining both the issues and their potential solutions. The two main issues are related but also separate. They are: 1) the growing gap between adults and their children at all levels of American society; 2) the very special and aggravated problem of increasing poverty and its damaging effects on children and young families. There are also two main strategies, likewise related yet separate: the strategy of local initiatives devised to meet a community's particular needs and the broader strategy of state or national interventions.

The gap between adults and the young is mainly, but not entirely, an issue that might be addressed through efforts that fall under President Bush's happy phrase, "a thousand points of light." Local efforts fashioned to fit local circumstances and using local resources in large part will be dominant in dealing with it. But the fiscal burden of local efforts will grow steadily heavier as the services needed are delivered to groups on the lower rungs of the economic and social ladder. For them to receive meaningful assistance will almost certainly require state funding or federal funding, or both.

Two examples of local efforts are youth community service programs and mentoring programs. Both of these are ways of bringing youth into new contacts with adults; both are efforts to augment the social capital available to the young through community action; both tend to enhance the opportunities families would like to provide if they could; and both are deeply concerned with educating young people in ways that are not always found in schools, yet help to improve school performance. Also, it must be said that both have a certain bandwagon appeal. They are increasingly seen as *solutions* to social problems, rather than as what they almost certainly are — constructive contributions to living with such problems.

Youth service in communities, or more widely in states and even on a national level, has immense appeal. When combined with efforts to improve learning skills and work habits, as well as to inculcate responsible personal conduct, youth service offers a wonderfully balanced menu of constructive adult contact and worthwhile growth

223

experiences. It holds the rich promise of turning anti-social youth into responsible citizens, while also improving communities through the work that they do. There are working models of local and state initiatives for youth corps, and a federal program has been approved by both Congress and the President.

Mentoring is a strategy for helping young people to get control of their lives and to mature by bringing them into regular contact with a caring, volunteer adult. It attracts as much enthusiasm as youth service, maybe more. Although mentoring can serve all types of people, today it is seen mostly as a way to help at-risk children and youth subject to the vicissitudes of poverty or neglect or special family problems. We know much less about mentoring than we know about youth service, but that does not seem to affect its popularity. Mentoring is a component of many school-business partnership programs; and schools sometimes help by arranging mentorships, as do churches and other agencies. There are a variety of experiments with retired persons as mentors. They have the time, and there is evidence that the mentorship relationship also enriches their lives. College students also frequently become mentors for the young and combine the role with that of tutor.

Mentoring is an example of one type of intervention with the potential of adding community leverage to the lives and education of the young. When it is successful, it may be able to bring confidence and self-esteem into young lives that lack them; but whether that will happen is very much a matter of how individual relationships work out. We know that mentoring relationships are difficult to establish, that many of them don't succeed, and that chances of success are greater when mentors receive some form of training. If mentors are to get the training and support they need, the costs of mentoring programs may be much larger than its enthusiasts perceive. Although mentoring and youth service have much to offer, neither is a quick and easy solution to fill the vacuum of adult attention among America's children and youth.

Shifting now to the problems of poverty, which include but add to those of the gap between generations, I would modify my earlier statement about dealing with these problems through local efforts. Poverty among children and young families must be addressed mainly with resources provided by the national and state governments. The "thousand points of light" are not sufficient. Indeed, the idea that local voluntarism can deal effectively with poverty is both a myth and a cruel hoax.

224

To deal with the various effects of poverty, we currently have a mix of strategies at the federal level. The mix includes food stamps, subsidized housing, Medicaid, AFDC (Aid for Dependent Children), and a few other programs, with basic support coming from the federal government but partly conditioned by the willingness and ability of states to match federal funds. Poor states contribute less than rich states; neither states nor the federal government keep up with inflation. For the older poor, the most successful program by far is Social Security; but it does relatively little for children, youth, and young families.

This mix of strategies is supposed to help people in poverty to live decent lives or to become self-sufficient. However, our feelings about poverty keep us from being generous. We tend to blame poverty on the poor and conclude that they should be responsible for finding their way out of it. In a nutshell, we are not willing to mount programs that will come anywhere near providing decent lives for the American poor. We do much less than many other countries.

The Domestic Policy Council of the Bush Administration reviewed the options for a constructive effort on poverty among children in the summer of 1990, and agreed that major social gains were possible. But it decided to do nothing because of the costs and the length of time needed to show any gains. My guess is that this ostrich-like political decision is a reasonably valid measure of the mood of Americans today. We are unlikely to make much progress in terms of new programs until we have a greater awareness of the long-term implications of continuing poverty and a better fix on the moral and social implications of the growing inequities in American society. There is no question but that the rich have been getting richer and the poor poorer and more numerous over the last 10 years. In our cities these trends are moving us toward a loss of civility that is daunting; but so far the main response has been to build more prisons.

In the realm of training people for better jobs, we have a mixed picture. There is real hope in the provisions of the Family Support Act of 1988. If the states move vigorously to do their share, this program can be very productive. That, however, is a very large "if." The Job Training Partnership Act is inadequately funded and can't do the job it promised, although it has useful provisions for a limited number of youth seeking to develop the skills to qualify for good jobs.

The prospect for programs to deal with children of poverty that would be as helpful as Social Security is for older people seems unlikely. Therefore, families, schools, and communities must live with an inadequate and uncoordinated national policy on poverty and do the best they can. Although there is some leadership in Congress for national action on the poverty problem, the odds are against it, as they are for governors who pick up the challenge.

The School Reform Movement and the Broader View of Education

There is no question but that the school reform movement in the U.S. has been vigorous. Even before the National Commission on Excellence in Education sounded its trumpet blast in 1983 with its report, *A Nation at Risk*, there was a growing awareness that the promise of our schools was not being fully realized. Evidence from the National Assessment of Educational Progress showed limited improvement in student achievement; the high school graduation rate, which increased steadily over the past 50 years, leveled off; and college enrollments by minorities dropped a bit in the late 1970s and early 1980s. A business community worried about its need for better-prepared workers was aware of these trends and turned to the schools — first criticizing them and then joining in a variety of school reform efforts. Governors became the leaders of educational change, and the federal government became its cheerleader — providing free advice but not much else.

Throughout the early years of school reform, there was very little interest in the family and community as educative institutions. An exception to this by the mid-1980s was the work of the Committee on Economic Development (CED), an organization supported by corporate interests. It promulgated the idea that unless children come to school ready to learn, they aren't going to learn much — an unarguable proposition. It supported Head Start vigorously and recommended adding funds for the health of mothers and infants and for disadvantaged students. Although the CED did not fully take on the cause of helping families and communities to be the educative institutions they need to be, it did recognize the need for national efforts to alleviate the damaging effects of poverty on children. CED's efforts in this area are in sharp contrast to those of the National Commission on Excellence in Education, which barely mentioned the role of parents, gave no recognition at all to the effects of poverty on children's learning, and in general, assumed the narrow view that *education* and *schooling* are synonymous.

The work of CED in calling attention to the research on the special significance of the early years in children's development was augmented by numerous other studies making the same point. The result has been that school readiness is first on the list of six National Goals of Education announced by President Bush and the National Governors' Association in February 1990. And with it has come some welcome increases in federal funding for several programs serving the early childhood years. But these helpful actions simply do not go far enough to provide the consistent support needed for the offspring of poverty-stricken families. Indeed, these efforts could lead us to a second erroneous assumption: that early interventions will suffice to overcome the effects of poverty. They will help, but counteracting the effects of poverty will almost certainly require special efforts throughout both childhood and adolescence. A strong argument can be made that the costs of such continued preventive interventions are much less than the costs of dealing with the social pathology that poverty helps to create. This argument received strong support from a February 1991 study by CED titled *The Unfinished Agenda: A New Vision for Child Development and Education.*

Many other studies about what was wrong with schools and what to do about them appeared after *A Nation at Risk*. They, too, focused on schooling but tended to ignore the lives of children in families and what changes in the economy were doing to families. When they did bring up the topic of families, they invariably did it in terms of parents and not families. They were strong on the idea of parental cooperation with schools, supporting school objectives at home, and even having parents help run the schools. But they had little or nothing to say about how poverty's grip on families prevents them from carrying out their normal functions, or about how parents' roles have changed radically because they are so busy commuting and working.

Another aspect of school reform in the 1980s that deserves comment here is the frequent comparisons made between achievement of students in Japan and of those in the U.S., and of attributing the differences to the *schools alone*. There is a massive myopia in school reform literature that fails to take into account a key factor when making such comparisons. I am referring here to the key role the Japanese family, particularly the mother, plays in the learning achievement of the Japanese child.

The school reform reports have used such comparisons to build a powerful case for changes only in the schools, when what is required is recognition of the needs of families and communities, as well as schools, in educating children. Education is a culture-based endeavor. The family is at the center of it. There is no way to transplant the Japanese family to the U.S., even if we wanted to do so. But by recognizing the Japanese family as a central component of its education system, we can then begin to consider ways to make American families more effective.

Japan is a society very different from ours. It has experienced no massive waves of immigration as we have; it has negligible cultural minorities. Our society has been built on the immigration of varied cultures over 400 years, a goodly proportion of it under conditions of slavery or peonage − conditions hardly conducive to academic achievement or even to the development of strong families in some instances. To expect schooling alone to overcome these phenomena is naive, a charge to which *A Nation at Risk* is wide open.

In ranging over these issues, I am not saying that school reform is not necessary. It clearly is. But what we do in its name will be conditioned by why we do it. The nature of school reform that will emerge if driven by a desire to beat out other industrialized nations in international economic competition will be very different from the reform that will emerge if the goal is to diminish the inequities in our society and bring its ideals and its reality closer together. In the latter mode, we can align the educational missions of schools, families, and communities into a new vision of America. Training a work force to beat our international competitors during a temporary economic slump is a distorted rationale for guiding our country toward a constructive role in an increasingly interdependent world.

True, the quality of schooling is important and needs attention for the benefit of both our economic system and the overall well-being of our society. But there are some other questions that must be added to school reform agenda: Do we plan to keep as a significant element of our economic system the thousands of low-paying, poverty-level jobs that have been added in recent years? Who will hold these jobs? What will we do for the families involved in them − just keep them in poverty? What will be the commitment to social justice in our school reform endeavor? Will the new job opportunities so glibly promised in return for improved learning be fairly distributed, or will women and minorities continue to be shortchanged as they are now? Will anything be done about poverty?

With regard to stronger social supports for families, modern European economies provide us with some models. A review of history over the past 100 years suggests that in America social legislation designed to heal the human damage that capitalism inflicts comes about 35 years later than in western European countries. Will the recent moves in France to provide comprehensive programs to benefit young children and their families be a challenge to us that won't require 35 years for a response? Yes, we are now considering day care for children, an issue these countries faced many years ago. And in 1988 Congress passed the Family Support Act and currently is trying to muster the resources to bring it into operation as a way to moving poor families toward self-sufficiency. On the other hand, President Bush's veto of legislation to provide for parental leave from work at critical times in family life is not a positive signal. Yet this right for parents is a common feature of modern European economies, because they recognize the impact that work can have on families.

The reasons that we Americans are slow to act on these matters are many and complex. I will mention only three: 1) In our heart of hearts, we still believe that the reason people are poor is that they are lazy or improvident or otherwise flawed, in spite of unquestionable evidence that their misfortunes are almost invariably caused by events beyond their control. 2) We are both blessed and cursed with the myth of individual self-sufficiency, which is responsible for many of our achievements and for an increasing number of our social failures. Until we protect the victims of this myth from the risks of our competitive system, we will not be the land of opportunity that we profess to be. 3) A still powerful cross-current in American society is the suspicion we have of each other because of racial and cultural differences. We have come a long way toward reducing this destructive bias, but we have a long way still to go. In the meantime it reduces our capacity to care for and help each other.

There have been a few studies that have said some sensible things about the gap between schools and families, particularly poor and minority families. (A list of these studies appear at the end of this essay.) Two publications issued by the National Coalition of Advocates for Students touched on family needs and problems among minorities, the poor, and recent immigrants. The Hispanic Policy Development Project provided another such report, as did the William T. Grant Foundation study of older youth, with which I was involved. The recent overview of minority education needs by the Quality for Education Minorities Project gives a broad and useful perspective, although it pays scant attention to the special problems of recent immigrants. In spite of these insightful documents, the myths persist that the schools can do it all and that the school is the *only* place where a youngster gets educated.

In the last five years, more attention to families has crept into the peripheral vision of the school reform movement. More health services are being offered in schools – not paid for with school district funds, mind you, but permitted to operate in school facilities because that's where the youngsters are. Several national organizations are finding ways to link up with schools in order to help pressured families give children more attention. In 1984 Missouri piloted a program of parent education and family support services in several school districts, which has since been implemented statewide. Called the Parents as Teachers (PAT) program, it is targeted at parents of preschoolers. It provides health screenings and helps parents to promote their children's cognitive and social-emotional development, with a special emphasis on language development. PAT builds on family strengths and emphasizes parent empowerment. Home visits are a key feature of the program. The success of PAT has prompted other states to investigate the program. The "community school" concept first implemented in Flint, Michigan, in the 1920s with the largesse of the Mott Foundation is receiving renewed attention. Child psychiatrist James Comer of Yale University has developed a unique and promising plan for linking families and schools in New Haven, Connecticut, which is now spreading to other cities, with major foundation support. Some of the current school restructuring plans include the idea of a network that embraces school, community, and family as independent but related elements in the lives of children. In addition, some cities are experimenting with ways to coordinate the work of the many separate agencies and programs that serve children and families. Such efforts are being funded from private, local, state, and federal sources. While these developments cannot counteract the economic conditions that lead to poverty in families, they do signal a concern for the family and community roles in education and deserve our encouragement. Certainly, they can blunt the impact of poverty and make schooling more effective.

Conclusion

A special danger lurks in this entire argument about the key roles of families and communities and their relationship to education, schools, and children. This is the temptation of teachers and administrators to take the position that they can't be expected to deal with children whose development is retarded by inadequate homes and communities. Fortunately, this attitude is not typical of the country's educators. As with the medical profession, which is engaged in both the prevention and cure of disease, so do educators have a dual role, which is to work constructively with the children they have in school and to support social action for stronger families and communities.

We know from case studies of selected inner-city schools serving children who lack support at home that these children can achieve more with the right mix of high expectations and individual attention. We know that positive and respectful relationships among students, parents, and teachers in schools can make a difference. We know that if teachers understand the varied cultural backgrounds of their students and are committed to a pluralistic society, then the chances of school success are increased. We know that teachers can motivate learning with instructional strategies that awaken students' interests and encourage the exploration of ideas. But we also know that some students with the potential to succeed will not do so for lack of family and community supports. We can't allow this tragic fact to deter us from changing schools in ways that will benefit children and youth. We have the knowledge, but do we have will? Educators should not keep quiet on this matter. They know that what they do in their schools can be much more successful when families and communities are working well. And they should shout it from the rooftops. That message might then at least appear in the list of National Goals of Education, where it cannot be found today.

Significant Reports

Barriers to Excellence: Our Children at Risk (1985). National Coalition of Advocates for Students, 100 Boylston St., Suite 737, Boston, MA 02116.

New Voices: Immigrant Students in U.S. Public Schools (1988). National Coalition of Advocates for Students, 100 Boylston St., Suite 737, Boston, MA 02116.

Make Something Happen, 2 vols. (1984). Hispanic Policy Development Project, 1001 Connecticut Avenue, N.W., Suite 310, Washington, D.C. 20036.

Education That Works: An Action Plan for Education Minorities (January 1990). Quality Education for Minorities Network, 1818 N St., N.W., Suite 350, Washington, D.C. 20036.

The Forgotten Half: Pathways to Success for America's Youth and Young Families: Final Report of the William T. Grant Foundation Commission on Work, Family and Citizenship (1988). William T. Grant Foundation, 1001 Connecticut Avenue, N.W., Suite 301, Washington, D.C. 20036. (Many other related publications are available from this organization.)

Reflections on
Teaching Ourselves

BY PHILIP W. JACKSON

This essay reports on the history of my efforts to come to grips with a topic that should be of interest to educators everywhere. It has to do with the way teachers view the world, their outlook on life, one might say. There is, of course, no single view of anything that characterizes all teachers for all time. Yet there does seem to be a perspective that is sufficiently prevalent among the many teachers I have met over the years to make me want to understand it better. I have been trying to do just that for quite some time now with varying degrees of success and failure.

I begin with a description of how I gradually became convinced that this was a topic worthy of thought and investigation. This is followed by a brief account of my prior efforts to pin it down, both conceptually and empirically. I then conclude with an account of my recent participation in a series of discussions with a group of teachers in which this elusive topic became a recurrent theme.

My earliest sense that teachers may be different from other folks in ways that I had not anticipated emerged with a start during the early fall of my first year of teaching. The county superintendent of the southern New Jersey school system in which I taught had earned his doctorate in audiovisual education — or so it was rumored — and he had "suggested" (another rumor) that it would be highly desirable if all the teachers in the county were to join the state audiovisual education association (abbreviated as NJAVEA). The story that circulated in our school was that Dr. Eliot (not his real name) wanted

Philip W. Jackson is the David Lee Shillinglaw Distinguished Service Professor in the Departments of Education and Psychology at the University of Chicago.

to become president of NJAVEA, and one step in that direction was to ensure that all teachers under his supervision were members in good standing of the association and thus could exercise their voting rights on his behalf.

We teachers did not put up much of a howl in response to Dr. Eliot's strong-arm tactics, largely, I suppose, because the dues we paid to belong to NJAVEA were only fifty cents a year in those days. And for that paltry amount we got to take a day off with our chief administrator's blessing to attend the organization's annual meeting, which that year was held in Atlantic City. The cynicism of that bargain did not trouble me as much then as it does today, which I would like to interpret as a sign of moral growth.

I can't believe the schools actually closed for a day to allow all of the teachers in the county to attend the annual meeting of the NJAVEA that year, but I do recall that a number of us from my school, which had only about a dozen classrooms, drove to the meeting together. What must have happened was that quite a number of substitutes were hired to cover for us. Whatever the arrangements, I was among the many curious souls who converged on Atlantic City that bright October day, hoping to be brought up to date on the latest goings-on within the world of audiovisual education. My own curiosity was probably a bit higher than most, for this was my very first educational convention. I shall never forget it.

The meeting was held in a huge auditorium within Atlantic City's Convention Hall. At the registration tables we were given a packet of the usual informational materials plus a white card about three or four inches square to serve as an identification badge. On the card was printed a cartoon-like figure of a smiling man with his arm raised in greeting. Above that in huge block letters, it said: HI! I'M _____. I was a bit surprised by the chumminess of the smiling figure and the informality of the HI!, but I thought little of it at the time. I simply filled in the blank as indicated and turned to enter the auditorium. I did notice, however, on my way in that several of my fellow conventioneers had filled out their badges with their first name only. Indeed, many used nicknames, like "Irv" or "Dennie" or "Marge," whereas I had printed my full name and even included my middle initial! My feeling of being an outsider, already present because of my status as a new teacher, began to intensify.

Upon entering the auditorium I encountered my second unsettling experience, which turned out to be much worse than the first. Just inside the door I was met by a woman wearing a kelly-green dress with a name tag that said "Liz." She handed me a sheet of paper from a stack she was carrying on which were the lyrics to four or five songs, a couple of them familiar, the others not. One of the familiar ones was "A Bicycle Built for Two." One of the unfamiliar ones was titled "The A-V Blues," with lyrics having mostly to do with audio-visual equipment that malfunctioned. I had no desire to read further. I wanted only to bolt the hall at once for I feared things were going to get worse. However, having driven all that distance and not knowing where else to go, I decided I had no choice but to put my fears to the test. They passed with flying colors.

I sat down toward the back of the auditorium and looked around somewhat desperately for the teachers from my school, from whom I had become separated for some reason. Suddenly a woman walked to the center of the stage, stood before the microphone, and said "Good Morning!" in rather too loud a voice. She then turned her head to one side and cupped her hand behind her ear, as if waiting for us to say "Good morning" in reply, which a scattering of those seated proceeded to do. The microphone lady then said in a sing-songy voice, "I can't heeeear you," and cocked her ear again. This time a considerable portion of the audience obliged by shouting "Good morning" at the top of their lungs, or so it seemed to me. "That's better," said the microphone lady, who proceeded to introduce herself. Her name was Sandra Bradshaw, and she was a music teacher from Red Bank. She had gladly accepted the honor, as she put it, of leading the opening session in song, "To get us all into the right spirit before we get down to serious business," she added.

There was more. Before turning to the songs on our sheets, we were going to become acquainted with the strangers immediately around us by giving each other a musical greeting. "And we are going to do this in harmony!" our vocal director enthused. The audience moaned in mock disquietude, but one sensed its secret delight. I headed for the door. On my way out I heard Sandra from Red Bank say something about dividing the hall up into thirds and that she would use her pitch pipe to give each section its tone to make a tonic chord as it sang the word "Hello." Then, while sustaining that note everyone was to shake the hand of the person on their right and then do the same with the person on their left. There was probably more to it than that, but I never learned what it was. I reached the exit and heard the door bang closed behind me before Ms. Bradshaw could finish her directions.

I don't remember now whether I returned for any portion of the day's program after the sing-a-long was over. But if I did, it certainly did not lodge in my memory with anything like the vividness of those opening exercises. For days afterward I thought about my sense of discomfort in that situation and wondered why everybody else seemed to be having such a good time. There probably were others there just as uncomfortable as I was, but I didn't look around to find kindred spirits. I mostly kept my head down so people wouldn't see me wince with embarrassment.

What was I to make of the difference between my reaction and that of the others? What did it say about me? Or about them? I did not bother to ask at the time whether that difference might have something to do with the nature of teaching and with the kind of people who choose to teach, but such thoughts could not have been far from my mind. It took a couple of other experiences, however, to prod them into consciousness.

The second such experience occurred a few years later when I was a graduate student. This one was nothing like the sing-a-long that morning in Atlantic City. Rather, it occurred in the sedate and cloistered environment of a university library. I was doing some reference work that required my poring over entries in successive volumes of *Education Index*. In one of them I chanced upon an entry labeled "Verses by teachers." The item had nothing to do with what I was interested in at the time, but it intrigued me all the same. "Verses by teachers," I thought, What a peculiar item to find listed in a reference work of this kind. If I were to look in *Chemistry Index* (assuming there is such a thing), would I find an entry called "Verses by chemists"? Surely not. Or in a volume of legal abstracts, would "Verses by lawyers" be listed? I doubt that, too. Why then, "Verses by teachers"? What could such an entry signify? Did it mean that teachers were much more likely to write poems than were either chemists or lawyers? And if that were true, what might that mean?

Spurred on by such musings, I flipped to the letter "P" in the volume of the *Index* I was using; and there under the heading "Poetry" I found literally scores of entries, most of them titles of single poems that had appeared in educational publications of one kind or another over the two-year period covered by the index. Judging from their titles, many of these poems were the kind that grade-school teachers might actually use in class. They had titles like "The Wind in March" or "Farmer Brown's Hitching Song," and most had appeared in magazines like *Instructor* or *Grade Teacher*. But there also were dozens of poetry entries that obviously were meant to be read and enjoyed solely by teachers. Many of these seemed to be about the experience of teaching, which likely meant that they were written by teachers, though I couldn't tell for sure. Again I found myself thinking about comparisons. "Why so many poems about teaching?" I asked myself, which was a slightly different question than the one about why so many teachers might be versifiers. Why are poems such staple items in so many education journals? Is there a heartier appetite for poetry among teachers than among chemists or lawyers? Is it that teaching somehow lends itself to poetry more than do the activities of those other professions? If that were so, what would it mean? I don't remember how long I continued to think along these lines, probably not very long because I had other work to do that afternoon. But those thoughts stuck with me for years and would surface from time to time like an unsolved riddle that one keeps turning over in one's mind.

A third piece of the puzzle (perhaps one might better say a third push toward the puzzle) came in the form of an exclamation from a teacher whose name I no longer remember and may not even have known at the time. Her outcry wasn't all that unusual, but its ordinariness turned out to be memorable all the same. This event took place on a late March morning in Chicago, a few years after I completed graduate school and had joined the faculty of the University of Chicago. I was by then the father of two children, an infant son and a four-year-old daughter, whom I walked to nursery school in the morning on my way to work.

The routine at the school was for parents who dropped their children off to wait around until their youngsters had been examined by the school nurse. If a child showed no sign of a sore throat or a runny nose or any other kind of respiratory ailment, the accompanying adult was then free to leave. If, on the other hand, the nurse judged the child to be unfit for school, he or she had to be taken home or cared for elsewhere.

During the nurse's inspection, for which the children had to line up, the parents would either chat with one another in the hall or, if it were a nice day, step outside to the playground where they could watch those children who had already been cleared by the nurse. On such days two or three of the school's teachers were always present supervising the playground activities.

This particular morning was one of those rare March days that native Chicagoans dream of throughout the long dark winter months. The temperature was already in the upper-forties and promised to go even higher as the day wore on. Several of the children had un-

236

zipped their snowsuit jackets, and two or three had been bold enough to discard theirs, causing teachers to rush over and insist they be put back on. There were still patches of soot-blackened snow in the playground areas that received little sun. We all knew we could expect more cold and nasty days in late March and even into April, but on this morning it was clear that such days were on the wane. Spring was in the air.

As I stood there waiting on the playground for my daughter to be cleared by the nurse, one of the teachers gave a shout of surprise. "Ohhhhhh LOOK!" she exclaimed, "Look what we have here!" The children came running from all sides, dropping balls, abandoning tricycles, and sliding off rocking horses. I resisted the temptation to run and walked over to see what was going on. What the teacher had discovered, to the delight of everyone present, was the very first crocus of spring, at least the first one to appear on the school playground. There it was, a small lavender flower with spiky green leaves nudging its way through the sooty topsoil. The teacher looked around at everyone and smiled with satisfaction. "Isn't that wonderful?" she said. We all nodded and smiled back.

As I left the school that morning and proceeded to my office, I could not erase from my mind the memory of that tiny drama − the teacher with her ecstatic "Ohhhhhh LOOK," the running children, our shared smile of delight. The whole thing was a genuine pleasure to recall. But it was more than pleasure that kept it on my mind. It was as though that charming sequence of events, which couldn't have lasted more than a minute, contained some message that I was supposed to heed, something about teaching and teachers. What was it?

"One thing is certain," I said to myself, "I could never have done what that teacher did. I couldn't have spontaneously cried out with delight at the sight of that crocus, no matter how pleased I might have been to have come upon it." As a matter of fact, I probably would have stepped on the damned thing before I saw it, given my tendency to have my head in the clouds much of the time. But still, wasn't I glad that the teacher brought that delicate, solitary flower to our collective attention? You bet I was. And wasn't that just the kind of teacher I hoped my daughter would be spending her mornings with − and my son, too, as soon as he was old enough? Definitely so.

As my thoughts ran along in this direction, my memory of the two other experiences I have just related slowly began to revive and to mix in with what I was thinking. Though markedly different, these three memories, the last one only minutes old, seemed to cohere as though all of a piece. I felt they all had something to do with what teachers are like. Yet they clearly were not signalling the same thing, as was clear from my initial reaction to them.

In the sing-a-long situation, I had felt a kind of snobbish contempt for those members of the audience — my fellow teachers no less! — who went along with Ms. Bradshaw's corny enthusiasm. In the library reading the *Education Index*, I had felt puzzled but emotionally neutral as I mused about the prevalence of poetry in educational publications. And this latest situation of the teacher discovering the first crocus of spring evoked genuine admiration and gratitude (tainted with a trace of envy, I must add). What was I to make of these differences? If there was a single quality or characteristic these three experiences revealed about teachers, they certainly did so in ways that produced markedly different reactions on my part.

I didn't get very far in my thinking about these matters on that day. But a few months later I happened to be reading C.M. Bowra's *The Romantic Imagination* (1961) in which I came across the line: "The beauty of visible things carried Keats into ecstasy." It immediately brought to mind the image of the nursery school teacher espying the crocus. I then recalled Wordsworth's famous first line: "My heart leaps up when I behold" and his poem about wandering "lonely as a cloud" and coming "all at once" upon "a host of golden daffodils." I turned the page and there were some lines from Blake's *Songs of Innocence*. They, too, picked up the same theme. They spoke of seeing heaven in a wild flower and of piping songs of glee. Poetry, flowers, song — that was what my three experiences had been about. The coincidence was too obvious to ignore. My excitement began to mount; and as I read on in Bowra's book, I started to sense all kinds of connections between features of the Romantics' world view as explicated by him (their focus on the individual, their suspicion of science, their delight in products of the imagination) and those qualities of teachers that I had been trying to put my finger on for such a long time. Moreover, many of those same qualities turned out to be ones I possessed myself in fair measure, which may help to explain why I picked up Bowra's book in the first place.

Was that it, I wondered? Did the three parts of the puzzle fit together as easily as that? Did it suffice to say that teachers everywhere, but especially teachers of the young, tended toward a view of the world that characterized the Romantics of the eighteenth and nineteenth centuries? My interpretation was perhaps simplistic and certainly incomplete, but at least it was a start.

Armed with that hunch, I began to spend more time talking with teachers about what they believed and about how they looked at their work. I also began to spend a lot of time sitting in the back of elementary school classrooms, trying to figure out what was going on there.

The fruits of those conversations and observations were reported in my book, *Life in Classrooms* (1968). I did not specifically mention Bowra and the Romantic imagination in that book (I probably should have done so), but I did talk abut the way teachers become absorbed in the immediacy of classroom events and in the well-being of individual students. I also spoke about how they eschewed technical terms and how they relied heavily on intuitive approaches to classroom events. I described them as being like amateur art lovers, "who knew what they liked, even if they did not always know why they liked it." I pointed out that there was "something romantic, even sentimental perhaps," about the image of teachers I was presenting. Indeed, at one point I referred to the teachers I had been interviewing as "tender-minded romantics," pure and simple. But then, as if to make amends, I went on to suggest that "the persistence of this tender-mindedness in generations of teachers is surely no accident" and "may have its adaptive significance." I hinted that these romantic qualities might help to remedy the harshness and impersonality of schools, might serve as "antidotes to the toxic qualities of institutional life." Finally, I concluded that "As we look more carefully at what goes on in an institution we begin to see how our present cadre of elementary school teachers, with all of their intellectual fuzziness and sticky sentimentality, may be doing the job better than would an army of human engineers."

Looking back on what I wrote then, I now sense the ambivalence I must have felt toward what I was trying to understand. I say "must have felt" because I don't recall experiencing any internal struggle while writing that section of *Life in Classrooms*. But the conflict is evident in the language I used: "Sticky sentimentality" facing "an army of human engineers." The battle lines are sharply drawn, and what a pair of opponents! How could one choose sides? The truth is I privately sided with both.

I recall a kind of slogan I used to rattle off in those days when asked what I thought might improve American education. "What is sorely needed," I declared back then, "is a tough-minded defense of a tender-minded view." I still believe that to be so in a way. But I realize now that I personally yearned for something more than a strong defense of tender-mindedness. I sought the best of both worlds. I wanted to be tough-minded *and* tender-minded at the same time. Moreover, I wished the same for all of my fellow teachers. I guess I still do.

But I now see some things I didn't see back then. I now realize, for example, that the dichotomy in which the tough-minded is pitted against the tender-minded reflects a bias in favor of the former point of view. The emotional overtones of the labels, not to mention their latent sexism, give that away. "Tough-minded" is flattering, "tender-minded" is not. One connotes strength, the other weakness. Thus, as soon as we begin to think in those terms, we have already adopted a biased view.

I also have come to realize that bi-polar conceptions such as these are too extreme and too sharply drawn to describe real-life circumstances, whose manifestations are far more complicated and subtle than can be expressed by a dichotomous construct. Such conceptions, in other words, are mere caricatures. Though helpful as heuristic devices, these thumbnail sketches reinforce the habit of thinking in stereotypes, which is one of the great drawbacks of using them. This is not to say that stereotypes never hit the nail on the head; but the people who fit them almost perfectly are usually a bit odd, if not downright laughable, like my Ms. Bradshaw from Red Bank.

Thoughts such as these led me gradually to turn from thinking about what makes teachers alike to become interested in some of the key differences among them. I should insert here that in the meantime I had become a school administrator, first as a nursery school principal and later as director of the University of Chicago Laboratory Schools, two positions that afforded me yet another perspective on teachers and teaching and enabled me to become much more closely involved with a much broader spectrum of teachers than I had ever had contact with before. I frequently visited classrooms during those years, as I had done previously; but my reasons for doing so were more often related to my official duties as an administrator than for scholarly pursuits.

During this period I continued to read sporadically about Romanticism as a literary movement and about the Romantics as individuals. I also developed a new interest in philosophy, particularly the writings of Wittgenstein and other philosophical critics of the social sciences. Out of that amalgam of experience and continued study came *The Practice of Teaching* (1986), a book whose individual chapters focused on a variety of different topics related to the conditions of teaching, the complexities that teachers face in their daily work, and their ways of coping with those complexities. In the final chapter I introduced a dichotomy whose explication echoed many of my earlier thoughts about the Romantic world view and its resemblance to an outlook I discerned to be prevalent among teachers. The two halves of that dichotomy referenced a pair of traditions that have flourished for millennia within the teaching profession and remain vibrantly alive today. One of them I called the *mimetic*, the other the *transformative*. This is not the place to elaborate on the distinction between the two, except to say that the transformative tradition is the one that comes closest to the qualities of teachers that I previously had called "tender-minded."

In essence, teachers who self-consciously ascribe to what I call the transformative tradition seek to bring about changes in their students that extend far beyond the acquisition of knowledge and skills. Indeed, in extreme cases such teachers may forsake entirely the conventional pedagogical goals associated with subject matter mastery. (In *The Practice of Teaching* I go on to suggest that all teachers partake of this tradition to some extent, albeit without knowledge of doing so. But that qualification need not concern us here.) What draws this perspective close to the province of Romantic thought is its concern with levels of pedagogical influence that mirror a layered conception of human affairs and of reality in general. Those who teach within this tradition — Socrates being the classic example — aim to modify attitudes, values, interests, character, personality, the depths of the soul. In short, the goals of this way of teaching cover all of the psychic "stuff" of which we humans are said to be made — leaving aside, but by no means excluding, what we are said to know. Another way of putting it is to say that such teachers seek to have an effect on their students analogous to the influence of a memorable work of art, though ideally with much greater and more enduring impact than any single work of art.

That is about as far as I went with my exploration in *The Practice of Teaching*, though I did say a lot more than I have here about the distinction between the mimetic and the transformative traditions. One of the most heartening outcomes for me when I had completed the book was the feeling that my dual interests in the arts and in teaching, both of which I had nurtured for a very long time, were finally beginning to converge. I also sensed that a missing element in my work on teaching (and in my thoughts about art, for that matter) had

241

something to do with morality and the moral. I vowed to correct that deficiency as soon as possible.

That vow led to the project in which I have been engaged for the past three years or so. It is called *The Moral Life of Schools Project*, a title that signals its substantive focus. The project's participants comprise 18 teachers in five schools (two public, two parochial, and one private), two research assistants, and myself. Basically, my assistants and I observe the teachers in their classrooms and talk with them at length about their educational views. For the past two-and-a-half years we have also met bi-weekly with the teachers as a group for an evening's discussion on subjects ranging over a broad spectrum of educational topics, mostly having to do with teachers and teaching. The fruit of those discussions is what I shall report on here briefly.

As the title of our project would suggest, our group has spent many evenings over the past couple of years discussing the moral nature of teaching and the many different ways in which teachers might affect the moral conduct of their students. Concerning the latter, the group has spent very little time addressing formal programs of moral education; in fact, we have hardly done so at all. Instead, we have chosen to focus on the many informal and often unconscious ways in which teachers make known their own moral positions and values to their students. What lies behind this choice is our conviction that teachers are continually transmitting moral messages of one kind or another, whether they intend to do so or not. Of course, the same could be said of everyone else, for as Emerson tells us: "Character teaches above our wills. Men imagine that they communicate their virtue or vice only by overt actions, and do not see that virtue or vice emit a breath every moment" (p. 266).

Teachers are specially positioned to play the role of moral model for the young and immature as few other adults are situated to do, save parents obviously. They are continually being looked up to for guidance on matters that extend far beyond their subject matter expertise. This may be truer of teachers who work with younger students than those who work with adults, but even the latter cannot fully escape being viewed as the embodiment of qualities they may or may not actually possess.

In the process of teaching subjects like science or math or a foreign language, teachers at all levels also teach, through example and through shared forms of social exchange, the virtues of diligence and persistence, of commitment to truth, of listening to and caring for the contributions of others — the list could easily go on. But they

242

do more than that. They also teach what it is like to be a certain kind of person, a person who not only possesses this or that combination of virtues (and vices) but also one who puts those qualities to work, meshing them with the demands of reality and molding them into an effective way of life. These observations may not be very profound. Nevertheless, they strike us as fundamentally true and as terribly important. In our group discussions we summarize our feelings with what has become our very favorite expression: "Teachers teach themselves," we are fond of saying.

Teachers do indeed teach themselves, but that pithy generalization, true as it is, needs immediate qualification. What happens to most of us as teachers is that we put our best foot forward in the classroom. We project to our students not who we are but the kind of person we would like to be or what we would like others to think of us as being. We show our students our better selves, or try to. Again, teachers are not alone in this kind of posturing. Parents do the same, as do ministers, rabbis, judges, police officers, and everyone else in a position of social responsibility, including, one might add, authors of literary works. The critic Wayne Booth (1988) refers to this tendency among authors as a form of "hypocrisy upward." Here is how he speaks of it:

> Everyone knows that the character implied by the total act of writing any literary work (the implied author) is always (but always) an "improved" version over the flesh-and-blood creator — not necessarily improved by your standards or mine, but improved by the standards of the author. (p. 254)

Booth's term, "hypocrisy upward," became yet another expression that our discussion group found useful when trying to put into words what it felt like to be a teacher. We teach ourselves, true enough, but we also try to be on our good behavior when so doing. After years of such trying we often wind up better than we were at the start, which is surely one of the great rewards of teaching.

That is about where I am today in my understanding of what teachers are like as persons and how they differ from folks who do other sorts of things for a living. It's a long way back from here to that day in Atlantic City, when I wasn't really sure whether I was a teacher or wanted to be one. I did give up teaching young children (for which I was not very well-suited to begin with, I fear); but I have never given up teaching, nor would I want to. Teaching has taught me too much. And so have teachers. I plan to go on learning from both for as long as possible.

References

Booth, Wayne C. *The Company We Keep*. Chicago: University of Chicago Press, 1988.

Bowra, C.M. *The Romantic Imagination*. New York: Oxford University Press, 1961.

Emerson, Ralph Waldo. *Essays & Lectures*. New York: Viking, 1983.

Jackson, Philip W. *Life in Classrooms*. New York: Holt, Rhinehart and Winston, 1968.

Jackson, Philip W. *The Practice of Teaching*. New York: Teachers College Press, 1986.

Reflections on
Children and Books

BY NANCY LARRICK

There was a time when a period of 25 years seemed an eternity — certainly a lifetime — and, indeed, it was for me then. But having survived several of these 25-year cycles, I find that each succeeding quarter of a century whirls by with greater and greater speed — fast enough to get the overall view, not too fast to weigh and measure, compare and question.

What have been some of the distinguishing features of the 1965-1990 cycle? How might these affect the next quarter-century? With my professional interest primarily in children and their reading, I will focus my "reflections" for the past quarter-century on these areas. (I rejoice that I have been asked to reflect, not to provide solutions.) So what are some of the issues that have taken center stage? How have we responded? Where are we heading?

Family Disruption and Poverty. In looking at the status of children, I think we must first face up to the cataclysmic changes in the home scene. At all economic levels, there are more one-parent families than ever before. More mothers are working outside the home. One estimate is that 75% of mothers with school-age children will be in the labor force by 1995. Most latchkey children, with estimates ranging from two to 12 million, come home after school with only the voices of television to greet them.

The weakening job market and scarcity of housing for low-income families have dislocated hundreds of thousands of households. This means frequent moves, often as many as four different schools for

---

Nancy Larrick is Adjunct Professor Emeritus at Lehigh University and author of A Parent's Guide to Children's Reading.

a child in one school year. In my small town — clean, prosperous, conservative — elementary teachers have learned to expect a 47% turnover in their classes each year. As one teacher put it: "This makes it hard to cultivate team work and for children to learn or to establish friendships that contribute to learning."

Nationwide, more and more children are becoming part of the hidden homeless, those crowded in with neighbors or relatives until family stress forces another move. When all else fails, the hidden homeless become part of the growing multitude of homeless, living on the streets or in public shelters, often on a day-to-day basis. One estimate puts the nation's homeless at 3,000,000, with 500,000 being children under age 10. Families with children constitute the fastest-growing segment of the homeless population. According to Senator Patrick Moynihan of New York, "The United States is the first nation in history in which the poorest group in the population was the children." Today, the poorest children are also the youngest children.

Teachers interviewed in the 1989 Metropolitan Life Survey reported that social problems are getting worse in their schools and classrooms. These teachers are especially concerned about latchkey children and the increase of absenteeism. Not surprisingly, they plead for more social services in their schools and for more social workers and family services for both elementary and middle-grade pupils.

The Television Take-Over. Television is unquestionably the most time-consuming interest of all our children. It is a steady source of entertainment — perhaps even companionship. According to the 1990 Nielsen Media Research Report, 92.1 million households in the United States have at least one television set. In 1989 households with children had television turned on an average of 58 hours, 43 minutes each week. In the same period, the average weekly viewing time of children age two to five was 27 hours, 49 minutes; for the six- to eleven-year-olds it was 23 hours, 39 minutes per week. Of the two-to-five age group, 21% were watching TV during primetime hours, along with 29% of the six-to-eleven age group. Four percent of these groups were still watching at 1:00 a.m.

Favorite programs of the children range from "Cosby Show" to "Roseanne," "A Different World," and "Who's the Boss?" Many children are also watching "Star Trek," "Love Connection," and a choice of such movies as "Alien Warrior" and "Love and Hate: A Marriage Made in Hell." On Saturday mornings millions watch cartoons interspersed with advertising done in the same cartoon style, frequently selling the very toys shown in the entertainment sequence.

Much of the television world is harsh, brutal, shrill, distorted. Violence, terrorism, drugs, and sex are played out in vivid detail in some of the shows that children watch. How do these young viewers interpret what they see; and what are they thinking as they are bombarded by images of violence and brutality? When asked about her favorite program, one fourth-grader said, "I don't know. I was only watching." Another frowned and then asked, "Do I have to say it in words?" One psychotherapist suggests that kids have seen such extraordinarily powerful images on television that they are completely jaded. Real life is a let-down, so "What's the thrill?" they say.

How does a steady diet of television affect children's reading? Clearly, those watching TV for four to six hours a day have little time left for reading. Innumerable research studies show that heavy viewers are usually poor readers. (No one has attempted to determine whether they are poor readers because they watch television or whether they watch television because they are poor readers.)

We do know that many children who see a program based on a children's book rush out to get the book and read it. One youngster who was an avid fan of the TV series, "Little House on the Prairie" based on the Laura Ingalls Wilder books, was disappointed, however. "The book's not right," he said. "I know because I saw it on television."

At every turn we see that television is revealing new worlds to children. But it is also raising new problems that are unresolved for many a silent viewer. Yet in 1990 I find the television take-over in children's lives is seldom mentioned by writers in professional magazines and by speakers at professional meetings. Has television become so much a part of our daily lives that we take it for granted with no questions asked?

Education Before Age Five. Few school systems have a planned program for all children under age five. Head Start programs serve only a minority of children eligible to attend them. Day-care centers vary from personal and highly stimulating play-and-learning centers to mere holding pools where children are fed and watered but little else. In one community, visitors to a day-care center found the children sitting before the television screen sucking their thumbs. There was no plan for stories, singing games, or one-to-one conversation.

Several early childhood advocates have proposed that the mandated public school entry age be pushed back to age four. But what sort of program would be provided for these four-year-olds? In some communities kindergarten no longer is focused on enrichment through play, group activities, stories, and oral language experiences but, instead, has become a highly structured skill-drill program. Will the new program for four-year-olds be just as highly structured? Will it be school-based or home-based? What about the role of the parents?

Enlisting Parents as Partners. Certainly one of the most positive influences in the 1965-1990 period has been the concerted effort to enlist the support of parents in introducing children to oral language, stories, and reading in general. It may be hard to believe, but there was a day — within my memory — when schools gave parents the "hands off" treatment. "You take care of the children at home," went the message, "and we'll take care of them at school." Perhaps the PTA conducted bake sales and raised money for playground equipment, but parents were not expected to be part of the teaching-learning program either at home or at school.

Now schools are saying, "Parents, we need you! You are the ones who can enrich the child's learning in infancy and give support throughout the child's schooling." How could it have been otherwise at any time? Traditionally, at least one parent was with the child almost full time during the first five years, sometimes called "the peak language learning years." This is when the child begins to meet the language arts of listening, speaking, singing, storytelling, and sometimes reading. This also is the time when interest in books can begin, when story sense can develop, when conversation can flourish. All of this can happen before children enter kindergarten or first grade — if they are exposed to enriching language experiences.

Of course, many parents, influenced by their own childhood experiences, have given their young children a rich introduction to the language arts through reading aloud, story-telling, singing, and conversation. But until the late Fifties, there were no books directed to parents to encourage this kind of home enrichment for infants, toddlers, and school-age children. Now, in 1990, we have a proliferation of books addressed to parents, beginning with *Babies Need Books* and *Children's Reading Begins at Home* on to innumerable parents' guides giving suggestions for helping children of all ages.

Many school systems are now sending home parent newsletters with this kind of information and guidance. In some communities, visiting teachers go into the homes to show parents how to provide rich language experiences for their children. Many parents are hungry for this kind of help. Witness the success of Jim Trelease's book, *The Read-Aloud Handbook* (1982), which is reported to have sold 70,000 copies in one week after Dear Abby endorsed it in her column.

(Trust Dear Abby to have her finger on the pulse of the American public!)

Ironically, the big outreach to parents did not come initially from the schools. In Orlando, Florida, for example, it was the public library that launched a program called "Catch'em in the Cradle" to show parents how to read aloud to their infants and why. Another program from the Orlando Public Library, "Sharing Literature with Children," shows parents, grandparents, day-care teachers, even teenagers, how to read aloud to preschool children and involve them in stories and nursery rhymes.

In Nassau County, Long Island, the Family Service Association initiated a unique outreach to parents in 1967 and now has longitudinal studies to show the positive effect of this home-based Verbal Interaction Project. The director, Dr. Phyllis Levenstein, notes that with one-to-one guidance, mothers are able to increase a young child's vocabulary, oral language facility, and interest in stories and books. On the average, youngsters of two to four in her project increase I.Q. scores by 17 points. Later in school these youngsters — largely from dysfunctional families — have higher academic achievement scores than would have been predicted for them. They have held their own in the school setting. The key to the success of this program, says Levenstein, is the mother-child bond. Mothers learn how to talk to their two- and three-year-olds and how to draw them into questioning and conversing. Older siblings benefit at the same time.

After viewing tapes of parent-child interaction produced by Dr. Burton White of Harvard and studying the transcripts of mother-child conversations in Levenstein's Verbal Interaction Project, both of which are home-based, I find myself wishing that every young child might have similar advantages of learning at home through parent-child interaction.

The Trade Book Bonanza. At a time when children's television viewing averages more than 23 hours per week, it is encouraging to report that children's trade book publishing has made extraordinary growth. In 1989, 5,000 new children's trade books were published, almost double the figure for 1984. In the same period, the number of bookstores handling children's books exclusively is reported to have grown from a baker's dozen to close to 500. Predictions of a "paperless society" have not been borne out — at least for the youngest segment of the population.

By 1990 the baby boomlet phenomenon has brought 19 million preschoolers into the market, a fact that publishers think will guarantee purchasing power through the year 2000. One analyst heralds "Glorious years ahead for children's books!"

For those 19 million preschoolers there are quantities of new full-color picture books, many of them produced on printing presses in Hong Kong and Singapore. There are many new easy-to-read books with full-color illustrations that avoid the old baby-book look. Non-fiction is flourishing, too. More titles are in larger format with lavish full-color art as well as more elegant design. As one book reviewer put it, "We are in the middle of a renaissance which has been a long time coming!"

With continuing inflation, it is not surprising that book prices have increased dramatically. A full-color picture book now may cost as much as $17.95, but such books seem to sell very well, nonetheless. One explanation is that there are now more educated parents with two paychecks in the family. Unfortunately, few of these luxury books will reach homes with only one paycheck or no paycheck. To help children from these homes, Reading Is Fundamental (RIF), a non-profit, nationwide organization, has distributed 100,000,000 free books since 1965 to children who might otherwise never own a book to read and reread.

Balancing the high-price books are more and more quality children's paperbacks. Many are well written, attractively illustrated, and well printed. Prices range from $2.50 to $6.50. School paperback book clubs, which offer books at reduced prices, are flourishing.

Use of Trade Books in the Teaching of Reading. The extraordinary growth in the publication and distribution of children's books in both hardcover and paperback has come about in part because of new approaches to the teaching of reading in the United States, Australia, and New Zealand. By and large, these reading programs advocate the use of trade books (children call them "real books") instead of basal readers and their accompanying workbooks, activity sheets, and skill-drill paraphernalia. Many of these literature-based reading programs encourage children to select the books they want to read instead of requiring all children in the class to proceed simultaneously in goose-step fashion through the basal reader.

These newer approaches provide time for storytelling, reading aloud, sustained silent reading, impromptu dramatization of stories and poems, and creative writing, or, in the case of the youngest, dictating their stories. The term "whole language" used to describe many of these programs reflects the linking of all the language arts, each strengthening and enriching the others. Instead of being asked to check lists of words or questions in a workbook, children are being encouraged to raise their own questions, to compare the stories being read by different children in the group, and to get the reactions of other children. Thus reading one book leads to the reading of another and another, while building the skills of oral language and critical thinking.

Anyone whose experience goes back to the Forties and Fifties is well aware that these current approaches are not really new. In the early Thirties, Lucy Sprague Mitchell was advocating the use of children's creative writing or their dictation as the basis for learning to read the colorful "here and now" stories being created at her Bank Street School in New York City. Teachers at the Lincoln School at Teachers College, Columbia University were using "whole language" long before the term was invented.

Such valiant leaders as Laura Zirbes at Ohio State, Roma Gans at Teachers College, Columbia University, and Alvina Treut Burrows at New York University were among the early advocates of integrating the language arts through literature in the classroom. Burrows' book, *They All Want to Write*, published in 1939, is a blueprint for the writing side of today's "whole language" approach. In the Fifties, Jeannette Veatch was advocating what she calls "individualized reading," where each child selects and reads his or her own book, talks about it with the teacher and classmates, and then follows up with writing, questioning, and further reading.

Concurrent with these new — and not so new — approaches to teaching reading have come research studies reporting that children who have been read to and who have had the opportunity to read lively, exciting, challenging "real books" are the ones who do well as independent readers, the ones who learn to enjoy reading. I am thinking of the carefully designed study by Dorothy Cohen (1972), replicated a few years later by Cullanan, Jaggers, and Strickland, and more recently the longitudinal study of Gordon Wells in England as reported in his book, *The Meaning Makers: Children Learning Language and Using Language to Learn* (1986). Wells concludes that "it is growing up in a literate family environment in which reading and writing are natural occurring daily activities that give children the particular advantage when they start formal education. And of all the activities that were characteristic of such homes, it was the sharing of stories that we found most important." Many teachers have noted the same "particular advantage" of children growing up in a literate classroom environment.

For those who were students of Roma Gans and Alvina Treut Burrows, the growing use of children's trade books in the teaching of reading is cause for rejoicing. We know it can work. Children's enthusiasm has convinced us! Children are hearing and reading stories, nonfiction, and poetry in the language they hear all around them as opposed to the stilted, awkward, unnatural language of the basal readers. (As someone said long ago, "The language of the basal readers is the only written language that has never been spoken by anyone anywhere.")

While authors of the basal readers have been restricted to lists of acceptable "easy" words for each grade, authors of trade books have been free to use such exciting words as *alligator, helicopter, rhinoceros, television*, and *satellite*, words almost every child has heard and spoken dozens of times and recognizes quickly. Children learn that reading is the voice of real life, the "here and now" philosophy in modern narrative.

Now children are reading whole books about such unforgettable characters as Pippi Longstocking, Ramona Quimby, and the Great Gilly Hopkins. They have wept over *Bridge to Terabithia*. They feel the emotional tug of Eve Bunting's deceptively simple picture book, *The Wall*, which raises ethical questions about the Vietnam War. This leads to further reading and probing.

Children like to become emotionally involved. They respond eagerly and ask for more. The basal readers are notoriously lacking in feelings, emotions, problems of any kind. The literature-based program, at its best, invites children to think, to question, to ponder, to feel.

Yet old ways of teaching and thinking about reading are difficult to put aside. For years elementary teachers have been told in the basal teacher's guides to ask certain questions and to accept only one correct answer for each question. Those who have used one basal reader series for a number of years find it hard to cope with a wide range of books and pupil-initiated questions (with no assurance as to the "right" answer).

In some school systems, teachers know that their professional rating — even their jobs — depends on how well their pupils perform on mandated standardized reading tests. Not surprisingly, many teachers feel more secure when they follow the step-by-step directions provided in the basal teacher's guide.

Now the overly prescriptive teacher's guide is infiltrating the trade book approach and spawning a whole new publishing industry. These new guides list vocabulary words to study in advance and questions to be asked (with the correct answer given for each, of course). They include forms to be duplicated with instructions for each child to carry out such questionable practices as drawing lines to connect related ideas, rewriting the final chapter of the book to provide a different ending, rewriting the title of the book using just six words, or translating the last paragraph into a poem. How can we expect children to enjoy reading a book when they are forced to do such activities?

There are, of course, many teachers who do a very creative job of integrating the language arts using trade books. But when I saw a demonstration of the way one group of teachers attempted to integrate poetry into the language arts, my heart sank. One poem after another — all delightful poems by outstanding poets — was displayed on the screen with an overhead projector. The first was used for a lesson on adjectives with the children being asked to identify the adjectives in such phrases as "blue sky," "sparkling water," and "giant tree." The next poem provided a lesson on finding the "-ing words." Another was the basis for a lesson on homonyms, another on compound words. And they called it "integrating poetry into whole language." How can anyone do this to the poems of Eve Merriam, Theodore Roethke, Robert Frost, and Carl Sandburg, I wondered. Where was mention of the rhythm, the imagery, the emotional pull, the sheer beauty of these poems?

I am coming to realize that there are many interpretations for each new approach in education. But unless individual teachers are vigilant and willing to evaluate critically, these approaches can often be counter-productive.

Where Do We Go from Here? A thoughtful look at the past quarter-century shows that the changes in our society have made the education of our children ever more complex. While we know that children's education begins at birth and is influenced by home experiences long before they reach school, we must accept the fact that outreach services to children will have to begin earlier. Prenatal clinics are needed to ensure a healthy start for a child's formal education. Family services are needed to help parents provide for each child's physical and mental development from infancy.

Children from low-income and disrupted families must have the same opportunities for physical and intellectual development as other children. Those from non-English-speaking homes must receive special care and instruction so they can enter the mainstream comfortably. This may mean home-based services or a system of quality day-care centers where physical and intellectual growth can be cultivated all day, every day.

Such responsibilities go far beyond the services currently provided by most public schools. Indeed, it may necessitate restructuring the entire school program in order to provide children of all ages with the special services needed to achieve maximum growth — physically, intellectually, emotionally, and socially. This will require greater cooperation among parents, community agencies, and the schools. It calls for a central coordinating plan that focuses on improving the quality of life in individual homes and in the community as a whole.

Most important in achieving this goal will be the continuing education or "recharging" of the personnel who are responsible for making it happen: parents, day-care workers, classroom teachers, social workers, family counselors. All must be constantly evaluating and innovating as society changes.

Then . . . someday . . . I hope all children will be reading and thinking creatively, eagerly asking questions, and seeking solutions for the betterment of all.

Reflections of a Foundation Executive

BY EDWARD J. MEADE, JR.

A little more than 30 years ago, my professional life changed dramatically. Until then I had been a schoolman: a teacher, a director of school and community service projects, an assistant principal, president of my teachers' organization. I had a couple of degrees and was completing a doctorate in education at Harvard. I had left the public schools for graduate study, in part, because of differences with some of my colleagues and supervisors about the purpose of public schools. I went to graduate school to find good answers; I left with better questions.

I expected to return to the public schools and get on the track leading to a superintendency. But first I wanted to broaden my perspective. Much of the leadership of the schools in which I had worked struck me as narrow in outlook and lacking in vision. If there was a vision, it looked inward as though schools were islands unto themselves. Maybe that was an unavoidable occupational hazard, but I was determined to avoid it. To do so I wanted experiences that would arm me against narrow-mindedness and broaden my perspective on and my vision of education. And broaden I did.

That broadening began after graduate school when I joined the education program staff of the Ford Foundation in 1960. The foundation was a good place in which to acquire a sharper and more comprehensive perspective on education. Its programs were both national and international in scope and its interests were varied and many. By the time I left in the fall of 1989, I had what I had come for and much more — though I never went on to be a superintendent.

Edward J. Meade, Jr. was formerly Chief Program Officer at the Ford Foundation, where he served for 30 years, and currently is an educational consultant to foundations and other nonprofit and educational institutions.

The educational challenges to which the Ford Foundation responded over those many years were the result of massive demographic changes taking place; of major social, political, and economic events in America and on the world scene; substantial additions to our knowledge about human development and learning; and a gradual but profound realignment of the goals of education in America, particularly the rise of the equity issue as a goal as critical as excellence.

The first of the demographic forces having a major impact on the schools was the post-World War II baby boom phenomenon. As a result, starting in the 1950s, schools needed the three "F's," funds, facilities, and faculties. The agenda was to get more money, build more buildings, and hire more teachers, all to serve the growing number of students. Thanks in part to the now-defunct National Committee for the Support of Public Schools, citizens and state legislators mobilized to secure better funding for public education. Concurrently, the Ford Foundation created the Educational Facilities Laboratories, whose mission was to assist schools and colleges to meet more effectively the demands for expanded physical plants as well as to make better use of existing facilities.

The baby boom also had its impact on the demand for teachers. Teacher education programs expanded dramatically to prepare more and more teachers to staff the new classrooms and the children in them. Some years later colleges and universities would face similar faculty shortages as the babies grew into young adults.

By the mid-1970s, school enrollments were beginning to decline. The babies were gone; more than a few of them were now in college. Schools were closing and the teacher ranks were reduced by early retirement incentives or reductions in force, often dictated by collective bargaining agreements of "last in-first out." While school enrollments were declining generally, enrollments of poor, minority, and otherwise at-risk students were increasing and represented a higher percentage of the enrollment, especially in our cities. Thus schools overall had fewer students, but they had more students with diverse and special needs than ever before.

The pressures for quantitative growth in the 1950s were followed by demands for quality or educational "excellence." Still largely absent from the education agenda was attention to the needs of children of widely diverse backgrounds and to those with handicaps. School desegregation was inching along "with all deliberate speed." And the term "dropout" was barely on anyone's mind, much less a major problem to be dealt with.

256

The Soviet Union's launching of Sputnik in 1957 resulted in an electrifying spurt in the drive for "excellence." The nation responded in many ways. One was the 1958 report, *The Pursuit of Excellence: Education and the Future of America*, commissioned by the Rockefeller Brothers Fund. Another was passage of the National Defense Education Act (NDEA) with its combined thrust of "excellence" and concerns about national defense. NDEA's mission was directed largely at the more academically oriented students. The focus was on improving the quality of instruction in science, math, and foreign languages — areas that received renewed attention in the "excellence" movement of the 1980s, but for different reasons. The goal was to enrich schools academically in order to prepare students to compete with the Russians and their daunting technology.

Some look back on the NDEA years and say it "creamed the cream," that is, it skimmed the top of the cream from the rest of the cream and never dealt with the milk. There was not much ferment in the country then about dealing with the milk, that is, equal educational opportunity. Rather, there was a kind of unspoken agreement to focus our resources on the more able. For the rest, the standard fare of schools and colleges was good enough.

So, National Merit Scholarships were created, along with programs to accelerate the able, such as Early Admission to College and Advanced Placement, both based on the premise that if students have the academic capacity to advance, they should be allowed to do so. The Early Admission to College program, while judged a success, soon abated as high schools objected to losing their academic "cream." But Advanced Placement, which began in the mid-Fifties, has continued to grow, now serving about 200,000 academically able students each year.

Also during that time came what I call the "New Deal" in curricular reform (others called it the alphabet soup curriculum). Remember PSSC, BSCS, SMSG? When translated they mean, respectively, Physical Science Study Commission, Biological Sciences Curriculum Study, and Stanford Mathematics Study Group. These curricula and others were developed by academicians in the disciplines. These programs had integrity with respect to mathematics and the sciences, but critics argued that they did not take into account sufficiently the cognitive development of children and youth or their "teachability." Some of these curricula were billed as being "teacher proof." As a result, they did not take hold in schools as expected. To put it in the words of Charlie Brown, "You can't teach new math with an old math mind." Nonetheless, this earlier excellence movement sought to upgrade the academic quality of schools by targeting talented students and devising better curricula.

As the nation entered the 1960s, looming large were the civil rights movement, the women's movement, collective bargaining for teachers, and what was then thought to be a modest war in Southeast Asia. At that time, too, the Supreme Court's 1954 decision in *Brown* v. *Board of Education* declaring segregated schools unconstitutional was viewed largely as a regional issue, a problem in the South and not much elsewhere. Early desegregation efforts were limited to moving students among the schools but not doing much to change instructional programs for them.

The nation was also becoming aware of what had been going on for some time: the erosion of our cities. More middle-class people were moving, or trying to move, to the suburbs; the cities were in trouble and so were the lives of some of the people in them. Slowly, initiatives emerged to meet the needs of a formerly invisible group, those we were later to call the "disadvantaged." These children and young adults were not a new population; we used to call them poor because many of them were, and often so because of discrimination. Finally, education leaders started to pay attention to them under the rubric of urban school reform.

I remember working with a preschool experiment in Baltimore in 1961. (Could Head Start be far behind?) Remedial education also began to be institutionalized in our schools. Then, it was the conventional wisdom that what schools were doing was pretty good; but if some students couldn't make the grade, then they were to be "remediated." So they were given more help, but more of the same did not work. The effort to help disadvantaged students – later to be called "compensatory education" – was, and continues to be, as challenging an instructional mission as our schools have ever faced. To help those we now call "at risk" is the most serious test of the pedagogical power of our schools.

Throughout the 1960s and beyond, the social agenda of the schools was becoming more dominant. The drive to desegregate and integrate schools continued with more force and vigor, first in the South and later in the North. The law was clear: our schools must be integrated – something we were not willing to do in our neighborhoods. As a result, schools needed to become more directly engaged in fostering social harmony. They also needed to provide services that went beyond formal academic instruction. Increasingly, schools were expected to feed kids, give them clothes, provide health services, transport more of them, and expand counseling and social support services. And gradually, with support from federal laws, the schools began to provide education for those who are physically, emotionally, or mentally handicapped and for those speaking a language other than English.

Civil rights for minorities, for women, for the handicapped, separately and together, has generated a sea change in education. How different our schools are as a result. One need only look at any school to find affirmative action, handicap access ramps and elevators, cultural pluralism, equal access, women's studies, ethnic studies, captioned television, mainstreaming, talking books, ethnic and gender mix in faculties and staff, bilingualism, equal opportunity policies, traditional curricula now sensitive to race and gender issues, and on and on.

The earlier push for quality in education in the 1950s and early 1960s was limited because it was targeted largely at the more academically able. Similarly, the later and much more pervasive push for equality was also limited because it did not take academic quality fully into account. But together they add up to what education needs to provide, namely, both equality and quality. Indeed, they are not separable, certainly not for the society we aspire to be and constitutionally must be.

As we moved into the 1970s, educational technology was making a comeback. Not television this time; instead, it was programmed instruction, sequenced workbooks, and teaching machines. A little later it was computer-assisted instruction and computer-managed instruction; now it is interactive video joining computers with sound and picture − in glowing color and "user friendly." Time and experience will tell us whether these technologies will make greater contributions to the quality and equality of education than their antecedents.

Another important new thrust in education was the issue of accountability. States and local schools established programs to improve basic skills, often with added funds for testing to measure the outcome of the the programs. The intent was, and still is, to ensure that students acquire solid learning in basic skills and to hold teachers and students accountable by a test − more often than not, a standardized one.

More recently school/business partnerships have flourished. Some are promising; others are not. At the very least, the level of public understanding about education is rising as more people outside schools get involved, particularly those who have some voice and power in their communities and can make a difference in the schools. Increasingly, the public is realizing how essential schools are to the health and well-being of their communities. Other kinds of partnerships include schools and health service agencies and school/college collaboratives. The latter is *deja vu* for me, since years ago I was involved in a number of Ford Foundation-supported efforts to bring schools and universities together. Then they did it because it was "innovative." Now colleges and universities collaborate with schools because they need students; and improved schools should produce more of them. Also today, the development of magnet schools are providing broader options and signify a new diversity in public education.

Moreover, there now is a larger and more significant body of knowledge about learning, about child development, and about instruction and teaching. For example, there has been a renewed emphasis on what makes a school effective, what makes it work for students. We are coming at last to learn how important it is to bring decision-making authority for instruction to the individual school level and not have all the shots called at the central office, much less the state house or the nation's capital. We now know how important it is for those at the building level (principals, teachers, other staff, and parents) to have a greater role in deciding what the school should do and, certainly, how to do it. But first they have to have resources to carry out their responsibilities; and they need to be held accountable for the outcomes.

The call for educational excellence began with the publication of *A Nation at Risk* in 1983 and sparked numerous studies and reports about education. However, these renewed calls for excellence had to take into account the equity gains that had come about in the 1960s and 1970s. For example, a group of hard-headed business executives studying the schools for the Committee on Economic Development spoke to the need for both educational excellence and equality in two reports, *Investing in Our Children: Business and the Public Schools* and *Children in Need: Investment Strategies for the Educationally Disadvantaged*. These two studies were but a sample of many that have appeared in recent years. With few exceptions, all spoke to excellence in education in a context of equality. Whether the impetus for a study was the need to improve America's workforce, to increase the level of literacy, or to enhance civic participation, recommendations took into account all students and underscored the need for an open, accessible, but still rigorous system of education. An analogy comes to mind when thinking about excellence and equity: A quality meal is nutritious and tasty but is of little consequence unless all are allowed to come to the table and eat it. What is needed is a quality meal to which all have access and all can eat. In short, we cannot separate excellence from equity.

The 1980s also brought a reaffirmation of the centrality and significance of education to America's economic, political, and social future. Equally significant was that this reaffirmation was made by a cross-section of our nation's leadership, from business and corporate executives to labor leaders, governors, legislators, scholars, and artists – and, yes, even educators.

Now in the 1990s, the challenge to improve education to meet the dual goals of excellence and equity is even greater. Today, perhaps more than before, we must rely on the creativity, productivity, sensitivity, and civility of individuals working together in order to be effective workers, responsible citizens, good neighbors, caring parents, and sensitive persons. As our nation and the world grow more interdependent, we need to rely on the judgment of the people – individually and in groups. The capacity to make sound judgments and difficult decisions is a function of education. Education is the way that we develop the knowledge and the wherewithal to understand, to analyze, to think, and to decide – all in the context of a free and just society. Lofty as it may sound, that is the essence of what education needs to do for this society and for each one of us in it.

The Ford Foundation's activities aimed at improving education have ranged widely. Sometimes they were aimed at improving access to schools, colleges, and special programs for students who might otherwise have been excluded. Others were aimed at enabling education to meet changes in the workplace, to reflect cultural and gender diversity, to serve learners who need special assistance or those who are capable of advancing beyond the norm. Work along this line also supported research, seminars, and the development of degree programs in new academic disciplines. Still other activities were aimed at improving the quality of schools and college curricula, including different instructional arrangements, applications of new technologies, and additional student services.

Since education is largely a public enterprise, many of the Ford Foundation's activities were aimed at enhancing public participation in and support for education. These activities included developing new arrangements for managing and governing public schools and

261

for financing them more equitably. It sponsored research on the processes of teaching and learning and helped to generate new forms of evaluation and assessment. These activities often were targeted at those directly involved in education: teachers, professors, administrators, counselors, paraprofessionals, trustees, board members, state and federal education officials. They took the form of fellowships, on-the-job training, formal degree programs, informal workshops and conferences. Whatever the form and whoever was involved, the expected outcome was always to improve education qualitatively, quantitatively, and humanely, and to do so in ways that were consistent with the nature of our democratic society and within its means.

As a foundation executive who granted funds for all kinds of projects, I have learned many lessons. For one, I learned that ideas and innovations won't take hold unless the conditions are right for them to be understood and implemented. As an illustration, I offer the Ford Foundation's early investments in instructional television. Some years later and after the outlay of millions of dollars in grants, there was little residue to be found in and around schools and colleges. In some instances, implementation was hurried and not thorough; in others, the commitment was greater in the funding agency than it was in the grantees in the schools and colleges.

But today instructional television is a fact of life in many places. Why? For one thing, the technology has improved. Initially classes had to be scheduled around broadcast times; now there is the VCR. Also, through years of experience, we know better how to put together programs that both inform and instruct. Look at the motivational and pedagogical qualities of such efforts as "Sesame Street," the National Geographic specials, and countless other TV series now in use in schools and colleges. Television is embedded in American life — for better or worse. To the extent that it plays a role in education, it will be for better.

Some of the most painful — and lasting — lessons arose from the attempt to devise and apply innovations designed to somehow improve education. Sometimes the innovation was to be a "model" program. That is, if it accomplished what it was intended to do, say in a school or a college, the program could be transported, perhaps with some adjustments, to a similar setting. The adjustments might involve the training of program participants in the new setting. Or sometimes the adjustment meant tinkering with, if not changing, the "model" to accommodate the context of a setting that differed from that of the original site.

262

Training was always necessary but, unfortunately, rarely done as thoroughly as necessary in order to enable the trainees to understand the model fully and to implement it effectively in the new setting. Often the designers and implementers of the original model resisted tinkering with, much less changing, the model. They argued, with some justification, that too much tinkering would "corrupt" the model, altering it in ways such that it no longer could be expected to accomplish what it was intended to do. More often than not, however, the developers of the model gave little thought to *who* participated in the original pilot testing or to the *setting* in which it took place.

One lesson is that few model educational programs are easily rooted and grown elsewhere (or diffused, as the federal government prefers to call the process). It is difficult to replicate models neatly because all educational programs involve people: teachers, students, administrators. But people are different. A model that works with some people might work with others who are properly trained, but it may never work with still others, trained or not. The characteristics of the student and teacher population originally involved in the model are never quite the same elsewhere; nor is the context, no two of which are precisely alike. Settings affect what goes on in them.

Simply put, the first lesson is to learn what the essential features of the model are — what I have come to call the integrity factors — that cannot be compromised. If these factors are largely to be found only in the characteristics and capacities of the persons originally engaged in the model program or only in the nature and context of the original setting, then beware. Replicating it elsewhere will be difficult if not impossible. Social innovation is never perfect. Rather, it often is quite messy. Understanding and dealing with that fact is essential.

Another lesson I have learned from working with model programs comes from those who wish to use models. Over the years, I have seen leaders of schools and colleges — both professional and lay persons — eagerly adopt a model in the belief it will solve a problem or quickly improve their school, college, or program. They often see the model as a "quick fix." If they try a particular model and it does not quite do the job (typically the decision to use the model is made in haste and after only a cursory study of the problem the model is intended to address), then they try another model, then another, hoping to find the right one. The search for the quick fix becomes an addiction to find *the* model program, *the* model curriculum, *the* model organization. Sadly, the search and not the model becomes the goal. And the search goes on, mindlessly in some cases, to find that "perfect" fit or, if not that, to keep up with kindred institutions and agencies that are lost as well in their searches for the "right" model. What should really matter more is why we are searching and what we are learning from the model programs that are being tried out. That is where the learning occurs, not in the search itself.

Still other lessons I have learned cluster around teachers. Take the so-called "teacher proof" curriculum programs. In my experience, the more able and pedagogically nimble the teacher, the better the use and outcomes of any curriculum program will be. More often, it is the less-able teacher who makes a curriculum "teacher proof" by rigidly applying it to students. As a result, the outcomes are disappointing and fall short of expectations. Able teachers make curriculum programs succeed, sometimes with better results than could reasonably be expected. Less-able teachers do not.

Modifications in school staffing also taught me a lesson. Some years ago, the Ford Foundation, through its Fund for the Advancement of Education, supported the idea of using teacher aides to assist the regular teacher in the classroom. At first the idea was widely criticized with the argument that it would undermine the authority of the classroom teacher. Today, teacher aides are commonplace. Indeed, they are now organized and are represented by the same teacher unions that originally criticized them. Later, there were experiments using lay volunteers to assist the school staff in many ways. They, too, were suspect for a time. Today, the school volunteer movement is well established in the schools nationally.

In this instance, the lesson is that improving schools and colleges in any real and lasting way takes time. Unlike factories, which can quickly change the equipment and manufacturing process on the assembly line to put out a different product, educational institutions have no assembly lines to change. Educational institutions are more people than they are machines. Also, the "product" or the so-called "bottom line" in education cannot be so clearly defined as it is in business and industry. Further, there are differences — even when there are agreements — about what the outcomes of our schools and colleges ought to be. The recent action by the nation's governors and the White House announcing national educational goals is laudable. Still, those goals, as general as they are, represent only some of what we expect from our schools and colleges. Some people would argue that those goals, while important, may be no more important than, for example, learning to live with and care for others in families, neighborhoods, workplaces, and other cultures and nations. Others might argue that a goal of developing informed, active, and participating citizens is every bit as important as the goal set for student performances in mathematics.

School and colleges are more labor dependent and labor intensive than are technologically driven industries. I have been puzzled over the years by the number of innovations and programs to improve schools and colleges that ignore that education is a human enterprise. It is an enterprise that succeeds best when its rich human resources are recognized and used. Too many efforts — and I helped to fund some of them — have tried to harness people into a specific mold of sameness and, as a result, failed to capitalize on the visions and energies of the people themselves. The outcomes may be more uniform but are minimal compared to the potential of what education can be. Slowly we have come to recognize that our schools and our colleges are driven by people. Therefore, they need to be empowered with more authority; and with this authority, they can be held more accountable. By doing so, I believe we can expect higher levels of performance from them and, in turn, get better results in student learning.

In this human factor lies the paramount lesson I have learned over my many years participating in varied activities aimed at improving education. It goes something like this: The good idea, the best strategy, the most thoughtful innovation or intervention — even in the most receptive setting and at the most appropriate time with the right amount of support — still need people to see them through. In the foundation world, we use a cliché: You don't fund projects, you fund people. This is especially true when it comes to the leadership of a project. I have worked with all kinds of people, from the prominent and powerful to the little known and powerless, from those carrying vast responsibilities to those who carry very few, from those with a track record of success to those who have none. These known factors (power, responsibility, track record) served only as partial indicators of what leaders could and would do when the time came for me to make recommendations for funding grants. There were other traits I came to rely on, traits that made awarding a grant a true opportunity and a risk worth taking.

The persons who stand out as leaders, those who were good bets, shared some common traits. While each may not have had all of these traits or not to the same degree, the following baker's dozen could be found among most of the truly effective leaders with whom I have worked over the years.

1. They had a solid sense of a real issue or problem, one that was fundamental to the mission of their organization or program and often to that of similar organizations elsewhere. Rarely did they deal with a contrived or artificial issue or problem or with trivial matters. Rather, they saw deeply into the heart of a matter of concern or need.

2. They had a vision of what could be, a vision that was lofty yet practical. They wanted things to be better for the program or organization for which they were responsible. Their vision was coupled with hope, not of the Pollyanna variety but a real and uplifting hope. To me, the expression of genuine hope is a sure sign of leadership.

3. They had a reasonable approach, if not a fully developed strategy, for dealing with the issue or problem that was within reach, one that was "doable," and, perhaps, one that involved risk but, nevertheless, stood a good chance of succeeding.

4. They had a firm commitment to do what they proposed to do regardless of whether they ever got a grant. Somehow they were going to go forward with or without this support. I always thought that effective grant-giving was like adding momentum to a wave about to crest, that is, the funds enabled the wave to be more forceful and, as a result, to yield more powerful results.

5. They had the capacity to stick to their project or program. This is not to say they were stubborn or blindly pushed forward whatever the circumstances. But they were tenacious, they held fast, they stayed strong. They were able to cope with big and little obstacles, to overcome lethargy in their organization, to make necessary adjustments and yet keep their eye on the target. And finally, they were tenacious enough to be patiently impatient.

6. They were people who, by and large, viewed what they were doing as bigger than themselves. The mission or the project was personal only in that they knew that they had an opportunity — almost an obligation, in some cases — to be part of a larger cause. They had confidence in themselves to do what was proposed. Rarely were they arrogant; more often than not they were humble about this confidence.

7. They were willing to learn from others, from experience, from research and study. They were discerning learners, persons not easily persuaded by just any evidence or judgment but open to anything relevant. They accepted — even sought — such knowledge or judgment, even when it might be critical to a point of being harsh. More importantly, they used criticism to make course corrections in the

266

come up with different recommendations that would better serve the state.

Most state coordinating boards have three fundamental responsibilities: 1) to develop and maintain statewide master plans for higher education, 2) to recommend adequate and equitable budgets for higher education, and 3) to approve new programs and new campuses for the state. If these three purposes are carried out responsibly, they are of substantial importance to the state and to the campuses. These are professional tasks, not political ones.

I have found that thoughtful legislators and state government executives expect and appreciate professional judgments. They expect educators to be educators, not novice politicians. Frank Newman (1987) did a study of state intrusion into the academic affairs of colleges and universities. He found examples of such intrusion but not as many as may have been predicted. A more important finding was that in most cases of state intrusion, the campuses had invited such intrusion. That is, having failed to achieve certain objectives through the established proposal and review process, some faculty or administrators tried to do an "end run" around the established process by using the political process. The lesson they soon learned was that when you invite political intervention for things you want, you can expect intervention on some things you don't want.

A state coordinating board can be enormously influential if it understands its roles and carries them out responsibly and professionally. The board is of inestimable help to the state legislature and administration. As the higher education planning agency, it addresses needs of the state and precludes "over-serving" through unnecessary duplication. As the fiscal agency, it determines equitable funding for each institution and is a buffer against personal-interest lobbying. As the program approval agency, it authorizes programs that are needed — and only those programs. Moreover, the coordinating board executive officer can, without the burdens of campus operation responsibilities, look across the state and address those matters that can improve higher education and the state.

Coordinating boards, by definition, are protectors of campus autonomy. They neither hire nor fire presidents or other campus personnel, nor do they stipulate line-item budgeting. They do, however, adhere to campus missions; thus, they can be frustrating to an expansion-minded president whose aspirations go beyond the campus mission. Some coordinating boards fail to adhere judiciously to coordination and unwisely get enmeshed in governance. Freedom from governance responsibilities is what makes a coordinating board an exciting incubator for ideas.

Some matters in higher education that need to be addressed are: 1) making college attendance financially affordable for all academically qualified students, 2) providing an adequate cadre of well-trained manpower for the state, 3) developing a reservoir of "know-how" for the state through research and public service, 4) developing the effective use of telecommunications and other technology for the delivery of higher education, 5) providing academic articulation with K-12 education and between two-year and four-year institutions, and 6) defining the role of higher education in developing civic responsibility.

The state must be assured that its higher education needs are being met, that its tax investments are used well and wisely, and that quality performance is demonstrated. In Tennessee, the coordinating board addresses these matters through goal-setting and performance-based incentive funding. The successes have been most satisfying. Most quality improvements exceed national norms, with respect to academic aptitude of beginning students, performance of seniors on tests of general education knowledge, performance of students in professional fields of study on licensure examinations, placement of occupational students in relevant jobs, and alumni satisfaction with their educational experiences.

On Higher Education Organization

Any discussion of higher education would be incomplete without addressing the highly visible and volatile topic of organization. The trend in governance organization of higher education in recent years has been toward so-called "super boards." This trend is misguided and needs to be reversed, in my judgment.

American higher education has no peer in the world. Unfavorable comparisons of this country with other industrially developed nations in such areas as K-12 performance in mathematics, science, and geography, industrial product quality, and worker productivity never include higher education. There are institutions of marginal quality to be sure; however, collectively, our colleges and universities clearly are the best in the world. Students from other countries clamor to study in America, and American-based research — most of which is done at our universities — is far superior to research in any other country.

We became world leaders in higher education by prizing autonomous campuses under the oversight of lay boards. These lay boards

300

initially provided campuses the freedom for teaching and learning and for conducting research without their being controlled by prescriptive ideology and doctrines of the church. Later, the same principle of lay boards became a part of public colleges and universities to buffer them from partisan politics. We still have lay boards, but a single public college or university with a single board is becoming rare. Rather, we are seeing a single governance board whose authority encompasses several campuses. Many states are adopting "super boards" with one board for all of the public colleges and universities in the state. Because of the scope of responsibilities of these multi-campus boards, they cannot be guardians of single campus autonomy. Rather, they can attend only to the non-academic trustee functions that promote look-alike homogeneity on all the campuses.

In higher education we seem to be unlearning what the best-run businesses and industries are beginning to learn; namely, that creativity and productivity are fostered in small autonomous units with lots of freedom to experiment and with lean centralized management dedicated to goal setting and quality assessment.

On Intercollegiate Athletics

Perhaps the most talked about and written about topic in higher education is intercollegiate athletics. No other program in higher education is depicted in a full section of daily newspapers and in a segment of the nightly news broadcasts.

Many observers believe that intercollegiate athletics is "out-of-control." With increasing frequency we hear reports of institutions cheating on the rules and of academic compromises through transcript tampering and "baby courses" for athletes. Many presidents and governing boards seem to be powerless to control the integrity of athletics on their campuses.

The National Collegiate Athletic Association (NCAA) requires that its representatives and officers be affiliated with member colleges and universities. Each year, prior to the annual NCAA policy-making convention, the presidents are asked to name convention delegates from their respective institutions. Typically, the delegates are directors of athletics and faculty representatives. Few presidents bother to involve themselves in the work of NCAA.

When I was a university president, I decided that I must become involved in athletic policy making, so I named myself as one of the delegates from my university. For the first several years of attendance, I saw only a handful of other presidents. Presidents claimed they were

301

too busy to be involved in NCAA matters. They seemed not to be too busy, however, to attend the annual American Council on Education meeting and other meetings in which they were interested.

During my involvement as a delegate, I was elected to the NCAA Council, the governing body of the organization, and later to the Executive Committee as Vice-President for Division I, the major universities. During that time, two highly visible actions were the enactment of Proposition 48 and creation of the Presidents' Commission.

Proposition 48 set academic performance requirements in high school as a prerequisite for a student athlete to be eligible to compete in intercollegiate athletics. The hue and cry across the country was loud — and embarrassing. There was much anguish expressed that talented athletes would be academically ineligible and thus not allowed to compete; that the policy discriminated against blacks, particularly black males; and that the NCAA was interfering in university academic policy.

The NCAA exhibited extraordinary leadership on this issue. A study was conducted during the time between passage of the policy and its implementation to determine differential impact on student athletes. That study was one of the most definitive ever done on high school academic preparation for college and on college academic performance and survival. The findings were clear: Student athletes performed at a higher academic level in college if they took basic core courses in high school. And, indeed, black males who scored low on standard college aptitude admission tests (ACT and SAT) were more likely to perform at a satisfactory level in college than did white males who scored low on these tests. The embarrassment was the minimum level of the new requirements. ACT and SAT score requirements were below the predicted level for satisfactory academic performance, and the high school core curriculum requirements stipulated completion with at least a grade of C.

Proposition 48 made no policy regarding college admissions. Institutions could admit any student they wanted to admit regardless of academic aptitude. The policy only stipulated minimum academic requirements for a student athlete to compete in intercollegiate athletics. Student athletes who were admitted but did not meet the academic requirements could not compete nor practice in intercollegiate athletics during their freshman year. Their subsequent participation in athletics was allowed only if their academic performance was satisfactory during the freshman year. That college and university officials complained so loudly about this minimum academic requirement was indicative of their lack of academic backbone.

302

The experiment of Proposition 48 has a happy ending. It works. When students know what the requirements are for participating in intercollegiate athletics, they will meet those requirements. After the first couple of years of Proposition 48, student athletes, for the most part, are coming to college having met the minimum academic requirements. Now, I think it is time to strengthen Proposition 48.

This experiment in intercollegiate athletics policy making has wider implications for secondary education. For example, colleges and universities can influence the nature of courses taken in high school by being unequivocal about what is required for admission to higher education institutions. In Tennessee the public colleges and universities have stipulated rather extensive high school core curriculum requirements for students admitted in the fall of 1989 and later. High schools had five years to get the curriculum in place and advise students of the new requirements.

Some college and university presidents predicted gloom and doom; their enrollments would plummet; high schools couldn't offer the courses; teachers were not available to teach the required high school courses. What happened? College and university enrollments increased at a rate greater than had been the case in the previous 15 years. Student enrollment in high school geometry and advanced mathematics increased by 116%, foreign languages by 138%, and natural and physical science by 44%. Again, the message is clear. If you expect students to be prepared academically, tell them. They will get prepared.

The formation of the Presidents' Commission within NCAA was the second important event influencing college athletics. The absence of presidential involvement in the affairs of the NCAA was a matter of great concern to the NCAA Council. To remedy this, the council designed a plan for creating a Presidents' Commission patterned somewhat like the council, with powers to develop agenda items for the annual meeting, to call special meetings of the delegates, and to prescribe roll-call votes on certain agenda items.

The roll-call vote issue was an interesting one. Presidents claimed that their delegates were not voting the way they (the presidents) wanted them to vote. By calling for roll-call votes, the presidents could check up on the votes cast by their delegates. The NCAA is perhaps the most democratic of all the associations with which I have worked. All of those NCAA rules and regulations were developed by the membership. Although presidents claimed to be powerless in NCAA, they were, in fact, all-powerful and could exert absolute control if they chose to. All they had to do when the request came to name delegates was to name themselves as the voting delegates, thus giving them the authority to vote on all the issues. Clearly, the presidents were not interested; but neither did they trust their own staff whom they appointed as delegates to represent them.

In the meantime, the American Council on Education (ACE) decided to take matters in hand and show the NCAA who was boss. They loaded a chartered airplane with presidents and took them to Vail, Colorado, to develop their own plan for reorganizing the NCAA. In their position paper, they complained that the NCAA was composed of persons whose only interest was athletics and that they were not representing the presidents' interests. They acknowledged that there were a few presidents on the NCAA Council (there were three of us at the time) but accused us of being co-opted by the athletic interests.

I was incensed that a planeload of presidents flew over Mission, Kansas, the headquarters of NCAA, on their way to Vail, Colorado, to develop a plan for the NCAA. None of those presidents had a record of working within NCAA. Indeed, only one or two had ever attended an NCAA convention over the previous 10 years. And they had the temerity to criticize me and the other two presidents on the NCAA Council who had become involved with policy making.

The plan developed by these presidents was to establish a Presidents' Council under the auspices of the American Council of Education, which would have veto power over actions taken at the NCAA conventions. They would not dirty their hands working with NCAA, but would rise above the organization and exercise vetoes over actions taken by their appointed delegates whom they didn't trust.

Derek Bok, president of Harvard, was selected to be the convention mouthpiece for the ACE position. The NCAA Council asked me to represent the council's plan on the convention floor. Although the ACE had lobbied hard for its plan and reported that it had the votes to win, the vote wasn't even close. The ACE plan was overwhelmingly defeated and the council's plan overwhelmingly adopted. Ironically, one of the speakers on behalf of the ACE was the president of Southern Methodist University. That great university's shameful athletic scandals soon became public knowledge, and the president was soon gone.

Although my comments may not sound like it, I have great respect for college and university presidents. They carry enormous responsibilities. What all of us have learned regarding problems in intercollegiate athletics is that not all presidents ride white horses. There are no short cuts for presidents; they are responsible for academics *and* athletics on their campuses, and they must get involved and let their positions on ethical issues and academic integrity be known. On this issue, the American Council on Education suffered from an omnipotent/omniscient complex. That may be a chronic illness of the American Council, which acts as if the headwaters of the education stream is in Washington, D.C. It is not. The action is in the states.

On Values

As I said in the beginning of this essay, reflections come easily when you have experienced a lifetime love affair with education. There are problems to be sure, but they pale in comparison to the joys of learning new things and teaching new things and seeing the country rally around education. The National Governors' Association has issued goals for education for the year 2000, and reforms are under way in many states. These goals are exciting and we must achieve them.

And we must take seriously Orin Graff's thesis on values. For 20 years, we have seen a declining interest among college students in community service, international relations, and race relations. These value commitments have been replaced by an obsession with making a lot of money and being in administrative control of others. Also, the steady decline in voting habits of all citizens is an embarrassment in a nation that calls itself a democracy. We all need a liberal portion of Graff's values, which refute the attitude that "what is to be will be." Rather, let us direct our actions so that what is to be will be based on human values.

There has never been a time when American education was more prized than it is now. There is a determined coalition of governors, other political leaders, and business leaders, which offers the best chance in our history of effecting far-reaching educational improvements. Let's be on with the task. This is the time for leaders in education to step forward, to abdicate their self-appointed positions as Chairmen of the Grievance Committee of the American Paranoia Society.

305

References

Kerr, Clarke, and Gade, Marian L. *The Guardians: Boards of Trustees of American Colleges and Universities; What They Do and How Well They Do It*. Washington, D.C.: Association of Governing Boards of Universities and Colleges, 1989.

Newman, Frank. *Choosing Quality: Reducing Conflict Between the State and the University*. Denver: Education Commission of the States, 1987.

Reflections on the Functions of Schools

BY J. GALEN SAYLOR

On the first Monday in September 1907, my two older brothers and I trudged our way "catty-corner" across a section of Nebraska farmland to the little white schoolhouse that served the educational needs of our community. Ever since that day, except for two short breaks, I have been involved extensively in the educational process as a student, teacher, school administrator, researcher, college professor, author, and just plain observer.

I was elected to membership in Phi Delta Kappa in 1937 by the University of Nebraska/Lincoln Chapter. At the time, and continuing to this day, I regard that act of recognition as a highlight of my professional life. Our monthly PDK meetings were held in a small hotel near the campus, which served us the best chicken dinner in town for 50 cents. During my residence at Teachers College, Columbia University as a graduate student, I participated in the activities of the fraternity and served as president of the chapter there in 1939-40. When I returned to Nebraska in 1940, I again attended the meetings of the chapter there and, except for several years when I was heavily involved in parent-teacher work, have continued to do so ever since.

Two significant developments in Phi Delta Kappa during the 54 years since I became a member have made it the foremost association of professional educators in the nation. These were the election of women to membership beginning in 1974 and the outstanding publications issued in recent years. Also, in the past few years the fraternity's journal, the *Phi Delta Kappan*, has had outstanding articles

J. Galen Saylor is Professor Emeritus of Secondary Education at the University of Nebraska-Lincoln.

on the broad issues of school reform, on promising developments in particular schools, and on the basic concepts that should guide school planning. And the fraternity has published numerous monographs and fastbacks covering the same and additional topics, which are practical, stimulating, thought-provoking, and valid in doctrine.

In recent years there has been continuing discussion and endless proposals in both educational and political circles of this nation for educational reform. Proposals range from demands that the schools reinstate the classical course of study that characterized the high schools and academies of the early 1900s to those calling for an almost complete restructuring of the present-day school program. This nationwide movement for reform is promising for the future of our country and augurs well for the present and coming generations of our children and youth. The schools of the future will be even better.

But how is one to select from all of these proposals? Which of them should educators, parents, and our political leaders adopt as valid and most promising for the carrying on the best possible programs of education in our schools and cultural institutions? In pondering what actions to take, let us first establish a philosophical base for decision making.

During the four centuries of this nation's history, we Americans have taken the necessary steps to ensure that every child should have an opportunity to obtain schooling. The first such action was the passage of the "Old Deluder Satan" Act of 1647, adopted by the governing body of the Massachusetts Bay Colony. It required every town of 50 families to establish a school that provided instruction in reading and writing to all children. Even earlier in 1635, the citizens of Boston had founded the Boston Latin Grammar School for advanced schooling at the secondary level. True, many Massachusetts towns over the years failed to establish the required primary school; and laws passed in 1787 and 1824 released all but seven communities from the requirement. Nevertheless, the basic concept of free, public schools for the children of the community had been clearly established.

The next major effort to provide an appropriate education for the youth of the nation was the founding in 1751 of the Philadelphia Academy and Charitable School, which was in keeping with Benjamin Franklin's famous "Proposals Relating to the Education of Youth in Pennsylvania." It offered a broader course of study than the Latin grammar schools and a more meaningful program for a broader segment of the youth of America.

308

One of the early actions of our newly established Republic was the enactment by Congress of the Northwest Ordinance in 1787. This ordinance captured the utmost importance of education for the children and youth of the nation with these words: "Religion, morality, and knowledge, being necessary to good government and the happiness of mankind, schools and the means of education shall forever be encouraged." In support of this obligation a section of land in each township (later increased to two sections, and then to four sections) was retained in public hands and administered by the respective states to support the founding of public schools.

The action of the School Committee of Boston in 1821 was another landmark event in this nation's efforts to provide a proper and adequate education for its youth. It authorized the establishment of the English High School, the first free public high school in the United States. The committee, in justifying its actions, stated the basic concept undergirding the development of public education in this nation as follows:

> The mode of education now adopted, and the branches of knowledge that are taught at our English grammar schools, are not sufficiently extensive nor otherwise calculated to bring the powers of the mind into operation nor to qualify a youth to fill usefully and respectably many of those stations, both public and private, in which he may be placed.[1]

The addition of the high school to the public education system for all children and youth was firmly established by the acclaimed Kalamazoo Decision rendered by the state supreme court of Michigan in 1874. The court upheld an 1850 law that established a system of public education extending from the primary school to the secondary school and on through to the university. Thus, complete programs of schooling were to be made available to all children and youth in Michigan by public agencies.

The states separately took two other very important actions to ensure that the children of America would have the opportunity to obtain an education: passage of child labor laws and compulsory school attendance laws. These legal steps further made certain that all children, regardless of parents' views and actions, would be able to develop their intellectual powers, a basic tenet of American democracy.

Two other important developments during the early decades of the 1900s further illustrate the efforts by governing agencies to provide schooling that would serve the educational needs and interests of children and youth. They were the establishment of the junior high school and the passage of the Smith-Hughes Act of 1917. The first was an effort to improve education for the critical early adolescent years; the other was an attempt to offer a broader, more diversified curriculum. Other movements, legislative acts, and official actions by state and national bodies could be added to this list of major efforts to ensure every child and youth the opportunity to be educated in free public schools.

Notwithstanding the tremendous efforts made by the state and federal governments over some 300 years to provide every child and youth a free education in public schools, substantial numbers did not take advantage of these opportunities. In 1950 the federal census began collecting information on the years of schooling completed. At that time 54.2% of persons 20 years of age had completed high school. Of those 25-29 years of age, 51.7% had completed high school. For all persons 25 and older, only 33.4% had completed high school. The median years of schooling completed by this 25 and older age group was 9.3 years.[2] This figure, of course, includes many immigrants. In the absence of any official census data, one may reasonably assume that during the period of 1910-1920 not more than one of every three or four youths graduated from high school.

In the years following World War I, several developments occurred that contributed to a gradual increase in secondary school attendance. One was the introduction of vocational training courses under the Smith-Hughes Act or by action of local authorities. Another was drastic changes in the requirements for high school graduation and corollary action by colleges and universities to change entrance requirements. Over time, these developments brought about many major changes in high school course offerings. Some examples include: a course called General Mathematics that could be used to meet graduation requirements; General Biology replacing separate courses in Botany and Physiology; World History replacing Ancient History, English History, and European History; Social Studies replacing Geography and Civics; dropping of foreign language requirements; and other changes in course titles and content.

High school attendance did increase quite remarkably. By the 1960 census, 41.1% of all persons 25 years of age or older had completed high school; by 1970 the percentage had risen to 52.3%; and in 1980 it was 66.5%. The median year of schooling completed by all persons 25 or older was 10.5 years in 1960, 12.1 years in 1970, and 12.5 in 1980. But the overall situation is still very disturbing when a third of the adults of this nation have not completed a program of schooling that was designed to provide the basic skills necessary for carrying on the social, economic, and political functions in our American democracy.

It should not be necessary to review the 1980s here. We are all too familiar with the reports, the senseless charges, the threats, the proposals for action. Let's hope that the 1990s will be a period of genuine reform that will ensure each child and youth in America the most meaningful and appropriate education we collectively can plan and then provide. Such efforts for improvement must be based on a sound philosophical base, which is accepted by those participating in the planning and in the doing. Here is my base. I invite you to consider it.

The fundamental function of the public school is to contribute maximally, within its resources, to the development of the capabilities, talents, and interests of all children and youth entrusted to its care. Planning an educational program to fulfill this function requires consideration of these basic and all-encompassing factors:

WHOM am I teaching?
WHAT am I to teach?
HOW do I teach?[3]

Obviously, the three factors are interrelated; but to facilitate planning, we may postulate that a school's program of studies and learning experiences for all students falls within eight broad domains of subject matter and learning experiences:

1. Communicative Arts
2. Humanities
3. Social Sciences
4. Sciences and Mathematics
5. The Arts
6. Health and Physical Well-Being
7. Human Relationships and Parenthood
8. Special Individual Interests[4]

All students, from kindergarten to the senior year of high school, should have appropriate learning experiences in each of these domains. The WHOM and WHAT factors determine the nature and extent of such instruction for each year of schooling. The HOW factor is the essence of teaching. Thus teaching embodies the utmost understanding, insight, and skill in making sound judgments at any particular time and with any particular group.

A basic consideration in planning and carrying out a program of schooling for children and youth is the issue of equality. De Tocqueville, in his *Democracy in America*, based on his studies of American culture in the 1830s, makes this observation:

> There is, in fact, a manly and lawful passion for equality that incites men to wish all to be powerful and honored. This passion tends to elevate the humble to the rank of the great; but there exists also in the human heart a depraved taste for equality, which impels the weak to attempt to lower the powerful to their own level and reduces men to prefer equality in slavery to inequality with freedom.[5]

But de Tocqueville also makes this fundamental observation:

> The gifts of intellect proceed directly from God, and man cannot prevent their unequal distribution. But it is at least a consequence of what I have just said that although the capacities of men are different, as the Creator intended they should be, the means that Americans find for putting them to use are equal.[6]

Thus, in planning educational programs for all children and youth of this nation, we must provide 1) schooling for all; 2) equal opportunity to develop the talents, capabilities, and intellectual needs for each individual student; and 3) a planned program of educational experiences that enables each person to lead a satisfying, challenging, productive, and socially acceptable life.

Suggestions for Schooling

My own recommendations for school "reform" are two: 1) provide differentiated programs for students as they advance through the years of schooling, and 2) provide each student with an appropriate set of learning experiences in each of the eight domains mentioned earlier.

In our school organizational structures, in the curriculum, and in our teaching methods, we must give much more consideration to the capabilities, talents, interests, and developmental level of each student. As we plan and carry out our programs of schooling from kindergarten through high school graduation, we must provide differentiation throughout the program.

Recent professional literature contains many excellent suggestions on this whole matter of restructuring, differentiation, and serving more fully the needs of individual students. Many schools throughout the nation have been developing instructional programs that better serve the needs of students, ranging from those with serious disabilities to those with unusually high levels of some particular talent or capability.

Perhaps the best example of differentiation is what most schools have been doing for a long time. I am referring to the varied and challenging opportunities schools provide in the area of athletics and sports activities. From the games and activities on elementary school playgrounds and in physical education classes through the more highly organized interscholastic sports programs in high schools, schools have nurtured students' talents and interests of a physical nature. To those who demonstrate superior talent in athletics have come local, state, and national recognition and often scholarships to college.

Many school systems have other programs that provide for differentiation based on students' talents and interests. Although less common than in athletic programs, schools now provide programs for students with unusual abilities in the sciences, music, graphic arts, literary arts, mathematics, mechanical skills, and possibly others. A number of school systems have established specialized high schools, often designated as magnet schools. Professional literature is replete with descriptions and plans for differentiating instruction in schools.

Regardless of how students are grouped or assigned to class sections, ALL should have appropriate, meaningful, and stimulating educational experiences in terms of their needs, interests, and capabilities and to prepare them for their obligations in a democratic society. For example, kindergartners should have challenging and continuing learning experiences in the communicative arts so they can carry on conversations and discussions with classmates and teachers. They also should be experiencing the joy and creativity that come from participating in the domain of the arts. And an abundance of learning experiences in the other six domains should be undertaken during the school year. Similarly, each student, for the full 13 years in the common schools of the nation, should have appropriate learning experiences in each of the eight domains.

To carry out this function of the school, national commissions should be established for each domain and be charged with defining the instructional goals in each domain and specifying levels of attainment a student should achieve at the elementary, middle, and secondary school. The commissions should set minimum attainment levels for all students at each level of schooling and also desired attainment levels for students with the ability and motivation for higher levels of achievement. However, the recommendations of the vari-

313

ous commissions would not be prescriptive. Rather, individual schools, perhaps with some state guidelines, would use the recommendations as a resource for curriculum planning and would set the minimum levels of attainment to be reached by their pupils.

Whatever efforts are made in the years ahead to provide the best schooling possible, we all must continuously plan on the basis of the ultimate function of a school: to contribute to the maximum development of the talents, capabilities, and interests of each child and youth entrusted to its care.

Phi Delta Kappa, within the limits of its resources, should continue to assist those who provide schooling to our young to fulfill that function.

Footnotes

1. Boston School Committee, Minutes, 1821, quoted from E.P. Cubberley, *Readings in Public Education in the United States* (Boston: Houghton Mifflin, 1934), pp. 229-30

2. U.S. Bureau of the Census, *U.S. Census of Population: 1950, Vol. 2, Characteristics of the Population, Part. 1, U.S. Summary* (Washington, D.C.: U.S. Government Printing Office, 1953), Chapter C, Tables 114, 115.

3. Herbert M. Kliebard, "Problems of Definition in Curriculum," *Journal of Curriculum and Supervision* 5 (Fall 1989): 1-5. Discusses more fully these three factors in educational planning.

4. Two important similar lists of the essential areas for the schooling of youth are: Commission on the Reorganization of Secondary Education, *Cardinal Principles of Secondary Education*, U.S. Office of Education Bulletin No. 35 (Washington, D.C.: U.S. Government Printing Office, 1918), pp. 10-11; and Educational Policies Commission, *Education for All American Youth* (Washington, D.C.: National Education Association, 1944), pp. 225-26.

5. Alexis de Tocqueville, *Democracy in America*, Vol. 1, 53 (Garden City, N.Y.: Doubleday, 1969), p. 57.

6. Ibid. p. 56.

Reflections on Social and Educational Directions for the 1990s

BY HAROLD G. SHANE

The schools I attended as a youngster and many of those in which I taught had a physical setting and a curriculum similar to the ones that existed at or before the turn of the century. Although the Committee of Ten convened by the National Education Association recommended seven worthy Cardinal Principles of Education in 1918, their initial impact on instruction was modest. Those principles included:

1. Health
2. Command of Fundamental Processes
3. Worthy Home Membership
4. Vocation
5. Civic Education
6. Worthy Use of Leisure
7. Ethical Character

"Health" tended to be more the voicing of precepts rather than instilling good health practices. "Command of Fundamental Processes" often meant drill and repetition rather than understanding sources, weighing data, and seeing relationships. "Worthy Home Membership" meant fitting into traditional family patterns but failed to anticipate the changing work roles of women. "Vocation" focused on preparation in the traditional skills for earning a living — skills that even then were beginning to become obsolete. "Civic Education" involved introducing students to key democratic ideals and principles; but the schools themselves tended to operate on an autocratic basis, with administrators directing the teachers and the teachers mirror-

---

Harold G. Shane is Distinguished Rank Professor Emeritus in the School of Education at Indiana University.

ing this behavior with the students. "Worthy Use of Leisure" had little relevance since youngsters on farms, and even in towns and cities, had prescribed chores, which precluded most leisure activity. "Ethical Character" was often interpreted as little more than showing respect for elders and following the rules students received from adults.

Despite their perception as worthy goals, I would say that the Seven Cardinal Principles did not really have a profound impact on the schools I knew as a pupil and as a young teacher. In retrospect I would hazard the guess that much schooling as late as the 1930s resembled that of the 19th century more than it anticipated the educational ideas that slowly had been developing during the previous 50 years.

Awareness of the societal changes of recent decades becomes particularly important because our young people (as well as their elders) need to understand and come to grips with an increasing number of problems that are clouding our future and threatening our lives. Indeed, as a pioneer educational futurist, I would say that the Cardinal Principles, as interpreted in our schools during the 1990s and thereafter, must build *enlightened foresight* in our children and youth as they cope with problems that threaten our world.

Let us now consider a small roster of these problems and see what implications they hold for education. The difficulties that beset us, difficulties of particular potency insofar as our schools are concerned, have either come into being or worsened with such speed that the list that follows probably will need to be expanded even before these "reflections" appear in print.

Family disintegration. Although qualities in the family life of 50 years ago are not above criticism, the past 25 years have seen a shocking social disintegration in U.S. family life. What has happened to the family unit that once was characterized by a faithful, hard-working husband; a wife who looked after the children and was a diligent housekeeper; children whose success in school was promoted by loving parents who read to them, sang with them around the piano, planned holidays that were enriching, and encouraged Sunday school and church attendance and close relationships with grandparents and other relatives? Judging by data from a variety of sources, many of our children are now living under conditions that might best be described as "family rot." Consider the following.

As of 1990, approximately one child in five lived in a single-parent family, often with the one parent employed. The number of families consisting of an employed father, a homemaker mother, and two children declined by 21% between 1980 and 1989. Many children from single-parent households become latchkey youngsters, returning from school to an empty house. The cost of full-time child care in the home can run as high as $300 a week, a sum way out of reach for most single-parent families. Moreover, nearly 69% of adult females were in the workforce in 1989; and of this group, one-third had children five years of age or younger.

Teenage pregnancy. The increase in the number of children born to unwed mothers is alarming. According to a United Press report (9 October 1989) more than a half-million babies were born to mothers under 17 years of age, 96% of whom were not married. The *Milwaukee Journal* (14 September 1989) reports that by 1989 the total out-of-wedlock births in that city had passed the 50% mark — up from 39% in 1984.

In most cases these young mothers are left to raise their children by themselves, or more likely with the help of government subsidies from Medicaid, AFDC, and other welfare sources. The Center for Population Options (*Insight*, 27 November 1989) reported that it cost the federal government $20 billion dollars in 1988 in aid to one-third of the 364,586 teens who gave birth for the first time. Each will presumably receive an average of $49,230 in government aid over a 20-year period. Clearly, our youth need more sex education, including birth-control information, as well as education about AIDS. As controversial as such education is, the schools cannot abdicate their responsibility for teaching about responsible sexual behavior.

Drug abuse. The abuse of drugs, plus trafficking in crack and cocaine, has become a plague that is decimating our youth. A related problem is the violence associated with drug use and drug trafficking. According to *Time* (6 February 1989), handgun killings in 1988 in the U.S. totaled 8,092 compared to five in Canada, eight in Britain, and 121 in Japan. Indeed, in one day, Tuesday, 21 February 1989, lethal shootings in Washington, D.C., totaled 13. Labeled our "murder capital," the city had 75 handgun homicides during the first 45 days of 1989 (*Time*, 22 February 1989). A high percentage of these killings were drug-related.

Our schools cannot control killings on the street, but they can take steps to deal with the root causes behind the killings. This will require expanded drug education and counseling programs as well as rehabilitative services for addicted adolescents.

Growth of minority populations in the U.S. It is estimated that soon after the beginning of the 21st century, today's minority groups will outnumber the majority population from European backgrounds. Projections of enrollment trends show that by 2000, minorities will have become the majorities in the schools of 53 of America's 100 largest cities. Because of the influx of Hispanics and Asians in California, some of the schools in that state already have a majority enrollment of so-called minorities.

The problems presented to schools in serving minorities are many. For example, 15% of our minority-group children speak English as a second language. Some 20% come from families below the poverty level. Many have poorly educated parents, and about one in seven suffers from some form of handicap. Also, according to a Congressional Economic Committee report, as many as 50% of our four million Hispanic students are likely to become dropouts. For further analysis of changing student demographics, see Harold Hodgkinson's "What Ahead for Education" (*Principal*, January 1986).

Decline in academic competence. A recent Gallup Poll, conducted in 1989 for the National Endowment for the Humanities, produced distressing information regarding U.S. students' lack of general knowledge. I was startled to learn that if college seniors were to be graded on the questions in the poll, more than 50% would have failed. For example, the study revealed that 24% did not know the century in which Columbus landed in the Western Hemisphere, 58% did not know that Shakespeare wrote *The Tempest*, and 42% were unaware that the Civil War occurred after 1850. Ironically, 23% attributed Karl Marx's words, "From each according to his ability, to each according to his need," to the U.S. Constitution!

One explanation for the younger generation's lack of general knowledge ("cultural literacy" is the term used today) is that they are confronted with so much information they cannot assimilate it all. Be that as it may, this lack of basic knowledge and skills has become a major concern of U.S. corporations. And they are taking matters into their own hands. For example, in 1989 the Ford Motor Company had 8,500 of its blue-collar workers taking basic skills classes. Polaroid spent $700,000 to teach language and math skills to both new and old employees. Many other corporations from Planter Nuts to General Motors are doing likewise. These corporate educational efforts are likely to continue, since much of the growth in the workforce will be from the ranks of minorities, who traditionally have not mastered basic skills while in school. For more about corporate education, see *Workforce 2000* by William Johnson and Arnold Packer (Hudson Institute, 1990).

In addition to the problems associated with deteriorating family life and changing demographics, there are other major national and international issues that demand our attention. The following are representative.

Exploding global population. In 1990 the world population passed the five billion mark and, at the present rate of increase, could reach eight billion by the year 2025. There is reason to doubt that our already endangered planet could provide even a modest standard of living for so many people. The population explosion is even more alarming in some developing countries, where more than a third of the population is 15 years of age or younger − 45% in Africa. In Kenya in the late 1980s, the average birth rate was seven children for each woman. See Bill McKibben's *The End of Nature* (Random House, 1989).

National debt. In 1990 the total U.S. debt passed $7 trillion dollars, divided more or less equally between individuals and corporations. In addition, the federal government's debt amounted to $20,000 for every man, woman, and child in this country.

Aging population. In George Washington's day the average life span in America was 33 years. By 1900 it had increased to 44 years. At the present time, a man who reaches age 65 will probably live until he is 78, for women until 83. While increased longevity undoubtedly is desired by most people, it has presented some severe problems, including prolonged funding for Social Security, Medicare, and Medicaid; and for the family, the care of victims of Alzheimer's disease, which some estimate will affect 50% of those who live past age 85.

Foreign ownership of U.S. property. By 1990 foreign investors had purchased more than $170 billion worth of U.S. property. Japan and Great Britain have been the most aggressive purchasers, but other countries also are buying up our factories, shopping malls, and office buildings. Appreciable foreign ownership and control of our enterprises could pose a variety of problems in the future.

Adjusting to the computer age. The impact of computers on contemporary society is still being sorted out. But there is little question that the burgeoning presence of computers has made this a microelectronic era. Since the Bell Labs developed the transistor in 1947 and the complex multiple circuit microchip made its debut in 1959, we have been deluged with an array of microelectronic gear. By 1976 there were 400,000 computerized installations in our offices and homes. During the next 10 years this number zoomed to six million. It is estimated that at least half of our households will have computer systems by the early 1990s. For a fascinating account of this development, see J.N. Shurkin's *Engines of the Mind: A History of the Computer* (Norton, 1984).

In addition to inundating us with far more information than can readily be digested, the computer age has presented several educational challenges. One, in particular, is making sure that young learners continue to *think*, rather than merely punch a computer key, as they seek answers to problems.

Increase in serial employment. Advances in technology have made many jobs obsolete. No longer can workers assume they will have a lifetime job. The U.S. Department of Labor estimates that the coming generation of workers will need to be retrained for new careers three times in a lifetime. The advent of serial employment means that both industry and the schools must gear up to provide the retraining that will be necessary (including the retraining of teachers as well). This will require both updating of existing skills and learning other skills for entirely new jobs. Of course, the curriculum of the 1990s and beyond will need to be revised frequently to accommodate the changes brought by the computer age.

Media maladies. Of all the mass media, television is the most pervasive; and it presents a variety of maladies. As media ecologist Neil Postman observes in *Amusing Ourselves to Death* (Viking, 1985), one of the maladies is the immense amount of time consumed in viewing the videoscreen. While children spend approximately 12,000 hours in elementary and secondary school, they spend (or perhaps I should say squander) 16,000 or more hours televiewing, hours that might otherwise be spent on homework, leisure reading, sports, and other activities. Moreover, the time parents spend televiewing might better be spent with their children reading or on trips to the museum or zoo.

Another media malady is the distorted view television presents of world events and life in general. The situation is particularly troublesome on late-night TV shows with their depictions of sex, violence, and fraud, which are viewed after midnight by an estimated 600,000 school children. It would be progress, indeed, if network TV did not feel compelled to stress and exaggerate the social blemishes both in our country and overseas.

The short list of problems described above could be lengthened many times over. Edward Cornish, writing in *The Futurist* (January-February 1990), notes that the Union of International Associations in Brussels has compiled a substantial list of more than 10,000 world problems. Nevertheless, my short list provides a full agenda for educational directions in the 1990s.

Curricula in an Era of Social Change

The educational agenda for the 1990s and beyond calls for substantial changes with regard to curriculum planning and development. In thinking about curriculum in terms of contemporary issues and problems, I believe there are at least eight conceptions of curriculum (sources of learnings) in which all learners are enmeshed to some degree, although they overlap to some extent. Only one of these conceptions falls within the traditional notion of curriculum, that is, the subject matter that is taught. The conceptions include:

1. The *phantom* curriculum: information acquired from the media.
2. The *hidden* curriculum: what children infer from school policies (for example, discipline, promotion, and grading policies).
3. The *tacit* curriculum: what children infer from the school's social climate as reflected by pupil behavior, teacher behavior, extracurricular activities.
4. The *latent* curriculum: What is from learned from out-of-school social experiences (travel, parent and sibling contacts, clubs, church, etc.).
5. The *paracurriculum*: what is learned on one's own (independent reading, hobbies, games, puzzles, etc.).
6. The *societal* curriculum: positive and negative social learnings gleaned from other people, both young and old, at play, during meals, when guests are in the homes, at parties, etc.).
7. The *conventional* curriculum: subject-centered learnings derived from textbooks or a curriculum guide and directed by the teacher.
8. The *child-centered* curriculum: individualized learning experiences based on the teacher's understanding of each learner's needs, abilities, and purposes.

My purpose in listing these eight conceptions of curriculum is to emphasize the broad dimensions of learning that teachers, administrators, parents, and all others associated with educating children need to re-examine when planning the curriculum of the future. The problems of our times demand enlightened foresight of what is to come. Only in this way can we mold the future and not be molded by it.

321

Distance Learning for Tomorrow's Schools

When I juxtapose the increasingly complex and sometimes dangerous future with my views on curriculum change or restructuring in the coming decades, I find the concept of distance learning to be a promising approach. (For a succinct explanation of distance learning, see my interview with Lord Walter Perry in the July-August 1989 issue of *The Futurist*, pp. 25-27.)

Distance learning had its origins in Great Britain. The concept was first suggested by then Prime Minister Harold Wilson in 1963. He proposed that a "University of the Air" be created in order to pull his country into the 21st century. However, the driving force behind distance learning was Lord Walter Perry. He initiated Britain's University of the Air in 1969, with the first courses being offered in 1971 via television. For a full account of this program, see Perry's *Open University: A Personal Account of the First Vice Chancellor* (Priority Press, 1986).

In essence, distance learning is a form of microelectronic continuing education. It has some of the features of correspondence courses of yesteryear. Students are able to take courses in the humanities, social sciences, education, technology, and mathematics. Instruction is offered via television combined with semester-long seminars. These programs currently serve tens of thousands of students seeking a degree or diploma from London to Hong Kong.

I have visited Britain's University of the Air several times since the early 1970s and am convinced that the instructional strategies used provide a model that could be replicated in the U.S. to deal with some of the problems discussed earlier in this essay.

Here are my conjectures about some of the functions distance learning could perform under the auspices of elementary and secondary schools and colleges and universities:

1. Retraining persons whose jobs are terminated or threatened with obsolescence as a result on new technology, thus preparing them for serial employment.
2. Enabling high school dropouts to complete secondary school and obtain their diploma.
3. Assisting the flood of new immigrants in adjusting to a new environment; for example, by teaching English as a second language or consumer education skills.
4. As in Britain, opening up higher education for older adults who decide they want to pursue a degree.

5. Creating an array of programs for seniors (60 years or older) who want cultural enrichment, information about health matters, or advice about finances.

6. Offering, on a continuous basis, short courses or seminars to professionals in medicine, nursing, education, law, or social work to keep them up to date on developments in their respective fields.

7. Providing cultural programs to enrich the life of the public in general.

8. Providing children at the preschool and primary levels, particularly those from underprivileged or immigrant families, with readiness activities and enrichment experiences.

9. Providing direct instruction to learners in their homes or in electronic study halls; for example, dramatized nursery rhymes and stories for young learners; courses in geography, literature, science, or foreign languages for older students; and an array of college-level courses for adults.

The potential of distance learning for alleviating some of the problem areas mentioned above is only now being realized. It holds great promise for enriching, broadening, and diversifying education in our country. It is, of course, but one of many approaches that might be tried in the context of the eight conceptions of curriculum described earlier.

Reflections on Forty Years in the Profession

BY ALBERT SHANKER

I have spent almost 40 years as a teacher and a trade unionist. The majority of those years were spent in fighting to gain collective bargaining rights for teachers and in using the collective bargaining process to improve teachers' salaries and working conditions. But during the past decade, I've devoted most of my time and energy working to professionalize teaching and to restructure our schools. Some of the people who hear me speak now seem to think this represents an about face on my part. They are surprised at this message coming from a union leader – and one who has been in jail for leading teachers out on strike, at that – but they probably put it down to my getting mellower in old age or maybe to wanting to assume the role of "elder statesman." Some union members, too, believe they are seeing a shift in my positions. Perhaps so. But it's not that I have abandoned any of my former views, and it's certainly not an attempt to go back to the good old days before collective bargaining when teachers and administrators in a school were supposedly one big, happy family; and teachers behaved in a "professional" manner. As a matter of fact, memories of those days still make it hard for me to talk about professionalism without wincing.

"That's Very Unprofessional, Mr. Shanker!"

The word *professional* was often used then to beat teachers down or keep them in line. I can remember my first exposure to it as a teacher. I started in a very tough elementary school in New York

---

Albert Shanker is President of the American Federation of Teachers.

City and had great doubts that I would make it; the three teachers who had preceded me that year with my sixth-grade class had not.

After a couple of weeks, the assistant principal appeared at my classroom door. I remember thinking, "Thank God! Help has come." I motioned him in, but he stood there for what seemed like a very long time, pointing at something. Finally, he said, "Mr. Shanker, I see a lot of paper on the floor in the third aisle. It's very unsightly and very *unprofessional*." Then the door closed and he left.

Soon after that, I went to my first faculty meeting. In those days, not many men taught in grades K-8; there was only one other male teacher in my school. The principal distributed the organizational chart of the school with a schedule of duties — who had hall patrol, lunch patrol, and so forth, including "snow patrol." By tradition, snow patrol, which involved giving up lunch period and walking around outside warning kids not to throw snowballs at each other, was a job for a male teacher. And, sure enough, Mr. Jones and Mr. Shanker found themselves assigned to it. Mr. Jones raised his hand and asked, "Now that there are two men on the faculty to handle snow patrol, would it be okay to rotate — you know, the first day of snow, he goes and the next day I go?" The principal frowned at him and replied, "Mr. Jones, that is very *unprofessional*. First of all, the duty schedule has already been mimeographed, as you see. Secondly, I am surprised that you aren't concerned that one child might throw a snowball at another, hit him in the eye, and do permanent damage. It's very unprofessional of you." That was my second run-in with this new and unusual use of *professional* and *unprofessional*.

Of course, I subsequently heard principals and others use these words many times, and I became accustomed (though not reconciled) to the fact that, in the lexicon of administrators, "professional" had nothing to do with teachers exercising "professional judgment" or conforming to "professional standards." The words were — and still are — used to force teachers to obey orders that go against their sense of sound educational practice and, often, their common sense. Professionalism, in this Orwellian meaning of the word, is not a standard but a threat: Do this, don't say that, or else.

The Fox and the Grapes

Many teachers were also victims of their own definition of professionalism. They believed it was somehow unworthy and undignified (unprofessional) for teachers to try to improve their salaries and working conditions through organizing and political action. I came up against this definition of professional when I went from school to school as a union organizer, arguing that teachers ought to have a right to negotiate. At first, very few teachers would even come to meetings. I remember that Brooklyn Technical High School had 425 teachers, and only six showed up at the meeting. One of them explained it to me: "We think unions are great. My mom and dad are union members. That's why they had enough money for me to go to college. But they sent me so I could do better than they did. And what kind of professional joins a union?"

This professionalism was not professionalism at all. It was the willingness of teachers to sacrifice their own self-interest and dignity — and the interests of their students — in order to maintain a false feeling of superiority. The issue was really one of snobbery; and in those days, when I was trying to persuade teachers to join the union, I often told Arthur Koestler's version of the Aesop Fable about the fox and the sour grapes.

According to Koestler, the fox, humiliated by his failure to reach the grapes the first time, decides to take climbing lessons. After a lot of hard work, he climbs up and tastes the grapes only to discover that he was right in the first place — they are sour. He certainly can't admit that, though. So he keeps on climbing and eating and climbing and eating until he dies from a severe case of gastric ulcers.

The teachers who heard this story usually laughed when I told them that it was the sour grapes of professionalism the fox was after. He would have been better off running after chickens with the other foxes — just as they would be better off joining a union with other workers — instead of continuing to eat the sour grapes of professionalism that were filled with lunch duty, hall duty, snow duty, toilet patrol, and lesson-plan books.

The basic argument for unionism and collective bargaining is as true today as it was when I went around to New York City teachers talking about the fox and the grapes. School systems are organizations, many of them quite large; and individual employees are likely to be powerless in such organizations. They can be heard and have some power to change things only if they are organized and act collectively.

Can anyone doubt how teachers felt about themselves when school boards, superintendents, and principals could do whatever they wanted without consulting teachers — or even notifying them? Some teachers would be assigned to be "floaters" in a school and had to teach in a different classroom each hour. A few teachers were always given the most violent classes, while other teachers were out of the classroom most of the time on "administrative assignments." Some teachers got their pay docked if they were a few minutes late because of a traffic jam, but others could come late as often as they wanted because they had friends in high places. Some teachers were always assigned to teach the subject they were licensed in and were given the same grade each period so they would have the fewest possible preparations. Others almost always taught several different grades, often out of the fields in which they were licensed.

So there should be no hankering to go back to the good old days, because they weren't good at all. The spread of collective bargaining has not made everything perfect, of course. Some people even blame the growth of teacher unions for the problems in our schools and the difficulty we are having in getting school reform. But if that were so, schools would be much better in states where there is no collective bargaining (like Mississippi or Texas) than in states where it exists (like California or Connecticut), and that's plainly not the case.

Collective Bargaining and Educational Issues

When I went to work for the New York City schools in 1953, I joined the New York City local of American Federation of Teachers (AFT), the New York Teachers Guild, Local 2. The union, the predecessor of the United Federation of Teachers (UFT), had already been around for a long time. It was founded in 1917 (with John Dewey as a charter member). But it had organized only about 5% of the system's 50,000 teachers. And it was only one of 106 teacher organizations. There was a group for each division, each religion, each race – and each grievance. I remember one called the Sixth and Seventh Grade Women Teachers' Association of Bensonhurst. (Something must have happened there at some point, and they started an organization.) And there was a Bronx Teachers' Association, a Staten Island Teachers' Association, and so forth. Most of these groups were rather small, and most of them had very low dues, some as little as 50 cents a year.

It was difficult to create a single organization from these 106 different groups. As I've mentioned, most New York City teachers were cool to the idea of joining a trade union. Besides, what kind of power could a union have unless it could withhold the services of its members by striking. And strikes by public employees were illegal under New York State's Condon-Wadlin law. This law also said that any employee who went on strike was to be fired and, if hired back, was to remain on probation for three years and get no salary increase during that time.

Nevertheless, in 1960, when a merger with another group had increased our membership from 2,500 to 4,500, we had a strike. Only about 5,000 teachers (out of 50,000) went out, but the school board couldn't afford to fire that many so we didn't lose our jobs. As a result of the strike, we got more members, many of them teachers angry at the do-nothingness of the other teacher organizations. And that was the beginning of a dramatic period of growth. We also got a referendum on collective bargaining that took place in June 1961. Teachers were simply asked if they favored collective bargaining for New York City teachers; the majority said Yes.

We were the only organized group supporting collective bargaining. In fact, all the 105 other groups were strongly opposed, so more teachers joined our union. When the election was held in December 1961 to decide which group would become the collective bargaining agent, we won overwhelmingly; and more teachers joined. In April 1962, we had another strike in order to get adequate salary increases, and more teachers joined. In June 1962, we bargained our first complete contract, with a $995 salary increase; and more teachers joined. And as we administered grievances under the contract, still more teachers joined. In 1963 and 1965, we bargained two-year contracts with salary increases, increases in health benefits and choice of health plans, reduction of class size, and the elimination of every teacher's least favorite regulation: that they bring a note from their doctor every time they took sick leave. In 1967, we had a three-week strike to get salary increases and to keep an Effective Schools program that was working well, and more teachers joined. By 1968, when we had a long strike over due process in the Ocean Hill-Brownsville section of Brooklyn, 70,000 teachers stayed out between September and the middle of November. During this incredible period of struggle and vitality, the union had grown from 2,500 members (about 5% of the teaching staff) to a miraculous 97%. And by that time, teacher unions and collective bargaining had spread to many other states; although today there are still states where teachers do not have collective bargaining rights.

Teachers made great gains in the early years of collective bargaining. There were substantial increases in salaries. In addition, teachers were able to limit and reduce the old indignities, because contracts required that undesirable chores and assignments be shared by all the teachers in a school. And grievance procedures meant that management had to use its authority more prudently, because it was usually subject to external and independent review.

But even in those days, it became evident that the bargaining process was severely limited in its ability to deal with some of the issues that were most important to teachers. In addition to the traditional union goals of improvements in wages, hours, and working conditions, teachers wanted to use their collective power to improve schools in ways that would make them work better for kids. Most teachers entered teaching knowing they wouldn't be well paid; they were looking for the intrinsic satisfaction derived from doing a good job for their students. So they were concerned about conditions that would allow them to enjoy this satisfaction. But as soon as the words "good for children" were attached to any union proposal, the board would say, "Now you're trying to dictate public policy to us," and that was the end of that proposal.

The first time I sat at the bargaining table in New York City, the union submitted 900 demands, many of which were designed to improve learning conditions for students. We were shocked when representatives from the school board told us that they would deal with demands about improvements in wages, hours, and working conditions for *teachers* but would not entertain any demand justified as being good for *students*. The reason? Because we were elected by teachers to represent teacher interests, not by students to represent student interests. After all those years of being told by principals and superintendents and school boards that it was *unprofessional* to join a union because our primary concern should be the welfare of our students, it came as a shock when we were told that we could not, as a union, deal with educational issues, that they were not bargainable.

Critics have often said that a teacher union can't really be interested in educational issues and that the union's involvement in current discussions of reform are just a ploy for getting bigger salary increases. But from the earliest years of collective bargaining, issues of educational quality were part of the UFT and AFT agenda. And there were times when professional interests and union interests were in conflict. For example, as we headed toward the collective bargaining election in 1961, the issue of granting regular licenses to substitutes came up.

The school board was in a big bind at that time. A group of black parents were boycotting two predominantly black schools and refusing to send their children to school. When the school board went to court

329

to invoke the compulsory attendance law, the parents said they couldn't be compelled to send their children to inferior schools. They offered as evidence the fact that most teachers in predominantly white schools had regular certification whereas most teachers in predominantly black schools did not. They were what were called "permanent substitutes." Instead of trying to attract an adequate number of teachers who met the certification standards, the school board then went to the legislature to get the rules for certification changed.

At this time, the New York City system employed some 20,000 of these permanent substitute teachers on a regular basis. A disproportionate number supported the union, and we needed their votes to win the upcoming election. Nevertheless, after an extensive debate, we opposed the proposal to water down the license standards. And, recognizing that paper requirements were not adequate anyway, we proposed internships for new teachers. These internships would have involved coaching and evaluating the classroom performance of new teachers instead of just giving them a paper-and-pencil test. They would have been a step toward the kind of professionalism associated with the medical and legal professions. Our proposal didn't get anywhere. It was 20 years before a school district did implement an internship program like the one we suggested. I'm talking about the Toledo, Ohio, Peer Review program, which was also devised and proposed by an AFT local.

Although educational issues were an important part of our agenda from the beginning, it was difficult to make headway on them. Even efforts to reduce or limit class size ran into snags. Was class size a working condition for teachers or was it an educational issue? (Where can you draw the line between the two, especially since teaching is inextricably linked with educational issues?) Certainly a very large class could be, and was, viewed as an onerous working condition. But the question of the proper class size for effective teaching and learning was considered outside the scope of bargaining. In some states, any consideration of class size was excluded from the list of appropriate subjects for bargaining.

The Treadmill

When we first went into collective bargaining, we were very optimistic. We would bargain one- or two-year contracts so we could get back to the bargaining table believing that, with each new set of negotiations, we would make great gains. But as we got to the late Sixties and early Seventies, the union began promoting three-

year contracts. Each time we went to the bargaining table, management would try to take away what we had won in the last round. And as we went through a number of years and a number of rounds of bargaining, it became clear that while bargaining gave teachers voice and dignity, the normal bargaining process was not likely to do what teachers believed needed to be done, even in terms of salary and working conditions. Salary gains were made, but then in the Seventies the economy turned sour at the same time as the need for teachers dropped off when the baby boom turned into the baby bust. During those years, we saw many of the gains we had won through collective bargaining wiped out.

For me, the biggest shocker was the day in 1975 when 13,000 New York City teachers lost their jobs. The city was basically in receivership. Other cities were suffering from fiscal crises, too. In that one year, New York City teachers and teachers from Chicago and Philadelphia were all out on strike at one time. And it became very clear that our bargaining power was being weakened by a poor economy and a rapid reduction in demand for teachers because the baby boom was over. More and more, it looked as though we would have a hard time regaining what we had lost, much less pushing ahead with demands we had not been able to achieve earlier.

Our whole outlook changed from the optimistic Sixties when we had been buoyed up by the climate of economic growth, the war on poverty, federal aid to education, and putting a man on the Moon. It had seemed in those days that all we had to do to get what we wanted was to push harder. Now, we were in a period that did not look as though it would be over soon, and we knew we would be lucky to hold on to what we had. In fact, if we were realistic, we had to admit that we might lose a good deal of it.

Indeed, during the ensuing years of tremendous inflation, teachers' salaries were seriously eroded, because salary increases didn't nearly keep up with inflation. We ran very hard to try to stay even but fell behind anyway. Teachers lost 15% of their income in real dollars during that period of recession, and we didn't get back to where we had been in 1973 until about 1988. Now, we are in a new recession. And it's clear that, if we continue to organize our schools and our profession as we have in the past, teacher salaries will never equal those of other professionals, no matter how skilled union negotiators nor how willing school boards. It's just not possible.

For 20 years, the union's agenda was to increase salaries and reduce class size and class loads. As we saw it, salary increases would attract and retain qualified teachers, and reductions in class size and class loads would give teachers more time to work with students individually and creatively. They also would give teachers what members of other professions take for granted: time to confer, to share ideas, and work with colleagues. This program was widely accepted by school boards, parents, and communities as a strategy for school improvement. But by the early 1980s it became clear that carrying out the program would call for an amount of money and a level of staffing that, realistically, we could not expect to get.

Bringing the average teacher's salary to $45,000 per year — a respectable but by no means extravagant amount — would mean an increase of $10,000 to $15,000 per teacher. Multiply this by 2.5 million teachers, and it comes to something in the neighborhood of $30 billion dollars a year more than what the U.S. currently spends on elementary and secondary education. And this is before adding in the cost of fringe benefits. Decreasing class size to the extent that it would make a real difference in the way teachers deal with students runs up against the same arithmetic.

If we were to cut class size by one-third, this would give teachers more time to coach and work with students. (According to Theodore Sizer, it would still take an English teacher with five classes of 20 students each, 17 hours to grade a set of essays.) But to get this kind of reduction nationally, we would need another 800,000 teachers. That represents an enormous amount of money, even with salaries at their current levels. And we would not be able to find qualified people to fill the jobs anyway. We don't have a host of well-qualified candidates who are standing in line to be teachers. In fact, we already have some people in the classroom who are at the borderline of literacy and numeracy; hiring more would mean digging deeper into the talent pool.

So the price for getting smaller class size on a national (as opposed to a local) level would be putting huge numbers of kids in classes with poorly qualified teachers. Or we could try to attract people who now go into better paying professions by raising teachers' salaries. But that's unrealistic, too, because these other professions or lines of work would raise their salaries to remain competitive.

Rethinking Goals

The arithmetic of salaries and availability of qualified teachers suggests that we need to rethink the traditional goals of teacher unions. There isn't going to be enough money to raise all salaries in all districts to a professional level. And even if we somehow found the money, where could we find the people to accomplish what we wanted? Unions could continue repeating the same slogans – even if union leaders didn't believe them anymore. Or we could tell members there was no way of reaching the goals we originally set for ourselves. Or we could find some other ways of accomplishing these goals. We could change the way teachers teach; we could change the structure of schools and the structure of the teaching profession.

If all the people working in hospitals had to be doctors, we would have seven million doctors instead of 500,000 – and they would all be paid like teachers. There would be too many to educate as rigorously as we do now, so the standards of medical practice would probably be much lower than they are. And undoubtedly we would have superintendent doctors, principal doctors, and department chairman doctors standing over ordinary doctors telling them what to do, because with seven million doctors, we would be dipping down pretty deep into the talent pool. But the medical profession isn't organized that way. So why not follow the model of a hospital instead of the model of an assembly-line factory in organizing schools and the professionals who work in them?

Why not reserve the title of teacher for those who are highly qualified, and pay them accordingly? This arrangement need not mean having fewer adults working with kids. We could have more than we do now: a large number of paraprofessionals, intern teachers, and resident teachers (going through the kind of training doctors get), and parents and other volunteers.

In a system like this, teachers could leave the drill-and-practice and the administrative, clerical, and custodial duties to others. And they wouldn't have to stand up in front of a class of 35 and try to get everybody to learn the same thing at the same time. Instead, they could spend their time working with small groups or individual students, stimulating them, helping them manage their work, and figuring out ways to customize their learning. And they would finally have the time to meet with colleagues to discuss cases and strategies – something that is taken for granted in other professions but virtually unheard of in teaching. Restructuring teaching and schools would also allow teacher unions to make progress toward one of their original, but often frustrated, goals: making schools work better for students.

There is plenty of evidence that schools are not working very well for many of our students. One example is the scores on National Assessment of Educational Progress (NAEP) exams over a 20-year period. True, recent NAEP results offer some encouragement. Nearly all students who are ready to graduate from high school are able to read simple materials, write a simple paragraph, and do simple arithmetic. Moreover, NAEP scores show that African-American and Hispanic children are closing the gap in achievement between them and white children. For instance, in 1980 only about 45% of African-American and 60% of Hispanic 17-year-olds still in school could read beyond the level of rock-bottom literacy (compared to about 88% of white children). By 1988 nearly 75% of African-American and 73% of Hispanic 17-year-olds had reached beyond that rock-bottom level.

But encouraging though this progress is, few high school graduates perform well enough to qualify for an entry-level job at a top firm. And fewer still reach the level necessary to do real college work. In 1988 only 1% of 17-year-olds still in school could write a really good, brief discussion comparing modern food and frontier food after reading a paragraph on frontier life. And only 7% could solve multi-level arithmetic problems. Compare this with student achievement in other industrialized nations where students have to be able to write an excellent essay and handle complex math problems in order to get into a university. And 16% to 30% of those young people achieve at these levels compared to no more than 6% of U.S. students who achieve at NAEP's top − but much lower − levels. These results and others confirm what experience has told us for a long time: schools as they are now structured don't work well for large numbers of kids. They may be adequate for young people who can sit still and learn by listening to the teacher talk. But people − and kids − learn in many different ways and at different rates. Some need to see pictures before they can understand a concept; some need to manipulate things; some learn best in groups; and some want to go off and explore by themselves. So our lock-step system that requires everyone to learn in the same way at the same time is inefficient. It can also be cruel to kids who can't play by these rules and who feel stupid because they are constantly being compared unfavorably with those who can.

Nor can teachers responsible for 30 kids with different ways and rates of learning − or even 30 different kids every period − do much to accommodate these differences. There is a certain amount of material to be covered, probably in a certain way. And there is little time left over from doing what is required to diagnose the individual needs of individual children and to try to find ways to meet those needs. Teachers themselves are constrained by the structure of our schools.

Restructuring Schools

What can be done? There are, in fact, plenty of ideas, even models, for more effective ways of structuring student learning — and not all of them are new. In the late 1950s, Tam Dalyell, a member of Great Britain's House of Commons and also a teacher, worried about what would happen when the school-leaving age in Great Britain was raised from 15 to 16. What would they do with these kids, who had already signed off on school and couldn't wait to leave, if they were forced to stay on another year? Dalyell's solution was to create "ship schools" where students could learn geography, economics, and history by sailing to different foreign countries, as well as by reading about them, and could learn math from shipboard activities as well as through books. But another, less exotic educational institution offers kids a chance to learn by doing and offers even more flexibility than Dalyell's ship schools. I have in mind the Boy Scouts and Girl Scouts.

There are various levels of achievement in scouting. For example, in the Boy Scouts a boy begins as a Tenderfoot and then, when he gains the skills required, he becomes a Second Class Scout, then First Class, and so on, up, perhaps, to Eagle Scout. Scouts move up the ladder of advancement at their own pace; at any level, they can choose from among a variety of tasks to reach the next level. Scouts can work individually or with friends. If they need help with something they are reading or doing, they can ask a peer or the scoutmaster. They may learn a particular skill from a volunteer. They can go for information to a community agency or the local museum or the Audubon Society. If they choose, much of their learning can be private; but in the course of scouting activities, they will have many experiences working together in groups.

Besides being self-paced and individualized, the scout's learning is broader and less abstract than what kids usually get in school. It simulates the real world more closely because it involves more than the manipulation of words and numbers, which make up so much of what kids do in our schools. Perhaps most important of all, this system makes students responsible for their own education.

I often think of my experience earning the Boy Scouts' bird-study merit badge — the experience of a city kid who wasn't very interested in birds — and I think about the difference between school learn-

335

ing and what happened in Boy Scouts. If I had learned about birds in school, my teacher probably would have had flashcards and pictures of birds all over the room. Eventually we would have had a bird test: The teacher would have asked us the birds' names, and we would have filled in some kind of chart to show we knew what part of the country the birds came from. I know I would have forgotten the birds within three weeks of taking the test — and that would have been no loss because I probably would have come to hate them anyway.

But to earn the merit badge, we actually had to see 40 different kinds of birds, *see them*. And we weren't going to be able to do it by looking out a window or by taking a walk in Central Park. We had to get up at five o'clock in the morning so we could be in a swamp as the sun was coming up. Or we had to go at sunset to a hill or mountain. And, of course, since most of us didn't want to go by ourselves, we invited a couple of friends. When we looked through the binoculars, the birds we saw weren't at all like the stuffed specimens in the Museum of Natural History. We would see a certain shape and certain identifying marks — a red crest or a prominent black stripe across the wing — and we would start looking through our field guidebooks. Someone would say, "There it is, that's the one." And someone else would say, "No, you dope, that says Texas; we're in New York." We were learning to look for different things, to use a reference book, to think together with friends.

The final assessment wasn't a multiple-choice test. It was what would now be called a "performance-based assessment." We had to use what we had learned in a number of different ways. We had to build something. I built a birdhouse and tried (unsuccessfully) to attract birds to live in it. The most important part of the test was a walk with one or two people who really knew birds, where you had to identify every bird you spotted that was on your bird list. That's the kind of knowledge that doesn't leave you. It becomes part of you. I don't know of anybody who got a bird-study merit badge who didn't maintain an interest in birds for many years after. Could our schools be restructured to incorporate some of these features of scouting? Of course. The Holweide School in Cologne, Germany, which I visited a couple of years ago, incorporates many of them. So do the medical schools at McMaster University in Hamilton, Ontario, and at Maastricht in the Netherlands. There are many learning models to try, but we won't be sure which ones will work best until people in schools experiment with them.

Incentives for Change

I have participated in my share of commissions and task forces where we talked about education reform and even drafted bills that were supposed to transform public education. But I've become convinced that no scheme imposed from on high, no matter how wonderful, will do the job. Nothing works right the first time you try it, not even a mechanical device. The success of a plan depends on people making a big effort to get it to work. And people won't do that unless they want to — or have to.

I remember years ago getting into a rowboat with an outboard motor for the first time and trying to start it. It didn't start when I pulled the cord out slowly, but pulling it out rapidly didn't work either. Through trial and error, I learned I had to use a certain flick of the wrist to start the motor. You can give people a general idea about reforming their schools, but they have to figure out the specifics for themselves.

This means giving them the freedom to experiment and to make changes. They need to be released from regulatory constraints (except for those dealing with health, safety, and civil rights); and they need to be given control over the budgets in their individual schools so that, when they figure out what they need, they can get it. But the freedom to do things is not sufficient. People have to want to do them enough to seek out the knowledge they need and to keep on experimenting until they get it right. I would never have persisted in trying to start that outboard motor if I hadn't wanted to go somewhere.

So there have to be incentives. But what kind? No doubt the greatest incentive is the intrinsic satisfaction people feel when they get something right, but that's not the whole story. There are extrinsic satisfactions like recognition from peers, from leaders in the community, from experts in the field. And most people are powerfully moved by financial rewards and punishments: the fear of losing their shirts or the chance of making it big.

No single incentive moves everybody all the time. Businesses understand this. Though they appreciate the importance of external incentives, successful companies also know that intrinsic satisfactions are important. So they use a whole array of incentives to reward the results they are after. If we want people in the schools to put their utmost effort and imagination into restructuring American education, if we want them to experiment and take risks, we will have to provide as many incentives as possible moving in the same direction at the same time.

I'm always surprised that people in public education have a hard time recognizing the importance of incentives, and particularly extrinsic ones. In most other areas, people immediately see how incentives − or the lack of them − cause problems that a change in incentives can solve. For instance, when we hear about companies that are run into the ground by managers looking for short-term profits (and the big salary increases that go with these profits), we say that extrinsic incentives were perverted and became destructive to the enterprise. When we talk about how Americans are still driving gas guzzlers, we say the price of gas in the U.S. is too low to provide an incentive for switching to cars that get 45 miles to the gallon.

Many people outside the field of education think we can solve its problems by applying extrinsic incentives, which is why they propose simplistic plans for testing and merit pay, for retaining kids, for vouchers and school choice. We can't counter these simplistic − and often destructive − proposals by arguing that extrinsic incentives are not important; no one will believe that. We have to come up with a system of incentives that will produce the results we want. And we do not have much time.

There is increasing dissatisfaction with the pace of school reform and increasing support for various radical solutions to our education problems, like the massive administrative decentralization program in Chicago or radical privatization plans of the kind we are beginning to see in Milwaukee and Epsom, New Hampshire. In Milwaukee, low-income children are being allowed to attend private schools at state expense. In Epsom, taxpayers are being offered an incentive, in the form of a substantial property tax abatement, if parents send their child to a private or religious school. Moreover, proposals like these are beginning to attract a broad base of support, from poor and minority parents whose children suffer particularly in inadequate inner-city schools to middle-class taxpayers and conservatives. If we are not able to produce − and quickly − a credible plan for moving school reform, we may have reached the end of public education.

Public Education and a Multicultural Society

Why do I continue when so much of what I've worked for seems threatened? To a large extent because I believe that public education is the glue that has held this country together. Critics now say that the common school never really existed, that it's time to abandon this ideal in favor of schools that are designed to appeal to groups based on ethnicity, race, religion, class, or common interests of various kinds. But schools like these would foster divisions in our society; they would be like setting a time bomb.

A Martian who happened to be visiting Earth soon after the United States was founded would not have given this country much chance of surviving. He would have predicted that this new nation, whose inhabitants were of different races, who spoke different languages, and who followed different religions, wouldn't remain one nation for long. They would end up fighting and killing each other. Then, what was left of each group would set up its own country, just as has happened many other times and in many other places. But that didn't happen. Instead, we became a wealthy and powerful nation — the freest the world has ever known. Millions of people from around the world have risked their lives to come here, and they continue to do so today.

Public schools played a big role in holding our nation together. They brought together children of different races, languages, religions, and cultures and gave them a common language and a sense of common purpose. We have not outgrown our need for this; far from it. Today, Americans come from more different countries and speak more different languages than ever before. Whenever the problems connected with school reform seem especially tough, I think about this. I think about what public education gave me — a kid who couldn't even speak English when I entered first grade. I think about what it has given me and can give to countless numbers of other kids like me. And I know that keeping public education together is worth whatever effort it takes.

Reflections on My Life and How It Grew

BY JULIAN C. STANLEY, JR.

For forty-odd years in this noble profession,
I've harbored a guilt and my conscience is smitten,
So here is my slightly embarrassed confession —
I don't like to write, but I love to have written.
— Michael Kanin

The Background Years

The period that made a great difference in my life lasted 44 months. It began on 6 January 1942, less than a month after the Japanese bombed Pearl Harbor, when I beat the draft by enlisting in the Chemical Warfare Service of the Army Air Corps. My service ended on 6 September 1945, 18 days before I began coursework toward a master's degree in educational and vocational guidance and counseling at the Harvard Graduate School of Education. That "stretch" as an enlisted man in a service outfit — 28 months of it overseas in England, Algeria, Italy, and Corsica — changed me from a routine high school teacher to an almost incredibly achievement-motivated graduate student who ever since has found his greatest professional satisfaction in study, research, writing, and other scholarly activities.

In the school system of a small, contiguous suburb of Atlanta, Georgia, where academic competition was slight, I had skipped the fourth grade. In high school I was studious but not scholarly. I took physics, chemistry, four years of Latin, and the other standard college

Julian C. Stanley, Jr. is Professor of Psychology at Johns Hopkins University and Director of the Study of Mathematically Precocious Youth (SMPY), which he founded in 1971. The author thanks Linda E. Brody and Barbara S.K. Stanley for their editorial assistance.

prep courses and made excellent grades without doing much work. I managed to be graduated as the "best all-round boy" in a class of 177 students while still 15 years old (my birthday was in July and there were only 11 grades). The year was 1934, in the middle of the Great Depression.

I could claim that lack of money led me to enroll at the nearby, unselective, state-supported residential West Georgia Junior College rather than a more appropriate institution such as Emory or Harvard, but that would be untrue. Unlike many in the Depression years, my father was much more prosperous from 1933 on than he had been earlier. To be frank, my low aspiration was due to lack of initiative, poor judgment, and a great desire to get away from home. And I had no suitable academic models or advisers.

As I look back now, my two years at junior college were fairly well spent, even though I studied too little but still made A's and B's. Good teachers were plentiful in those days, and the school had a number of them. The social life was really heady for me, and I had all the time in the world for it. I received a junior college certificate while still 17 and felt infinitely learned, but my bad academic judgment persisted.

A friend at the only teachers college in the state (then South Georgia Teachers College, now Georgia Southern University) persuaded me to enroll there that summer. Except for organic chemistry and one other subject, this proved to be an intellectually uninspiring atmosphere, so I took extra courses (as I had done in junior college) and completed requirements for a B.S.Ed. degree in August of 1937, one month past my nineteenth birthday.

A history professor suggested graduate school at the University of Chicago, but that did not appeal to me at the time. My other professors assumed that the main, and perhaps the sole, purpose of a teachers college was to produce public school teachers. So I took the line of least resistance and set about to find the best available position as a high school teacher. The Fulton County (Atlanta) School system saved me from entombment in a small south Georgia town. There I taught a total of ten different subjects, including science and mathematics, over a period of 4½ years. At the time of my departure for military service, I was 23 years old.

That brings me back around to the long service in the military during which my ambition grew, and I came to see the life of student and scholar as preferable to that of a high school teacher. In retrospect, I am glad that my assignment to Officer Candidate School came too late — after I was already in England — so I remained an enlisted man throughout the war, my top rank being staff sergeant.

The utter intellectual vacuum of an isolated company storing mustard gas and handling incendiary bombs gave me time to think. The petty indignities to which any enlisted man is constantly exposed made me determined to rise in the occupational hierarchy after the war. I am particularly glad that 10 months in Algeria, where I was a company clerk, and 10 on Corsica as the Wing Chemical NCO were virtually devoid of stimulating activities, other than opportunities to read a great deal, learn to touch-type, and take a couple of USAFI courses.

Upon my return from overseas in late 1944, I was processed through the Air Corps returnee station in Miami and selected to be a counselor of returnees. Though a luxurious assignment for a sergeant, it proved to be boring in expensive Miami Beach. So I soon transferred to Third Air Force Headquarters in Tampa to wait out the war — but not before I delved into some career materials at the returnee center in Miami and decided to study guidance under the G.I. Bill at a great university such as Chicago, Columbia, or Harvard as soon as the war ended. Having chosen undemanding colleges earlier, I decided that this error of judgment would be avoided as a graduate student.

It occurred to me that with my eight-year-old degree from a less than illustrious teachers college, I might find the curricula at a major university difficult, but I threw caution to the wind and chose Harvard (because to me it seemed the most prestigious of the lot). I was a well-conditioned 27-year-old and worked furiously. We ex-GI's brought consternation to regular-age Ivy League students because of the vigor and seriousness with which we attacked every assignment.

By the end of the first semester, it became obvious that work at the Harvard Graduate School of Education was well within my competency, and I found it fascinating. I discovered educational psychology, including measurement and statistics, under Professors Truman L. Kelley and Phillip J. Rulon. The second year I continued, aided by a $600 fellowship (Tuition then was $200 per semester!), the G.I. Bill, and a half-time instructorship in psychology at a local municipal junior college. That year I took 10 psychology courses, wrote 10 term papers, and made 10 A's. The pattern was firmly set. I received the Ed.M. degree in 1946 in educational and vocational counseling and guidance, after two semesters of study. The Ed.D. degree in experimental and educational psychology came after three

342

more years, during the last of which I was an extremely hard-working, full-time instructor in education at Harvard.

The intellectual vacuum of my war years interacted with the lure of 44 months of G.I. Bill support to launch me into the university orbit. Without both, I probably would have retired from public school teaching in 1967 with 30 years of routine service. It seems most unlikely that I would have become the author and/or editor of 13 books and some 450 other published articles, or active in national professional associations.*

The Years After Harvard

On 12 June 1949 my wife, Rose, our 15-month-old daughter Susan, and I piled most of our belongings into our new Ford V8 sedan (the first car we'd had since World War II began) and headed for George Peabody College for Teachers in Nashville, Tennessee. I was less than a month short of being 31 and had had many varied experiences since age 19. Besides the 4½ years of high school teaching and the nearly four years in the Army Air Corps, I had taught general psychology at Newton Junior College in Newton, Massachusetts, in 1946-1948, been chairman of the Editorial Board of the *Harvard Educational Review*, president of the study body of the Harvard Graduate School of Education, editor of the published version of the Inglis Lecture delivered by noted black social anthropologist Allison Davis at Harvard in 1948, acting director of the Harvard Psychoeducational Clinic, master of Palfrey House, in charge of master's degree candidates in guidance, busy teacher of graduate students, and much more — all while doing the arduous research for my doctoral dissertation (Stanley 1950). As if this were not enough, during the year as an instructor at Harvard (1948-49), I collaborated with my major professor on a long review article about a new area of psychology (Jenkins and Stanley 1950).

This arduous pace I set for myself served me well at George Peabody College and at Vanderbilt University; at both institutions I soon came to be regarded as *the* specialist in statistics, testing, and research methods. The four eventful years there were fruitful preparation for my next move. Also, they allowed my wife to earn a master's degree in child psychology from Peabody and to gain much experience in nursery school education at the Vanderbilt University Cooperative Nursery School, which benefited our daughter as well.

---

*The preceding section is adapted from Stanley (1969).

In 1953 the University of Florida offered me a full professorship in educational foundations, and the University of Wisconsin offered me a tenured associate professorship at the same salary. I chose Wisconsin, feeling that its research orientation and cold weather would be more conducive to rigorous work than would sunny Florida. This proved to be a wise decision. At Wisconsin I could specialize in the design of experiments in the social sciences, my newly emerging interests (see Campbell and Stanley 1966). Also, there would be time for test theory (Stanley 1971a).

For the 14 years at Wisconsin (1953-1967), with visiting appointments along the way at Michigan, Chicago, Louvain (Belgium), Hawaii, Harvard, and Stanford, I worked hard to further the fields of educational psychology and experimental design nationally. Under my leadership at Wisconsin, the Department of Educational Psychology was created in 1962. A year earlier I had started the Laboratory of Experimental Design. Both flourish to this day.

In rapid succession in the mid-1960s, I was president of the National Council on Measurement in Education, the American Educational Research Association, and the Division of Educational Psychology of the American Psychological Association (APA). A few years later I served as president of the Division of Evaluation and Measurement of the APA. During that time I, in close collaboration with Richard E. Schutz, was instrumental in starting the *Journal of Educational Measurement* and the *Educational Psychologist*, with Ellis B. Page.

The two years 1965-1967 were spent as a Fellow of the Center for Advanced Study in the Behavioral Sciences, located on the campus of Stanford University. Because of my numerous national professional commitments this was a somewhat hectic period, with much flying to Washington, D.C. But being at the Center was about as near to heaven for Rose and me as most mortals get before they die. Ralph W. Tyler, the Center's superb director, created an atmosphere extremely conducive to unstressful, prolonged creative work.

After being at the Center, I feared it was going to be difficult for my wife and me to return to Wisconsin, from which I was on leave without pay. The University of Wisconsin had been growing too rapidly to assimilate its hordes of new students, and the 30-below-zero winters were becoming unpleasant for Rose, who had lived in Atlanta until we married in 1946. Thus in 1967, when I received a fine offer from smaller Johns Hopkins University in warmer Baltimore, it looked tempting. Daughter Susan had already completed two years of college in California, so she did not need to be involved in the decision. I had been a full professor at Wisconsin for 10 years, so rank was not a concern. Rather quickly, we made the decision to leave our beloved Madison for the East. This, too, proved to have been a good choice, despite some unhappy times at first because of an extremely unpleasant department head. It took three years to "neutralize" him.

I tend to view my life as five phases: 1918-1942, growing up and teaching high school; 1942-1945, the war years; 1945-1949, graduate study; 1949-1971, educational psychology, especially statistics, testing, and experimental design; and 1971 to the present, finding youths who reason extremely well mathematically and helping them to get the special, supplemental, accelerative educational opportunities they sorely need and, in my opinion, richly deserve. Although not quite the "five faces of Eve," it is almost as if I have lived five different lives. Each has had its distinctly interesting aspects, and I can see how each has led logically to the next phase. I enjoyed the challenges of creating the Laboratory of Experimental Design and training a large number (about 18) of Ph.D. recipients in statistics and measurement during the years 1961-1968 and doing research in those areas myself. However, probably my greatest satisfaction (but not greatest professional recognition) has come from the Study of Mathematically Precocious Youth (SMPY), which arose rather adventitiously in 1971. The events leading up to it may be worth sketching.

How SMPY Started

During the summer of 1968 on the Homewood Campus of Johns Hopkins University, a program on computers was being offered for junior high school students. One of them was 12-year-old Joseph Louis Bates, who had just completed the seventh grade. Joe was a whiz when it came to computers; he helped some graduate students who were learning to use the FORTRAN computer language. Joe's knowledge and performance so impressed one of the instructors, Doris K. Lidtke, that she cast about for someone to help him. Lidtke had heard of me when she was a graduate student in computer science at Michigan State University. Thus, she called and told me about Joe.

I was busy that summer and fall and didn't have a chance to talk with Joe until January of 1969. He seemed so able and advanced that I administered several difficult tests to him and also had him take the SAT and several of the College Board's high school achievement tests. His scores were remarkable. I might have believed he was the ablest kid in the United States, perhaps one of a kind, had I not known of Leta Hollingworth's work on above-level testing during the 1920s and 1930s (Stanley 1990*a*).

It was obvious to Joe, his parents, and me that enrolling in high school as a regular ninth-grader in the fall of 1969 would not provide the depth or breadth of subject matter he needed and was capable of handling. I tried to find a public or private school in the Baltimore area that would let Joe take mainly 11th- and 12th-grade honors courses but encountered strong skepticism that he could handle them. Finally, in desperation, I suggested to Joe and his parents that they consider enrolling him as a regular freshman at Johns Hopkins that fall at age 13 (he was born in October) and perhaps take a light load in subjects likely to be relatively easy for him: 13 semester credits of physics, honors calculus, and computer science. We were apprehensive about this but willing to give it a try.

I approached Dean Carl Swanson and described Joe's abilities without telling him Joe's age and grade. The dean was impressed. When I told him that Joe was just 13 years old and had completed only the eighth grade, he didn't turn a hair. His response was "Tell Brinkley [the Johns Hopkins Director of Admissions] I said admit him."

That first semester Joe astounded all of us with his fine grades, achieved without undue effort. He went on to receive his B.A. and M.A. in computer science and began advanced graduate work at Cornell University while still 17 years old, where he earned his Ph.D. in computer science. Currently, Dr. Bates is a researcher in computer science at Carnegie Mellon University.

Another youth, also 13 and just as able as Joe, heard about this early admission and insisted on coming to Johns Hopkins. He did well, too. Two years later, in 1972, a local boy came to Hopkins at age 16, two years younger than typical. He made 40 credits of A the first year, then transferred to Princeton University, where he graduated Phi Beta Kappa and *summa cum laude* in mathematics at the age of 20. This precocious young man is now an outstanding cardiologist.

These three cases were enough to suggest that there were quite a few extremely talented youths who needed far more stimulation than could be provided by almost any high school. They should be identified and given special, supplemental educational opportunities in mathematics and related subjects. (For a current update, see Brody and Stanley 1991.)

Fortunately, in 1970 I heard of the newly created Spencer Foundation in Chicago. A quickly prepared, 4½-page proposal yielded me $266,100 to use over a five-year period to start the Study of Mathematically and Scientifically Precocious Youth (SMSPY), later shortened to SMPY but without de-emphasizing its involvement with scientifically talented boys and girls. This grant enabled me to get started on a substantial basis, officially as of 1 September 1971 but actually in June of that year, when Daniel P. Keating arrived from Holy Cross College as a beginning graduate student and SMPY's first research assistant. He and I spent that summer reading or rereading publications about gifted children, especially Lewis M. Terman's famed five-volume *Genetic Studies of Genius*, Terman's pioneering longitudinal studies of high I.Q. youths.

Lynn H. Fox, a mathematics teacher and educational psychologist from Florida, also joined us early that fall as a graduate student. She, Dan, and I and several others began searching for good ideas to try out on youths who reason exceptionally well mathematically. We remembered the old saying, "If you want to have rabbit stew, you must first catch a rabbit. Otherwise, you'll have squirrel stew, chicken stew, or perhaps no stew."

This led in March 1972 to conducting a systematic talent search for quantitatively apt boys and girls and starting a fast-paced precalculus class three months later. In that initial talent search, 450 able students in the Baltimore area, most of them seventh- and eighth-graders, took two mathematics tests (Scholastic Aptitude Test—Mathematical and Level I of the College Board mathematics achievement test) and/or both forms of the Sequential Tests of Educational Progress Science test, college freshman level. In most of SMPY's talent searches, we administered the Scholastic Aptitude Test (SAT) ourselves and scored it by hand, that being much faster and a bit more accurate than sending off the answer sheets to be scored by machine.

Via the talent search we found a large number of highly talented youngsters. Our results were reported promptly at professional meetings and in the professional literature (especially Stanley, Keating, and Fox 1974). We continued the talent searches with ever-increasing geographical diversity and numbers in January 1973, January 1974, December 1976, January 1978, and January 1979 (see Benbow and Stanley 1983).

The first fast-paced math class was highly successful. All of the students who persisted in attending the Saturday morning sessions beyond the summer of 1972 learned at least two years of algebra or geometry by June of 1973. More than half of them learned much more by June or August of 1973, with some completing the 4½ years of pre-calculus from Algebra I through analytic geometry in a total of about 120 class hours. Further details and references are contained in Stanley and Benbow (1986) and Stanley (1990*b* and 1991*a*).

This class led SMPY to experiment with various ways to help mathematically talented boys and girls learn mathematics and related subjects such as physics, chemistry, and biology much faster and better than they could in nearly any regular school class (see Stanley and Stanley 1986). Those early innovative days were thrilling experiences. We knew we were breaking new ground and finding better ways to till it.

SMPY's staff remained small, consisting chiefly of me, with a full teaching load not much related to SMPY work; William C. George, the assistant director; several graduate students; one or more undergraduate work-study students; and Lois S. Sandhofer, our 80%-time secretary and administrative assistant from October of 1971 to the present. SMPY's many developmental, research, and service activities, such as publishing a newsletter 10 times per year, constituted a great operational load.

In 1979 I decided to give up overseeing the annual talent search and the fast-paced classes and helped to establish a new group to handle them on the Johns Hopkins campus. In about 15 minutes of conversation, President Steven Muller and I set up the Office of Talent Identification and Development (OTID), to start that fall. A few years later its name was changed to the present form, the Center for the Advancement of Academically Talented Youth (CTY). OTID and CTY have always been independent of SMPY, and vice versa.

Under William C. George's directorship initially, OTID was an instant success. It farmed out the SAT testing to the regular local testing centers operated by the Educational Testing Service, thereby getting rid of the chore of administering and scoring its two parts. OTID enlarged the talent search area to 13 Eastern states, plus the District of Columbia. (Later, CTY added Alaska, Arizona, California, Hawaii, Oregon, and Washington.) Criteria for entering the search were changed to include students talented verbally but not necessarily mathematically. A residential summer program of quantitative and verbal-oriented courses was held for three intensive weeks during the summer of 1980 at St. Mary's College in southern Maryland, a state-supported liberal arts institution. Another was held there in 1981. From 1982 onward, CTY has operated its summer program on campuses across the country and in Switzerland. It seems likely that a similar program will soon be set up in Ireland, with CTY's and SMPY's assistance but administered independent of them. The current director of CTY is William G. Durden.

In 1980 I encouraged William Bevan, then the Duke University provost, to set up there an organization similar to OTID. It has functioned ever since as the Talent Identification Program (TIP). Soon thereafter, I helped Joyce VanTassel-Baska set up the Midwest Talent Search at Northwestern University, now called the Center for Talent Development. The University of Denver set up the Rocky Mountain Talent Search soon thereafter. These four regional talent searches and their residential summer programs serve all 50 states and several foreign countries.

There also are some local searches and providers of fast-paced classes. Among the earliest were the Association for High Potential Children at the University of Wisconsin in Eau Claire and the Project for the Study of Academic Precocity at Arizona State University in Tempe (now known as the Center for Academic Precocity). In 1973 Halbert and Nancy Robinson founded a program at the University of Washington that allowed quite young students to enroll in that institution and, after a transition year, to become full-time college students. Terry Thomas runs a talent search and largely commuter academic summer program in the Sacramento, California, area. The State of Illinois has long conducted an annual math talent search, followed up by provision of advanced programs for the high scorers. There also has been considerable activity of this sort in the Minneapolis-St. Paul area, which William C. George helped start, as he had done for the State of Illinois.

SMPY itself now has four parts: SMPY at Johns Hopkins University, still headed by me, which focuses its efforts on boys and girls who score at least 700 on the mathematical part of the SAT before age 13, representing the top 1 in 10,000 of their age group; SMPY at Iowa State University, directed by Camilla P. Benbow; SMPY at the University of North Texas, headed by Ann E. Lupkowski; and SMPY at Tianjin, People's Republic of China. Benbow was a predoctoral and postdoctoral staff member of SMPY at Hopkins for a number of years before going to Iowa in 1986. Lupkowski was a postdoctoral fellow with us, 1986-1989. Another postdoctoral fellow (1988-1990), Susan G. Assouline, is now at the University of Iowa, specializing in kindergartners through sixth-graders who reason extremely well mathematically. This is one of Lupkowski's specialties, too.

Success of the SMPY Idea

I have been both greatly surprised and extremely pleased by the extent to which SMPY's conceptualizations have been disseminated successfully. No group using SMPY ideas has yet failed. Amazingly, all have flourished. The talent searches and academic summer programs since 1980 have been largely self-supporting through fees charged the participants. SMPY at Johns Hopkins, however, has provided nearly all its services without any cost to its "protégés." This was made possible by a series of grants from a number of foundations, notably the Spencer Foundation for 13 consecutive years, 1971-1984, and a generous donor more recently who does not want his name or organization revealed. SMPY has had only three government grants, two short-terms ones from the National Science Foundation a decade ago and one later from the U.S. Department of Education.

The success of these various enterprises is mute testimony to the intellectual hunger that many academically talented youths feel. Well-meaning individuals may offer goodies in the form of "enrichment" programs for gifted students. But these efforts are not attuned to the specific intellectual needs of these highly talented youngsters (Wallach 1978). Superior mathematical reasoning ability calls for systematic opportunities to learn mathematics at the right level and pace. An interesting social studies discussion or a session on the greenhouse effect can hardly give this type of student the intellectual thrill, stimulation, and satisfaction for which his or her special quantitative talent cries out.

Repeatedly, my associates at SMPY and I decry this mismatch in professional meetings, at conferences, in articles and letters to editors, in books, by telephone, in letters responding to things we've read — anywhere and anyhow we might make an impression on educators, parents, and especially the talented youths themselves. We started off with three Ds, the subtitle of our first book (Stanley, Keating, and Fox 1974): Discovery (finding the talented), Description (learning more about them), and Development (providing them special educational opportunities, including much information). Soon we added a fourth, equally important, D: Dissemination. Besides our newsletters, correspondence, and conferences, we send out, without charge even for postage, about 500 sets of reprints and memoranda each year. We are ever alert to opportunities to influence and help those who subscribe to SMPY's goals, even when they have not solicited our assistance.

When we began in 1971, probably fewer than a dozen boys and girls aged 13 or less took the SAT in a given year. In 1990 about 100,000 did. Most were tested in late January. Walk into an SAT testing site in your locality in January and see for yourself. In residential, academic summer programs during 1990 there were about 5,000 enrollees. Drop in next summer at Dickinson College, Franklin and Marshall College, Skidmore College, the University of Redlands, Duke University, Northwestern University, Iowa State University, or elsewhere and see for yourself how eagerly the young students there pursue their studies — for example, pre-calculus mathematics five or six hours each day for three weeks or intensive German. It is likely to amaze you.

Of course, SMPY's work thus far has been only a drop in the bucket. Even yet, many talented boys and girls have never heard of the talent searches or summer programs. Many parents cannot afford them. Much dissemination, development, and research must still be done.

Summing Up

I've had a most interesting life, 73 years thus far. Forty-five years have elapsed since I was inducted into the Phi Delta Kappa Chapter at Harvard. That seems to be the demarcation between my rather routine first 27 years and my more intensely professional ones thereafter. Although at the initiation ceremony I did not feel a sudden transition, clearly it was beginning to occur. Not, however, until that summer, when I married Rose Sanders, with whom I had taught mathematics for several years before the war, did the shift become complete. For 32 years, including the first seven of SMPY, she inspired me to have a full professional career and made it possible for me to do so. After Rose's untimely death in 1978, I married Barbara Kerr, who for more than a decade has assisted me greatly with the ever-changing, ever-expanding nature of SMPY and its offshoots.

In order to develop SMPY properly, I had to give up test theory, experimental design, and applied statistics at the time I was being most successful in them. Sometimes I've missed the challenge of research in these methodological areas. Yet the satisfaction of seeing youths helped enormously to use their special talents has been compensation enough.

Besides SMPY, what were my most satisfying accomplishments and honors? As for publications, I cite Jenkins and Stanley (1950), Stanley (1955, 1961, 1971a), Campbell and Stanley (1966), Glass and Stanley (1970), and Hopkins, Stanley, and Hopkins (1990). One of my earliest major awards was being made a Fellow of the American Statistical Association in 1967, an unusual honor for a psychologist. Of course, I was delighted to receive the Edward L. Thorndike Award for Distinguished Psychological Contribution to Education from the Division of Educational Psychology of the American Psychological Association and the American Educational Research Association Award for Distinguished Contributions to Research in Education. The most overwhelming honor accorded me was being awarded an honorary Doctor of Educational Excellence degree by the University of North Texas in 1990. Chancellor Alfred Hurley staged a full convocation of the faculty, a large reception, and a seated dinner for about 100 dignitaries, solely for me.

I've already mentioned presidencies of national organizations. For a while I seemed to become the president of almost anything. Upon arriving in Nashville in 1949, I attended a meeting of the Middle Tennessee Vocational Guidance Association and was immediately elected president of it. Within a year or so I was president of the Tennessee Psychological Association and of the Faculty Association of George Peabody College for Teachers. Even at Harvard, upon my arrival in 1945 as a complete stranger to everyone there, I was elected president of the student body of the Graduate School of Education. I attribute these honor-burdens partly to the influence of my mother, who presided over virtually everything social in East Point, Georgia (population about 3,000 then): Woman's Club, Missionary Society, Sunday School classes, several PTAs, etc. She served them all, unstintingly and without seeking praise. I like to think that some of her altruism carried over to me.

My career has not been without controversy, however. In the 1960s I was one of the first to show that scholastic aptitude and achievement measures predict grades of blacks at least as well as they do for whites (see Stanley 1971b). Also, in 1980 Camilla Benbow and I became deeply embroiled in the controversy about gender-related differences in scores on nationally standardized achievement tests (for the full story, see Benbow 1988). Although this was only a minor part of our work at the time, it has received disproportionate attention in both the public and the professional press for 10 years.

Portents for the Future of Education

As I write this, the daily news carries reports of a savings and loan scandal that will be astronomically expensive for all taxpayers, a huge and ever-increasing national debt, large annual federal deficits that can only become larger, problems with AIDS that are sure to get much worse, crippling Lyme Disease, severe substance abuse problems, great increases in illegitimate births and single-mother homes, much homelessness, and poor educational performance of American youth, many of whom work too many hours at dead-end jobs in order to indulge in the rampant materialism hyped by TV and other media. Why should one bother to care about idealistic enterprises such as SMPY in the face of this pessimistic outlook?

Perhaps we should remember that the United States has almost always been in terrible shape of one sort or another. Are we worse off now than at the end of the Civil War, than during the Great Depression? Time will tell. Meanwhile, there are some reasons to be guardedly optimistic about the education of the ablest. For example, in the 1990 International Mathematical Olympiad (IMO), involving high school teams from 53 countries, the United States ranked third, behind China (first) and the Soviet Union. Five of the six students constituting the U.S. team were members of SMPY's "700-800 on SAT-M Before Age 13 Group." During the five-year period 1986-1990, 18 of the 30 of them were. We inform our "protégés" from age 12 or younger about the annual IMO competition and let them know that some of them are able enough to be among the six chosen for the U.S. IMO team from about 400,000 examinees. Information, encouragement, and role modeling are powerful tools for aiding the academically talented.

For me, the message of SMPY is simple: find youths who reason extremely well mathematically before age 13 and help them get the special, supplemental, accelerative educational opportunities they must have in order to make optimal use of their abilities and to move toward satisfying personal and professional lives. That formulation gives me the same kind of exquisite pleasure that creating an intricate experimental design and analyzing data from using it once did.

References

Benbow, C.P. "Sex Differences in Mathematical Reasoning Ability in Intellectually Talented Preadolescents: Their Nature, Effects, and Possible Causes." *Behavioral and Brain Sciences* 11 (1988): 169-232.

Benbow, C.P., and Stanley, J.C. *Academic Precocity: Aspects of Its Development*. Baltimore, Md.: Johns Hopkins University Press, 1983.

Brody, L.E., and Stanley, J.C. "Young College Students: Assessing Factors that Contribute to Success." In *Academic Acceleration of Gifted Children*, edited by W.T. Southern and E.D. Jones. New York: Teachers College Press, 1991.

Campbell, D.T., and Stanley, J.C. *Experimental and Quasi-experimental Designs for Research*. Boston: Houghton Mifflin, 1966.

Glass, G.V., and Stanley, J.C. *Statistical Methods in Education and Psychology*. Englewood Cliffs, N.J.: Prentice-Hall, 1970.

Hopkins, K.D.; Stanley, J.C.; and Hopkins, B.R. *Educational and Psychological Measurement and Evaluation*. 7th ed. Englewood Cliffs, N.J.: Prentice-Hall, 1990. (This is the lineal descendent of J.C. Stanley's 1954, 3rd edition revision of Clay C. Ross' 1941 textbook, *Measurement in Today's Schools*.)

Jenkins, W.O., and Stanley, J.C. "Partial Reinforcement: A Review and Critique." *Psychological Bulletin* 47 (1950): 193-234.

Stanley, J.C. "The Differential Effects of Partial and Continuous Reward upon the Acquisition of a Running Response [by rats] in a Two-Choice Situation." Doctoral dissertation, Graduate School of Education, Harvard University, 1950.

Stanley, J.C. "Statistical Analysis of Scores from Counterbalanced Tests." *Journal of Experimental Education* 23 (1955): 187-207.

Stanley, J.C. "Analysis of Unreplicated Three-Way Classifications, With Applications to Rater Bias and Trait Independence." *Psychometrika* 26 (1961): 205-20.

Stanley, J.C. "Interaction of Intellectual Vacuum with G.I. Bill." *Theory Into Practice* 8 (1969): 318-19.

Stanley, J.C. "Reliability." In *Educational Measurement*, 2nd ed., edited by R.L. Thorndike. Washington, D.C.: American Council on Education, 1971. *a*

Stanley, J.C. "Predicting College Success of the Educationally Disadvantaged." *Science* 171 (1971): 640-47. *b*

Stanley, J.C. "Leta Hollingworth's Contributions to Above-Level Testing of the Gifted." *Roeper Review* 12 (1990): 166-71. *a*

Stanley, J.C. "Finding and Helping Young People with Exceptional Mathematical Reasoning Ability." In *Encouraging the Development of Exceptional Skills and Talents*, edited by M.J.A. Howe. London: British Psychological Society Books, 1990. *b*

Stanley, J.C. "An Academic Model for Educating the Mathematically Talented." *Gifted Child Quarterly* 35 (1991): 36-42. *a*

Stanley, J.C. *My Many Years of Working with the Gifted: An Academic Approach*. Fourth Lecture in the School of Education Alumni and Friends Distinguished Lecture Series. Williamsburg, Va.: School of Education, College of William and Mary, 1991. *b*

Stanley, J.C., and Benbow, C.P. "Youths Who Reason Extremely Well Mathematically." In *Conceptions of Giftedness*, edited by R.J. Sternberg and J.E. Davidson. Cambridge, England: Cambridge University Press, 1986.

Stanley, J.C.; Keating, D.P.; and Fox, L.H., eds. *Mathematical Talent: Discovery, Description, and Development*. Baltimore, Md.: Johns Hopkins University Press, 1974.

Stanley, J.C., and Stanley, B.S.K. "High School Biology, Chemistry, or Physics Learned Well in Three Weeks." *Journal of Research in Science Teaching* 23 (1986): 237-50.

Wallach, M.A. "Care and Feeding of the Gifted." *Contemporary Psychology* 23 (1978): 616-17.

Reflections on My Experiences in and Observations of Education

BY RALPH W. TYLER

My recollections of my early childhood include listening to frequent discussions about education by my parents. They both perceived education as the chief, if not the sole, means by which individuals develop their talents and learn to use them effectively. The development of civilization has been brought about by leaders having a vision of a humane society and by establishing schools to help people to learn how to transform this vision into reality.

My parents appreciated education because it had transformed their lives. My father was born in 1867 on a farm in western Illinois, two years after his father returned from serving in the Civil War. In 1868 his family moved to Thayer County, Nebraska, to homestead virgin land. My father attended the local public school at times when he was not needed to work on the farm. He liked school and did well in his studies. When he completed the program of the common school, he took a position as a teacher in that school. Formal education for teaching was not required in those days.

In 1888 my father and his brother went down to Fort Scott, Kansas, to attend a summer session at the Fort Scott Normal School to learn more about teaching. While in Fort Scott, they were informed of many jobs available in Washington, D.C. It seems that Congress had enacted a law providing pensions for Civil War veterans, but there was no list of veterans in the federal records. The soldiers in the Civil War were paid by the states from which they came, since the Constitution at that time permitted the federal government to col-

Ralph W. Tyler is Director Emeritus of the Center for Advanced Studies in the Behavioral Sciences.

lect only excise and custom taxes, far too small an amount to support the Union Army. In order to pay the federal pensions, it was going to be necessary to copy the state records. So my father and his brother went to Washington to work as clerks in the War Department. Since there were two shifts, the Tyler brothers chose to work the night shift and during the day attended the medical school associated with George Washington University.

In 1895 they graduated from the medical school. My father returned to Nebraska and began his practice of medicine. By 1898 he had an annual income of more than $5,000, a large sum in those days. Both he and mother were deeply religious and worried that they might become addicted to money rather than being of service to God. Furthermore, as father worked with patients with various physical illnesses, he became deeply aware of their psychic or spiritual illnesses. Finally, he and mother decided that he should give up medicine and become a preacher. They moved to Chicago for a four-year training program at the Garrett Biblical Institute, associated with Northwestern University.

I was born in Chicago in 1902, while father was studying at Garrett. After graduating in 1904, he moved his family back to Nebraska. He never received more than $3,600 in salary, but he was a very happy man. He called himself a teacher of the moral and spiritual life. As I listened to their discussions over the years about the great importance of education and teaching, I knew I wanted to be a teacher.

I had the opportunity to teach in the high school sooner than I expected. I graduated from Doane College in Nebraska in the spring of 1921. On July 4, 1921, I went home to spend the holiday with my parents. A house guest, the son of an old friend of my father, was the principal of the high school in Pierre, South Dakota. When he heard that I had majored in science and mathematics, he exclaimed, "What, you have all this science and math, and we haven't been able to get a math and science teacher since 1917. (They had all been drafted to serve in the war.) It is your duty to use your education to teach, and I can offer you a teaching position in our high school." So, I became an "instant" teacher.

When school opened in September, I was confronted in the science room by two young men from the nearby Indian reservation. They said, "We are going to beat you up. We don't want to go to school." "You can beat me up," I said, "but you still have to do your science." They asked, "Why do we have to do science?" I replied, "You want to play football, don't you?" Their reply was "Of course, that's the

357

only reason we go to high school." My response was, "To play on the high school football team, you have to be eligible. To be eligible, you've got to do your science; so let's go into the lab and get out the equipment."

They liked working with the lab equipment and did well in their science classes. They got so interested that they stayed in school and graduated. I greatly enjoyed working with them and found teaching to be a profession that never grows boring. There are always moments of excitement when students enthusiastically exclaim, "Oh, I see, so that explains it." I'll always be a teacher.

During that first year of teaching, I encountered many problems that were new to me. Pierre was the capital of South Dakota but had a population of only 3,000, and the state was sparsely settled. The nearest high school to the one in Pierre was more than 100 miles away. One-fourth of our enrollment came from the three Indian reservations, one-fourth from the children of state officials, one-fourth from the children of ranchers (these students roomed in Pierre, going home on weekends), and one-fourth were children of the townspeople who provided the local services: merchants, blacksmiths, barbers, etc.

Students coming from these varied backgrounds had different aspirations on which motivation for learning could be built; different experiences on which understanding, skills, and aptitudes could be developed; and different opportunities to practice what they were learning in school. But how I could take advantage of these opportunities and help the students to solve their problems was not at all clear.

I decided to return to Nebraska in the summer of 1922 and enroll in a program of science education at the University of Nebraska. This program was directed by Herbert Brownell, a superb "hands on" teacher of science. The subject of science as he saw it was not found in books but in natural phenomena. Observation, manipulation, and interpretation were the course materials of science, not memorization of textbook material.

I did not return to Pierre. Professor Brownell offered me an instructorship, teaching in the University High School, supervising practice teachers, and the opportunity to work on a master's degree, which I was awarded in 1923. I learned a great deal about education in the four years I worked with Professor Brownell. He was the most effective teacher of science I have ever observed. He became my mentor.

The University High School was situated in an industrial area of Lincoln, and its enrollment included a large number of children from families of migrant farm workers. Most of the teachers thought these children had little intelligence and could not learn much, but Professor Brownell was able to arouse their interest, to stimulate their efforts to understand biology, physics, and chemistry. Their performance was not inferior to that of the children of middle-class families. Working with these students taught me that all children can learn; in fact, all children are learning every day. The problem is not the lack of intelligence but our inventiveness in developing activities that stimulate and reward the learning that schools are expected to teach.

After four years working with Professor Brownell, he suggested that I continue graduate work and earn a Ph.D. He advised me to go to the University of Chicago and work with Charles Judd. "Judd," he said, "works as a scientist, studying human learning." In my first class in educational psychology at Chicago, Judd said, "This course provides an opportunity for you to study children's learning in classrooms and on playgrounds. I have made arrangements for you to visit two nearby schools and observe children's activities in and out of the school buildings. Try to understand what they are doing, what they are learning, and how they are using what they learn. After you interpret what you observe, we will then read how other scholars interpret school learning."

My work with Brownell and Judd helped me establish a basic conception of educational studies, which has guided me throughout my professional career. In addition to Judd, at the University of Chicago I studied with W.W. Charters (who later became my mentor), Franklin Bobbit, George Counts, Frank Freeman, William Gray, and Karl Holzinger. It was an exciting time and place for me to develop. When I received my Ph.D., I accepted a position at the University of North Carolina in Chapel Hill, where I spent half time on campus and half time out in the schools, where I worked with teachers on their curriculum problems.

From North Carolina, I went to the Ohio State University in the Bureau of Educational Research to head the Division of Accomplishment Testing. My responsibility was to help faculty members who wished to improve their instruction and their testing. While at Ohio State, I had the privilege of directing the evaluation of the famous Eight-Year Study. This enabled me to work with a large-scale, school improvement project that involved developing interschool cooperation, directing summer workshops, and conducting follow-up evaluation studies.

359

In 1938, on the retirement of Charles Judd from the University of Chicago, I was appointed his successor as well as University Examiner, responsible for the comprehensive examination system of the university. While at the University of Chicago, the American Council on Education asked me to direct its Cooperative Study in General Education, which was another fine opportunity for learning and development.

In 1953 the Ford Foundation established the Center for Advanced Study in the Behavioral Sciences, and I was asked to serve as the initial director. My experience in this position was a unique one, and I learned many things that I had not learned in my previous work with teachers and students in schools and colleges. In 1967, at age 65, I retired from full-time academic appointments and have been working on special educational projects. It is on this experience of teaching that my reflections are based.

Education in Early Childhood

Our family was closely knit. Father, mother, and the four sons did many things together. We also learned much from each other, including some of the content of school learning. We learned to read as we followed the printed pages from the bedtime stories mother read to us. Also, we learned from the school materials of our older brothers, and we learned from our older brothers' efforts to teach us what they were learning in school.

When I was in high school studying algebra, my oldest brother was in college. He brought his calculus book home and showed me his homework. I tried to do his homework and learned a good deal of calculus in the process. In my adult years, I have observed a great deal of teaching in the home by children working with their younger brothers and sisters. When working in Indonesia, I encouraged retired elders to carry on informal teaching of children, since the supply of teachers was inadequate to provide for all the students. Young people also can help by teaching their peers.

As I have observed families, it seems clear that the family's efforts in stimulating and rewarding the learning of children strongly influences their school achievement. Parents in a city slum who tell their children, "The only way we can get out of this slum is to get an education and a good job. Learn all you can in school," strongly influence the attitudes and efforts of their children. However, the motivation developed in the home must be reinforced by the classroom experiences.

Many children from families in which the parents have had little education lack the confidence necessary to work hard to learn what the school is expected to teach. When they are not successful in completing a classroom assignment, many give up, believing that school assignments are too difficult for them. Thus, the teacher needs to be supportive and encouraging. The teacher may say: "Come on, let's try again. You can do it. I'll show you again how to do it. I'll show you and then you can show me." In this way confidence can be built.

There are other ways in which experience in the home can strongly influence learning in the school. My mother was a preacher's wife. She was busy with church matters: Ladies Aid Society, Home Nursing Society, visits to the homes of congregation members, etc. She gave her four sons responsibilities for household duties and expected them to learn to do their jobs well. We learned to do the household chores and also the seeding and cultivating of the vegetable garden and the food marketing. Since we were given responsibility, we were eager to learn.

The transition from learning in the home to learning in the school was an easy one for us. Early in our lives, mother read us fairy tales and other children's stories in a half-hour period before bedtime. We enjoyed hearing these stories and began to look over her shoulder to see the printed words and pictures there as she spoke. By the time we were four years old, we could read some of the stories to visitors. We were well along in reading stories when we entered kindergarten.

But there is a problem in transferring what one learns in school to life out of school. For example, we learned to compute in our arithmetic class but seemed unable to use these skills when we had to compute the total cost of the school supplies we needed. We learned to write compositions, but two years later we were unable to write a meaningful letter to the editor of the rural newspaper. For many students there seems to be two worlds of experiences, the world of school and the world outside of school, with few connections between them. To some students the school world is neither a pleasant one nor one that helps them learn things of value in achieving their aspirations for the "real world." They can hardly wait to get out of the school world in order to devote full time to the "real world." This is a serious problem. Some schools seem to be solving it by developing a school world that acknowledges students' aspirations and provides opportunities to develop the knowledge, skills, and attitudes to achieve their aspirations.

One of the characteristics I have observed in children that seems to have a strong influence on their school success is their attitude toward exploring new experiences. Some children actively explore their environment and seek new experiences. Others seem afraid of new experiences and limit their activities as far as possible to those with which they are familiar. The former appear to be more actively involved in their school work than are the latter. It seems likely that these attitudes and habits are developed in the home and in the early years in school.

Exploring new experiences is very important to learning. To educate is to develop new behaviors, new ways of thinking, feeling, and acting. If one is actively engaged in exploring new experiences, one is open to new ways of thinking, feeling, and acting. If one continues habitual behaviors without exploring new experiences, education is difficult if not impossible. This suggests that parents and teachers should encourage exploration and seek to identify and remove obstacles to this exploration.

When children enter school for the first time, there are differences among schools in the receptions they receive. Some schools are inclusive communities providing a warm welcome to all children, rich and poor, from all racial and ethnic backgrounds. Other schools are exclusive communities, welcoming some children and making other children feel unwanted. Often when students feel unwanted, they attempt to disrupt school activities. Most young people want attention and respect. If they are not able to get respect for behavior valued by the school authorities, they develop behaviors that get attention by being disruptive. Some schools deal with these problems by organizing the total school staff into counselors, whose role is to identify the problems and to develop plans for resolving them.

Parent Education

There are many families in America in which the parents have not had the benefits of school learning. They do not know how to provide the home conditions that can stimulate, reward, and guide the learning of their children. To deal with this problem, some schools have established short-term parent education programs. For example, Sam Redding has developed a number of these programs, called Parent Academies, in Chicago and Lincoln, Illinois. The programs focus on such topics as how the school can help your children be successful in life, why your children's homework is important, or how you can help your children do their homework.

Redding has an advisory committee of well-known educational researchers who are conducting studies of the effects of these Parent Academies on the school achievement of their children. Their studies show that these programs have helped the participating parents guide their children's schooling and that these children perform somewhat better than children in a control group.

Redding is also working on the development of "learning communities" involving not only parents but other persons, organizations, and institutions in developing activities that stimulate desirable learning in children and youth as well as parents. The learning community includes such groups as the Scouts, YMCA, YWCA, 4-H Clubs, Junior Achievement, libraries, museums, and the like.

School Improvement

The public schools of the United States have been relatively effective in helping to develop citizens for a democratic society. Today, however, the schools are faced with new demands; they are faced with new kinds of students. Clearly, schools must make changes in order to remain effective. However, many of the proposals for school improvement are being made without considering the resources required or the constraints under which schools operate.

The particular improvements needed are not the same for all schools, partly because the problems are not the same and the resources for solving the problems are not the same. These resources include the teaching staff, the families, community resources in the form of volunteers and social agencies, and, of course, money. Ultimately, however, school improvement depends on the efforts of teachers and parents. If they do not perceive the problem as important, they will not put forth the whole-hearted effort to solve the problem. They may respond to proposals from outside commissions and reports, but the necessary commitment will not be there. In some school districts the board of education may be able to employ additional staff to work on the problems, but with most districts today facing budget constraints, improvements will generally have to be carried out by existing staffs.

A better way to institute a program of school improvement is to involve teachers and parents in a series of discussions to identify the serious problems in the school and what impedes solving the problems. The object of these discussions is to identify a problem that all or nearly all can agree is interfering with student learning in school. This problem does not necessarily need to be the most serious problem, but it should appear to the teachers and parents to be important enough to justify a serious effort to solve it. In my experience, that serious effort needs to be maintained for five to seven years to get the problem solved.

The problem needs to be carefully studied in the context of the particular school and community before developing a proposed solution. Teachers and parents will need to acquire information and knowledge to guide their efforts. Some may need to develop new skills. In some cases, new materials of instruction may need to be prepared. Time is also required to implement these ideas effectively. Pilot projects may be needed and their results appraised in order to insure proper implementation. The time needed to carry out these steps may discourage reforms, but this step-by-step procedure has been characteristic of lasting improvement in schools. Short-term efforts achieve little permanent reforms and are soon abandoned. Patient, continuing effort accompanied by comprehensive evaluation has been characteristic of effective school improvement.

Local School Management

The legislation recently enacted in Chicago appears to provide a structure that facilitates the monitoring of student learning and the development of school improvement programs. The new law establishes local school councils at each school with the responsibility of management of the instructional programs. Each school council consists of five members, two parents elected by the parents, two teachers elected by the teachers, and the school's principal. The school council is expected to meet regularly to review the progress of the school improvement program, to identify problems, to revise the school improvement program, if necessary, and to establish annual goals to guide the progress of the improvement program.

This structure was developed in an effort to remedy the deficiencies in the previous structure, which operated top-down from the central administration. Monitoring local school programs and developing improvement plans were the responsibility of the city school superintendent and his staff. They could not easily identify the resources of persons, organizations, and institutions that could help in the improvement of student learning in each school, nor could they easily discover the significant problems the school must solve. The new legislation seeks to involve parents and teachers in efforts to improve the learning of their students.

There is, of course, the danger that the local councils will not accept the responsibility for developing and managing a program for school improvement and will become instead a forum for political power shifts. Thus it becomes important for the local leadership to urge cooperation of parents and teachers in helping their children to learn what schools are expected to teach. This may be difficult in some districts.

School Dropouts

In 1910 when I was in the elementary school, half of the children in America's public schools had dropped out by the time they had completed the sixth grade; 10% completed high school; and 3% graduated from a four-year college. Today, about 75% of American students graduate from high school and 34% graduate from college. An analysis of these statistics reveals great variation in school attendance among particular populations and particular communities. On the one extreme are the districts in which many students are from families of uneducated migrant farm workers, who often come from countries where educational opportunities are not easily accessible to poor people. Some of those parents have high educational aspirations for their children, but many have no such concern. At the other extreme are the school districts enrolling the children of doctors, lawyers, teachers, business managers, and the like. Most of these parents have high educational aspirations for their children; and, in fact, few of their children drop out. Those that do have not found their high school studies relevant or have not been successful in their high school studies, or both.

There is an additional factor to consider when interpreting dropout statistics. Some schools label students as dropouts because school records show that after enrolling in the ninth grade their name did not appear on the graduating list four years later. Actually, some of these students have moved to another high school from which they graduated, have enrolled in college early, have returned to high school after laying out for one or more years, or have completed a high school equivalency program. So they are not really dropouts. To work constructively on the dropout problem, we must go beyond the official school records and contact students or those who know them to find out their true status.

International Comparisons of Student Achievement

Student achievement has become a concern of those who worry about the U.S. competitive position in the international marketplace. The leaders of all modern nations expect their schools to develop good citizens as the leaders define it. Both the Soviet Union and the People's Republic of China developed a curriculum that their leaders believed would produce the ideal communist citizen. Thomas Jefferson, in his plan for education in Virginia, argued for public support of schools for the new republic: "Because our nation is a democracy and the American people are the rulers, they must be informed and educated in order to rule intelligently." Japan's democracy appears to be a patriarchal one in which the common people are expected to respect the wisdom of their leaders. In America, the common people need to develop the understanding, skills, and attitudes of citizenship in order to participate fully in a democratic society. In such a society, free and extended discussion informs the public and the leaders on matters to be dealt with by policy makers and decision makers. In a democratic society, the most important skill for citizen participation is the skill of critical reading.

In the project called the International Evaluation of Educational Achievement involving 16 nations, the reading achievement of 14-year-old Americans is exceeded only by their cohorts in Finland and New Zealand. These two countries have relatively small and homogeneous populations. This seems to indicate that the American schools are relatively successful in skills of communication. On the other hand, in mathematics and sciences, the scores of American students fall within the lower third of the 16 nations, with the scores of the Japanese students being the highest.

The Importance of Being an Active Kappan

Some 30 years ago, the faculty of the Medical School of Case Western Reserve University undertook a comprehensive study of the professional activities of their graduates. They found that 80% continued to improve their professional knowledge and skills for seven years after graduation. But then, for 66%, the quality of their practice began to decline. Only 34% of their graduates maintained impeccable procedures for the diagnosis, treatment, and follow-up of their patients. It seems likely that the details of medical practice had become routine and boring for many physicians, causing them to lose interest. When this happens, they may not be alert to new symptoms and fail to think about solutions to new problems they are encountering.

In my own teaching and in observations of other teachers, I have noticed how easy it is to get into a rut and no longer be actively engaged in studying the problems of education and the possibilities for improvements. In medicine, one means for remaining an active professional is membership in a society of colleagues where one's problems are discussed and possible solutions explored. For me, active participation with members of Phi Delta Kappa in projects that are interesting and important is my chief means of maintaining my professional life. I have been able to write for the *Kappan*, participate in the work of national committees, and to speak at local chapter meetings. For me, Phi Delta Kappa provides the means to gain greater understanding of the field of education.

Reflections on America's Inter-Generational War

BY CAROLYN WARNER

The Parable of the Hole in the Boat: A man was a passenger on a ship a few miles out to sea when he was told that there was a hole in the starboard side of the ship. He listened to the news, thought about it, then smiled and said, "Oh, thank God. I'm on the port side." He didn't know, but would soon find out, that a hole in the boat is a hole in the whole boat.

Introduction

As a child, a "Dust Bowl baby" growing up in Oklahoma, the 21st century seemed about as remote as one of the planets. Yet, as I write this reflection, we are less than 10 years away from that time. From that perspective of age, combined with more than 20 years in education governance and policy making, I sense some disturbing trends that affect my attitude about both age and education.

A look at key demographics suggests a realignment of political, social, and economic power, shifts that do not bode well for education, for schools, and for the ability of the institution of public education to carry out its mission in the new century. I sense a redrawing of the political map, with divisions of political power being exercised less along regional, ethnic, or even ideological lines and more along *generational* ones.

This "social Balkanization" is resulting in spheres of interest that pit a numerically fixed, relatively affluent and aging, predominantly Anglo population — the "un-young" — against a growing non-Anglo (predominantly Hispanic, black, and Asian) population that is much

---

Carolyn Warner is former Arizona Superintendent of Education (1974-1986) and currently President of Carolyn Warner and Associates.

less affluent and a great deal younger — the "young." And in the middle is my own generation of Depression-era babies, along with the World War II crop just a little younger.

In this competition of age-interest, America is thus divided into essentially three generations:

- the young, the current "first generation";
- the un-young, the current "last generation";
- the "middle generation," which is caught in a pincers that will grow ever tighter in the early years of the 21st century.

The nature of the pincers is political. It is based on the fact that essentially every domestic issue that demands our attention — education, child care, health care, employment, equity, housing — all have common threads. Not only are they key human-need issues, they are generational issues in terms of interest. And they are costly.

This is a time of economic and political tension, combined with uncontrolled (and seemingly uncontrollable) federal and state budget deficits. These factors together impose genuine constraints on government spending at all levels. The result is that the amount of attention— and funding — received by areas of need are in reality based on the political potency of the constituencies seeking the funds.

Thus, these basic human issues become issues in which are embedded the seeds of severe generational conflict. To put the worst case forward, they are issues whose current lack of societal consensus could lead, by the end of this century, to an inter-generational "civil war" in American society. We could actually be facing a domestic conflict in which the interests of the young are basically sacrificed to serve those of the un-young, with the "middle generation" caught helplessly in the political crossfire.

The challenge that confronts us when we attempt to address these problems is rooted in our generational fragmentation. It has left us a society in which, by and large, each generation seems to think that its needs and issues are paramount. Like the man in the parable, each generation believes that the holes in the boat are on the other side and do not, therefore, have the slightest thing to do with their generation's safety on the ship.

The relevance of these concerns to education in America is twofold. First, if these conflicts are not resolved, they will ultimately pauperize and fragment out of existence one of the great keystone institutions in American history — public education. But it may well be that the institution of public education (and those who devote their life's work to it) is the only social "engine" with the necessary know-how to bridge the generational gaps.

What Are the Generations?

We can't properly understand this inter-generational civil war that I sense is brewing, let alone do anything about it, unless we understand something about the two key generations in the equation: the "first generation" young and the "last generation" un-young.

Everyone who works in education futures has studied statistic after statistic dealing with the changing demographic face of America. However, we seldom, if ever, look at these numbers from a historical or, more specifically, from a generational perspective.

In this context, who are the young? They are the generation of Americans who essentially lack economic and political clout and are, for the most part, *tax consumers*. (Yet it is upon this generation that my aging "middle generation" will depend for the payment of our Social Security, Medicare, and other tax-supported entitlements.)

Who is this "first generation," historically-speaking? In the 1988 presidential election, about 20 million Americans between 18 and 21 were eligible to vote. They represent about 12% of the voting-age population, and the youngest of them were born in 1970!

If we accept the hypothesis that one's opinions on social and political affairs are molded to a great extent by personal experiences or memories, and if we consider that age 10 is when an event creates a lasting, memory-forming impression, then we are dealing with a generation that shares almost none of the memories that have shaped the lives of today's generation of economic and political leaders.

Using 10 years of age as a benchmark "memory key," when we look at America today, we see a nation of almost 250 million, of whom:

- more than 80% don't remember the "Crash" of 1929, and the decade of the Great Depression;
- approximately 70% have no personal memory of World War II, and more than 60% don't remember the Korean conflict and the beginnings of the Cold War;
- over two-thirds cannot remember life before television;
- more than half aren't old enough to remember the launching of Sputnik and the beginning of the "Space Race" in 1957;
- almost half don't remember the assassination of John F. Kennedy in 1963;

370

- and 32% are too young to remember when man first walked on the Moon in 1969 — a year before today's 21-year-olds were born!

Those are pretty remarkable numbers. But even more remarkable as numbers go is that the fastest-growing age group in America today are people who can remember all of those events, *people over 100 years old!*

When we look at the un-young at the opposite end of the spectrum, we see a generation that has one almost identical characteristic to the young, and two that are totally opposite. Like the young, they are in great part *tax consumers*. But, unlike the young, they not only *can* vote, they *do*. In fact, they have the highest voting record of any age group in America. As a generation, they consume the highest percentage of the federal budget of any segment in our society; and they hold most of the wealth. Those 55 and older comprise slightly more than one-third of U.S. households, but they hold two-thirds of the deposits in banks.

Those of us who support a full and constant national commitment to education have traditionally made much of the power of the "military-industrial complex" vis-a-vis the federal budget. But even during the hot "cold war" Reagan years, only about 20% of the federal budget went to the Pentagon. In contrast, more than 30% of the federal budget is allocated to programs for 12% of the population — people over age 65!

To put that figure into a trans-generational perspective, much less than 10% of the federal budget goes for education; and it is estimated that not much more than 10% directly affects the generations that are left — the taxpaying, "middle generations."

There is a politically popular — and politically potent — myth about the un-young. The myth has it that those "senior citizens" so dear to campaign strategists are an impoverished group, living precariously on "fixed incomes," and are thus deserving of subsidization by every level of government and of being protected from any hint of increased contributions to the revenue generation side of the equation.

Of course, the other face of the myth is that the young are not so much receiving their just share of society's benefits but, rather, are simply feeding at the trough of government "giveaways." The reality, however, is that the "safety net" for the un-young has far fewer holes than the "safety net" for the young.

In truth, it is *voting power*, not economic need, that drives budget decisions. And budget drives policy, not vice versa. Therefore,

371

government spending on programs for the un-young translates into a disproportionately lower level of spending on the young. Neither need nor numbers drives the decision. Only voting power.

In relating voting power to corresponding shares of the federal budget, it is instructive to look at the most recent presidential election. In the 1988 election, slightly more than 50% of the voting-age population actually voted. Thus, George Bush's "landslide" actually meant that only about 27% of eligible American voters chose him, as opposed to 23% for Michael Dukakis. It also meant half the electorate said they didn't give a damn one way or another! But contrasted with the meager 50% of *all* Americans who vote, upwards of 70% of Americans age 55 and older vote.

What this means in terms of practical politics is pretty simple. People vote their issues. Older Americans vote, and they vote in numbers far greater than their percentage of the general population. Consequently − and regardless of any economic or societal need − Social Security, Medicare, and other forms of government benefits (not to mention a plethora of "Senior Citizen discounts" on everything from movie tickets to Caribbean cruises) are protected as entitlements, regarded as almost sacred and certainly as politically sacrosanct.

Yet, when it comes to federal support for programs dealing with "first generation" needs, such as family planning, prenatal care, early childhood education, food and nutrition, drug and AIDS treatment, summer jobs for youth, Pell Grants for college students, or even aid to elementary and secondary education, an even crueler myth persists. In this "first generation" myth, Congress and the Administration − with the consent of a majority of American voters − find it much easier to talk of "fat" in the federal budget and to point out that most programs for the young just happen to be "state and local" responsibilities. Crueler still, this myth is often reinforced by pious concerns about governmental "interference" with the "rights" of the family!

We're a strange nation. As individuals, families, and communities, we are, for the most part, a caring, kind, and decent people who try to do the right thing. But, generationally, we have major blind spots.

Even though centenarians are our fastest growing age group, we think of ourselves as a youth-oriented society. We are a dynamic society, priding ourselves on our "individualism"; but we are generous with our subsidies for politically potent voting blocs. We pride ourselves on our "historic" institutions (at 214 years old, we are the world's oldest unchanged democratic system); but from an historical perspective, the United States is only four lifetimes old:

- Thomas Jefferson was 33 when he signed the Declaration of Independence in 1776.
- When Jefferson died in 1826, Abraham Lincoln was 17 years old.
- Lincoln, who guided our nation through its most painful times, died in 1865, when Woodrow Wilson was 9 years old.
- In 1924, the year in which Woodrow Wilson died, George Bush was born.

Now in 1991, we are a young nation that is steadily aging; a nation that says it cares but a nation deeply divided in the ways it cares for its young and its un-young; a nation with a cohort of dual-loyalty men and women (the "middle generation"), who are at the same time the parents of the young, the children of the un-young, and the caregivers of both.

If we take another look at America, this time as a macrocosmic family of three generations — children, parents, and grandparents — we see a family that is in trouble. Of the three generations, 14% of the grandparents live in poverty, as do 20% of the children. And the generation in the middle is in the no-win situation of trying to support both ends of the spectrum with very little help and, in many instances, active hostility from almost every level of government.

The Saving Remnant

I am by nature an optimist. I think there is no room for pessimism in public life. Realism, yes; but we must always look forward in faith, never backward in fear. During our Bicentennial celebration in 1976, I saw a bumper sticker that read, "America Ain't Perfect — But We Ain't Through Yet." The grammar was a little faulty, but the attitude was visionary. And to me it sums up much about our country and why it really should be impossible to be a pessimist about our future.

My optimism is fueled by the fact that I have spent most of my public-service life in education, the most frustrating and the most hope-inducing institution in American society. Frustrating, because so much needs to be done in this arena. Hope-inducing, because the capacity exists now, as it always has, for the institution of education to provide both the motivation and the remedy for ending America's generational "cold war."

I should, and do, feel guilty about assigning yet more tasks to the institution of education. The greatest problem our schools face at present — and, I believe, the principal reason for their current "failure" — is that they have taken on every single task assigned them by American society. Schools today are charged with raising the undisciplined children of undisciplined parents and with righting every social wrong that society as a whole lacks the courage to deal with. They have accepted these burdens, succeeded for the most part in carrying them, and have never yet refused one of society's challenges, or cast aside one task in order to deal with another one.

However, the dangers facing America as we near the year 2000 make taking on two more tasks a special case. They are special because if public schools, public educators, and those who believe in the public school concept can succeed in meeting these challenges, they will succeed in not only saving American education, they will succeed in saving American society as well.

It is said that, in each generation, there is a "saving remnant," a group of people, no matter how disparate they may otherwise be, whose dedication to a principle or devotion to a cause enables them to transcend the challenges that face them, allowing them to achieve the otherwise unachievable.

I believe that in America at the dawn of the 21st century, our saving remnant is the people who have retained their faith in the democratic process. It is the people who believe in the power of universal, free, public education. It is the people who see the realization of those two concepts in the American public school. It is to this saving, public-school-believing remnant that I would assign these two additional tasks.

First, I assign them the task of reminding the rest of their fellow citizens that America is, indeed, a multi-generational society. I further charge them with doing what they do best. I charge them with educating Americans that a hole in the boat of one generation is a hole in the boat of every generation. And if one generation declares social or economic war on another generation, every generation is the loser.

Is it important for the un-young to vote support of the young via school bond and millage levies or school budget override elections, even when it means a raise in taxes? Is it important that they write their elected representatives in support of, rather than in opposition to, funding for "first generation" needs? Before un-young Americans think that they are voting in their own best interest by voting against the institutions of the young, such as schools, they need to be reminded of some demographic facts of life. In the 1970s, for every person 65 and over (tax consumers) there were five working-age Americans (taxpayers). But by the year 2000, the ratio of taxpayer to tax consumer will be down to less than three to one.

If the "last generation" is convinced that it is voting for its economic best interests when it votes against education and other types of "first generation" spending, it seems to me we have here a classic case of confusing short-term gain with long-term loss. Putting it bluntly, when the old use their economic and political power against the young, they are standing on their own oxygen tubes!

Compounding the short-sightedness even more is the fact that in the 21st century's information/technology age, the relationship between quality and equality of educational opportunities and a healthy economy (and, therefore, a healthy society for all generations) depends on a continuum of education. From kindergartens to graduate schools, from pre-school to pre-med, from basic educational needs of the very young to the vocational/technical education needs of adults, there will be no genuinely "healthy" generation if other generations are not equally "healthy."

So, the saving remnant has another challenge: It must make the un-young understand that we can no longer keep black children in the ghetto, Hispanic children in the barrios, Native American children on the reservations, and immigrant children out of the mainstream. It must educate the un-young that they cannot allow the gradual whittling down of educational and economic opportunities for the young or for the current tax-paying generation.

The un-young must understand it is the taxes these children and young adults will pay as workers that will fund Social Security, Medicare, and various other entitlements. The un-young further need to understand, before they vote their reflexive "No," that if the "first generation" reaches adulthood under-educated and under-employed and thus becomes a permanent underclass and clients of our criminal justice and social service systems, then they, too, will be tax consumers and not tax *payers*. And they, too, will become a clamoring lobby, competing with the un-young for those hotly contested subsidy dollars.

Our saving remnant also needs to communicate the fact that young people who grow up believing themselves to be looked down upon and not worthy of support by the un-young upper classes, who have the vote and the clout, are not likely to feel inclined toward participatory citizenship. And, if they do become politically involved, how likely are they to vote for legislators (or aspire to be legislators) who are sensitive to the needs of the elderly?

If the young are denied their piece of the "American pie" and decide to take it out at the polls, who is the most logical target? Most likely it is the generation that is perceived as having "hogged" more than its share, I suspect. It is quite possible that shrewd politicians might one day see as much to be gained by exploiting the fears and frustrations of the young as they do now in pandering to the un-young.

The reality of trans-generational conflict demands that we provide for a quality education for all of our children and help them become participating, fully functioning, fully-integrated members of society. If we fail to do this, then *every* generation of Americans will suffer the consequences.

Second, we need to start raising some hitherto politically untouchable issues. If the politicians are afraid to raise them, then the saving remnant should. After all, the dictates of realpolitik say that if your political adversaries aren't going to vote with you anyway, what do you have to lose by advocating policies that further discomfit them?

There are several issues that need to be put on that table here. For instance, should people be rewarded for early retirement? As a matter of national policy, and perhaps good economics, maybe we ought to look at some sort of economic levers to keep people in the workforce longer — paying taxes instead of consuming them. Or perhaps it might be time to consider raising the minimum age for beginning Social Security benefits, thus providing a disincentive for leaving the tax-paying force at an earlier age. (It is thought to be a "health-enhancer" if one is making a contribution to an enterprise and thus feels needed. Perhaps this is an issue on which medical and economic policy could join forces for a change.)

Periodically, some brave (or foolhardy) politician brings up the notion of a "means test" for certain entitlement programs for the un-young. Up to now, the political fallout for such temerity is swift and certain. Is such a policy really a form of patricide, as the "last generation" lobby and their political allies would have us believe? Political education can take many forms. For instance, the claim that so-called entitlement payments are actually "getting back the money you put into the system" is still another myth badly in need of debunking. The truth is, those entitlements are being paid for by today's taxpayers, the "middle generation." And my generation's entitlements will be paid by tomorrow's taxpayers, the "first generation."

As every generation ages, it needs to be systematically educated by every available institution to which the saving remnant has access about the Parable of the Hole in the Boat, because the generations coming along behind us are the only support system we've got.

Conclusion

A few years back, Arthur Schlesinger commented in an interview that he saw a "new idealism blowing in the wind." This was still during the Reagan years, which says a great deal about Schlesinger's own idealism. Let us hope that he is right. Let us also hope that implicit in this new idealism is a renewed sense of the need for equality between and among people – specifically equality of educational opportunities – and for an understanding of the importance of educational opportunity to all ages of society.

This understanding is essential if we Americans are to have some grounds for commonality, some basis for mutuality, among the "first generation," the "middle generation," and the "last generation." We must come to understand that there are much greater commonalities than there are differences and that genuine social need is multigenerational in nature. If we fail, then I have not presented nearly a dark enough picture of our nation at the turn of the century in these reflections.

If John Kenneth Galbraith was correct in calling California's Proposition 13 a "revolt of the rich against the poor," we cannot allow today's inter-generational social and economic inequities to escalate into a revolt of the working class against the young and the un-young. That would be a tragedy of indescribable proportions.

Can the saving remnant, then, make a difference? Do the people who understand the secret of the Parable – that a hole in the boat is a hole in the whole boat – have the determination and vision to achieve the almost unachievable? I believe they do. Education and educators have taken up every challenge heaped upon them so far and have converted each challenge into an opportunity. I pray that they can do it again.

At some point, we are going to run out of time to deal with these problems. At some point, America's social fabric is going to become so tattered that no amount of hard work and good intentions can mend it. Our generational selfishness could finally catch up with us.

I believe that the years between now and 2000 are the watershed ones in which this work must begin. And I also believe that the saving remnant, as represented by public education and its practitioners, is the only likely institution that can carry out this task successfully.

Why education and why educators? Distinguished historian Henry Steele Commager expressed it best when he wrote, "There is a final quality . . . that our schools . . . must encourage. It is one that embraces, in a sense, all the others. It is the quality of faith — faith in society, faith in country, and faith in mankind. Here, of all places, our schools cannot do what we ourselves will not do. They cannot supply faith, if we repudiate faith. If we exalt reason, enterprise, imagination, boldness, tolerance, pluralism, freedom and faith, we may be sure that the schools will inculcate these things, and that the next generation will prize them."

There is no better rallying cry to ensure that Americans of every generation can be at peace with each other and with themselves.

Reflections on Life as an Educational Researcher/Reformer

BY ARTHUR E. WISE

This essay is a welcome opportunity to reflect on the issues in education that have been important to me personally and professionally. For nearly all my adult life, since I wrote a paper questioning education finance laws in 1964, I have been active in public elementary and secondary education as a scholar, an advocate for reform, or both. In many ways my career is linked closely with some of the major developments in recent American educational history: school finance reform, the changing federal role, the increased regulation of schools, and teacher professionalism. My discussion of these issues will hopefully prove useful to those who want to understand several of the major trends in American education during these past 25 years.

My reason for embracing a career in public education was really straightforward. I wanted a life of service, old-fashioned though that sounds these days. Very early, I realized I wanted to help those less fortunate than I. That desire stemmed, in part, from my background, which was not one of privilege. I was raised in Roxbury, Massachusetts, a working-class Boston neighborhood. My father was a pharmacist who owned a small drugstore. I worked for him and in other drugstores while growing up. That experience helped me empathize with people who were constantly struggling to survive economically and who were trying to provide their children with a chance for a better life.

My family was always supportive of education. Unlike many in my neighborhood, whose futures were uncertain, I always knew I

Arthur E. Wise is President of the National Council for Accreditation of Teacher Education.

would go to college. After a classical education at Boston Latin School, the city's most selective public high school, I won a scholarship to Harvard College and then went to the University of Chicago, where I earned a Ph.D. in educational administration, along with an M.B.A.

Without that education, and the opportunities it gave me, I would have a very different life today. Education has opened doors for me. My desire to open doors for others has impelled me to try to improve the public education system in this nation. I believe that education may set anyone free. But what kind of education can set someone free? Surely not one that only teaches students to read well enough to fill out applications for jobs in fast-food restaurants but fails to encourage them to love books. Surely not one that teaches children how to spit out bite-sized pieces of information but fails to teach them how to think deeply and critically. Surely not one that teaches them what they need to pass a standardized test but fails to instill a life-long desire to learn.

If the purpose of education is liberation, as I believe it is, then education must help every child maximize his or her potential. That goal should not be only for the academically talented. Every individual must be brought to the point of maximum intellectual functioning consistent with his or her talents. Students should be prepared to exercise informed judgment and should be free, as a result of education, from bias and prejudice. Students should be aware of their options and should understand that they can go as far as their talent and effort can take them.

It is important for society to have a literate and knowledgeable citizenry. It is important that we create a democratic society in which people can compete but also live in harmony. It is important that we educate students not merely to accept society but to challenge it. This country has always had a belief in the importance of the individual. Other nations place a higher priority on the importance of the group and elevate the primacy of the state. That is not the American way. So we must re-engineer our public education system to maximize individual potential. That is the only kind of education that is acceptable in a capitalistic democracy. Anything less is immoral. That perspective on education has guided me through many years of work; it has been the lens through which I have recognized, evaluated, and influenced many developments.

In my first year of graduate studies, I became interested in the subject of education finance. The more I read and studied, the more outraged I became over public school financing. While studying the Warren Court and how public schools are financed, I suddenly realized that the way we pay for public schools would probably be declared unconstitutional. For a course in education and the law, I wrote a short paper suggesting that disparities in per-pupil expenditures within a state might violate federal and/or state constitutional guarantees. I argued in this paper that the courts could use federal and state constitutions to compel states to distribute public school funds more equitably.

That little paper attracted some attention; and later, it became the basis for my doctoral dissertation, which was published as a book titled, *Rich Schools, Poor Schools: The Promise of Equal Educational Opportunity*. That book, I believe it is fair to say, became both a legal and philosophical basis for the school finance reform lawsuits that are forcing many states to overhaul their school financing methods.

The essence of my argument is that inequalities in funding constitute denial of equal educational opportunity. They are a denial of constitutional guarantees. We know that schools with more money can buy more and better resources, including textbooks, buildings, and teachers. Yet, we have invented a system of school finance in which we spend much more on children in wealthy communities than we do on children in poor communities. Many citizens and policy makers from wealthy communities have been reluctant to change that system, since they like to preserve the advantages they have. But it is simply not fair that an accident of geography should determine the quality of science instruction a child receives, or whether a class has 35 or 20 students in it. Why should the future computer programmer in East Orange, New Jersey, share her computer with 42 classmates while her counterpart in Moorestown shares hers with 10? The answer is simple: because her community's property wealth − the assessed valuation of each house − is a fifth that of most cities. To shortchange a child's education on the basis of where he or she goes to school is not only unfair, it's shortsighted and, ultimately, harmful not only to the individual but to the nation as a whole. We lose part of each generation of students whose potential contributions to our nation are stunted by the inadequacy of the education they receive.

After *Rich Schools, Poor Schools* was published in 1968, I gained some attention in legal circles but found myself in a rather awkward position since I was not a lawyer. In 1973, I learned that a major school finance reform case, *San Antonio* v. *Rodriguez*, was going to be argued before the U.S. Supreme Court. I was eager to hear the case, but lacking any political influence or legal credentials, I failed to get a reserved seat to listen to the arguments. When I arrived at 6:45 a.m. for an unassigned seat, I found many people in line ahead of me. Fortunately for me, I met a Harvard law professor who had come to hear the case with students in his class. When he learned who I was, he asked me to brief his class about the case right there on the steps of the Supreme Court building. When my informal seminar was over, the professor put his arm around me and we walked in together to a special section of the Court reserved for members of the Federal bar. I was able to hear the historic debate, which I believe my book had helped shape.

As time went on, I came to be regarded as "expert" on certain education issues and was invited to testify in court cases and to provide strategic guidance to many of the major participants to state lawsuits. Recently, I testified before a congressional subcommittee in support of a federal bill that would create additional incentives for states to equalize their resources. Although I enjoy the chance to present my point of view in court or on Capitol Hill, I consider that I made my intellectual contribution to the school finance issue long ago with the publication of *Rich Schools, Poor Schools*; and I leave it to others to carry on the struggle in state courts. However, even though I now have moved into other areas of education, my philosophical commitment to school finance reform remains strong.

I am pleased to see that finance reform efforts, which became derailed in the 1980s after a promising start in the 1970s, are increasing. The New Jersey Supreme Court recently declared that state's school funding system unconstitutional, noting that students in poorer districts do not receive the "thorough and efficient" education required by the state constitution. That decision followed similar decisions in Montana, Texas, and Kentucky. Advocates for poor districts in many more states are contemplating legal action. We have seen that equitable school financing can be attained and sustained. California, chastised by its Supreme Court in *Serrano* v. *Priest* more than 12 years ago, has equalized finances so that most students in that state now receive nearly an equitable share of state resources to develop their individual abilities.

We will, however, seriously have to rethink school finance issues in the 1990s. It would be political folly to attempt to reform school finance simply by redistributing existing monies. A radical redesign of the system is in order. We need to recognize that, in many communities as the population ages and becomes less interested in the education of young people, there will be an unreceptive environment for passage of school bond levies and tax rate increases. We will need to broaden the tax base support for public education by decreasing our reliance on local property taxes and increasing our reliance on state sales and income taxes.

While I recognize the need for the state to have a key role in school finance reform, I continue to be wary of its influence in other areas of education. I want the state to pay the bill for education but largely keep hands off the schools. That position is not as contradictory as it may sound. The state does need to intervene in equity issues such as finance, since local districts cannot solve those problems on their own. But when it comes to determining the quality of schools, the teachers, administrators, and local boards of education should have more power. One tenet of my educational philosophy is that schools must be responsible to the people they serve. The closer the decision makers are to the clients they serve, the better.

I first began to ruminate about these issues while I was associate dean at the University of Chicago's Graduate School of Education in the early 1970s. Everywhere I looked, education was becoming more regulated; the federal government was asserting more control, and state governments and courts were taking a more active role. In the mid-1970s, while I was a visiting scholar at the Education Policy Research Institute of the Educational Testing Service, I wrote a book titled *Legislated Learning: The Bureaucratization of the American Classroom* (1979), a book that foreshadowed the emergence of reforms such as restructured schools, school-based management, and greater parent participation. In the book, I described a world in which state government called the shots and local boards of education became irrelevant. It was an educational world best described by sociological jargon – bureaucratization, centralization, and hyperrationalization. I defined "hyperrationalization" as a process of educational decision making that involved excessive rules, regulations, and red tape that did not attain intended policy objectives. I concluded that we needed higher levels of government to regulate issues of equality, but when government strayed from pursuing the goal of equality and tried to regulate quality, it was writing a prescription for disaster.

The growth in regulation and centralization in many states has led to mandated standardized testing, mandated curriculum, mandated curriculum alignment, and mandated teaching methods. There are moves in Congress now to require a national assessment of educational progress for all children, so we can compare state to state, district to district, school to school, classroom to classroom, and perhaps even child to child. These tests have long-term consequences. With high stakes involved in testing, school personnel do change their behaviors. They do what external authorities expect them to do. Instead of teaching children in a liberating way, they will teach for the right answers on the tests. I am not opposed to standardized testing, but I would like people to realize that the act of administering a test fundamentally alters the educational process in ways that are counterproductive and sends a strong signal that what counts is not performance but test scores.

What happens to teachers in this age of increasing regulation and centralization? They worry that multiple-choice tests cannot assess all that they teach or all that they should teach. They also worry that tests alter the curriculum. Testing takes time, and preparing students for tests takes time away from teaching. Some teachers begin to emphasize the content they know will appear on the test. The result for teachers often is ethical conflict and guilt. If teachers follow their own instincts about what to do in their classrooms, they are violating the policies they are supposed to be following; and their students may perform less well on the examinations.

On the other hand, if teachers follow mandated policies, they worry that they are shortchanging their students, even if the students perform better on the standardized tests. As a result of this ethical conflict, many teachers leave the field or adopt coping strategies designed to meet the letter of the law. But teachers continue to feel guilty because they know that, as test scores rise, the quality of education is deteriorating. And so legislated learning, an effort to regulate the schools to make them better, actually reduces the quality of education.

As I studied these issues, I concluded that there is one major reason why we as a society have been doing so much testing: We don't trust teachers. At the heart of the movement to regulate schools is a deep mistrust of teachers; as a result, we have created a bureaucratic monster in public education. Only as we overcome that mistrust can we move forward in education. How can we do that? By professionalizing teaching. We must find ways to attract high-quality candidates to the teaching profession, to prepare them in the most effective ways we know, and then allow them to teach.

At the Rand Corporation, where I served as senior social scientist, I launched the Center for the Study of the Teaching Profession

384

in 1985. The center conducts research on policies that affect teachers and teaching and helps to design, implement, and evaluate reform efforts. As chief consultant to commissions in Connecticut and New York, I helped develop major new legislative proposals to professionalize teaching and testified in Congress and in several state legislatures on policies related to teachers. I came to the conclusion that to make teaching a profession like law or medicine, we must make five critical changes in policies and practices. Those include: improved standards for teacher education, more rigorous teacher licensing and certification, increased teacher decision making, increased professional accountability, and higher pay and better working conditions.

Teacher education and teacher licensing need to evolve together. Teacher education programs must be strengthened. Schools of education play a critical role in preparing the vast majority of teachers who staff the nation's schools; thus they must be a target for reform. There is an emerging consensus that teachers should have a strong general education background as well as in-depth preparation in the subjects they teach. That means three basic changes should take place: 1) require every prospective teacher to have a broad liberal education; 2) extend teacher education so that students can acquire a solid knowledge base in pedagogy and professional subjects; and 3) provide a supervised internship. A report I co-authored on the teaching internship recommends that the intern have a variety of direct experiences and didactic instruction and be exposed to at least two different kinds of teaching situations in the course of the year. For example, the student might intern both in a poor urban school and in a wealthy suburban community.

I am pleased to note that there has been progress in the area of teacher education. A few states now require that teachers have a subject major and a master's degree in education to qualify for a full license.

We also need to continue working toward an effective system for licensing teachers through the creation of professional standards boards in each state. The path to be followed is well trod and has been used in other fields. The pivotal event in the professionalization of medicine, for example, was the development of professional standards boards with the power and responsibility to decide which individuals were qualified to practice medicine. Teaching is about 100 years behind medicine.

Right now, teachers in most states are not licensed in the true sense of the word. They are merely certified as having completed an approved program of teacher education. Simply because one has completed a program does not mean that the person is a competent professional. I would like to see a real licensing system that would assure the public that a person who is awarded the title "teacher" is, in fact, prepared to teach. Like the professional standards boards that license doctors, lawyers, architects, and other professionals, boards for the teaching profession would set and enforce standards and determine who is admitted to practice. Standards boards have existed in California, Minnesota, and Oregon since the 1970s and have recently been established in Kentucky, Iowa, and Nevada. A number of other states are redesigning their teacher licensing processes.

Those are all steps in the right direction. But at the same time, alternate certification systems also are gaining currency. Some states and large school districts are already hiring people with bachelor's degrees and giving them on-the-job training. If teacher preparation outside the university becomes the norm, it would remove any hope of truly professionalizing teaching.

Many forms of alternate certification allow a person to attempt to learn how to teach while teaching on-the-job under supervision. But on-the-job training doesn't develop the intellectual capacity teachers need to exercise judgment. No true profession can exist without being linked to the knowledge production and knowledge dissemination functions of the university. Supporters of alternative certification have misdiagnosed the problems facing teachers and fail to realize that alternative certification merely masks problems, such as the need to make teacher licensing performance-based and to make teaching a more rewarding career.

In addition to supporting more rigorous academic preparation and a meaningful licensing system, I believe we must also take other steps to ensure a professional cadre for teachers. Schools must be restructured to allow teachers to participate in decision making. Teachers can't be responsible members of a profession if they don't have some role in setting the conditions in which they work. School systems also must make provisions for continued professional development for teachers who need to stay apprised of current research and teaching methods.

Let's think about what would happen to central mandates, regulations, and standardized tests if we had professional teachers that the public really trusted. We might involve those teachers, for example, in the design of curriculum and examinations. Let's say that all the history teachers in one school district got together to decide on curriculum and to design an examination. The whole school system would know the teachers' expectations for their students' mastery of history. The examination likely would be one that causes students to think rather than fill in blanks.

Teachers would grade the examinations, but not grade their own students' work. Thus students' performance on the exam would be a measure of a teacher's competence and would reflect what the district said was important to know in history. The state could, if necessary, inspect the testing process in each district to ensure its integrity.

Many aspects of teacher professionalism need attention, and in 1990 I decided to focus my energies on the accreditation process for schools of education by taking a job as president of the National Council for Accreditation of Teacher Education (NCATE). This is the non-governmental agency responsible for the accreditation of schools, colleges, and departments of education in both public and private institutions of higher education. It currently accredits teacher education programs in some 500 institutions, which collectively prepare the majority of the nation's new teacher graduates. NCATE's formal activity is to establish a set of standards that individual teacher-preparing institutions must follow if they are to receive accreditation.

One of my goals is to begin to strengthen the ties between the accreditation process of schools of education and the licensing process for individual teachers. Standards for teacher licensing and NCATE's standards should be complementary and reinforce each other. They have functioned too independently in the past.

I became convinced of NCATE's strategic importance when I realized that comparable accreditation agencies have played a major role in the professionalization of their respective professions. Since I have always enjoyed an opportunity to shape events, I had been waiting for the right situation to come along where I could exercise my activist spirit. I believe through NCATE that I can help transform my vision of teacher professionalism into a reality in years to come.

I also want to comment on one other major interest in my professional life: education research. I have always believed that research has had a more powerful impact on educational practice than most people realize, but it has a great way to go. Hoping to influence the expansion of education research at the federal level, I came to Washington in 1973 to become associate director of the old National Institute of Education, an agency created under the Nixon Administration. Many people hoped that this new agency would energize education research and create a serious federal investment in it. But

NIE had political difficulties from the beginning (it was in some sense almost too visible for its time), and it became clear to me that the agency was not going to go very far very fast.

I left my government position to become a visiting scholar at the Education Policy Research Institute of the Educational Testing Service. While there I was contacted by the Carter White House and asked to help create a new U.S. Department of Education. That invitation was hard to refuse, even though at the time I did not think the creation of a federal education department was the most pressing issue in education. I believe I made two critical contributions to the process. The first was my suggestion that a provision for an intergovernmental advisory council be included in the legislation for the new department. The inclusion of the council, a high-level permanent committee, helped to assuage fears that the new education department would encroach on the responsibilities of states and local school districts.

I also designed the first Office of Educational Research and Improvement (OERI). However, its structure was fundamentally redesigned in the Reagan Administration. Recently, I have argued that OERI is not very effective because it is not mission-oriented; its structure does not directly engage the nation's educational problems or goals. The time is ripe to replace that research structure with a new and better one. I have proposed that Congress create a set of research institutes modeled after the National Institutes of Health and called, perhaps, the National Institutes of Education. As a starting point, the new institutes could take the educational goals that President Bush and the nation's governors have established, with each institute focusing on a major educational goal while mobilizing the interests of practitioners, policy makers, and researchers around areas of common concern.

The cost of such a structure might be $300 million, about three times the current level of federal funding for research. But the money would be exceedingly well spent, since the institutes would generate new knowledge and products that educators at all levels could use. High-tech industries spend up to 20% and more of their gross revenues on research and development. In education, we spend a miniscule fraction of 1% on research. In fact, the research budget has continued to decline in real terms. The amount spent on education research today is only about 20% of what it was in 1973. The $300 million I have suggested would be only a start. We could productively spend a billion dollars within a few years. It's tragic, really, that at a time when new approaches to education are desperately demanded, the research and development establishment is funded at its lowest point in decades; and the federal government seems unconcerned.

I'll admit, however, that even if all my goals — for more effective and better funded research, for a more equitable school finance system, and for greater professionalization among teachers — were met, we would still need to do more. What I have been talking about so far can make a difference in the education of most youngsters, but we have a class of youngsters for whom much more is required. There are some youngsters in such desperate straits that even well-financed schools cannot adequately address their needs.

For the education of the disadvantaged, our schools need to become more encompassing social institutions. We need to extend the school day and school year and to integrate social, health, and recreational services into school life. I propose that we bring into school buildings a broader array of professionals such as health care and social workers, and that we incorporate into the school day music and dance lessons and other recreational activities that middle-class Americans routinely provide to their children. We need to creatively rethink the best way for children to spend a 10-hour day.

I have not yet written on the topic of restructuring schools to better serve disadvantaged children, because my approach is to study an issue for a long while before I present solutions. For the moment, I am content to tackle the challenge of professionalizing teaching and to continue to have the chance to influence the course of the greatest social experiment of all time — a high standard of public education for all children in a large, culturally diverse nation.